A Catechism of Chemistry

CATECHISM

OF

CHEMISTRY.

A

CATECHISM

OF

CHEMISTRY:

BY

SAMUEL PARKES, F.L.S. G.S. &c.

A NEW EDITION,

REVISED THROUGHOUT, CORRECTED, AND CONSIDERABLY ENLARGED,

BY

WILLIAM BARKER, M.B.

OF TRINITY COLLEGE, DUBLIN.

LONDON:

PRINTED FOR SCOTT, WEBSTER, AND GEARY,

CHARTERHOUSE SQUARE.

1837.

ADVERTISEMENT.

HAVING undertaken to prepare, for the press, a new edition of Mr. Parkes' Chemical Catechism, the Editor has carefully kept in view the objects for which the work was originally designed, and endeavoured to render it suitable for those who are desirous to become acquainted with the first elements of the Science. As many and important changes have taken place in the different branches of Chemistry, especially in nomenclature and classification, since the publication of the last edition prepared by Mr. Parkes, the present Editor, as far as was consistent with retaining the character and plan of the original work, has altered and revised it throughout, so as to adapt it to the present state of chemical science.

In the late editions of this work the text was much encumbered with a mass of notes, sometimes useless, and frequently trifling and irrelevant, the notes have consequently been considerably curtailed in the present edition, and none retained or added which did not seem necessary to illustrate or elucidate the text.

The order of the chapters has been also altered ; the chapter on Chemical Attraction, which, in the former editions was placed at the end, has been placed in the beginning of the work, and the chapters on Atmospheric Air and Water have been incorporated with those which explain the nature of the elements which compose them. The additional notes have been almost wholly omitted, and in their place an Appendix has been substituted, containing details of some important chemical manufactures, and the discussion of some subjects which could not, with propriety, have been introduced into the text.

Dublin, June, 1837.

PREFACE TO THE THIRD EDITION.

THE very flattering reception which " THE CHEMICAL CATECHISM" has met with from the public, two large impressions having been sold within a very short period, and the respectable character it has received in the reviews, and other periodical publications, have encouraged the author to devote a large portion of his time to the correction and enlargement of the work ;—a third edition of which he now offers, in a form that he trusts will be approved, and with a confidence that he did not at first allow himself to entertain.

The late highly interesting and truly important discoveries of Mr. Davy having thrown new light upon many branches of chemical science, it became necessary to review every part of the following sheets with great care, that no opportunity might be overlooked of recording the new facts and opinions, in order that the whole of the text and the notes might be accommodated to the present state of chemical knowledge.

The author, however, is very far from claiming any merit on this account; for he conceives that he could never deserve the continuance of that patronage which the public has so liberally bestowed, were he to neglect giving that public a faithful detail of all such discoveries of importance as have transpired since the former editions were prepared for the press.

A 2

In the hope of rendering the present impression still more acceptable, a variety of new matter has been added, particularly in the notes; the accounts of some of the manufactories have been entirely re-written; and the collection of "*instructive and amusing Experiments*" has been improved by the addition of several new ones that were thought likely to interest and instruct the student.

Though the author might now, perhaps, be justified in omitting to state the motives that first induced him to engage in such an undertaking, it may nevertheless be observed, that, in considering the great importance of chemistry to the arts and manufactures, it occurred to him, that an initiatory book, in which simplicity was united with perspicuity, would be an acceptable present to a variety of persons, who have not had leisure or opportunity to study more elaborate treatises; and especially to those parents who are not qualified by previous acquirements to instruct their children in the elements of this science, than which there can be nothing more essential, in whatever line of life they may be destined to move. As an attempt, therefore, to supply this desideratum, " The Chemical Catechism" was first prepared for the eye of the public,—the author having, at the same time, had it in his contemplation to exhibit, in a popular form, a body of incontrovertible evidence of the wisdom and beneficence of the Deity, in the establishment and modifications of those laws of matter which are so infinitely and beautifully varied, and whose operation is too minute to be the object of general notice. For if it could be proved to the satisfaction of youth, that matter is subject to a vast variety of laws which escape common observance, and that, in the adjustment of those laws, the utmost attention, if it may be so expressed, has been paid to our convenience and comfort,——such a detail, it was imagined, would tend to make a more indelible impression on the young mind, than the display of the same goodness in the operation of causes which come under our daily notice and observation.

With these views it naturally occurred to the author, that the work would be very incomplete, should he neglect to offer to the student some of those moral reflections which spontaneously arise in every contemplative mind, when considering the magnificent system of nature: and though such remarks may be regarded by some as irrelevant to chemical science, yet to repeat the former apology, it may be observed that, in compiling any initiatory book, no writer, as a parent, could lose sight of the necessity of embracing every favourable opportunity of infusing such principles into the youthful mind, as might defend it against immorality, irreligion, and scepticism.

For the accommodation of schools, and to render the generality of parents and preceptors more competent to explain and expatiate upon the variety of facts which the science of chemistry presents, and to qualify them in some measure to afford such answers to a number of questions, which the young pupil, in proportion as he advances and becomes more interested in the experiments, will not fail to demand, the author has added a variety of explanatory notes. Many of these will be found to contain new matter, or, at least, what is not generally known or published; others, and perhaps the majority, were drawn from various sources; but as many were quoted from memory, and still more from the commonplace-book of the compiler, he was obliged, in some instances, either to omit the authorities, or entirely forego the advantages he had derived from the works, experiments, and opinions of some of the most enlightened chemical philosophers of the age. Here, however, he has constantly been guided by one rule—to produce rather what is useful than original.*

* With this view, not only a succinct account of the different branches of chemical knowledge has been given, but the author has uniformly endeavoured throughout the work to direct the reader to

It may also be remarked, that the catechetical form, which was first chosen for this work, has been found to possess at least all the advantages that any other mode of instructing youth in chemistry can claim, the work having already been introduced with advantage into several of the most eminent seminaries in the kingdom; and, that, if the author's original intention be followed, the progressive improvement of the student will be pleasant, rapid and correct.

The author assuredly never expected that the answers should be committed to memory *verbatim* by the pupil, nor indeed, that the language of the questions should always be literally adhered to by the tutor; but merely that the whole should be comprehended by the parent or tutor, which, with the assistance of the notes, is no difficult task, and then to allow the student to employ his *own language* to explain his ideas, and form the responses.

Thus, this treatise, the author confidently hopes, possesses every requisite to render it a *first book* for the chemical student; and that, whether it be employed as a catechism, as a set of dialogues, as matter for familiar conversation, or as a book for the closet, still the original design—a correct initiation into the science of chemistry—will be the result; for if these rudiments of chemical knowledge have been drawn in such a form as to invite the young to study larger and more extended works, and to prepare them to adopt that theory only which can be substantiated by their own experiments, the chief intention of the author will then be fully accomplished.

the best treatises in each department of the science, with a view to facilitate higher attainments; and to render "The Chemical Catechism" a kind of text-book for the student.

CONTENTS.

AN ESSAY

OBJECTS AND ADVANTAGES OF CHEMISTRY.

THE present state of chemical knowledge, and the daily improvements which are making in our arts and manufactures, by the judicious application of its principles, render it absolutely necessary to make CHEMISTRY a regular branch of general education; and that every youth should be acquainted with its elementary principles, whether he be designed to move in the higher ranks of life, or is likely to be concerned in any of the manufactures of his country.

I have therefore imagined that I should render an acceptable service to society by enumerating a few of the advantages which arise from the acquisition of this department of knowledge; for, as a large proportion of the community is not apprised of its real value, that general attention to it which it deserves, can never be expected until its utility be demonstrated.

It would, however, be no difficult matter to show that the world might derive great advantages even from the

B

diffusion of a *theoretical* knowledge of philosophy and chemistry. An instance or two will place this assertion in a clear point of view. Two thousand years ago Archimedes was ridiculed for his attention to mathematics and the abstruse sciences; yet by this knowledge he was enabled to invent such mechanical engines as were sufficient to resist the whole Roman army. And such a dread had the soldiers of this man's science, that if a rope only were let down from the walls of the city of Syracuse, the whole army would retire from before it in the utmost consternation.

A further proof of the importance of the dissemination of useful knowledge may be taken from the construction of the *Steam Engine*. Mr. Watt often acknowledged that his first ideas on this subject were acquired by his attendance on Dr. Black's chemical lectures, and from the consideration of his theory of latent heat and the expansibility of steam.

The people of France are so satisfied of the importance of chemical knowledge, that chemistry has long been an essential part of education in their public schools, and one of the most important branches of university education; in the different colleges in Germany this science is likewise taught as essential to the education of all persons designed for the liberal professions, and for those intending to devote themselves to manufacturing pursuits. It shall be our business, in this place, to endeavour to demonstrate it to be of *equal* importance to the various classes of our countrymen, that the science should be cultivated with the same ardour in these kingdoms. The science here recommended has for its objects every substance of the material world, and, therefore, is equally interesting to every civilized nation upon earth.

Is your son born to opulence—is he the heir to an extensive domain; make him acquainted with the principles of chemistry, and you enable him to appreciate the real value of his estate, and to turn every acre of it to the best account. Has he a barren or mountainous tract of country, which has been unproductive from generation to generation; he will explore its bowels with avidity for hidden treasures, and will probably not explore it in vain. By analysing the minerals which he discovers, he will ascertain with facility the geological character of the district he inhabits, and learn the probable success which may attend a search after valuable mineral productions, the true value of which can only be ascertained by mineral analysis. Thus he will operate on sure grounds, and be prevented from engaging in expensive and unprofitable undertakings.

Chemistry will teach him also how to improve the *cultivated* parts of his estate; and by transporting and transposing the different soils, how each may be rendered more productive. The analysis of the soils will be followed by that of the waters which rise upon, or flow through them; by which means he will discover those proper for irrigation: a practice, the value of which is sufficiently known to every good agriculturist.

A person occupying his own estate, and the cultivator of his own land, must, of necessity, be a chemist before he can be an economical farmer. It will be his concern not only to analyse the soils on the different parts of his farm, but the peat, the marle, the lime, and the other manures must be subjected to experiment, before he can avail himself of the advantages which might be derived from them, or before he can be certain of producing any particular effect. The necessity of analysis to the farmer is evident from a knowledge of the circumstance, that some kind of lime is injurious to land, and would render land hitherto fertile actually sterile. Besides, a knowledge of the first principles of chemistry will teach him when to use lime *hot* from the kiln, and when *slaked;* how to promote the putrefactive process in his composts, and at what period to check it, so as to prevent the fertilizing particles becoming effete, and of little value. It will also teach him the difference in the properties of marl, lime, peat, dung, mud, ashes, alkaline salt, soap waste, sea water, &c. and, consequently, which to prefer in all varieties of soil. A knowledge of the chemical properties of bodies will thus give a new character to the agriculturist, and render his employment rational and respectable.[a]

The practitioner of MEDICINE, if not a scientific chemist, must be prepared to meet many painful disappointments, and to witness very unexpected results from the effects of compound medicine. A slight knowledge of chemistry would have informed him that many of the formulæ in the Pharmacopœia, which are salutary and efficacious, are rendered totally otherwise if given with certain other medicines—not to say often destructive. We need not here adduce particular examples, as we shall have frequent opportunities of directing attention to them in the subsequent pages.

The student of medicine must make himself master of the chemical affinities which subsist between the various articles of the Materia Medica, if he wishes

[a] Lavoisier cultivated 240 acres of land in La Vendée, on chemical principles, in order to set a good example to the farmers; and his mode of culture was attended with so much success, that he obtained a third more of crop than was procured by the usual method, and in nine years his annual produce was doubled.— *Lalande's Life of Lavoisier.*

to learn the art of prescribing medicines with accuracy and precision. This will inspire him with professional confidence; and he will be as sure of producing any particular *chemical* effect upon his patient, as he would if he were operating in his own laboratory. Besides, the human body is itself, *in certain respects*, a laboratory, in which by the varied functions of secretion, absorption, &c. composition and decomposition are perpetually going on: how, therefore, can he expect to understand the animal economy, if he be unacquainted with the effects which certain causes chemically produce? Every inspiration we take, and every pulse that vibrates within us, effects a *chemical* change upon the animal fluids, the nature of which requires the acuteness of a profound chemist to perceive and understand.[a] Neither can a physician comprehend the nature of the animal, vegetable, or mineral poisons without the aid of chemistry. Many thousand lives have been lost by poison, which might have been saved had the physician been in possession of the knowledge which he may now acquire by a cultivation of chemical science. And though the operation of many of the poisons upon the system be in these days well understood, nothing but a knowledge of chemistry can enable the practitioner to administer such medicines as will counteract their baneful effects, or to detect the poison where the administration of it has been the cause of death; in which case the physician's character and the life of a fellow creature may both be placed in jeopardy from ignorance of the mode of testing for poison ; from which evils a

[a] The reader who wishes to see this subject treated at large may consult Dr. Prout's Bridgwater treatise, where he will see the importance of the study of chemistry to the physician most ably illustrated by one of the first philosophers of Europe.—ED.

very trifling knowledge of this science would in general
be a sufficient guard.

If we look to the MANUFACTURES of the kingdom,
there is scarcely one of any consequence that does not
depend upon chemistry, for its establishment, its improvement, or for its successful and beneficial practice.
In order to see the connexion which subsists between
chemistry and the arts, it will be necessary to take a
short view of the principal trades and manufactures
which are carried on in these kingdoms.

One of the staple manufactures of the country is
that of IRON: and it will be found that, from the smelting of the ore to the conversion of it into steel, every
operation is the effect of chemical affinities, and dependant on chemical laws. In the first place, it requires
no small share of chemical knowledge, to be able to
appreciate the *value* of the different ores, and to erect
such furnaces for their reduction as may be contrived
in the best possible manner for facilitating their fusion,
and for producing good metal. The subsequent processes to convert this into *malleable* iron are entirely
chemical, and will be conducted to the best advantage
only by those who have acquired a knowledge of the chemical changes which take place in these operations. The
making of CAST-STEEL, which has been kept so profound
a secret, is now found to be a simple chemical process,
and consists merely in imparting to the iron a portion
of carbon, by fusing it in crucibles with carbonate of
lime, or by cementation with charcoal powder, in a
peculiar kind of furnace constructed for that particular
purpose.

The manufacturers of *utensils, &c.* in cast-iron (called
IRON-FOUNDERS) will also acquire some valuable in-
mation by the study of chemistry; as it will teach

them how to mix the different kinds of metals; how to apportion the carbonaceous and calcareous matter; and how to reduce the *old* metal, which they often receive in exchange; many hundred tons of which are annually sent away as ballast for ships, for want of that knowledge which would enable them to convert it into good saleable iron.

The WOOLLEN, the COTTON, and the CALICO manufactures are also become of paramount importance to these kingdoms. In order to preserve these sources of national wealth, the utmost attention must be paid to the beauty, the variety, and the durability of their several colours, as it is well known that the monopoly England at present enjoys in the calico manufacture arises, in great measure from the superior knowledge we possess of the art of calico printing. Now of all the arts, none are more dependent upon chemistry than those of DYE-ING and CALICO-PRINTING. Every process is chemical; and not a colour can be imparted, but in consequence of the affinity which subsists between the cloth and the dye, or the dye and the mordant which is employed as a bond of union between them. It is surely then evident how valuable a chemical education must be to that youth who is designed for either of these trades, and how necessary is that portion of knowledge which shall enable him in a scientific manner to analyse his different materials, and to determine the kind and the quantity necessary for each process. After all, his colours will be liable to vary, if he do not take into the account, and calculate upon, the changes which take place in them by the absorption of oxygen; a knowledge of which, and of the different degrees of oxidizement which the several dyes undergo, requires no small share of chemical skill: and yet this skill is absolutely ne-

cessary, to enable either the dyer or the calico-printer
to produce in all cases permanent colours of the shade
which he intends. Moreover, these artists must be indebted to chemistry for any valuable knowledge which
they may acquire of the *nature* of the articles they use
in their several processes; not to say that they are
wholly dependent upon this science for the artificial
production of their most valuable mordants, and for
some of their most beautiful and brilliant colours.[a]
They must also possess a knowledge of chemistry to
enable them to examine the purity of the several articles required in dyes, as without this they may be
subject to most injurious frauds when purchasing the
dyeing materials; many of which, from their cost and

[a] An instance or two will render this evident. Formerly a
calico-printer required many weeks to produce a printed cotton
with some colours, such as an olive ground and yellow figures;
a scarlet pattern on a black ground; or a brown ground with
orange figures:—but, by means of chemical preparations, the
whole of this work may now be done in a few days; patterns,
more delicate than ever, may be produced; and all with a degree
of certainty of which former manufacturers had no idea; the
system being now entirely altered. According to the former
practice, the mordant was first applied to those parts of the cloth
that were intended to be olive, brown, or black; it was then necessary for the piece to remain some time before it could be dyed,
and afterwards to be exposed in a bleaching ground a sufficient
time to clear those places from the colouring matter of the dye
which had not been acted upon by the mordant: a different mordant was then applied by the pencil; and it was necessary to pass
the whole piece through the dyeing copper a second time, in order
to give the desired colour to those particular parts and finish the
pattern.

Now, all these effects are produced by dyeing the cloth a uniform
colour in the first instance, and afterwards merely printing the
pattern with a chemical preparation which discharges a part of
the original dye and leaves a new colour in its stead. Thus a
brown may be changed in an instant to an orange; a dark olive
to a yellow; or a black to a bright scarlet. In consequence of
similar improvements, rich chintz patterns, which formerly required two years or more to be completed, are now commonly
finished in a few weeks.

the difficulty of manufacture, are peculiarly liable to adulteration.

The art of BLEACHING, which is so intimately connected with calico-printing, has also received such improvement from the science of chemistry, that no man is now capable of conducting it to the best advantage, without a knowledge of the principles on which the present practice is established.

A few years ago the art of bleaching was carried on by merely exposing the cloth to air and light; this process generally occupied several weeks; in consequence of chemical discovery the whole process is now concluded in as many days, and a new source of national wealth has sprung up in the manufacture of the bleaching liquor which chemistry has taught us to apply to this branch of manufacture.

The manufactures of EARTHENWARE and PORCELAIN, which were so much improved and extended by the ingenious and industrious Wedgwood, are dependent upon chemistry for the successful management of all their branches, from the mixture of the materials which form the body of the ware, to the production of those brilliant colours which give a value to the manufactures by their permanency and beauty.

Mr. Wedgwood was so sensible of the importance of chemistry to these arts, that he devoted a great part of his life to the study of this science, and not only attended to those branches which practically bore upon his own manufactures, but successfully cultivated the more advanced parts of this science, and added many new facts to chemistry which have rendered his name distinguished among the successful cultivators of the science.

A faint idea of the advantages which he derived from

B 2

these sources may be conceived from the following circumstance :—Dr. Bancroft, in his "Philosophy of Permanent Colours," when treating on iron, says, "I remember having been told by Mr. Wedgwood, that nearly all the fine diversified colours applied to his pottery were produced only by the oxides of this single metal." This one fact is sufficient to show with what assiduous application he must' have studied chemical science, and how insufficient every attempt to bring his manufacture to the perfection which it has now attained, would have been, without this attention.

The sister art, that of making GLASS, is also entirely chemical, consisting in the fusion of siliceous earth with alkali and the oxides of lead. In this trade, as well as in many others, the chemical manufacturer, and the man of enlightened experience, will have many advantages. He will not only know how to analyse his alkalies and to ascertain their exact value before he purchases, but will be enabled on chemical principles to ascertain the exact quantity necessary for any fixed portion of silex, which to those who are ignorant of our science must always be a matter of uncertainty, and must repeatedly subject them to losses and disappointment. And it is probably solely owing to the insufficient chemical education of the glass manufacturers of this country, that we are unable to produce in Great Britain any glass capable of bearing comparison with that manufactured on the Continent for optical purposes.

The TANNING OF HIDES is a process which·was formerly carried on by persons who merely followed a routine of operations, to which they had been accustomed, without knowing the real cause of any of the changes produced. It has now, however, been well ascertained, that the whole art consists in impregnating the animal matter with that peculiar principle taken from the vegetable kingdom, called *tan* (or *tannin*), the effect of which may be explained entirely on chemical principles. It is also now known that many substances besides oak bark, as the gallnut, horse-chestnut, &c. contain tan; and to chemistry we are indebted for the means of discovering with accuracy the *quantity* of tan which the several astringent vegetables contain. Besides, this principle having been formed *artificially* by union of the elementary substances which compose it, it is not improbable · that, whenever these manufacturers pay a proper attention to the science we recommend, they may be able to direct us how to prepare for them, in our laboratories, the article in question, so as entirely to supersede the use of oak bark. This would be an event of great national importance, as the demand at present is so great, that it is not only imported from the continent, but trees, it is well known, have been actually cut down on purpose to obtain the bark. Should the tanner not be fortunate enough to make a discovery of the kind just mentioned, he will at least be able to analyse the substances now in use, and by experiments of the most simple kind to appreciate their *relative* value; a matter of no small moment to a man who operates upon a large scale. Chemistry will enable him also to combine the tanning principle with the skins, so as to form leather the most impervious to moisture; and to give the hides the greatest increase of weight in the least possible time :— and these are the main secrets on which the profit of the trade chiefly depends.

The manufacturers of MOROCCO LEATHER, an article entirely new in the productions of this country, have had the utmost reason to regret the want of chemical knowledge. Till within these few years, the consumers of morocco depended entirely on a foreign supply, many fruitless attempts having been made to prepare the article in this country. Later trials with various chemical mordants, have, however, so far succeeded, that several manufactories have been established in the metropolis, where the most beautiful moroccos are now prepared at prices which have superseded the necessity of all foreign importation.

The manufacture of SOAP, an art of considerable importance, and which materially aids the revenue of the country, has in general been conducted, like many of the foregoing, without any regard to system : and yet, perhaps, there is no manufacture which can be benefitted in such various ways by chemistry as this. To those who are designed for this trade we have no hesitation in recommending the study of the science as a matter of the first importance. Many thousands per annum, now lost to the community, would be saved, if the trade were in general carried on upon scientific principles. Make a soap-boiler a good chemist, and you teach him how to analyse barilla, kelp, potash, &c. so as to ascertain the proportion of alkali in each—the only sure guide to purchasing with advantage and profit, which with the common manufacturer is mere chance. When these articles are at a high price, he will have recourse to various residuums, which he will decompose by *chemical* means, and make use of as substitutes. He will learn, in choosing his tallows, how to avoid those which contain a large portion of sebacic acid, which require much *more* barilla than good tallow, and yet produce *less* SOAP. He will know how to oxidize the common oils and oil dregs, so as to give them consistence, and render them good substitutes for tallow,—

and how to apportion his lime so as to make his alkali perfectly caustic, without using an unnecessary quantity of that article.   He will be aware of the advantage to be derived from oxidizing the soap while boiling.   A knowledge of chemical affinities will teach him how, at a cheap rate, to make as good and as firm soap with *potash*, as with the mineral alkali; and how to take up the heterogeneous salts, so as to give the alkali full opportunity of forming a chemical combination with the oils, tallows, &c.   And, lastly, he will know how to make use of the *waste* lyes so as to decompose the salts which they contain, and convert them to good and serviceable alkali, fit for future operations.[a]

The manufacture of CANDLES, which is often connected with the foregoing, though it is of less importance, derives great advantages from chemistry. Foreign tallows frequently contain a large portion of acid, which renders them inferior to the English; these may be purified at a trifling expense by chemical means; and by the proper application of chemical agents, other brown tallows may be rendered beautifully white, and fit for the best purposes. In consequence of the attention recently bestowed upon the investigation of chemical character of fatty matters, a substance has been discovered, which by union with $\frac{1}{8}$ part of wax, yields a compound almost equal to the best wax for the manufacture of candles ; and we shall probably ere long be able to procure *stearine* candles of a quality fully equal to wax, and at a far lower price.

In connection with this subject, we may mention the application of gas to the purposes of illuminating our

[a] It was experiments carried on with this object which gave rise to the discovery of the important substance Iodine, which was found to exist in soaper's waste, by a manufacturer in Paris.—ED.

streets and houses, the discovery and application of which are entirely due to the cultivation of chemistry ; by means of this discovery we are enabled to make use of a clean and economical mode of supplying our houses with light, and of making our streets during the night safe and convenient for business; while at the same time, by diminishing the demand for oil and tallow, these substances can be more extensively used in other branches of trade, especially the manufacture of soap, an article on the cheapness of which the cleanliness and comfort, and consequently the health of the community so much depends : the use of gas also in our manufactories has proved highly beneficial, from the safety attending it compared with the former modes of supplying light ; and we may sanguinely expect, that ere many years, owing to the industry of chemists, it will altogether supersede every other method of supplying artificial light.

The BREWING OF FERMENTED LIQUORS, a trade of considerable consequence in the metropolis, is altogether a chemical process. To those persons, whose concerns are so large that it would require a princely fortune to purchase even the *utensils*, it must surely be of the utmost importance to acquire some knowledge of the principles of bodies, and of the nature of those changes which take place in the materials upon which they operate. I would therefore say to such persons, give your sons a chemical education, and you will fit them for conducting, in the best possible manner, the business which you have established. Hence they will learn how the barley, in the first instance, is converted to a *saccharine* substance by malting; how the fermentative process converts the saccharine to a *spirituous* substance ; and how the latter, by a continuation of the process, becomes changed into *vinegar*. The nature of fermentation (which till lately was entirely unknown) will be studied and understood; and they will not only have learnt the means of promoting and encouraging this process, but how to retard and check it, whenever it is likely to be carried too far; so that the scientific brewer will be as sure of uniformly obtaining satisfactory results, as he would be if he were operating on a matter by mere mechanical means.[a]

In like manner the DISTILLER, the maker of SWEET WINES, and the VINEGAR MANUFACTURER, will all receive benefit from the cultivation of the science we are recommending. Till the promulgation of the new chemical doctrines, the making of vinegar was carried on like many other trades, in which the makers themselves had no idea of the nature of their process. An acquaintance with chemistry will teach them many important matters; particularly how it is that the spirituous fermentation is succeeded by the acetous; and how the liquor acquires the substance necessary to produce this change. When this is once known, they will soon find by experiment how to oxygenize their wash at the least expense, and in the least possible time. Indeed, when chemical knowledge is more advanced, the process which now takes several months will probably be completed in as many days.[b]

[a] *Vide* the article Brewing, in the Library of Useful Knowledge, Nos. 57 and 60. This is considered one of the best essays on this subject yet published.—ED.

[b] At present the best vinegar is made by the destructive distillation of wood in close iron retorts. By this process an article is produced superior in many respects to that formerly manufactured, and at a cost far less than vinegar or acetic acid could be obtained of the same quality.—ED.

The REFINING OF SUGAR is also a chemical process, every branch of which depends upon laws well known to chemists. The separation of the sugar from the . molasses; the absorption of the superabundant acid ; the granulation of the purified sugar; and the crystal- lization of candy, will all be conducted most econo- mically, and with the least difficulty, by those who have studied the science with a view to the improvement of their art.

In France and Germany, they have recently com- menced this branch of manufacture, and owing to the improvements in the theory of sugar making, and the exclusive duty levied upon Colonial produce, they are now able to produce an article capable of vying both in quality and cheapness, with foreign manufactured sugars.   The experiment of producing home-grown sugar is also being tried in England and Ireland; we know not, however, with what prospects of success.[a]

The REFINING OF GOLD AND SILVER may appear to be merely a mechanical operation ; but even in this trade the artist cannot produce a single effect which is not attributable to the play of the chemical affinities. Besides, there is great reason to believe that a con- siderable portion of silver is often lost in the process which succeeds that of *quartation*, by the blue water being removed to the verditer-vats before the whole of the silver has been precipitated. A knowledge of

---

[a] The quantity of sugar from beet-root and chestnuts made in France and Germany at present, is said far to exceed that im- ported from the colonies, owing to the high duties levied on West Indian sugar; and it is probable that, ere many years, its manu- facturers will be able completely to supply their own market ; there are a number of manufactories of sugar already established on the Rhine, which consume several million pounds of beet annually. —ED.

chemical principles would suggest to the refiner a mode by which, without the aid of any apparatus, he might in an instant detect even a tenth of a grain of that metal, if left in the solution.

The manufacturers of ALUM, of COPPERAS, of BLUE VITRIOL, and of all other SALTS, would likewise do well to become chemists, before they attempt to bring their several arts to the perfection of which they are capable. The crystallization of salts depends upon so many adventitious circumstances, that no small share of knowledge is necessary to enable a manufacturer at all times, and in all seasons, to produce the article he intends.

· Even science itself is now reaping the benefit of its own discoveries. Many years ago the MANUFACTURERS OF PAPER were apprehensive that it would be impossible to supply a quantity of that article fit for printing upon, adequate to the increasing demand. Necessity, however, often the source of new inventions, had recourse to chemistry ; and in this science, of universal application, found the means of improving the colour of the very coarsest materials ;—so that rags, which formerly would have been thrown aside for paper of the lowest description, are now rendered subservient to the progress of truth, and the promulgation of knowledge. And so easy is the application, that an immense quantity of the materials can be bleached in a few hours at a trifling expense.

In like manner it might be shown that the making of BREAD, SUGAR, STARCH, VARNISH, and OIL OR VITRIOL, the REFINING OF SALTPETRE, and the MANU-FACTURES OF PRUSSIAN BLUE, CUDBEAR, ARCHILL, and other colours, are all dependent upon chemistry for their improvement and successful practice :—but we

flatter ourselves that the examples already adduced are
sufficient to show that chemistry is now a necessary
branch of the education of youth.   Even the management of a GARDEN may receive improvement from the
cultivation of this science, as it explains the growth of
vegetables, shows the use of the different manures, and
directs the proper application of them.

The various operations of Nature,[a] and the changes
which take place in the several substances around us,
are so much better understood by an attention to the
laws of chemistry, that in every walk of life the chemist
has a manifest advantage over his illiterate neighbour.
And it may be remarked, that in case of failure or disappointment in any particular line of commercial manufacture, the scientific chemist has resources as various
as the productions of the country in which he lives, to
which the uneducated man has no access.

Were parents aware of this truth, that sordid maxim
primò vivere, deindè philosophari, would not be heard,
but every youth would be instructed in the first principles of natural philosophy and chemistry, as *the
means* of qualifying him for conducting with advantage
the concerns with which he might be intrusted. If
" knowledge is power," surely the *love* of knowledge,
and a taste for accurate investigation, is the most likely
way for conducting to opulence, respectability, and
rational enjoyment.

Moreover, it is the necessary consequence of an
attention to this science, that it gives the habit of *investigation*, and lays the foundation of an ardent and

---

[a] " Man should observe all the workmanship and the particular
workings of Nature, and meditate which of these may be transferred
to the arts."—Lord Bacon's *Advancement of Learning*, book v.
148.

inquiring mind. If a youth has been taught to receive nothing as true, but what is the result of *experiment*, he will be in little danger of ever being led away by the insidious arts of sophistry, or of having his mind bewildered by scepticism or superstition. The knowledge of *facts* is what he has been taught to esteem; and no reasoning, however specious, will ever induce him to receive as true what appears incongruous, or cannot be recommended by demonstration or analogy.

TO THE READER.

The pupil is advised to go through the catechetical part of each chapter before he attends to the notes; for, as the questions generally arise out of the preceding answers, the connection of the whole will be best perceived, and more likely to be remembered, by this method.

CHEMICAL CATECHISM.

CHAPTER I.

INTRODUCTORY AND MISCELLANEOUS.

1. WHAT is Chemistry ?[a]

Chemistry is the science which enables us to discover the peculiar properties of bodies, either in their simple or compound state.

[a] The following definitions of chemistry have been given by some of the most celebrated writers on this science. That in the text was chosen on account of its conciseness, and the facility of being committed to memory:—

Chemistry relates to those operations by which the intimate nature of bodies is changed, or by which they acquire new properties.—*Sir H. Davy.*

Chemistry is the science which teaches us the composition of bodies and their mutual relations.—*Berzelius.*

Chemistry is that science which treats of those events or changes in natural bodies which are not accompanied by sensible motions.—*Thomson.*

Chemistry is that branch of natural knowledge which teaches us the properties of the elementary substances, and of their mutual combinations; it inquires into the laws which affect, and into the powers which preside over their union; it examines the proportions in which they combine, and the modes of separating them when combined, and endeavours to apply such knowledge to the explication of natural phenomena, and to useful purposes in the arts.—*Brande.*

Chemistry is that science, the object of which is to examine the relations that affinity establishes between bodies, ascertain with precision the nature and constitution of the compounds it produces, and determine the laws by which its actions are regulated.—*Turner.*

2. How are the properties of bodies examined?

The chemical examination of bodies is in general effected by producing a change [a] in the *nature* or *state* of the body under examination.

3. By what means do chemists effect a change in the qualities or states of bodies?

This is generally effected by means of *heat*,[b] or by the *mixture* of some other matter with the matter intended to be examined.

4. How does the application of heat and mixture enable chemists to examine the properties of bodies?

[a] To the eye, many substances appear similar to other substances, though they possess different, and perhaps opposite, qualities; it therefore became necessary to discover the means of analysing these substances, and of ascertaining wherein their difference consists. This we find in chemical *re-agents*.

It may, with few exceptions, be considered as an axiom in the science of which we are treating, that *whenever chemical action takes place, a real change is produced in the substance operated upon, and that its identity is destroyed.* An example will place this in a clear point of view. If a little carbonate of lime (powdered chalk) be put into a glass of water, the chalk will sink to the bottom of the vessel. Though it should be mixed with the water, if left at rest it will soon subside. No chemical action has taken place; therefore the water and the carbonate of lime both remain unaltered. But if a small quantity of muriatic acid be added to a glass of chalk and water, a violent effervescence will commence when they come into contact with each other; in consequence of this *chemical* action a complete change is effected in the characters of the chalk and acid, the chalk dissolves in the water and acquires a sharp taste, and the acid has lost its sourness; in fact, a new substance (muriate of lime) is produced.

[b] Heat has a tendency to separate the particles of bodies from each other. Hence nothing more is necessary to effect the decomposition of many bodies than to apply heat, and collect the substances which are separated by that means. We have a familiar example of this in the burning of common limestone; in this operation the carbonic acid of the limestone is expelled, and the lime remains in its caustic state; a complete *chemical* change has been produced in this case by *heat* alone; the lime will no longer effervesce in vinegar or any other acid, as limestone will, and it will have acquired a sharp acrid taste, the limestone before burning being perfectly tasteless: magnesia undergoes a similar change. Many other instances will occur hereafter.— ED.

By these means we effect the *decomposition* of a compound body, and thus acquire a knowledge of the nature, of its ingredients.

5. What is meant by decomposition?

In chemical language, decomposition means the art of dividing a body into its simple elements. Thus water may be decomposed, and reduced into oxygen and hydrogen, which are simple substances, incapable of further decomposition.

6. What is analysis?[a]

Analysis is the separation of the parts of a compound body from each other, by means of *reagents*, so as to present the constituents either in an uncombined or a new state of combination.

7. What is synthesis?[b]

Synthesis is the *putting together* or combining the separated constituents of a body so as to reproduce the original compound.[c]

[a] This term is derived from the Greek words which signify to separate.

[b] This is derived from the Greek to put together or combine.

[c] Recourse is had to these two methods of investigation whenever it is possible, in order to arrive at certainty respecting the nature of any compound. We first by analysis separate the elementary substances from each other, and then verify our result by combining these elements so as to reproduce the compound. There are, however, numerous cases where this cannot be done. We may take the following example of analysis and synthesis: If we make a solution of sulphate of magnesia (Epsom salt) in boiling water, and pour into it a little of a solution of carbonate of soda, the soda will precipitate a white powder, which on examination will be found to be carbonate of magnesia. When settled, decant the supernatant liquor, evaporate it till a pellicle rises on its surface, and set it aside to crystallize. When cold, crystals of sulphate of soda (Glauber's salt) will be found in the vessel. In this decomposition, the sulphuric acid of the Epsom salt combines with the soda to form sulphate of soda, and the carbonic acid of the soda combines with the magnesia to form carbonate of magnesia. Thus Epsom salt may be analysed, and shown to consist of sulphuric acid and magnesia. In order to prove the composition of this salt by *synthesis*, dissolve magnesia in

8. Give an example of these modes of examination ?

Water may by *analysis* be resolved into oxygen and hydrogen gases, and we can verify this *analysis* by uniting oxygen and hydrogen so as to reproduce water.

9. What are the most general properties of matter ?

Extension, or the property of occupying space, and *impenetrability*, or that property of matter in consequence of which no two portions of matter can co-exist in the same portion of space.

10. Has matter any other properties ?

Yes, it is susceptible of rest or motion,[a] divisible and indestructible.

11. What do you mean by divisibility ?

That property by which portions of matter may be subdivided into parts almost infinitely small.[b]

---

diluted sulphuric acid, saturate the liquor, and crystallize. Epsom salt will be the result.

It may be remarked, that chemists have not only the power of decomposing natural bodies, but of producing, by combinations, various other substances, such as are not found in the kingdoms of nature. Alcohol and ether are of this class.

[a] This is expressed by the term *vis inertiæ*, or the resistance of matter to any change when in a state of rest or motion.

[b] It can be proved mathematically that matter is infinitely divisible, and indeed we cannot conceive any particle of matter so minute as not to be capable of division into two separate parts; however, that there is a limit to division of bodies, or ultimate particles incapable of further division appears now established in consequence of the discovery of the atomic theory, of which we shall speak in a subsequent chapter.

That matter is capable of *almost* infinite division may be shewn in many ways: a single grain of gold is capable of being extended into a leaf of fifty square inches surface, and this surface is capable of mechanical division into two millions of parts visible to the eye: one ounce of gold may be extended upon a silver wire to such an extent, that the wire will be capable of division into 140,000,000,000 visible parts. Extraordinary as this mechanical division may appear, we can exhibit the divisibility of matter by chemical experiment yet more remarkably: if we take a grain of silver, and dissolve it in nitric acid, and add this to 40,000 times its weight of water, in which a small quantity of common salt (muriate of soda) has been dissolved, we shall find distinct traces of the silver

12. What is meant by indestructibility?

That though the particles of matter are continually undergoing changes, yet that none of these particles ever cease to exist.

13. How can you explain the many instances that occur of apparent destruction of matter, such as by the combustion of fuel, candles, &c. &c.?

In all these cases matter merely assumes a new form, no portion being destroyed; if in the cases adduced we collect the matter passing away as invisible vapour, we find it equivalent to the quantity of solid matter which disappears.

14. What are the different states in which bodies exist or their states of aggregation?

All bodies exist either as solids, liquids, or gases.

15. Is there not another class of bodies?

Yes; the imponderable substances, heat, light, and electricity; we are, however, ignorant of the state in which these exist, or whether or not they are material substances.

16. What do you mean by a solid body?

Solidity is that quality of bodies whereby their parts resist impression.

17. From what does this quality of solid bodies arise?

in the hundredth part of a grain of the fluid, or the grain of silver has been divided into four millions of visible parts.

A grain of iron, dissolved in nitro-muriatic acid, and mixed with 3137 pints of water, will be diffused through the whole mass. By means of the ferro-cyanuret of potassium, which strikes one uniform blue tint, some portions of iron may be detected in every part of the liquid. This experiment proves the grain of iron to have been divided into rather more than twenty-four millions of parts; and if the iron were still further diluted, its diffusion through the whole liquid might be proved by concentrating any portion of it by evaporation, and diluting the metal by its appropriate tests.

Dr. Thomson states, in his chemistry, that the smallest *chemical* particle of lead cannot weigh more than the 310 billionth part of a grain, or exceed in size the 888 trillionth part of a cubic inch: inconceivably minute as this seems to be, it may far exceed the size of the chemical atom.—ED.

C

From an attraction[a] between the particles of matter or the *force of cohesion.*

18. What are liquids?

Liquids are substances whose particles have free motion upon one another, their cohesion being prevented by a repulsive force existing among them.

19. What are gases?

Gases are substances possessing no cohesive attraction, and whose particles are kept asunder owing to a repulsive force existing among them.

20. What is the difference between liquids and gases?

Liquids are almost incompressible fluids, gases are highly elastic fluids; the particles of liquids attract each other to a certain extent; the particles of gases repel each other to an indefinite extent.

21. Is fluidity an essential state of matter?

It seems probable that solidity is the natural state of all bodies, and that fluidity is owing to the union of solid or liquid matter with heat.

22. Can you give any proofs of this?

By union with heat almost all solid substances can be converted into liquids or gases, and *vice versâ,* by abstraction of heat most liquids can be made to assume the solid form.[b]

23. What are vapours?

---

[a] Attraction is named according to the modes in which it acts, either gravitation, cohesion, capillary, or chemical attraction; the attraction of gravitation is the force which acts at sensible distances upon masses of matter; cohesion the force which acts at imperceptible distances upon the ultimate particles of matter, and keeps its particles together; capillary attraction is the force exerted between a fluid and the pores of a solid: we shall detail the nature of chemical attraction in a subsequent chapter.

[b] Not only fluids, but all those substances which are soft and ductile, owe these properties to the chemical combination of caloric. Metals owe their malleability and ductility to the same cause; for its very intense artificial colds, the most ductile metals, such as gold, silver, and lead, lose their malleability and become brittle, as Van Mons has shown.—*Annales de Chimie,* tom. xxix. 300.

Vapours are substances which exist usually as solids or fluids, but which are changed to the aëriform state by increase of temperature or diminished pressure.

24. What substances do you call fluids?

All substances whose particles have free motion amongst each other are natural fluids; all liquids, gases and vapors, are therefore fluids; for example, water, the air of the atmosphere, and steam.

25. What is the cause of bodies swimming in fluids?

Because they are specifically lighter than the fluids.

26. What do you mean by this? [a]

That a body which floats in a fluid must be lighter than *its own bulk* of the fluid; for as the particles of a liquid press equally in every direction, when a body is immersed in a fluid it displaces so much of it as is equal to itself in bulk, and this quantity was supported in its place by the pressure of all the adjacent fluid, and, therefore, the solid will be subjected to the pressure which was necessary to support its own bulk of the fluid, or will lose as much weight as its own bulk of the fluid, therefore, if its own bulk of the fluid weigh more than the weight of the solid, it will float in the fluid. Any solid which weighs less than its own bulk of a fluid will float in that fluid. [b]

[a] This may be shown to a child at the breakfast table, by placing a tea-cup upon a basin of water, and informing him that it swims there because it is specifically lighter than a body of water of its own bulk. Water may then be gradually poured from the tea-pot into the cup; and he may be directed to observe how the cup sinks in the basin as it becomes loaded with water, until the united weights of the water and the cup are too great for the water in the basin to support, and the whole sinks.

[b] Here the pupil may be informed that it is on this principle that ships and other vessels are constructed, and that it is this property of fluids which enables us to float a vessel from one country to another. The weight of goods in a vessel is indicated by the depth to which the vessel sinks in the water. In canal boats this is shown by graduated metallic plates affixed to them. An account of a curious method of ascertaining the tonnage of ships, hydrostatically, may be seen in the first number of the Retrospect. It is founded on the

27. What, then, is the reason that a piece of cork will float upon the surface of water and a piece of iron will sink in it?

Because the cork weighs less and the piece of iron weighs more than its own bulk of water, consequently the cork is supported in the water and the iron sinks.[a]

28. What term is made use of to express the relative weight of bodies?

Specific gravity. Thus the specific gravity of one body may be much greater than that of another, though their absolute weights be the same.[b]

29. How do you explain the difference in the specific gravity of different bodies?

When one body is larger, or takes up more room, than another of the same weight, the first is said to be *specifically* lighter.

different draught which a ship will have in salt and in fresh water, owing to the different specific gravity of the two fluids. That nautical men should be acquainted with this hydrostatical axiom, is certainly of importance; for, should a captain load his vessel with a *full* cargo at any seaport, his vessel would inevitably sink when brought into the Thames.

[a] It is an axiom in hydrostatics, that every substance which *swims* on water, displaces so much of the water as is exactly equal to its own weight; whereas, when a substance *sinks* in water, it displaces water equal to its bulk, and less than its weight.

Take a piece of hard wood, balance it accurately in a pair of scales with water, and then place it gently on the surface of water in a vessel exactly filled with that fluid, and it will displace a portion of the water, which will flow over the top of the vessel. If the wood be now taken out with care, it will be found that the water in the scale will exactly fill the vacancy left by the wood.

[b] The specific gravity of bodies is denoted in chemical writings by comparing it with the specific gravity of pure water, in decimal figures, water being always considered as 1.000. Thus the specific gravity of the strongest sulphuric acid of commerce is said to be 1.900, or nine-tenths heavier than water. Iron is 7.650, or more than $7\frac{1}{2}$ times heavier than water; that is, a cubic inch of iron, if put in a scale, would require $7\frac{1}{4}$ inches of water to balance it; silver is 10.478; gold, 19.300; and platinum 23.000, or 23 times heavier than water. The specific gravity of bodies is noted in the same way throughout this work.

· 30. How do you ascertain the specific gravity of a substance?

If possible, I take equal bulks of the substance whose specific gravity I want to ascertain, and some standard of comparison, and the proportion of their weights gives me the specific gravity.

31. What substance is generally used as a standard of comparison?

Water is usually employed for solids and liquids, and atmospheric air for gases.

· 32. How can you obtain the specific gravity of a solid compared with water?

As I cannot compare the weights of equal bulks directly, I make use of the hydrostatical principle already mentioned, "that solids lose by immersion in a fluid a portion of their weight equal to the weight of their own bulk of the fluid." I, therefore, by taking a known weight of a solid, and ascertaining its loss of weight by immersion in water, can ascertain its specific gravity; for the loss of weight is to the absolute weight as the specific gravity of water is to the specific gravity sought.[a]

· [a] The following is the method of obtaining the specific gravity of a solid depending on this principle. We append the solid to the extremity of the arm of a beam, by a fine silk thread, and having weighed it first in the air we place under it a vessel (e) of pure water; on immersing it in the water we find that the beam is no longer balanced, but that the scale (c) preponderates, we therefore place weights in the scale (a) until the equilibrium is restored; the weight necessary to restore the equilibrium is the loss of weight sustained by immersion, or *the weight of an*  *equal bulk* of water: the weight of the body in air multiplied by 1000, and divided by the loss of weight, will therefore give us the specific gravity of the solid compared with water taken as 1000.—ED.

· 33. How do you find the specific gravity of a liquid?[a]

By weighing a vessel filled with the liquid, and then weighing the same vessel filled with water; as I have in this case the weights of equal bulks, I have at once the specific gravity, for the weight of the vessel filled with water is to its weight filled with the given liquid, as 1000 is to the specific gravity of the fluid.[b]

34. What definition do you give of the atmosphere which you spoke of in connection with this subject?

The air is that very light fluid which surrounds us every where; it is the medium in which we live, and without which we could not exist.

35. What is the specific gravity of atmospheric air?

A cubic inch of water weighs 252·458 grs.; a cubic inch of air weighs only thirty-one hundredths of a grain; a cubic foot of water, therefore, weighs upwards of 75lbs. and a cubic foot of air only 536 grs.; consequently water is more than 800 times heavier than air.

36. If the specific gravity of water be so much greater than that of atmospheric air, how is water retained in the atmosphere?

[a] The nations of antiquity were unacquainted with any method of ascertaining the specific gravity of bodies. A singular event was the cause of its being discovered by Archimedes 200 years before Christ. Having reason to believe that an unprincipled goldsmith had greatly debased the golden crown of Hiero II, king of Syracuse, he was anxious to ascertain the fact; but was perplexed by not knowing how to effect it. However, one day while bathing, the difference in the weight of his own body, when in the water and when out of it, gave him the idea that he might adopt *that* method for discovering the specific gravity of the king's crown; and it is related of him that he was so rejoiced at the discovery, that he leaped from the bath in an ecstacy, and ran naked about the streets of Syracuse, crying *I have found it! I have found it!*

[b] This word is derived from the Greek language, and signifies a body of vapour in a spherical form. By this name we understand the "entire mass of air which encircles all parts of the terrestrial globe, which moves with it round the sun, which touches it in all its parts, ascending to the tops of its mountains, penetrating into its cavities, and incessantly floating on its waters. It is the fluid which we inhale from the first to the last moment of our existence.

The water which is taken up by the atmosphere is not in an aqueous state, but is converted into vapour[a] by union with heat.[b]

37. How is it that heat converts water into vapour?

A large portion of the matter of heat combining with water, renders it specifically lighter; which is the cause of its rising, and mixing with the atmosphere.[c]

38. Is this effected in any of the great operations of nature?

Yes; the waters of the earth are continually undergoing the process of evaporation, by which they are converted into vapour, which rises in the air, and when condensed, forms clouds.[c]

[a] As it is of importance to demonstrate to a young person the truth of every thing we teach him, the opportunity ought never be omitted. This can be done, to prove the assertion in the text, by the simple experiment of inverting a glass goblet over a cup of hot water, when the vapour will be seen to condense upon the cold glass and run down the inside; which will show that steam is *real* water, and can become water again.

[b] Here the pupil may be informed that water not only becomes converted into steam by heat, but that, when it is received into the atmosphere, if the air be warm, it becomes so far changed by its union with the matter of heat as to be perfectly invisible. In this state it occupies a space 1700 or 1800 times greater than in its ordinary liquid state.

[c] It is of great importance to be able to ascertain the quantity of moisture contained in the atmosphere; to enable us to ascertain this point, three different species of *hygrometers* (or instruments to effect this) have been employed. The first is that of Saussure, who proposed the use of a human hair, the contraction and lengthening of which, from the air becoming dry or moist, enables us to form a rough estimate of its hygrometric state; this instrument depends on the property which almost all bodies have of attracting moisture, and which is found in a high degree to exist in *organized* substances. The second is that of Leslie, depending on the evaporation of water effected in a given time; the evaporation being slower or quicker in proportion to the quantity of water previously existing in the air. The third is that of Dr. Dalton, dependant upon the temperature at which moisture is deposited upon a cold body, or the *dew* point. When a glass of cold water is brought into a warm room we observe a deposition of moisture on it; now the temperature of the water at which this takes place affords us an indication of the quantity of mois-

39. What is the cause of the waters of the earth being thus vaporized ?

As the rays of the sun warm the earth, a portion of the matter of heat combines with a portion of the water, and converts it into vapour.[a]

40. But what causes the vapour to rise in the air ?

If a cork be placed at the bottom of a basin of water, it rises immediately to the top, because it is specifically lighter than the water ; so vapour rises in the air because it is specifically lighter than the air.

41. What becomes of the water which thus evaporates from the earth ?

It occupies the lower regions of the atmosphere, and is preserved there partly dissolved in air, and partly in the state of elastic vapour.

42. How is this vapour formed into clouds ?

---

ture contained in the air. The *hygrometer* of Professor Daniell, which is a very ingenious instrument, is constructed upon this principle, for the details respecting which we must refer to his meteorological Essays.—ED.

[a] Bishop Watson found that, even when there had been no rain for a considerable time, and the earth was dried by the parching heat of summer, it still gave out a considerable quantity of water. By inverting a large drinking-glass on a close-mown grass-plat, and collecting the vapour which attached itself to the inside of the glass, he found that an acre of ground dispersed into the air above 1600 gallons of water in the space of 12 hours of a summer's day.

The ocean loses many millions of gallons of water hourly by evaporation. The Mediterranean alone is said to lose more by evaporation than it receives from the Nile, the Tiber, the Rhone, the Po, and all the other rivers that fall into it. This water is conveyed by the winds to every part of the continents:—these it fertilizes in the form of rain, and afterwards supplies the rivers, which flow again into the sea.

In our climate evaporation is found to be about four times as much from the vernal to the autumnal equinox, as from the autumnal to the vernal. Heat facilitates all solutions ; and the greater the difference between the temperature of the air and the evaporating surface, the greater will be the evaporation.

In winter, the earth at eighteen inches depth is warmer than the air ; in summer, the air is warmer than the earth at that depth : these effects are owing to the earth being a bad conductor of heat.

After it has remained some time in the atmosphere, it becomes in a measure condensed by causes unknown to us ;[a] and the particles of water of which it is composed unite, and form small hollow vesicles, which accumulate together and produce clouds.[b]

43. What further changes take place in this aqueous vapour?

By the operation of causes which are also in a great measure unknown, the clouds after a time become further condensed, and are converted into water.

44. What is the consequence of this change of vapour into water?

When the vapour is condensed, it becomes too heavy for the air to support, and falls down in rain, hail, or snow,[c]

---

[a] This branch of meteorology is not yet perfectly understood. It is only understood that two masses of air of different temperatures meeting; the warmer being charged with moisture will cause rain ; many of these phenomena, however, remain as yet to be investigated.

[b] It is evident that water exists in the atmosphere in abundance, even in the driest seasons and under the clearest sky. There are substances which have the power of absorbing water from the air at all times ; such as the fixed alkalies, and sulphuric acid ; the latter of which will soon absorb more than its own weight of water from the air, when exposed to it.

There can be no doubt but that in general the vapours occupy the lower strata of the atmosphere : that they sometimes ascend very high, is also true ; for it is well known that clouds are seen forming above the tops of the highest mountains. Indeed, the clouds *begin* to form always at some considerable height.

Persons who have been in the habit of making observations on the clouds may have sometimes noticed a cloud, which appeared to be just in the act of precipitating, suddenly arrested by a warm current of air, and entirely dissolved, so that it soon becomes invisible. In the same manner warm air in passing over the sea and rivers dissolves and renders invisible much water, which on ascending to the colder regions of the atmosphere forms clouds. In the next chapter we shall more fully explain this subject, when we come to speak of the barometer.

[c] By the experiments of Saussure it appears that a cubic foot of atmospheric air will hold six grains of water in solution. From this property of the air we derive many advantages. It has a tendency to preserve every thing on the face of the earth in a proper degree of moisture. In one season of the year, in the interior parts of Africa,

45. Is this property of holding water in solution peculiar to atmospheric air ?

No; all gases have this property in common with
atmospheric air, as may be shewn by exposing them to
any substance having a strong attraction for moisture.

46. What is the use of this constitution of nature ?

This principle of evaporation is of universal importance
in all the operations of art, or of nature. It tends to
preserve the equable temperature of the human body in
consequence of the heat absorbed during the process,
and, by the formation of clouds, moderates the excessive
heat of the sun; by preventing the accumulation of
putrescent waters in the warmer regions of the earth, and
counteracting the effects of a tropical sun, it renders them
habitable by man; in the·most common-place employ-
ments recourse is had to its effects, and in the arts and
sciences we constantly have recourse to its agency.

47. What is the ultimate use of this principle?

The Almighty has contrived that moisture should
continually rise from the earth, and from the various
bodies upon its surface, to shield this world of ours from
the intense heat of the sun, and to return in rain to water
the ground, causing grass to grow for the cattle, and corn
and herbs for the service of man.[a]

a wind prevails called the *Harmattan*, which is so extremely dry that
household furniture is destroyed by it; the panels of wainscots split;
boarded floors are laid open; and the scarf-skin of the body peels
off, during its continuance. Were it not for the property which
atmospheric air has of holding water in solution, this would be the
case every where.

It appears from the experiments of some aëronauts, that the air is
much drier in the higher regions than it is near the surface of the
earth. Phil. Mag. vol. xix. 878.

[a] It may be observed that rain not only affords a proper degree of
moisture to the vegetable creation, but is of service in bringing the
soils into a proper state to perform their office. *Dry* earth of itself
has little effect; but when *moistened* it has the property of decomposing atmospheric air, and of conveying its oxygen to the roots of
those plants which vegetate within it. We are indebted to Humboldt
'or the knowledge of this fact.

CHAPTER II.

HEAT.

1. WHAT is heat?

Heat is the well-known sensation occasioned by touching bodies of a superior temperature.

2. What name is given to the cause of heat?

Chemists have agreed to call the cause of heat *caloric*,[a] when it is desirable to distinguish it from the sensation which this matter produces. Little inconvenience can however arise from using the term heat to express the cause producing the peculiar effects ascribed to caloric.

3. How do you show the advantage of distinguishing the cause of heat from the sensation?

Because, when I use the term heat for the sensation produced upon the human body, I am liable to err in consequence of my sensations deceiving me; for example, if I place one hand upon a hot body, the other upon a cold body, and then both hands upon a body of intermediate temperature, I shall feel the sensation of heat in the cold hand and of cold in the warm hand; so that judging by my senses the same body will feel at the same time hot and cold.

4. What are the different theories respecting the cause of heat?

Some have supposed it to be a material substance consisting of infinitely small and imponderable particles

---

[a] In order to give precision to chemical language, it was necessary to find a term to distinguish the matter of heat from its effect; for, whenever caloric becomes fixed or *latent* in a body, it loses its property of affording heat. Nothing can be more evident than that caloric may exist in many substances, without producing any of the effects which arise from the agency of fire.

thrown out by the heated body; others that it is an etherial fluid, pervading space and producing in us the sensation of heat by being thrown into a state of vibration; and some that it arises from a vibratory motion produced in the particles of matter. As none of these theories is yet established, we may adopt at present the first as the most easily understood.

5. What are the sources of caloric?

There are six sources from whence we procure caloric; viz. from the sun, by combustion, by friction, by chemical action, by means of electricity, and from vital action in organized beings.

6. Which of these is the principal source of caloric?

The sun is the first source which furnishes the earth with a regular supply,[a] and renders it capable of supporting the animal and vegetable creations.[b]

7. How is caloric furnished by combustion?

In the common cases of combustion, such as the burning of fuel, candles, &c. the heat is given out in consequence of the chemical action of the oxygen of the air upon the combustible substance.

---

[a] Taking it for granted that light and heat travel with equal velocity, it appears that caloric comes to us from the sun at the rate of 190,000 miles in a second of time; but as Dr. Herschel has proved, that the solar rays which produce heat are distinct from those which illuminate and produce vision, we cannot assert that the rays of heat travel with that velocity, though they must pass from the sun with very nearly the same velocity as light. It is exceedingly probable, from the similarity of the laws which regulate heat and light, that they are identical in composition, and their differences may only arise from the different velocities with which they move.

[b] According to the laws of nature, animal and vegetable life are both very much influenced by the temperature in which they exist; we therefore find different kinds of vegetables, and a different race of animals, appropriated to the different climates of the earth.

That caloric is as necessary for the support of vegetable as it is for that of animal life, may be proved by direct experiment. If in the midst of winter a hole be bored in a tree, and a thermometer put into it, it will be seen that the tree is many degrees warmer than the atmosphere.

8. How is caloric produced by friction or mechanical action?

The heat produced by friction is generally occasioned by the *compression* of the particles of the body, which compression forces out a portion of its latent caloric.[a]

9. In what way can heat be produced by electricity or galvanism?

By the discharge of an electrical battery, or by the galvanic apparatus, a more intense degree of caloric may be obtained than by any other means whatever.

10. How is heat communicated from one body to another?

Either by direct contact of the hot and cold body, or by radiation.

11. Whence does it arise that heat is communicated from one body to another?

From the tendency it has to equally diffuse itself, or attain a state of equilibrium.

12. How is heat communicated by contact?

By being slowly transmitted from particle to particle of the cold body; as for example, when I place a poker in the fire, the heat slowly passes from the fire through all parts of the poker in contact with it.

---

[a] We shall afterwards have occasion to refer to this subject. Count Rumford adduced this as one of the strongest arguments against the theory of the material nature of heat. He showed that by friction a piece of metal can be kept at a high temperature during an unlimited period, without any diminution of its quantity of heat; which he inferred could not be the case were heat a material substance in combination with the metal. As friction is one of the sources of heat most available to man in the savage state, we find that among the uncivilized human tribes it is constantly had recourse to for the purpose of producing fire; they have probably learned this by observing the instances where whole forests have been burnt down, by fires kindled from the violent friction of the branches against each other by the wind. Among the South Sea islanders and the inhabitants of California, wood is soon ignited by friction; the mode is either to make one piece revolve rapidly in a cavity in another piece, or simply to rub a stick for some time back and forwards on a plain surface of wood.—ED,

13. How is it communicated by radiation?

By being rapidly thrown off from the heated body in *rays* or right lines, as from the sun, the fire, &c. and so passing freely through the air.

14. Does heat pass with the same velocity through all bodies?

Radiant heat seems always to travel with the same velocity, but the heat communicated by contact travels with different velocities through different substances.

15. How are bodies named with respect to their power of transmitting heat by contact?

Conductors of heat; solids are the best conductors of heat, liquids and gases are the worst conductors of heat.

16. Have all solid substances the same power of conducting heat?

No; the metals are the best conductors, and in the following order: gold and silver conduct heat the best among the metals, copper, platina, iron, and lead—the last is the worst conductor of all the metals; woods, glass, clays, and wool are the worst solid conductors.

17. Can you shew the different conducting powers of different solids by any experiments?

If I hold a silver spoon in the flame of a candle, in the course of a few minutes it becomes so hot that I can no longer hold it, although I can hold a piece of wood, glass, or porcelain for a length of time in the flame without the heat being communicated to my fingers, which proves that the heat is conducted through the particles of the silver better than through the wood, &c.

18. You have said that fluids are bad conductors of heat: how does it happen that a vessel of water becomes soon heated when placed on a fire?

This is owing, not to the conducting power of the fluid, but to what is called its *carrying power;* in consequence of the particles of a fluid having free motion, when a vessel of water is heated *below,* these particles being rendered lighter than those above by being heated, ascend, and their place is taken by the cold particles, which when heated also ascend, and so the heat is conveyed through the fluid.

19. But can you prove that fluids are bad conductors?

Yes. If I place a piece of heated iron upon the surface of a vessel of water, and allow it to remain a great length of time, though the surface in contact with the iron is heated, I will find the water quite cold an inch below the surface. If I pour some ether over cold water and inflame it, after it has burned for some time the water below the surface still remains quite cold; proving that water is a very bad conductor of heat.

20. Do bodies, generally speaking, undergo any change by being heated?

Yes; all bodies increase their dimension or expand by heat; solids undergo the least change, fluids expand more than solids, and gases undergo the greatest enlargement of volume.

21. How do you prove this?

If I take a solid piece of iron capable, when cold, of passing freely though a hole in a plate of metal, and heat it, I find it will no longer pass through, shewing that its dimensions have increased; if I take a fluid, and when cold pour it into a vessel, so as to fill this completely, and then heat the fluid in the vessel, it will overflow, shewing that fluids expand by heat; if I take an air-tight bag, and having partially filled it with air, hold it before the fire, the air will expand, so as completely to fill the bag, proving that gases expand by heat.

22. Do you know of any practical uses to which the expansion of solids is applied?

Yes; there are many: one of the most obvious is the binding together the parts of machinery by iron hoops, put on when heated strongly, which on being allowed to cool contract and bind the parts they surround with great force.

23. Is there any use made of the expansibility of fluids by heat?

Yes; in the construction of the thermometer, in which the expansion of a fluid is made the measure of the quantity of sensible heat present in any substance.

24. What is the construction of a thermometer?

It is an instrument consisting of a glass ball connected with a hollow stem; the ball and part of the stem being filled with a fluid, the expansion of which serves as a measure of the quantity of sensible heat.

25. What fluids are employed in the construction of thermometers?

Mercury and spirit of wine; the former because the distance between the temperatures at which it boils and freezes is very great, and spirit of wine because it cannot be frozen, and is therefore well adapted for determining exceedingly low temperatures.

26. Are there any other thermometers in use?

Yes, the expansion of gases is made use of in the construction of thermometers. Sir J. Leslie made an instrument which he called a Differential Thermometer, in which he employed the expansion of air for measuring very slight differences of temperature.[a]

27. How is the thermometer scale divided?

Into a number of equal parts, which are named degrees; in this country the scale used is that of Fahrenheit, in which the interval between the freezing and boiling point of water is divided into 180 degrees.

28. From what temperature is the scale commenced?

From the temperature produced by mixing together

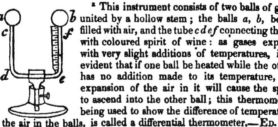

[a] This instrument consists of two balls of glass united by a hollow stem; the balls *a*, *b*, being filled with air, and the tube *c d e f* connecting them, with coloured spirit of wine: as gases expand with very slight additions of temperatures, it is evident that if one ball be heated while the other has no addition made to its temperature, the expansion of the air in it will cause the spirit to ascend into the other ball; this thermometer being used to show the difference of temperature the air in the balls, is called a differential thermometer.—ED.

ice and salt; this point was called zero, it being supposed that no greater cold could be produced than by
this mixture; Fahrenheit, therefore, imagined this to be
the point at which bodies are deprived of all heat; the
scale between this and the boiling point of water he divided into 212 parts, and the freezing point of water was
found to be in the 32nd division of this scale.[a]

29. Do all bodies expand when heated, and contract
when cooled?

No, some substances when cooling expand; the most
remarkable cases are some metals which expand when
assuming the solid form after fusion; of these iron affords
a good example, which when cast as it solidifies expands,
and so forms a perfect impression of the mould, and the
mixed metals used in the composition of printer's types,
which for the same reason assume accurately the form of
the matrix; some fluids also expand when cooling, the most
remarkable of which is water, which expands to a great

---

[a] There are different divisions of the thermometer used in different
parts of the world; that described above is that in use in these
countries; the following are used in different nations of Europe:

The centigrade thermometer of France places the zero at the
freezing point, and divides the range between it and the boiling point
into 100°. This has long been used in Sweden under the name of
Celsius's thermometer. The temperature, as given by this thermometer may be reduced to that of Fahrenheit by multiplying the
number of degrees by 9, dividing the product by 5, and adding
32: the reason of this is obvious; the scale in the centigrade is
divided into 100 parts from the freezing to the boiling points of
water, in Fahrenheit's thermometer into 180, and these are in the
proportion of 5 to 9, therefore the degrees in each thermometer are in
this proportion; and we add 32, as the scale of Fahrenheit commences
32 degrees lower than that of the centigrade.

In Reaumur's thermometer, which is at present in use in Germany,
the space between the freezing and boiling of water is divided into
80°, and the zero, as in the centigrade thermometer, placed at the
freezing point of water; the degrees of this thermometer are reduced
to those of Fahrenheit by multiplying by 9, dividing by 4, and adding
32; the reason is the same as in the former case.

De Lisle's thermometer is used in Russia. The graduation begins
at the boiling point, and increases towards the freezing point. The
boiling point is marked 0, and the freezing point 150°.

degree when changing into ice; at the temperature of
about 40° water has its greatest density; when cooled
below this, it begins to expand, and continues to increase
in bulk until the whole is solidified.

30. You have mentioned that heat is radiated from the
surfaces of bodies; does the *state* of a surface affect the
radiation of heat?

Yes; Leslie found that the colour and state of the
heated surface materially altered its radiating power; he
found that when a surface was black, it gave off heat
faster than when it was red or white—when rough better
than when polished.

31. How can this be shown experimentally?

By filling three vessels having surfaces in these three
states with water at the same temperature; we shall
find the black will cool more rapidly than the red or
white, and the roughened more rapidly than the polished
surface.

32. What practical uses are made of these discoveries?

When we wish to retain heat in bodies we always keep
their surfaces polished; this is of great use in parts of steam-
engines in which it is of importance to retain as much
of the heat as possible, and in different domestic utensils. When we wish to give off heat rapidly from a surface
we always have the surface blackened, as .this diffuses
the heat more quickly; thus in heating apartments by
means of steam or hot water, the surfaces of the tubes
are always blackened, and therefore diffuse the heat more
rapidly than if they were in any other state.

33. As heat is given off or radiated from bodies
with different degrees of celerity depending on the state
of their surfaces, we might expect to find that when
heat falls on a surface it would be absorbed with greater
or less facility according to the state of the surface; is
this the case?

.Yes; the *absorption* of heat is materially influenced by
the state of the surface upon which it falls; and we find

the best *radiating* surfaces are also the best absorbing surfaces; thus a black surface absorbs heat more rapidly than a red or white, and a rough more rapidly than a polished surface.

34. How is this demonstrated?

Dr. Franklin proved this many years ago by placing pieces of different coloured cloths upon snow, when he found that the snow melted more rapidly under a piece of black cloth than under a red, and more rapidly under a red than a white piece; in this way we shall find that with respect to colours, a black surface absorbs heat better than a white surface, and with respect to the state of surface, a rough better than a polished surface.

35. When heat falls upon a surface what are the different effects to which it is subject?

It may be absorbed as I have already mentioned; it may be reflected, or it may be transmitted through the body.

36. What do you mean by saying it may be reflected?

That it may be thrown off again from the surface, in the same manner as we know the rays of light are.

37. How was this proved?

By the experiment of Pictet; he showed that when a heated body was placed opposite a concave metallic mirror the heat was reflected from its surface and collected in the focus of the mirror; if, for example, we take two concave metallic mirrors *c d* and *e f*, and place them at the distance of several feet from each other, and place in the focus of one of them a heated ball *a*, and in the focus

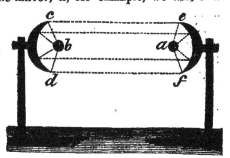

of the other a delicate thermometer, we shall find that

the heat radiated from the surface of the ball is reflected in parallel lines from the surface of the mirror *e f* and reflected to the focus *b* of the mirror upon *c d* the thermometer, which will immediately show a rise of temperature.

38. In speaking of the thermometer you stated that it showed us, by the expansion of the fluid within it, the quantity of *sensible* heat; does it show us the whole quantity of heat in a body?

No; it only shows that which is not chemically combined with the body: that it does not show the whole quantity of heat in a body is easily proved; if we place a vessel of snow before a fire, having placed a thermometer in it, the snow will gradually melt by union with the heat absorbed from the fire, and yet no change will take place in the fluid in the thermometer, because the heat does not become *sensible*.

39. How can you shew that bodies contain a large quantity of heat not appreciable by the thermometer?

Wrought iron, though quite cold, contains a large portion of *latent* caloric; and if it be briskly hammered for some time on an anvil, it will become red hot by the action of this species of caloric, which by the percussion of hammering is now evolved and forced out as *sensible* heat; while chemically combined with the iron, it only tended to give it malleability and ductility; but when converted to free caloric, it operates with as much activity as though it had never existed in a latent state.

If we mix a little sulphuric acid with about an ounce of nitric acid, and the mixture be poured into oil of turpentine, the whole will burst into flame. This is owing to the compound having less capacity for caloric than these separate fluids; consequently a part of their combined caloric is liberated, and produces the inflammation.[a]

[a] The phial containing the acids should be fixed to a rod, and its contents poured at once upon the oil in a cup, placed in the open air, or under a large chimney, to prevent any accident from the sudden combustion.

40. What substances contain latent caloric?

Caloric in a latent state exists in all substances that we are acquainted with.

41. Do all substances contain the same quantity of latent caloric?

No; caloric combines with different substances in different proportions; or, as Doctor Black, to whose discoveries we are indebted for our knowledge of this branch of science, expresses it, bodies have different capacities for heat; one body being capable of uniting with a greater quantity of heat than another.

42. Can you exemplify this curious property of matter?

If equal quantities, by weight, of water and mercury, cooled down to the same point, be afterwards separately heated to the temperature of boiling water, the water will be found to have required more than 23 times the quantity of caloric that the mercury did to bring it to that temperature. This property may be shown more readily by the following experiments:—Take 1 lb. of water at 100°, and mix it with 1 lb. of water heated to 200°, the mixture will be found to give the exact mean temperature of 150°; but 1 lb. of mercury at 100°, and 1 lb. of water at 200°, will produce a heat much higher than the mean temperature: mercury has not therefore so great a *capacity* for caloric as water. A metal plunged into an equal weight of water of a higher temperature, gains more degrees of thermometric heat than the water loses; and this takes place, in different proportions, for each species of metal. In all these cases it is necessary that there be no chemical action exerted between the bodies.

43. Is this capacity for caloric uniformly the same in the same bodies?

Yes; the same bodies have at all times the same capacity for caloric, unless some change takes place in the state of those bodies: as for example, when a solid changes its state and becomes a fluid or gas.

What change takes place in solids by change to the fluid state ?

44. Owing to their acquiring an increased capacity for heat, their sensible heat is absorbed and rendered latent, and consequently they indicate cold to the thermometer.

45. Give me some experiments in proof of this ?

If we dissolve certain salts in water a great degree of cold is produced; thus if we mix in a vessel of water muriate of ammonia, nitre and sulphate of soda, the solution of these salts will produce a degree of cold lower than that at which water freezes; on this principle all compound freezing mixtures are formed.

46. Does the contrary change take place when fluids become solids, or is the latent heat rendered sensible during this change ?

Yes; whenever a body changes from the fluid to the solid state, heat is given out; we have a good example of this in the slaking of quick-lime, in which case the heat escapes from the water in consequence of its changing from a liquid to a solid form by its union with the lime. The same effect is produced in making butter. When the cream changes from a fluid to a solid, a considerable degree of heat is produced.

47. According to this statement heat ought to be given out during the conversion of water into ice.

This we can prove to be the case; if we place a vessel of water in a freezing mixture and suspend over it a delicate thermometer, we find the thermometer will shew a rise of temperature at the moment the water begins to solidify. This may be shewn perhaps more clearly by the experiment first pointed out by Doctor Black.

If when the air is at 22° we expose to it a quantity of water in a tall glass, with a thermometer in it and covered, the water gradually cools down to 22° without freezing, though 10° below the freezing point. Things being in this situation, if the water be shaken, part of it instantly freezes into a spongy mass, and the temperature of the

whole instantly rises to the freezing point; so that the
water has acquired 10° of caloric in an instant. Now
whence came these 10°? Is it not evident that it must
come from that part of the water which was frozen, and
consequently that water in the act of freezing gives out
caloric?

48. How does this property of bodies operate?

Whenever a body has its capacity for caloric thus
increased, it requires a larger portion of the matter of
heat to raise it to a given temperature, than another body
does which has a less capacity for heat.

49. Is there any method of ascertaining the specific
caloric of different bodies, and comparing the relative
capacity of each for heat?

An instrument called a *calorimeter*,[a] is used for this
purpose. The substances to be tried are heated to the
same temperature, and then placed in this machine surrounded with ice. By observing how much ice each of
them melts in cooling down to a given point, the specific
caloric which each of them contained is determined.

50. What do you mean by heat becoming latent?

That when a body changes from the solid to the fluid
state, or from the state of fluid to that of a gas, that the
heat which combines with it in order to effect this change,
does not appear as sensible heat, but unites with the
body undergoing this change and remains latent.

51. Can you give me a familiar example of this?

In the case of ice thawing we have a good example;
all the heat we may communicate to a piece of ice or

---

[a] The calorimeter was first suggested by M. Laplace, and contrived by Lavoisier. Though this instrument be capable of measuring
what is called the *specific* caloric of bodies, no method has yet been
discovered of ascertaining the *absolute* quantity which bodies contain.
It is therefore unknown at what point a thermometer would stand, if
it were plunged into a substance entirely deprived of caloric. According to the experiments and calculations of Crawford, Irvine, and
others, the real zero is, probably, at least 1200 degrees below the
freezing point of water.

snow when thawing is rendered latent; the same thing occurs in the conversion of water into steam; for when the water begins to boil, its temperature never rises above 212° because the heat is carried off in a latent state by the steam, owing to its increased capacity for heat.

52. Why is the capacity of steam for heat greater than that of water?

Because water, by change into vapour, expands nearly 1800 times in volume, and therefore its capacity is increased.

53. Is the temperature at which water boils always the same?

No; the boiling points of all fluids depend on the pressure to which they are subjected; if we remove this pressure, the fluid will boil at a lower temperature; if we put a cup of ether under the receiver of an air pump, and remove the air, the ether will boil at a very low temperature; and this experiment will also shew, that a large quantity of heat is absorbed during the conversion of a fluid into elastic vapour, for the ether will become so cold during the ebullition, that if a tube be filled with water and placed within it, the water will be frozen.

54. What is the reason that steam issuing from high-pressure boilers, generally feels cold, when we know that the temperature of the steam and water within the boiler must exceed 212°?

Because the steam on coming into the air suddenly expands, and absorbs the sensible heat in consequence of its increased capacity.

55. What is the principle on which steam acts in the steam-engine?

Water when converted into steam forms a vapour, whose expansive force is proportional to its temperature; when, therefore, water is heated and converted into steam, this, in consequence of its expansion, is made to act as a moving power.

56. To what practical purposes is the fact of the boiling

point of water, varying with the pressure, made subservient?

It is often applied to the evaporation and concentration of solutions likely to be injured by subjecting them to a high temperature; in the refining of sugars, recourse is had to this law, in the concentration of the sirup, which, if boiled down at a high temperature, might suffer injury.

57. You have mentioned that steam contains a large quantity of heat; how is this shown?

When steam is reconverted into water the latent heat is given out; for this reason it is that a gallon of water in the form of steam will impart more heat to cold water than a gallon of water at the temperature of steam; for example, one part of water at 212° will raise the temperature of 100 parts of water at 50° only 1½ degrees: but one part of water as steam will raise 100 parts of water 11°. In consequence of the large quantity of heat contained in steam, it is used with advantage, on many occasions, to heat large quantities of fluids without the direct application of fire.

58. What do you call that portion of caloric which is a necessary part of fluids?

It is called the caloric of fluidity; and different fluids require different portions of it to preserve them in the liquid state.

59. Can you adduce any experiments in illustration of this?

If we mix together four parts of sulphuric acid, and one part of ice, both at the temperature of 32°, the ice melts instantly, and the temperature of the mixture rises to 212°, the heat of boiling water. But if four parts of ice and one of the same kind of acid at 32° be mixed, the temperature sinks to about 4°. In the first of these experiments, as the ice and acid combine, they become more dense than their *mean* density; consequently, they both give out a part of their caloric of fluidity, and retain only the caloric of fluidity which is necessary for the new

D

compound. In the other case, the ice, assuming a liquid form, requires a larger quantity of heat to give it fluidity; and the sudden fall of the thermometer is owing to the suddenness with which the ice absorbs the caloric from the acid, and which it requires before it can take a liquid form.

60. What are the particular effects of caloric on bodies?

It favours the solution of salts, and promotes chemical union. In other cases it serves to separate bodies already combined; so that in the hands of chemists it is the most useful and powerful agent we are acquainted with.

61. Mention some experiments in proof of these effects?

If sulphur and copper filings be mixed together in a Florence flask, no change is produced, but if they be heated, they instantly combine with combustion. The explosion of fulminating silver by heat affords an example of the effects of heat in separating substances already combined.

62. Is the chemical affinity of bodies for caloric in general very strong?

No: it is one of the weakest of all known affinities.

63. How does this appear?

From the facility with which heated bodies part with their sensible heat.

64. Is this universally the case?

Yes: it seems to be one of the laws of nature, that heated bodies should give out *part* of their free caloric to the neighbouring bodies at a lower temperature, till the whole become of an equal degree of temperature. This may arise from a repulsive force existing among the particles of heat, which, when not overcome by this attraction from the particles of matter, causes them to fly off.

65. Give me an instance of the operation of this law of nature?

When the temperature of the atmosphere is reduced

below 32° water gives out its superabundant caloric by degrees, till at length the cold atmosphere deprives it of its caloric of fluidity also, and it becomes ice. And this change can take place but slowly, owing to three circumstances; first, that heat is given out during the congelation in consequence of the change of state; and secondly, because the water is one of the worst conductors of heat; and thirdly, that water at the temperature of 40° is at its greatest density, and consequently the *carrying power* cannot operate in effecting this change.

66. Will you now enumerate to me a few of the advantages which have been derived from this branch of chemical study?

There is no necessity for enumerating the important effects produced in nature by this principle, for every change around us is either wholly or in part dependant upon its agency; in the arts and sciences we may also perceive how much has been effected, even within a few years, by the study of its laws, and its application to practical purposes; the invention of the steam engine alone, which is increasing the effective force of these countries to a degree hardly estimable, and giving us the power of vying with the very planetary motions in velocity, would establish its claims to our attention; by means of this agent man "makes the elements of air and water the carriers of warmth, not only to banish winter from his home, but to adorn it, even during the snow storm with the blossoms of spring; and like a magician, he raises from the gloomy and deep abyss of the mine the spirit of light to dispel the midnight darkness."[a]

[a] Mrs. Somerville.

CHAPTER III.

CHEMICAL ATTRACTION, OR AFFINITY.

1. What is attraction?

Attraction is an unknown force, which causes bodies to approach each other.

2. Which are the most obvious instances of attraction?

The gravitation· of bodies to the earth; that of the planets towards each other; and the attractions of electricity and magnetism.

3. Are you acquainted with other instances of attraction?

Yes; attraction subsists between the *particles* of bodies; and it is this kind of attraction which comes under the more immediate cognizance of chemists.

4. How is this kind of attraction described in chemical language?

· Whenever the force of attraction operates between particles of the same species, it is called the attraction of *cohesion*, or the attraction of *aggregation;* but when between the particles of different substances, it is called the attraction of *composition*, or chemical attraction or *affinity*.

5. Do·you mean that the attraction of cohesion cannot be exercised between particles of different kinds?

No: for we are aware that water will adhere to many substances, merely in consequence of cohesion; perhaps chemical attraction may be most properly defined to be an attraction exerted between the particles of matters by which their properties are completely changed, and the attraction of cohesion, that attraction which keeps the particles of matter together without effecting any change in their properties—an example may better explain my mean-ing; if we dip a piece of tallow in water, a small quantity of water will adhere to its surface, owing to the force of cohesion between the two substances; but no change will take place in the nature either of the water or tallow; we may boil melted tallow and water together for a length of time without effecting any alteration in the properties of either; but if we add to the water some potash or soda an immediate change takes place, and the tallow forms a white compound, which dissolves readily in the water, and cannot be separated from it by any simple means—in this case a chemical change has taken place, which has altered the property of the tallow and made it easily soluble in the water.[a]

6. Can you explain with more precision what is meant by attraction of cohesion?

The particles of all bodies are possessed of the inherent property of attracting each other, which causes them to adhere, and preserves the various substances around us from falling in pieces. The nature of this wonderful property is entirely unknown.

---

[a] A piece of loaf sugar broken into fine powder, or water in the state of vapour, is said to have its attraction of aggregation broken; but the smallest atom of the powder is still sugar, and the most trifling portion of the vapour is still water. In order to exemplify the latter kind of attraction, a little caustic soda may be put into a glass, and muriatic acid added to it. Both these are corrosive substances; but the compound resulting from them will be found to be our common table salt. Here we have an instance of two heterogeneous bodies producing, by their action on each other, a distinct substance, possessing the properties of *neither* of the bodies which compose it.

If several salts be dissolved in the same water, each particle, when they crystallize, will find its own kind, by a sort of innate polarity. To prove this, dissolve separately equal weights of sulphate of copper and crystals of nitrate of potass in sufficient quantities of boiling water; pour them together while hot into a flat pan, and when the water has evaporated a little, and the whole is suffered to cool, the salts will crystallize:—the sulphate of copper in blue, the nitre in white crystals, similar to what they were before they were dissolved.

7. Can you give me any examples of this force visibly acting?

If we carefully notice two small particles of mercury, while gently moved along a smooth surface towards each other, a mutual attraction of one to the other will be very evident at the moment of their union into one globule. Two bullets, if a small portion of each of their surfaces be freshly cut and strongly pressed together, will cohere with very great force.

8. How may the attraction of cohesion be measured?

The force of the attraction of cohesion, in solid bodies, may be measured by the weight necessary to overcome it. Thus, if rods of metal, glass, wood, &c. be suspended in a perpendicular direction, and weights be attached to their lower extremities until the rods break, the weight attached to each rod just before it broke, is the measure of its cohesive force.

9. What do you understand by chemical attraction?

The particles of every simple substance have not only an attraction among themselves, forming the aggregation of that body or substance, but they have also another attraction to such other substances with which they have an affinity; and, when presented, unite to them, and form a new compound.[a]

10. What are the laws of chemical attraction?

Chemical affinity can only exist between the particles of different substances; and this species of attraction is exerted with different degrees of force, according to the nature of such substances, and frequently in proportion to the mass. All bodies combine only in certain definite proportions. The new combinations acquire new proportions and are incapable of separation by mechanical means.

---

[a] This power was by Bergman called *elective* attraction, as though matter were endued with the ability to prefer one substance to another. *Chemical* attraction is a more definite term, and is now in general use.

11. Are there any circumstances which seem to modify chemical action?

Yes; heat has a remarkable effect in promoting chemical action of bodies on each other, as was mentioned in the preceding chapter: the state of aggregation of two substances has also a great effect; for example, two substances which in the dry state have no sensible action on each other, when made fluid immediately combine; this may be exemplified in the different alloys of metals with each other; copper and zinc may be kept in contact for ever without acting on each other, but by means of heat they are converted into the alloy brass; tin and copper also when heated are made to unite together; dry tartaric acid and carbonate of soda may be left in contact without undergoing any change, but if each be dissolved in water an immediate chemical action commences.

12. What are the most common effects of chemical action?

First, it produces a complete change in the properties of bodies; for example, when an acid and alkali combine, the properties of each are generally completely destroyed: smell and taste are both altered, and the characteristic properties of each can no longer be recognized. Secondly, change of form frequently results from chemical action. Thirdly, heat and light, or combustion, sometimes result from it. Fourthly, change of colour.

13. Give me an example of change of form resulting from chemical action?

The solution of a solid in water, the conversion of part of chalk into a gas by solution in an acid, and the solid matter produced by breathing through lime water, are examples of the three changes of form which may occur.

14. Do you know any cases of combustion resulting from it?

We have familiar examples in the burning of fuel, and candles, and the ignition of matches by dipping them in sulphuric acid.

15. Give me some example of change of colour?

If we make a solution of green vitriol in water, and add some ferroprussiate of potash we have a fine blue colour produced; common writing ink also affords us a good example of change of colour, the solutions which form it having one a light green and the other a brown colour.

16. How are the different kinds of chemical attraction or affinity distinguished?

Chemical attraction is of three kinds; viz. simple, compound, and disposing attraction.

17. What is simple attraction?

When two substances unite merely in consequence of their mutual attraction, they are said to combine by virtue of *simple* attraction. We have an example of this in the union of an acid and alkali or an acid and earth.[a]

18. What is compound attraction?

The action of two compound substances, whereby they mutually decompose each other, and produce two or more new compounds. For example, when we pour into a solution of sulphate of magnesia (Epsom salts) a solution of carbonate of soda, the sulphuric acid unites with the

---

[a] The following experiments will serve to exemplify some cases of simple attraction. Take a portion of acetate of soda, pour muriatic acid upon it in a retort, and distil it to dryness. The acetic acid will be expelled, and the muriatic acid will be found in combination with the soda, united so strongly that the most intense heat will not be able to separate it. This effect is owing to the soda having a greater attraction for muriatic acid than it has for the acetic. If a portion of nitric acid be now added to the muriate of soda, and heat applied, the muriatic acid will be again disengaged, and the nitric acid will be in possession of the soda. Lastly, if to the nitrate of soda sulphuric acid be added, and these exposed to a due degree of heat, the nitric acid will be expelled, and the sulphuric acid will be in possession in the alkali, forming a true sulphate of soda. These changes all take place in consequence of chemical attraction. By this attraction acetic acid combines with soda, and forms a salt called acetate of soda; but muriatic, nitric, and sulphuric acid, have each of them a stronger attraction for soda, and their respective attractions are in the order in which they have been named.

soda and the carbonic acid of the soda unites with the magnesia, forming carbonate of magnesia, which falls down.[a]

19. Are any other terms ever employed on the subject of chemical attractions?

There are what are called *quiescent* attractions, and *divellent* attractions.

20. What do you mean by quiescent attractions?

When two or more bodies are presented to each other, the attractions which tend to preserve their original arrangement of parts are denominated *quiescent* attractions.

[a] If into a solution of sulphate of ammonia there be poured nitric acid, no decomposition is produced, because the sulphuric acid has a stronger attraction than nitric acid for ammonia. But if a solution of nitrate of potash be poured in, we obtain by evaporation two new bodies, *sulphate of potash*, and *nitrate of ammonia*. In this case, the sulphuric acid of the sulphate of ammonia attracts the potass of the nitrate of potass, at the same time that the ammonia attracts the nitric acid; and to the agency of these united attractions the double decomposition must be attributed. The manner in which these combinations take place may be explained by the following diagram; let us suppose that all these forces are placed so as to draw the ends of two cylinders crossing one another, and fixed in the middle in this manner.

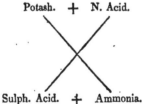

Potash. + N. Acid.

Sulph. Acid. + Ammonia.

In this form the compounds are nitrate of potash and sulphate of ammonia, when these are applied to each other double decomposition takes place, which may be represented by making the following change in the diagram.

Potash. Nitric Acid.

+ +

Sulph. Acid. Ammonia.

In which we have the sulphuric acid combined with the potash and the nitric acid with the ammonia.

21. Give an example of this?

If a solution of nitrate of silver be poured into a solution of chloride of sodium, two new substances will be formed; viz. nitrate of soda, and chloride of silver; the latter of which, being insoluble in water, will be precipitated. In this experiment the attraction of the nitric acid for the silver, and the chlorine for the soda, are the *quiescent* attractions; whereas the attractions of the nitric acid to the soda, and the muriatic acid to the silver, are the *divellent* attractions. Hence no new arrangement of parts in any mixture can take place, unless divellent attraction exist.

22. What is meant by divellent attractions?

Those attractions which tend to destroy the original compound, and to form new arrangements, are called the *divellent* attractions.

23. What advantage do we derive from the study of chemical attractions?

From all that has hitherto been explained, this seems to be beyond doubt the most important part of chemistry; for it is only from a thorough knowledge of the attractions which different substances have for each other, that we shall ever attain a complete analysis of the productions of nature.

24. How should a pupil proceed to acquire—what seems so essential to chemistry—a knowledge of these attractions?

Practice can alone give competent knowledge of these attractions; and a reference to the tables given in the different extended treatises on chemistry, will facilitate the acquisition.—The first tables were compiled by Geoffroy, a century since.

25. How are chemical attractions noted in these tables?

The name of the substance whose affinities are required, is always placed at the head of a column, and separated generally by a line; below this the other bodies are placed in the order of their attraction to the first substance, as in the following table:—

SULPHURIC ACID.

BARYTA.
STRONTIA.
POTASS.
SODA.
LIME.
MAGNESIA.
AMMONIA.
ALUMINE.
METALLIC OXIDES.
WATER.

From which we learn that baryta, which is the nearest, would separate strontia, potass, or any one of the succeeding substances, from sulphuric acid, which prefers baryta to all other bodies whatever.

26. Are these tables to be depended upon in every case of chemical composition and decomposition?

These tables, notwithstanding some exceptions,* are so extremely useful, that the study of them cannot be too strongly inculcated; since in most cases they may be safely trusted by the practical chemist.

27. What is repulsion?

Repulsion is a peculiar property, inherent in the par-

---

* The affinities of bodies are affected by the proportions in which they are presented to each other, by the cohesion of their parts, by chemical repulsion, temperature, &c. Berthollet has shewn that many substances are capable of decomposing each other reciprocally, if they be added respectively in the proper quantity. Thus sulphuric acid decomposes nitrate of potass altogether, by the assistance of heat. The nitric acid is driven off, and there remains behind sulphate of potass. But if nitric acid be poured into sulphate of potass in *sufficient quantity*, it takes a part of the base from the sulphuric acid, and nitrate of potass is regenerated. In like manner phosphoric acid decomposes muriate of lead, and muriatic acid decomposes phosphate of lead. We will also find that iron is capable of separating oxygen from hydrogen, and hydrogen will also decompound the compound of iron and oxygen.

ticles of all matter, which gives them a constant tendency
to recede from each other.

28. How is it proved that this force exists in matter?

We find that the particles of matter are not in actual
contact, which they would be if no such force existed.

29. How is it proved that the particles of matter are
not in contact?

The fact that most solids can, by mechanical pressure,
be made to undergo a diminution of volume proves this;
and the fact that liquids are capable of dissolving large
portions of solid matter without increase of bulk, proves
that there are spaces between their ultimate particles;
and the ready compressibility of gases is a proof of the
same theory.[a]

30. How does this property of matter operate?

It operates both at sensible and at insensible distances.

31. What instances are there of the former kind of
repulsion?

The only kinds of repulsion that can be exhibited to
the senses, are those of electricity[b] and magnetism;[c] but

---

[a] According to Boscovich, the atoms, of which all bodies are
composed, are mere mathematical points, destitute of extension and
magnitude, but capable of acting on each other with a force which
differs in intensity, and in kind, according to the distance.   At
sensible distances the force is *attractive*, and diminishes inversely as
the squares of the distance.   At the smallest distances the force is
repulsive; it increases as the distance diminishes, and at last becomes
infinite, or insuperable; so that absolute contact, of course, is impossible.

Some bodies have such a repulsion for water that it is difficult to
wet them.   The specific gravity of steel is much greater than that
of water; yet if a dry steel needle be placed with care upon the
surface of a basin of water, the repulsion of the water will prevent
its sinking.

[b] If two cork balls be suspended from an insulated body with fine
thread so as to touch each other, and we charge that body with
electricity, the cork balls will separate immediately.   The balls of
course *repel* each other.

[c] When we present the north pole of a magnet A to the same pole
of another magnet B, suspended on a pivot, and at liberty to move,

it is *insensible* repulsion with which chemists are more particularly concerned.

32. What instances have you of this latter kind, or of insensible repulsion?

The chief example that we are acquainted with is the repulsion of the particles of caloric[a] amongst them-selves; which repulsion would constantly tend to infinite separation, were it not for a chemical union, which by an irrevocable law of nature, they form with the first surrounding body: for by that law, it seems, the particles of caloric cannot exist in an isolated state.

33. How does this repulsive force operate upon other bodies?

It diminishes the cohesion of the integrant particles of all heated bodies, in consequence of the particles of caloric repelling each other; so that chemical unions, as well as chemical decompositions, are wonderfully facilitated by this species of repulsion.[b]

the magnet B recedes as the other approaches; and by following it with A at a proper distance, it may be made to turn round on its pivot with considerable velocity. There is then a *repulsion* between the two magnets—a repulsion which increases with the power of the magnets; and this power has been made so great, by a proper combination of magnets, that all the force of a strong man is insufficient to make the two north poles touch each other.

[a] It is now generally imagined that what is called insensible repulsion is owing to the presence of caloric. It is well known that the elasticity of air and all other gaseous bodies is increased by heat; that is, that the repulsion between the particles of air, the distance remaining in the same, increases with the temperature, so that at last it becomes so great as to overcome every obstacle which can be opposed to it.

[b] It is evident, that whatever diminishes the cohesion which exists between the particles of any body, must tend to facilitate their chemical union with the particles of other bodies. One reason why some bodies require a high temperature to cause them to combine, is, that at a low temperature the attraction of cohesion is in them superior to that of affinity; accordingly it becomes necessary to weaken that attraction by means of caloric, till it becomes inferior to that of affinity. In like manner bodies combine more easily when held

34. Endeavour to explain this action of caloric with more precision.

As chemical attraction takes place only between the ultimate particles of bodies, while the attraction of cohesion remains superior to that of affinity, no other union can take place; but whenever heat has sufficiently diminished this attraction in any substance, the particles are then at liberty to form new combinations, by their union with the particles of other bodies.

35. Can you illustrate this by an example?

The formation of the red oxide of mercury will exemplify the above chemical axiom. If mercury be submitted to a heat little superior to that of boiling water, no new combination will be formed, but the metal will remain unaltered. If the heat be increased to 600°, or thereabouts, the attraction of cohesion of the mercury will be broken; its particles will unite with the oxygen of the surrounding atmosphere; and a new substance, *red oxide of mercury*, will be produced. If this new substance be again submitted to the operation of heat, and the temperature be raised to 1000°, the combination will again be broken, and new affinities will take place. The attraction of oxygen for caloric will now be greater than that of oxygen for mercury; the oxygen will quit the mercury, and be expelled as oxygen gas; thus the mercury will consequently once more appear in its metallic state.

36. Is the addition of caloric always necessary to promote chemical affinity?

In order that the attraction of composition may take place between two bodies, it is generally necessary

---

in solution by water, or when they have previously been reduced to a fine powder, as these operations diminish the cohesion which exists among the primitive or integrant particles. Sulphuric acid has no action upon a lump of fluate of lime; but if that earthy salt be reduced to powder, a violent action will ensue on the addition of the lphuric acid, and the fluate of lime will be decomposed.

either that one of the substances should be in a state of fluidity, or that heat should be applied; so that caloric acts an important part, either sensibly or insensibly, in all cases of chemical affinity. .

37. Does chemical affinity operate in consequence of the universal law of attraction? .

We have reason to believe that every new compound is produced by virtue of the attraction to which all matter is subject, and which is equally operative on the most minute atom, as on a planetary system.

38. Do you recollect any familiar example of attraction of bodies for each other?

The attraction of the particles of bodies for each other is exemplified by small quantities of water, or mercury, which, when dropped upon a flat surface, form themselves into spherical masses.

39. Are there any other causes which seem to modify chemical action besides heat?

Yes. Elasticity, and the quantity of matter have both great effect in modifying it: many bodies having a strong attraction for each other when brought together in the elastic state will not combine: we have many examples of this; muriatic acid is composed of two gases having strong attraction for each other; yet if we mix these gases together in the elastic form we will have no chemical combination of them thus produced. Oxygen and hydrogen may be kept together for an indefinite period without combining; hydrogen and nitrogen cannot be made to combine directly by mixture, though having a strong attraction for each other, the attraction being overcome by the elastic force of these gases.

40. Can you give an example of quantity modifying chemical action?

A familiar example is afforded in the solution of substances in water, the greater the quantity of water in proportion to the substance, the more readily will the latter be dissolved.

41. When bodies enter into chemical combination, do they combine in determinate quantity?

It is a law of chemical combination that all bodies having an attraction for each other, combine and unite in fixed and definite proportions to form new compounds: that is, if two bodies, A and B, have a tendency to combine and form a third compound, C, whenever these bodies unite with each other they will always combine in the same proportion to form C: thus, if ten parts, by weight of A, combine with five parts, by weight of B, to form C, in every case where C is formed, its constituents A and B will be to the proportion by weight of 10 to 5.

42. Can a compound body ever vary in the proportion of its constituents?

No; under all circumstances, a compound body has its constituent parts in the same proportions: for example, sea salt, (chloride of sodium,) wherever it is found, or by whatever process it is produced, always consists of the same elements combined in a fixed proportion to each other.

43. Do you know any other facts relative to the combination of bodies?

The comparative quantities of substances combining chemically, may be represented by the same fixed number for each substance, in every compound of which it is an ingredient. Thus, the weights of the following simple or compound substances are, hydrogen 1, oxygen 8, chlorine 36, water 9, muriatic acid 37. Similar numbers have been accurately determined for a great number of simple and compound bodies.—See table, page 338.

44. When a body combines with another body in different proportions to form different substances, do we observe any remarkable fact relative to the proportions in which they combine?

When a body unites in several proportions with another body, we always observe that the second combination is some multiple of the first by a whole number, and so likewise of all the other compounds. A familiar example is afforded us in the combination of mercury with chlorine; 36 parts of chlorine, united with 202 parts of mercury, form calomel; in the compound formed by a larger quantity of chlorine with mercury (corrosive sublimate) we find the proportion of chlorine to mercury to be 72 to 202, or exactly double of the first quantity.

45. Do gases obey the same laws as other bodies in their combinations?

Yes; all gases when combining obey precisely the same laws. It is also found that the volumes in which gases combine are all multiples by whole numbers of the lowest combining volumes; thus water consists of one volume of oxygen and two volumes of hydrogen, muriatic acid of one volume of chlorine and one of hydrogen; and when two gases combine in different proportions all the new combinations will be multiples of one of these combinations by whole numbers; thus 1, 2, 3, 4, and 5 volumes of oxygen combine with one volume of nitrogen to form five different compounds.

46. What theory has been founded on these facts, and by which they are explicable?

The atomic theory[a] readily explains these facts, which supposes that chemical combinations are effected between the ultimate particles of matter, and that bodies combine either in single atoms of each to form new compounds, or two, three, or four atoms, &c. of one, to one, two, or three atoms, &c. of another.

47. What idea does this theory give us of the constitution of matter?

That matter consists of "solid, massy, hard, impene-

[a] To Mr. Higgins of Dublin is due the first attempt at applying this theory to the explanation of the laws of combination; but Dr. Dalton of Manchester so completely developed it, and shewed its applicability to all cases of chemical combination, that he may justly lay claim to the merit of one of the most useful and important discoveries of modern times.

trable particles," as was supposed by Newton and "that these primitive particles are so hard as never to wear or break to pieces, no ordinary power being able to divide what God made one in the first creation."

48. Has the chemical attraction existing between the particles of matter been referred to any known agent?

Yes, electricity has been supposed with great probability to be the cause of attraction between the dissimilar particles of matter, and Sir H. Davy suggested that all chemical attraction arose from these particles having opposite electricities, which caused them to attract each other and combine.

49. Can you mention any experiments in illustration of this?

The decomposition of water by electricity is an appropriate example; when we place a portion of water between two wires passing from the extremities of a voltaic battery, the water will be decomposed, one of its component parts passing to one wire of the battery and the other to the opposite wire, shewing that these bodies possess opposite electrical attractions; almost all compound bodies may be decomposed by the same means.

50. Has any classification of chemical substances arisen from this?

Yes: according to the side of the battery at which the different substances appear, they have been named electro-positive or electro-negative bodies, and we find that those bodies possessing opposite electrical relations have generally the strongest tendency to combination.

51. What are the practical uses of this theory?

From an acquaintance with this law of chemical action, and a knowledge of the relative quantities to which bodies combine, we are able to effect with the greatest certainty all chemical changes and decompositions. If we know the weight of one substance we can at once ascertain the quantity of another necessary to effect its decomposition or to form with it a new combination. We can also at once ascertain what proportion the elements bear to each other in a compound body from knowing its weight and being acquainted with the fact that the elements are always combined with each other in proportions fixed and invariable.[a]

[a] We give here a Table of the Atomic Weights of all the simple substances to which it will be necessary frequently to refer in the subsequent Chapters; in this Table the weight of hydrogen is taken as the standard of comparison.

TABLE OF THE ATOMIC WEIGHTS OF SIMPLE SUBSTANCES.

HYDROGEN I.

Substances.	At.Wt.	Substances.	At. Wt.	Substances.	At. Wt.
Aluminium	14	Iodine	126	Rhodium	52
Antimony	65	Iridium	99	Selenium	39
Arsenic	38	Iron	28	Silicium	7
Barium	69	Lead	104	Silver	108
Boron	11	Lithium	10	Sodium	23
Bromine	78	Magnesium	13	Strontium	44
Cadmium	56	Manganese	28	Sulphur	16
Calcium	20	Mercury	202	Tellurium	32
Carbon	6	Molybdenum	48	Thorium	60
Cerium	46	Nickel	29	Tin	59
Chlorine	36	Nitrogen	14	Titanium	24
Chromium	28	Osmium	100	Tungsten	95
Cobalt	29	Oxygen	8	Vanadium	67
Copper	32	Palladium	53	Uranium	217
Fluorine	19	Phosphorus	16	Yttrium	32
Glucinium	18	Platinum	99	Zinc	32
Gold	199	Potassium	40	Zirconium	34

CHAPTER. IV.

SIMPLE NON-METALLIC SUBSTANCES.

1. What is a simple substance?

Those bodies[a] which have never yet been decomposed nor formed by art, are called simple substances.

2. How many simple substances are there?

The simple substances at present known amount to fifty-two.

3. Can you enumerate the simple substances?

All the simple substances[b] we are at present acquainted with are; oxygen, chlorine, iodine, bromine, fluorine, hydrogen, nitrogen, carbon, sulphur, phosphorus, boron, selenium, and the metals.

4. Is it well ascertained that these are all simple substances?

It is extremely probable that some of these bodies may be compound; but as no mode has yet been discovered

---

[a] The most minute particles into which any substances can be divided *similar* to each other, and to the substance of which they are parts, are termed the *integrant* particles: thus the smallest atom of powdered marble is still marble; but if the lime, the carbon, the oxygen, and the hydrogen of this marble be separated, we shall then have the *elementary* or constituent particles.

Suppose a little common salt were reduced to powder, even though it be ground as fine as could be effected by art, still every single particle, however minute, would consist of a particle of sodium and a particle of chlorine; common salt being a *compound* body incapable of decomposition by mechanical means. But if we take a piece of sulphur, and pulverize that in the same way, every particle will be a homogeneous body, sulphur being one of the *simple* substances.

[b] If these substances were all capable of combining, the compounds formed by them would amount to many thousands; but several of them cannot be united by any means we know of.

of decompounding any of them, it will be more con-
ducive to science, to consider them, for the present, as
simple undecomposable bodies.[a]

5. What is oxygen?

Oxygen in a pure state is a gas, devoid of colour,
taste, or smell, resembling atmospheric air, but possessing
a slightly greater specific gravity, in the proportion of 17
to 15 nearly.

6. What are the properties of oxygen gas?

Oxygen gas is a supporter of combustion, and
is absolutely necessary for the support of animal and
vegetable life.[b]

7. How do you prove that oxygen is a supporter of
combustion?

Pour a little water on a flat dish, place two or three
lighted wax tapers of different lengths in the water, and invert a tall glass jar over them filled with oxygen gas. The
flame of the different tapers will soon be seen to grow
smaller, and at length will be extinguished in succession.
That which is highest will be extinguished first, and the
shortest taper the last, owing to the purer air occupying
the lower part of the jar. In this case the oxygen disappears, having combined with the tapers, and these no
longer burn when the oxygen is exhausted. If we take
a jar of pure oxygen, and put a taper in it, the taper will

[a] It is curious that most of those substances which were thought
by the old chemists to be the elements of all other bodies, are found
by our improved methods of experiment to be more or less com-
pounded; while, of those which were formerly ranked among the
class of compounds, there are a greater number that are really not
decomposable, and can only be placed among the simple bodies.
Air, fire, water, and *earth* were by the ancients called the elements
of the globe: modern chemistry has demonstrated, that these are all
really compound bodies. On the other hand, *sulphur, phosphorus,
carbon*, and the *metals*, which we call simple substances, were supposed formerly to be compounds.

[b] It has been proved by Mr. Hassenfratz, that oxygen is necessary
to promote the vigour of plants as well as that of animals.

burn with greater brilliancy and for a longer time than in the same quantity of air.

8. What is the nature of oxygen gas, when in a separate state?

Pure óxygen gas has the property of accelerating the circulation of all the animal fluids, and occasions the rapid combustion of most combustible substances; so that it is one of the most energetic and powerful agents that we are acquainted with.[a]

9. How may oxygen gas be procured?

By the action of heat on various substances; if we put into an iron retort black oxide of manganese, nitre, (nitrate of potass,) or chlorate of potass, and place the retort in the fire, oxygen gas may be produced of considerable purity, and received in proper vessels.[b]

10. What is chlorine?

Chlorine is a green coloured gas, having a sufficating smell, and heavier than atmospheric air.

11. How is it prepared?

[a] " Dr. Higgins having caused a young man to breathe pure oxygen gas for several minutes, his pulse, which was at 64, soon rose to 120 beats in a minute. The advantage which may be derived to the sick, by increasing or diminishing at pleasure this natural stimulus in the blood, may be easily conceived; for, by abstracting a part of the oxygen from atmospheric air, the pulse may likewise be lowered at pleasure."

[b] A retort fit for this purpose consists of two parts, the body *a*, made of cast iron, into which is ground a tube *b*; we introduce the materials 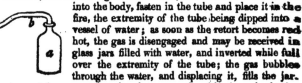 into the body, fasten in the tube and place it in the fire, the extremity of the tube being dipped into a vessel of water; as soon as the retort becomes red hot, the gas is disengaged and may be received in glass jars filled with water, and inverted while full over the extremity of the tube; the gas bubbles through the water, and displacing it, fills the jar. A piece of iron gas-tube closed at one end and having a lead tube luted in will also answer well.—ED,

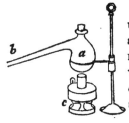 If we pour strong muriatic acid upon black oxide of manganese in a retort *a*, and having plunged the neck *b* of the retort in a vessel of water, apply heat, by means of a lamp *c*, we can procure this gas in the same manner as oxygen.[a]

12. What are its principal chemical properties?

It is a supporter of combustion, destructive to animal life, and destroys the colour of all vegetable substances.

13. Adduce some experiments in proof this?

Phosphorus plunged into a jar of chlorine, burns in it; copper leaf and several metals passed into this gas take fire, and water coloured by vegetable juice has its colour speedily destroyed.

14. Is chlorine used in the arts?

Yes; in the process of bleaching it is extensively used in combination with lime, in consequence of its efficacy in destroying vegetable colours; it is also frequently used as a disinfecting agent from its action on organic miasmata; and a small quantity disengaged in any place filled with offensive vapours quickly destroys them.

15. What are iodine and bromine?

The former is a solid substance of a brownish black colour, which when heated rises and becomes a violet coloured vapour;[b] the latter is a dense fluid, having a hyacinth red colour, and a smell resembling putrescent sea-wrack.

16. From what are they obtained, and are they applied to the arts?

[a] The rationale of this process is, that the muriatic acid, which consists of chlorine and hydrogen, is decomposed, the hydrogen uniting with the oxygen of the manganese, and the chlorine being set free.

[b] Hence its name from the Greek word which signifies violet coloured.

Both exist in sea-water and in certain springs; neither of them has been yet employed in the arts. Iodine has, however, been used in medicine, and is supposed to be useful in certain forms of disease.

17. How can you discern the presence of iodine in solution?

A solution of iodine in water (of which it requires 7000 times its own weight to dissolve it) may be at once recognized by its giving, with a solution of starch in water, a deep blue precipitate.

18. What is hydrogen?

Hydrogen in its pure state is a transparent, colourless gas, devoid of taste or smell, being the lightest of all known substances, and highly combustible when in contact with air or oxygen gas.

19. How is hydrogen obtained?

Hydrogen is easily procured by pouring sulphuric acid upon iron turning, or small fragments of zinc contained in a retort similar to that used for obtaining chlorine; an effervescence immediately commences, and hydrogen is given off.[a]

20. What is its specific gravity compared with atmospheric air?

It is 15 times lighter than atmospheric air; it is in consequence of its levity that it is employed in inflating balloons to make them ascend in the air.[b]

. 21. Does hydrogen enter into combination with the simple substances we have spoken of in this chapter?

---

[a] This arises from decomposition of the water, and affords a good example of what is termed disposing attraction; for in consequence of the attraction of the acid for the oxide of the metal we employ, the metal is enabled to decompose the water, unite with its oxygen, forming an oxide which is dissolved by the acid, and the hydrogen is liberated.—ED.

[b] Mr. Cavendish was the first person who examined hydrogen gas and pointed out its nature. Dr. Black then suggested the propriety of applying it to the inflation of air-balloons; and Mr. Cavallo was the first who put it in practice. 100 cubic inches of this gas weigh only 2·118 grains.

Yes, it combines with oxygen, chlorine, iodine, and bromine, and forms with each of them important compounds.

22. We shall consider the first of these at present: What compound does hydrogen form with oxygen?

Water is composed of these gases combined together.

23. How is the composition of water proved?

It is found that whenever hydrogen is burned in contact with air containing oxygen, that a quantity of water is formed, or if it be mixed with oxygen and the mixture ignited, that the two gases unite, and water is produced—if, for example, we pour some sulphuric acid and water into a flask *a* containing some iron turnings or small pieces of zinc, and fix into the neck a perforated cork *b*, in which a small piece of tube is fixed, and set fire to the hydrogen extricated from the mixture, on holding a glass bell *c* over the flame, the interior of the bell will be in a short time covered with moisture.

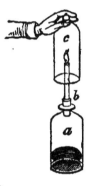

24. What phenomena attend the combustion of hydrogen and oxygen gases?

When these gases are mixed in the proportion of two measures of hydrogen to one of oxygen and inflamed, they unite with a violent explosion producing the most intense heat;[a] for this reason the greatest caution must be exercised in experimenting on hydrogen gas, as many

[a] The heat produced by these gases burned together is applied in the oxy-hydrogen blowpipe to effect the fusion of the most refractory substances, and also to produce the most brilliant light by the ignition of small portions of lime; this light has been found sufficiently intense to serve for the illumination of solar microscopes and has been applied to conveying signals almost incredible distances—the gases are safely used by being kept in separate reservoirs, and mixed together in very small quantities before they are inflamed, all risk arising from

accidents have occurred by incautiously applying flame to this gas when mixed with atmospheric air or oxygen even in small proportions.[a]

25. Can the composition of water be proved by any other means?

Yes, we can analyze water; if we pass steam over iron wire heated to redness in a tube, it is decompounded; its oxygen unites with the iron wire and forms oxide of iron, and the hydrogen is given off: water is also decompounded by electricity, and hydrogen and oxygen produced whenever we place a portion of water between the wires of a strong galvanic battery.

26. In what proportion do these gases combine to form water?

It is found that two measures of hydrogen and one of oxygen unite together to form water, or that one part by *weight* of hydrogen unites with 8 parts by weight of oxygen: the weights of the atoms of hydrogen and oxygen are therefore in these proportions, or if the atomic weight of hydrogen be 1, that of oxygen will be represented by the number 8.

27. In how many states do we find water?

In its ordinary state as a liquid, as a gas in steam, and as a solid in ice, or in chemical combination with different bodies, in which state it forms *hydrates*.

28. Which is the most simple state of water?

That of ice.

---

the explosion of large quantities being thus avoided. There have been many oxy-hydrogen blowpipes invented for obviating all danger in experimenting on these gases, for the construction of which the reader is referred to the different extended treatises on chemistry.

[a] It is related of Pilatre de Rosier, that, having mixed one part of common air with nine parts of hydrogen gas, and drawn the mixture into his lungs, it caught fire by accident as he respired it, and the whole of the gas exploded in his mouth and nearly deprived him of life. The shock was so violent, that at first he thought the whole of his teeth had been driven out, but fortunately he received no lasting injury whatever.

29. What is the essential difference between liquid water and ice?

Water contains a larger portion of caloric.

30. How do you define steam?

Steam is water combined with a still greater quantity of caloric.[a]

31. What are the properties of steam?

Steam, owing to the large quantity of caloric which is combined with it, takes a gaseous form, acquires great expansive force,[b] whence it has become a useful and powerful agent in its application as a moving

[a] However long we boil a fluid, in an open vessel, we cannot make it in the smallest degree hotter than its boiling point. When arrived at this point, the vapour absorbs the heat, and carries it off as fast as it is generated. Yet by continued heat, united with additional compression, both the expansibility and temperature of steam may be greatly increased; and some constructors of steam engines have availed themselves of this property, to augment the power and diminish the expense.

Those who have an air pump may easily see that water requires a large portion of caloric to convert it into steam: for, if a cup of *hot* water be put under the receiver, and the pump be set to work, the water will soon begin to boil furiously, and the receiver will be covered with vapour. If the receiver be now taken off, the water will be found barely lukewarm, owing to the vapour having carried off the greatest part of its heat.

Water, in being converted into vapour, combines with more than five times the quantity of caloric that is required to bring ice-cold water to a boiling heat, and occupies a space about 1,800 times greater than it does when in the form of water.

Owing to the quantity of caloric that liquids require to convert them into vapour, all evaporation produces cold. It has been remarked before, that an animal might be frozen to death in the midst of summer, by repeatedly sprinkling ether upon it; the evaporation would shortly carry off the whole of its vital heat. Water thrown on hot bodies acts in the same way; it becomes in an instant converted into vapour, and thus deprives these bodies of a great portion of the caloric they contain.

[b] The expansive force of steam is found by experiment to be much greater than that of gunpowder.

Some volcanic eruptions and earthquakes, it is supposed, owe their terrible effects to this power of steam; the water of the sea

power by means of the steam engine, which has so
far superseded animal labour, that we can hardly even
in imagination fix a limit to its applications.[a]

32. Does nature decompose water in any of her operations?

Certainly, by many: particularly by means of every
living vegetable; all vegetables having the power of
decomposing water.

33. For what purpose are vegetables endowed with
this power of decomposing water?

They combine part of its hydrogen, as well as of its
oxygen, with the carbon of the atmosphere and of the
soil, to form the vegetable compounds, oil, wax, gum,
resin, sugar, &c. while the superfluous oxygen is evolved
by the leaves with the assistance of the sun's light,
which seems essential to this decomposition.

34. Can you recapitulate what has hitherto been
detailed of the nature of oxygen?

Yes: oxygen is the basis of vital air, as well as one of
the constituent parts of water; it is the chief support of

finding its way to subterraneous fires. See an account of the dreadful
effects of the earthquake at Catania, in Sir Wm. Hamilton's Survey
of the two Sicilies.

In boiling oil, the workmen are very careful to prevent any water
coming near it; for a single drop coming among it would instantly,
by the excessive heat of the oil, be converted into vapour, and would
force part of the oil over the sides of the boiler. In casting iron and
other metals the greatest care is taken to have the mould perfectly
dry, as a drop of water by its sudden conversion into steam might
cause a formidable explosion.

It is to the expansive force of steam that the well-known motion
in water called boiling, is to be ascribed. The vapour is first formed
at the bottom of the vessel, and, passing through the water, causes
that motion in it which we call ebullition.

[a] The steam engine is brought to such perfection, that one bushel
of coals will raise 11,000 hogsheads of water ten feet high, and do
the work of 18 horses. Where there is no waste of steam, this work
may be performed continually with the consumption of only one
bushel of coals per hour.

life and heat; and performs an important part in most of the changes which take place in the mineral, vegetable, and animal kingdoms.

35. Is there any reason to suppose that water is thus formed in any of the great operations of nature?

Some persons have supposed that the torrents of rain which generally accompany thunder storms, may arise from a sudden combustion of hydrogen and oxygen gases.

36. How do they suppose that the atmosphere is furnished with this hydrogen gas?

Hydrogen is constantly emanating from, and is the consequence of every species of vegetable and animal decay or putrefaction; and it is also evolved from various mines, volcanoes, and other natural sources.

37. What is the specific gravity of water?

A cubic inch of water weighs 2,524 grains; a pint measure of water weighs one pound and a quarter avoirdupois: a cubic foot of water weighs nearly 1,000 ounces, or 62½ lbs. avoirdupois. It is 815 times heavier than atmospheric air.

38. What change does water undergo in order to be converted into ice?

The atmosphere, when its temperature is sufficiently low, deprives the water of a certain portion of its caloric —crystallization then ensues, and the water solidifies and becomes ice.[a]

* It is owing to the *expansion* of water in freezing, that rocks and trees are often split during intense frosts. According to the calculations of the Florentine academicians, a spherule of water, only one inch in diameter, expands in freezing with a force superior to the resistance of 13½ tons weight. Major Williams attempted to prevent this expansion; but during the operation the iron plug which stopped the orifice of the bomb-shell containing the freezing water, and which was more than two pounds weight, was projected several hundred feet with great velocity; and in another experiment the shell burst. The imbecility of man never appears so conspicuous as when he attempts to counteract the operation of laws which were designed by infinite beneficence for his preservation and comfort. The law

39. What do you mean by crystallization?

By crystallization is understood the concretion of certain substances into regular forms, occasioned by the loss of a portion of their caloric.

40. To what substances is the term usually applied?

The term is usually applied to compound bodies of the saline kind, and to their separation, in regular and peculiar figures, from the water in which they were dissolved. Simple substances, however, such as many metals, assume crystalline forms.

41. You have said that ice is the most simple state of water;—do you then imagine that water is naturally solid?

Yes; for near the poles it is eternally solid; there it is similar to the hardest rocks, and may be formed by the chisel of the statuary, like stone.[a]

42. Is this great solidity of ice at the poles, owing to its being frozen in such large masses?

The great solidity of ice at the poles is occasioned by the very low temperature of the circumambient air; and in very cold countries ice may be ground so fine as to be blown away by the wind, and will still be ice.[b]

in question is eminently important, and nature has made it unalterable.

This property of water is taken advantage of in splitting slate. At Colly Western the slate is dug from the quarries in large blocks; these are placed in an opposite direction to what they had in the quarry, and the rain is allowed to fall upon them; it penetrates their fissures, and the first sharp frost freezes the water, which, expanding with its usual force, splits the slate into thin layers.

[a] The ice at each pole of the earth forms an immense cupola, the arch of which extends some thousand miles over the continents; the thickness of which, beyond the 60th degree of latitude, is several hundred feet. Navigators have assigned to detached masses, which are met with floating at sea, an elevation of from 1500 to 1800 feet.

[b] "It is related that at the whimsical marriage of Prince Gallitzan, in 1739, the Russians applied ice to the same purposes as stone. A house consisting of two apartments was built with large blocks of ice; the furniture of the rooms, even the nuptial bed, was made with ice; and the icy canon, which were fired in honour of the day, performed their office more than once without bursting."—BISHOP WATSON.

43. Is ice the only instance of water existing in a state of solidity ?

No; water becomes still more solid in mortar and cements, having parted with more of its caloric in that combination than it does in the act of freezing.[a]

44. What other instances are there of water taking a solid form?

Water is combined in a state of solidity in many crystals, spars, gems, and in most alkaline and earthy salts. If water be thrown on quick-lime, it will be retained by it with such force that nothing less than an intense red heat will separate it. In its combination with lime it becomes much more solid than when in the state of ice; which may be proved by direct experiment. Calcined plaster of Paris, in a pulverulent state, becomes quickly solid by mixing it with water. Saussure has proved that alumine, when mixed with water, retains a tenth of its weight of that fluid at a heat which would melt iron.

45. What are the general and more obvious advantages which we derive from water ?

Water is a necessary beverage for man and other animals; is perpetually used as a solvent for a great variety of solid bodies; acts an important part in conveying nourishment to the vegetable world,[b] and giving

[a] Though water takes a solid form in its various combinations, such as with lime, saline crystals, &c., we know of no method of compressing it when in a fluid state. The Florentine academicians filled a globe of gold perfectly full of water, and submitted it to a very powerful press; but could not perceive that they were able to make it occupy less space than it did at first. They gave it such a degree of pressure, that at length the water exuded through the pores of the metal. Mr. Perkins states that he has succeeded in increasing the density of water 3·5 per cwt. by a pressure of 326 atmospheres. And Colladon, Sturm, and Oersted, state that for every atmosphere of pressure, water diminishes 51·3 millionths in bulk.

[b] Most stones and salts lose their solidity and transparency by being deprived even of a part only of the water which they contained, and generally become pulverulent. It is by a combination with water

salubrity to the atmospherical regions; and lastly, by its accumulation in the ocean, affords a ready communication with distant countries;—the whole of which evidently teaches how provident the great AUTHOR of nature has been in his attentions to the comforts and conveniences, as well as to the wants of his numerous creatures.

CHAPTER V.

SIMPLE NON-METALLIC SUBSTANCES.

1. What is nitrogen or azotic gas?

This gas is chiefly known by its negative properties: it does not support animal life; it extinguishes flame, and it is devoid of taste and smell, and something lighter than atmospheric air.[a]

2. How is this gas procured?

The atmosphere contains this gas united to oxygen. We may, therefore, procure it by the abstraction of

that some of the gases are rendered liquid substances, and that some liquids acquire the property of becoming fixed. This may be satisfactorily shown by boiling a few copper filings in concentrated sulphuric acid, with a small portion of nitric acid, till the copper is dissolved; then adding water, and leaving the mixture to cool gradually; when beautiful crystals of blue vitriol will be found, as hard as some minerals. Many other examples might be adduced of crystals owing their form to the water in a state of combination; carbonate and sulphate of soda both lose their crystalline structure by exposure to air, in consequence of giving off their water of crystallization. This change is called in chemical language *efflorescence*.

[a] Nitrogen enters into all animal substances, in combination with carbon, oxygen, and hydrogen. It is also the base of ammonia, and of the nitric acid. It appears to be favorable to plants, as they grow and vegetate freely in this gas. It seems to be the substance which nature employs in converting vegetables to animal substances; and to be the grand agent in animalization.

oxygen; which may be done by inverting a glass bell
filled with air in water, and placing under it a mixture of
iron filings and sulphur, which speedily absorbs the
oxygen, or by burning phosphorus in a vessel of air,
which has the same effect, or by the action of nitric
acid on fresh muscle.

3. Whence are the names nitrogen and azote given to
this gas?

It was formerly called azote, from its not being a supporter of respiration. This name is objected to because
this property is common to many other gases, and it is
more generally called nitrogen, because it enters into the
composition of nitric acid.

4. Does nitrogen combine with oxygen?

Yes; it forms with oxygen five distinct compounds:
nitrous oxide gas, nitric oxide, hyponitrous acid, nitrous
acid, and nitric acid. In these compounds the oxygen is
united with the nitrogen in the proportion of 1, 2, 3, 4,
and 5 atoms of the former to one of the latter.

5. Is there any other compound of oxygen and nitrogen?

Yes; the atmosphere is a compound of oxygen and
nitrogen; but in it these gases are generally considered
as merely mechanically mixed, not chemically combined.

6. What reason can you give for considering the
atmosphere as a mere mixture of these gases?

This appears probable from the facility with which the
two gases can be separated, as is proved in the modes I
have given for its preparation (2); and also that we can
form a gas resembling atmospheric air in all its properties
by simple mixture of the gases which compose it.

7. As we shall consider the chemical compounds of
oxygen with nitrogen when we come to speak of the
acids, we shall at present enter on the consideration of
the properties of the atmosphere; can you tell me its composition?

The atmosphere consists of oxygen and nitrogen gases
mixed together in the proportion of 20 parts of the former

to 80 of the latter; it also always contains a minute portion of carbonic acid.

8. What means have we of analyzing atmospheric air?

There are various methods, which all aim at the one object, namely,.to deprive it of its oxygen and carbonic acid.

9. How may we deprive it of carbonic acid?

By agitating a portion of air with lime water or a solution of pure potash, we deprive it of the whole of its carbonic acid.[a]

10. How do we estimate the quantity of oxygen it contains?

We can effect this by different means. If we enclose a piece of phosphorus in a portion of air confined over water, we shall find, in a few days, that the water has undergone a diminution in volume owing to the abstraction of oxygen by the phosphorus, and the quantity which has disappeared will be found to be nearly one-fifth of the whole quantity employed; another method consists in agitating air with hydrosulphuret of lime, or protosulphate of iron saturated with nitrous gas; which solutions have the property of absorbing oxygen.

11. What are the instruments used for these experiments called?

They are named eudiometers, a word derived from the Greek, and signifying instruments for measuring the purity of air.

12. Is hydrogen gas ever employed to analyze air?

Yes; this gas is most valuable for the purposes of eudiometry, as was first pointed out by the celebrated

---

[a] Each of these substances have a strong attraction for this acid. It is for this reason that lime water exposed to the air soon becomes covered with a white film (carbonate of lime) by attracting carbonic acid from the air.

Carbonic acid gas is found to exist in the atmosphere not only near the surface of the earth, but at the greatest heights. Saussure found it at the top of Mount Blanc, which is esteemed the highest point of the old continent.

Volta, who invented an instrument for this purpose. His eudiometer consists of a strong graduated glass tube, *a b*, closed at its extremity *a*, having two wires, *c d*, passing into its sides and coming within a short distance of each other, by means of which an electric spark may be passed through the gas contained in the tube.

13. How is hydrogen gas employed in this instrument?

I have already mentioned (chap. iv. 26) that oxygen and hydrogen gases combine in the proportion of one volume of oxygen to two volumes of hydrogen to form water. Now, from knowing this we can at once analyze atmospheric air by means of hydrogen gas; for if we mix 100 parts of this air with 40 parts of hydrogen, and pass an electric spark through the mixture (by applying the wire *a* to the conductor of an electrical machine, and the finger to the wire *b*), the mixture will explode, and 80 measures will remain, which, on examination, we find to consist of nitrogen, and of course the 20 parts which have disappeared are oxygen which has combined with the hydrogen to form water.

14. Having now explained the *chemical* properties of the atmosphere, will you mention what are its general properties?

Its general properties are fluidity, elasticity, expansibility, and gravity.

15. What do you mean by the elasticity of the air?

If atmospheric air be compressed into a small compass, it has the property of recovering its former state, as soon as the pressure is removed; which is called its elasticity.[a]

---

[a] The rebounding of a common foot-ball would be a familiar instance to explain the elasticity of air to a child.

Bubbles of air rising from the bottom of a glass of water will be seen to dilate as they rise to the surface; owing to the pressure of the liquor becoming less and less.

16. How do you show the elasticity of the air?

If a bladder be tied up with a very small quantity of air within it, and put under the receiver of an air pump, it will be seen to inflate gradually as the pump is exhausted, till it becomes of its full size; owing to the elasticity of the small quantity of air within the bladder, which dilates as the atmospheric pressure is removed. A wrinkled apple placed under the receiver of an air pump becomes plump and smooth, from the same cause. The elasticity of the air is proved by carrying a bladder half full of air to the top of a high mountain; for the air will be perceived to expand gradually as we approach the summit.

17. What is meant by the expansibility of the air?

The expansibility of the air is its property of being rarefied by heat, so as to occupy a larger space, its bulk increasing in proportion to the quantity of heat applied.[a]

18. How far does the atmosphere extend?

The atmosphere is several miles high, but how far it extends is not exactly known.[b]

The air gun and the forcing pump are constructed on this principle. It is by this property of air that fishes are enabled to rise and sink in the water; nature having furnished them with an air-bladder, which they have the power of contracting or dilating at pleasure. When the animal compresses this bladder, its whole volume becomes less, and it sinks in the water; when the pressure is removed, the air within the bladder instantly expands, and the creature is enabled to rise.

[a] If the neck of a bladder, containing a small quantity of air, be closely tied up and held to the fire, the swelling of the bladder, by the rarefaction of the air within it, will afford an idea of the *expansibility* of the air.

Mr. Robins has calculated, that the air which is disengaged in the firing of gunpowder is rarefied by the heat, so as to occupy a thousand times the space of the whole of the gunpowder employed.

[b] If the atmosphere were of the same density throughout, its height might be known by its effect in raising a column of water or mercury; but as it increases in rarity the higher it ascends, and is probably extremely rare in the higher regions, we cannot possibly tell how far it may extend. It was attempted to calculate the exten-

19. What are the principal uses of the atmosphere?

The atmosphere, which is the air we breathe, is necessary for the support both of animal and vegetable life; it is the medium of sounds, for they are produced by its vibrations. Without an atmosphere we should, the moment of sunset, be plunged into perfect darkness, and have no gradual approach of day at sunrise, but an instant change from total darkness to bright daylight; there are many other uses of the atmosphere too obvious to require enumeration.[a]

20. But what is the use of the atmosphere being extended so far above the surface of the earth?

It is this extension of the atmosphere which occasions its *weight;* and this great weight produces many important effects in the economy of nature.

21. How can you shew the pressure of the atmosphere?

The pressure of the atmosphere may be shown by a simple experiment. Place a card on a wine-glass *filled* with water; then invert the glass, and the water will not escape; the pressure of the atmosphere on the outside of the card being sufficient to support the water. It is the pressure of the air which enables the limpet to adhere firmly to the surface of rocks, and which acts in supporting the column of mercury in the barometer.[b]

---

sion of the atmosphere by ascertaining its comparative rarity at different heights; but this was also found to be impracticable. Since then, it has been estimated by the length of our twilight, and supposed to be about forty-five miles high. If we had no atmosphere, we should be in total darkness at the *instant* the sun sinks below the horizon; but as the sun illuminates the atmosphere for some time before it rises and after it has set, the light is refracted by the atmosphere to the earth.

[a] It is to the presence of air that water is indebted for its agreeable taste. Boiling deprives it of the greater part of it; hence the insipidity of boiled water.

[b] The same thing may be shown by a different experiment. Invert a tall glass jar in a dish of water, and place a lighted taper

22. What are the effects of the weight of the atmosphere?

It is owing to the weight of the atmosphere that we are enabled to raise water by the common pump,[a] and to perform many other useful operations.

23. What other advantages do we derive from this extension of the atmosphere?

If we had little or no atmosphere, we should have no water; for the waters on the face of the earth would 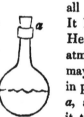 all evaporate at a very low temperature. It has been mentioned in the Chapter on Heat, that the boiling point varies with the atmospheric pressure, (chap. ii. q. 53.) We may here adduce the following experiment in proof of this fact. If we take a mattrass *a*, and having half filled it with water cause it to boil and suddenly remove it from the

---

under it. As the taper consumes the air in the jar, its pressure becomes less on the water immediately under the jar: while the pressure of the atmosphere on the water *without* the circle of the jar remaining the same, part of the water in the dish will be forced up into the jar, to supply the place of the air which the taper has consumed. Nothing but the pressure we are speaking of, could thus cause a part of the water to rise within the jar, above its own level.

[a] It is impossible for a youth to understand this, unless it be particularly explained to him; which may be done by telling him, that the atmosphere presses equally upon the whole surface of the water in the well, until the rod of the pump is moved; but that by forcing the rod down, the bucket compresses the air in the lower part of the pump tree, which being elastic, forces its way out of the tree through the valve; so that when the bucket is again raised, that part of the pump tree under the bucket is void of air; and the *weight of the atmosphere* pressing upon the body of water in the well, forces up a column of water to supply its place; that the next stroke of the pump rod causes another column of water to rise; and that, as long as the bucket fits the pump tree close enough to produce a vacuum, a constant stream of water may be drawn from below. In like manner the boy forms a vacuum between a piece of wet leather, tied to a string, and a pebble stone; and, by means of the pressure of the atmosphere, is enabled to lift the pebble from the earth and carry it about suspended by the leather. The common syphon is indebted to this pressure also for its action.

fire and cork it tightly, the water will continue boiling
for some time after it has been removed from the fire;
if when the ebullition has ceased we pour cold water
over the upper part of the mattrass the boiling will re-
commence; the reason of this strange phenomenon is,
that the pressure of the atmosphere is prevented by
corking the vessel, and the upper part of it is filled only
with the steam of water, which, by pressing on the
surface of the water, prevents the ebullition, but being
condensed by pouring cold water on the mattrass, the
pressure of this steam is removed, and the water boils
under the diminished pressure.

24. How are waters and other fluids preserved to us
by the weight of the atmosphere?

The weight of the atmosphere, pressing on the water,
binds it down as it were, and prevents the usual heat of
the sun from converting this and all other fluids on the
face of the earth into vapour.

25. What is the weight of the atmosphere?

It is about 1600 pounds upon every square foot. A
column of air an inch square weighs about 15 pounds.

26. How do you prove this?

The mercury in a barometer is supported by a column
of atmospheric air equal to itself in weight, and a column
of mercury of an inch square and 30.5 inches high weighs
about 15 pounds. Water can also be raised in a pump
33 feet by the pressure of the atmosphere, which gives
this pressure equal to 15 pounds on the square inch.[a]

27. What other advantages do we derive from this
immense atmosphere?

---

[a] Whenever I hold my hand out in this fluid, I feel no weight
upon it, because the pressure under and above my hand is equal; but
if I lay my hand on a hollow cylinder of glass, placed on the plate
of an air pump, and exhaust the air out of the cylinder, I become
immediately conscious of something that presses it so forcibly to the
glass, that I cannot release it. The prop is now gone; I have no

The atmosphere not only moderates the temperature of the earth and serves to render gradual the changes from light to darkness by its refraction of the sun's rays, but it also reflects those rays so as to give a lucid brightness to every part of the heavens, and serves to render the earth better adapted to the necessities of man by being the means of diffusing moisture in the form of rain and dew over all its surface. If there were no atmosphere surrounding the earth, only that part of the sky would appear light in which the sun was placed; and if a person should turn his back to the sun, he would directly perceive it as dark as night; for in that case there would be no substance to reflect the rays of the sun to his eyes. It is owing to reflection as well as refraction that the sun enlightens the earth some time before it rises, and some time after it sets.

28. What other substances are found in atmospheric air?

Besides carbonic acid gas, the air holds a portion of water in solution; and sometimes contains hydrogen and carburetted hydrogen gases.

29. What are the sources of these gases?

Carbonic acid gas is constantly formed by the respiration of animals and by combustion; and hydrogen and carburetted hydrogen gases arise from various sources, particularly from marshes, stagnant pools, &c. all which are prejudicial to the animal creation.

30. If carbonic acid gas and carburetted hydrogen are prejudicial to animal life, how are they corrected in the atmosphere?

pressure under my hand; a column of air, 45 miles high, forces it down by its weight, and I must let in the air under it, before the hand can be withdrawn.

Mr. Coates computed the weight of the air which presses upon the whole surface of the earth, and found it to be equal to that of a globe of lead sixty miles in diameter.

These gases, which would cause the death of any animal obliged to breathe them, are probably of use for the support of vegetables, which nature has endowed with organs fit for their decomposition.[a]

31. You have mentioned that nitrogen gas will not support animal life, what is the use of so large a quantity of it in atmospheric air?

Nitrogen gas has the effect of neutralizing, in some measure, the properties of oxygen gas, and rendering it fit for respiration and combustion. It prevents the rapid combustion of burning bodies, which we have shewn would take place in an atmosphere composed of pure oxygen, and moderates the action which this gas would have on organized beings; it also, probably, performs an important part in the production of animal substances; though we have not yet been able to investigate the mode in which it acts.

32. How does the oxygen of the air act in supporting life?

Oxygen seems essential to the performance of the function of respiration. "The internal surface of the lungs, or air vessels, in man, is said to be equal to the external surface of the whole body: it is on this *extended* surface that the blood is exposed, through the medium of a thin membrane, to the influence of the respired air, which undergoes a remarkable change in the lungs, the oxygen

[a] Vegetables are so constituted that carbon and hydrogen are the necessary food of plants, and conduce to the support of vegetable life: their vegetating organs seize the carbonic acid gas which comes within their reach, and while they appropriate the *carbon* to themselves, the *oxygen* is thrown off to renovate the atmosphere by its union with the nitrogen rejected by animal respiration. As all vegetables are in want both of carbon and hydrogen, there can be little doubt but that by their means the atmosphere is divested of carburetted hydrogen gas also. Thus, what is noxious to man is rendered beneficial to vegetables; and the oxygen which vegetables are not in want of, is separated by them in its utmost purity for the use of man.

of inspired air being replaced in the air when expired by carbonic acid gas."[a]

33. Does the oxygen of the air seem necessary for other living beings besides men?

Yes; both animals and plants require the presence of this element for their existence—even fishes require oxygen for their support: this they obtain from the water in which they live, which always contains a considerable quantity of air dissolved in it.

34. What is the cause of animal heat?

Different theories have been proposed to explain it; some have supposed that a low degree of combustion takes place in the surface of the lungs owing to the union of the oxygen of the air with the carbon of the blood; others believe that it arises from the change of form of the gas absorbed by the lungs, which gives out its latent heat; there is, however, no satisfactory theory as yet established to explain the cause of vital heat.[b]

35. How do clothes conduce to preserve the heat of the body?

As the temperature of the atmosphere in this climate is always below the animal temperature, clothes are

[a] " The blood is *purple* when it arrives at the lungs; but having there thrown off hydrogen and charcoal, it imbibes the vital air of the atmosphere, which changes its dark colour to a brilliant red, rendering it the spur to the action of the heart and arteries; the source of animal heat; and the cause of sensibility, irritability, and motion."—*Thornton's Philosophy of Medicine.*

Black venous blood, exposed to the air, becomes red on its surface; and air, remaining confined over venous blood, loses its oxygen, so that what remains is found to be unfit for combustion. These facts prove that the vermillion colour of the blood is owing to the inhalation of oxygen gas.

[b] Dr. Crawford instituted a series of experiments, with a view to discover the cause of animal heat. In the course of his inquiry, he found that blood contains a much greater quantity of *absolute* heat than the elementary substances of which it is composed, and that in its change from venous to arterial blood it acquires a greater *capacity* for caloric; by which admirable contrivance, any rise of temperature in the lungs which would be incompatible with life, is prevented.

necessary to prevent the sudden escape of the heat from the surface of the body. We clothe ourselves with wool, because it is a bad conductor of heat and retards its escape from the body. The inhabitants of Russia clothe themselves in fur, because fur is still a worse conductor of heat than wool. Sheep are natives of a temperate climate; but the bear and the ermine of the coldest.

36. What provision has nature made for restoring the vast quantity of oxygen which respiration and combustion are perpetually taking from the atmosphere?

The leaves[a] of trees and other vegetables give out during the day a large portion of oxygen gas, which, uniting with the nitrogen gas thrown off by animal respiration, keeps up the equilibrium, and preserves the salubrity of the atmosphere. All the oxygen is not given out by plants; part must be retained to form the sugar and acids which are found in vegetables.

---

[a] The *upper* side of the leaf is the organ of respiration; hence some vegetables (as they give out oxygen only in the day) close the upper surfaces of their leaves during the night. The multiplicity of the leaves of trees, &c. indicates the importance of the transpiration to a vegetable.

To show the production of oxygen gas from the leaves of plants, fill a glass bell with water, introduce leaves under it, and place the bell inverted in a flat dish of water. Expose the apparatus to the rays of the sun, and very pure oxygen gas will be disengaged, which will displace the water in the jar, and occupy its place. In like manner a sprig of mint, corked up with a small portion of carbonic acid air, and placed in the light, renders it again capable of supporting life. In bright sun-light a plant is capable of living in carbonic acid gas, though in the shade a very small proportion of this gas is found to be prejudicial to vegetation.

CHAPTER VI.

SIMPLE NON-METALLIC SUBSTANCES.

1. Having considered the properties of the simple substances which support combustion, we shall next proceed to those which exist in the solid state, which do not possess the characters of metals, and are combustible and capable of union with oxygen, uniting to this substance with the extrication of heat and light; can you enumerate these substances?

The simple non-metallic substances of this class are sulphur, selenium, boron, phosphorus, carbon.

2. How are these bodies electrically related with those already considered?

It is found that oxygen, chlorine, iodine, and bromine, when in combination with any of these bodies, appear at the positive end of the Voltaic battery, hydrogen, phosphorus, sulphur, &c. appearing at the opposite or negative pole. The former of these are therefore called electro-negative, and the latter electro-positive bodies, being supposed to possess electricities the opposite of the poles at which they appear.

3. What is sulphur?

Sulphur, or brimstone, as it is sometimes called, is a solid substance, of a pale yellow colour, insoluble in water, very brittle, and with but little taste or smell. Its specific gravity is 1·990, or nearly twice as heavy as water. It has various uses in medicine and the arts; it is a non-conductor of electricity; when newly melted it is transparent; it fuses at the temperature of 216, and by a higher temperature may be converted into vapour.[a]

---

[a] When sulphur is heated strongly, without contact of air, it rises in elastic vapour; and this vapour, on cooling, forms the flowers of sulphur, or sulphur in a state of minute division.

4. What is the origin of sulphur?

Sulphur is found in most parts of the world combined with metals, from which it is procured by roasting; it is found abundantly in the neighbourhood of volcanoes, especially in Sicily; it is sublimed from the sulphureous grounds in Italy, and is found in many mineral waters, combined with hydrogen.

5. Has sulphur any remarkable property when heated?

If sulphur be melted in an open vessel, by increase of heat it becomes thick, and has the peculiar property of becoming thinner as it cools, till it is nearly as thin as water. This is an exception to the general law, by which caloric causes the particles of bodies to recede from each other.

6. What compounds are formed by means of sulphur?[a]

Sulphur combines with oxygen, hydrogen, nitrogen, the alkalies, the metals, some of the earths, phosphorus, &c.[b]

7. What are the compounds of sulphur and oxygen?

If sulphur be heated sufficiently in oxygen gas it takes fire; it burns with a pale blue flame, and becomes converted to sulphurous acid. By burning sulphur with nitre (nitrate of potash) in vessels moistened with water, sulphuric acid is produced: these acids differ in the former containing less oxygen than the latter—16 parts of sulphur combining with 16 oxygen to form sulphurous acid, and with 24 oxygen to form sulphuric acid.

---

[a] " Nature employs sulphur in a great number of her operations; she presents it under many forms among fossils; charges it with waters denominated sulphureous; mineralizes with it the metals; causes it to pass into the vegetable and animal fibres; and exhibits it to chemists in an infinite number of combinations."

[b] Sulphur is used in large quantities for making gunpowder. When exhibited as a medicine, it penetrates to the extremities of the most minute vessels, and impregnates all the secretions; as may be perceived by those who have taken it for any length of time. Sulphur has many uses in the arts, and has been employed with advantage in stopping the progress of fermentation in wines and other fermented liquors.

8. What is the nature of the compound of hydrogen and sulphur?

Sulphur united with this gas forms sulphuretted hydrogen gas, which is a very fetid elastic fluid,[a] somewhat heavier than atmospheric air, and soluble in water;[b] the solution being readily decompounded by some metallic oxides dissolved in acids. The solution of this gas in water is consequently frequently used as a test[c] for the presence of certain metals in solution.

9. What are the properties of sulphuretted hydrogen gas?

Sulphuretted hydrogen gas possesses all the characters of an acid; it has an acid reaction, combines with earths, alkalies, and with several of the metallic oxides; and forms with them those substances called hydrosulphurets. It is combustible, and burns in contact with oxygen, with a pale blue flame; when set on fire at the mouth of a jar there is a deposition of sulphur on the sides of the vessel.

---

[a] This gas was long known by the name of hepatic gas, because the substances from which it was first obtained were called hepars, or livers of sulphur. It is decomposed by atmospheric air. The oxygen of the atmosphere combines with the hydrogen and forms water, while sulphur is precipitated. The sulphur which is found in the neighbourhood of mineral springs, originates from this cause. The fœtid smell which arises from house-drains is owing in a great measure to a mixture of this gas with other putrid effluvia.

[b] The waters of Harrowgate, Aix la Chapelle, and others of a similar nature owe their medicinal properties to sulphuretted hydrogen gas and muriate of soda. The salt of bitumen of the Hindoos, which is almost the only article of Hindoo physic, and is sold in every village, is chiefly composed of muriate of soda and sulphuretted hydrogen. It is taken by these people for every complaint.

[c] There have been instances, where people have taken frequent doses of mercurial medicine, of the human skin becoming suddenly quite black in a few hours after the outward application of sulphur-ointment; to the great terror and amazement of the patient. This was occasioned by the mercury exuding through the pores of the skin to unite with the sulphur, in consequence of its affinity to that substance; and a true Æthiops-mineral (sulphuret of mercury) was formed over the whole body.

10. How do we procure this gas?

If we introduce into a retort sulphuret of iron, and pour diluted muriatic acid upon it, sulphuretted hydrogen gas will be disengaged in abundance, and may be received in proper vessels, in the same manner as chlorine (chap. iv. 11.)

11. What are the properties of the hydrosulphurets?

The hydrosulphurets are soluble in water, and their solutions precipitate the metallic oxides from solutions in acids. Exposure to the air decomposes these hydrosulphurets when dissolved in water.

12. What is the composition of sulphuretted hydrogen?

It consists of 16 parts by weight, or one atom of sulphur, and one part by weight, or one atom of hydrogen.

13. What are the compounds of sulphur and the alkalies?

Sulphur, heated with potash, with soda, and the earths, forms compounds with their metallic bases by displacing the oxygen. Similar compounds may be formed by heating together sulphur and potassium, sodium, or any of the metallic bases of the alkalies or earths, and these sulphurets are decomposed by the acids, their bases being oxidized, combining with the acids, and sulphuretted hydrogen gas being disengaged.

14. What are the general characteristics of the alkaline and earthy sulphurets?

They are hard substances of a brown colour, resembling the liver of animals; they absorb water from the atmosphere, and emit a fœtid odour, similar to that of putrid eggs. By the action of acids, most of them are decomposed, sulphuretted hydrogen gas being disengaged.

15. What knowledge have we acquired of the combinations of sulphur with the earths and metals?

Sulphur may be combined artificially with most of the metals, and with some earths; but many of the metallic sulphurets are found native in great abundance.

16. What is selenium?

It is a solid opaque substance of a dark, brownish colour, in many of its chemical properties resembling sulphur, with which it is frequently found in combination;[a] at the temperature of boiling water it becomes soft, and may be drawn into threads which transmit a red light; at a higher temperature it is converted into vapour; it is also combustible.

17. How may we recognise selenium?

It tinges the flame of the blowpipe of a pale, blue colour, and produces by combustion an acid having a smell of horseradish.

18. Does selenium combine with oxygen?

Selenium forms two acids, the selenious and selenic acids, by union with oxygen gas; it also forms an oxide of selenium. Selenic acid resembles sulphuric acid in its strong attraction for water, and united with it dissolves most metals; even gold, which resists the action of most acids, dissolves in selenic acid.

19. Is there any other compound of selenium known?

Yes; Berzelius, the discoverer of selenium, has described a compound it forms with hydrogen, possessing the most noxious and poisonous properties—the selenuretted hydrogen, the minutest portion of which inhaled, produces the most injurious effects on the lungs, &c.

20. What is boron?

Boron is the base of the boracic acid, which exists in the well-known salt borax; it may be procured by decomposing boracic acid by means of potassium, when we obtain it as a chocolate coloured powder, without taste or smell, and unalterable by exposure to air; however, at a high temperature it burns in air or oxygen gas, and forms boracic acid; it is insoluble in water, and about twice the specific gravity of that fluid.

[a] It was discovered by Berzelius in the sulphur of Fahlun: it has since been found to exist in much of the sulphur of commerce; and also in combination with lead in some of the mines of that metal in Saxony.

21. What is the origin of phosphorus?

Phosphorus is a peculiar substance, chiefly of animal origin. It was formerly obtained from urine by a long and tedious process; but is now procured by the decomposition of the phosphoric acid which is found in bones.[a]

22. What is the nature of phosphorus?

Phosphorus is a solid inflammable substance, of a white colour, soft and flexible when slightly warm, which burns at a lower temperature, when in contact with atmospheric air, than any other combustible substance;[b] and, when combined with oxygen, forms peculiar acids. Its specific gravity is rather more than twice that of water. It is highly poisonous when taken internally.

23. What compounds are formed by means of phosphorus?

Phosphorus may be combined with oxygen, hydrogen, iodine, sulphur, and with many of the metals.

24. What is the nature of these compounds?

With oxygen, phosphorus forms an oxide of phos-

---

[a] Phosphorus was accidentally discovered at Hamburg, in 1669, by an alchemist of the name of Brandt; and two years afterwards one Kraft brought a small piece of this substance to London, on purpose to show it to the king and queen of England. Mr. Boyle afterwards discovered the process, which he described in the Phil. Trans. for 1680. Mr. Boyle instructed Mr. Godfrey Hankwitz of London how to procure it from urine, so that he was the first who made it for sale in England; and he continued to supply all Europe with it for many years.

[b] If a piece of phosphorus be placed on the surface of water, a little below the heat of boiling, it will immediately inflame. This is one characteristic of phosphorus, and distinguishes it from all other substances.

Phosphorus is used in forming phosphoric acid in various chemical experiments, and in making phosphoric match-bottles. These bottles may be prepared by mixing one part of flour of sulphur with eight of phosphorus. This requires caution, and should afterwards be handled with great care, lest any part of the mixture get under the finger nails, a small portion of which might occasion great inconvenience. When used to procure light, a very minute quantity is taken out of the bottle on the point of a match, and rubbed upon cork or wood, which produces an immediate flame.

F

phorus, also the phosphorous and the phosphoric acids;[a] with hydrogen, phosphuretted hydrogen gas; with sulphur, sulphuret of phosphorus; with chlorine, chloride of phosphorus; with the metals, metallic phosphurets.

25. What is the nature of the combination of hydrogen and phosphorus?

Hydrogen gas when combined with phosphorus forms *phosphuretted hydrogen gas*. This gas has the remarkable property of taking fire spontaneously whenever it comes in contact with atmospheric air.

26. How can we prepare this gas?

Phosphuretted hydrogen gas may be formed by boiling a little phosphorus in a solution of pure potash in a green glass retort. The water is decomposed, and furnishes the hydrogen. The retort should be nearly filled with the solution, otherwise the gas will inflame in the body of the retort and probably break the vessel: it may also be produced by using fresh slaked lime instead of potash, or by heating phosphuret of calcium in water.

27. What is carbon?[.]

Carbon is the base of common charcoal, divested of all impurities.

28. What is the most striking property of pure carbon?

Carbon is capable of crystallization, though not by art, and in that state it is called *diamond*.[b]

---

[a] The nature of these compounds will be explained in the chapter on the Acids.

[b] The diamond is chiefly found in the kingdom of Golconda in Asia, and in Brazil. It always occurs crystallized: indeed, if not, it would be carbon and not diamond.—See a note respecting the diamond under the article Steel, in the chapter on metals; where you have an additional proof that diamond is simple carbon. It is wonderful that Newton, who had no chemical means of examining the diamond, should have conceived the idea of its inflammable nature.

Mr. Tennant has satisfactorily shewn, that the diamond is pure carbon, carbon crystallized.—See Phil. Trans. for 1797. The diamond is the hardest substance in nature, and one of its rarest productions. From its hardness it is employed for sawing and boring

29. What is the origin of carbon?

Carbon in a state of purity is known only in the diamond; but it may be procured in the state of charcoal by burning a piece of wood covered with sand, in a crucible.

30. What compounds are formed by means of carbon?

Carbon combines with oxygen, hydrogen, nitrogen, sulphur, or phosphorus, and with iron.

31. What is the nature of these compounds?

Carbon combined with different proportions of oxygen forms carbonic oxide, or carbonic acid gases; with hydrogen, carburetted hydrogen gas, bicarburetted hydrogen, &c.; with nitrogen, cyanogen gas; with sulphur, sulphuret of carbon; with phosphorus, phosphuret of carbon; and with iron, plumbago, or carburet of iron.

32. What are the characters and appearances of charcoal?

Charcoal is generally black, sonorous, and brittle, very light, and destitute of taste or smell. It is procured whenever we burn animal or vegetable substances in close vessels without contact of air.[a]

the hardest stones. "Diamonds are usually found in an ochreous yellow earth, under rocks of grit stone; they are likewise found detached in torrents, which have carried them from their beds. They are seldom found above a certain size. The sovereigns of India reserve the largest, in order that the price of this article may not fall. Diamonds have no brilliancy when dug out of the earth, but are covered with an earthy crust."—Fourcroy. Diamonds are also found in considerable numbers in the island of Borneo. Whenever the mines are searched for them, an overseer attends, and watches the workmen with great care, that the largest may be secured for the sovereign prince. Notwithstanding, they are frequently conveyed away clandestinely by the workmen, who swallow them.

[a] Charcoal for common purposes is made by a less expensive process. The wood is disposed in heaps regularly arranged, and covered with earth, so as to prevent the access of any more air than is absolutely necessary to support the fire, which is kept up till all the water and oil are driven off; after which the fire is extinguished by shutting up all the air-holes. A more economical method is first to collect the acetic acid from the wood, by dry distillation in large iron cylin-

33. What are the properties of charcoal?

Charcoal is a powerful antiseptic;[a] has great affinity for oxygen; is unalterable and indestructible by age; and, if air and moisture be excluded, is not affected by the most intense heat.[b]

34. To what uses is charcoal applied?

Charcoal is used in large quantities in making gunpowder; it is employed as an antiseptic in purifying rancid oils, &c.; in decomposing the sulphuric acid, and for many other purposes, by the chemist and the manufacturer.

35. What other properties has carbon?

Carbon has the property of de-oxidizing the oxides of metals and other combustible substances, and of uniting with their oxygen to form carbonic acid.

36. Does carbon enter into any other combinations?

Carbon is formed abundantly in nature, forming the basis of coal and bitumen, and forming vegetable and animal substances.

37. Does carbon enter into combination with oxygen?

Yes, it forms two compounds with oxygen, carbonic acid, and carbonic oxide gases; the former of these is formed whenever charcoal is burned in contact with oxygen gas. If we introduce into a bottle filled with oxygen

ders; and then the residuum in the cylinders will be charcoal of the best quality. By this process, his majesty's gunpowder works have for some time past been supplied with charcoal.

[a] " All sorts of glass vessels and other utensils may be purified from long retained smells of every kind, in the easiest and most perfect manner, by rinsing them out well with charcoal powder, after the grosser impurities have been scoured off with sand and potash. Putrid water is immediately deprived of its offensive smell by charcoal. Meat, which is only a little tainted with putridity, may at once be made sweet by charcoal: and if common raw spirits be agitated with charcoal they will be deprived of their bad flavor."

[b] " The beams of the theatre at Herculaneum were converted into charcoal by the lava which overflowed that city; and during the lapse of seventeen hundred years, the charcoal has remained as entire as if it had been formed but yesterday, and it will probably continue so to the end of the world."

gas a piece of lighted charcoal, it will burn with increased brilliancy, and we shall find the oxygen has disappeared and a heavy gas which extinguishes flame and has acid properties, remains in the bottle; this is carbonic acid gas;[a] and consists of 6 parts by weight or 1 atom of carbon united to 2 atoms of oxygen, or 16 parts by weight. Carbonic oxide is formed by decompounding carbonic acid by means of some substance which will take away one of the atoms of oxygen:[b] this gas is not an acid, and is combustible, which properties at once distinguish it from carbonic acid.

38. What is the nature of the combinations of hydrogen with carbon?

The most important compounds of hydrogen and carbon are carburetted hydrogen and olefiant gas. The first of these is abundantly found in coal mines. In hot weather this gas is formed at the bottom of stagnant waters, and may readily be collected at their surface, by suspending a bottle of water over the pool, similar to the decanting of gases over a pneumatic trough, and stirring up the mud to disengage the carburetted hydrogen. It is found to consist of two parts by weight of hydrogen and 6 of carbon.

39. How is olefiant gas procured?

By the action of sulphuric acid on spirit of wine; if these fluids are heated together a large quantity of gas is disengaged, which may be received in jars over water: it is characterized by its burning with a more brilliant light than carburetted hydrogen, owing to its containing a larger quantity of carbon than this gas.

40. What are the gases used for the purposes of illumination?

[a] The properties of this will be more fully explained in the chapter on the acids.

[b] This may be done by heating to redness powdered chalk with iron filings, the carbonic acid of the chalk is decomposed and carbonic oxide is set free.

The gases procured from coal, resin, or oil, are all supposed to be mixtures of these two gases, the brilliancy of their light being proportional to the quantity of olefiant gas which they contain.

41. What is the use of carbon in the vegetable kingdom?

Carbon is not only a component part, but forms nearly the whole of the solid basis of all vegetables, from the flower of the garden to the oak of the forest.

42. If carbon forms so large a part of all vegetables, what occasions that infinite variety which we observe in the vegetable creation?

We are in a great measure strangers to the economy of vegetables; but much of this variety may be attributed to the different modifications of carbon, as well as of the other principles which enter into their constitution.

43. What products of vegetation are there which are indebted to carbon for their formation?

Carbon not only constitutes the base of the woody fibre, but is a component part of sugar, and of all kinds of wax, oils, gums, and resins, of which there are many varieties.

44. How are these substances formed by the vegetating organs of plants?[a]

---

[a] It has been discovered that the air which has been spoiled by the breathing of animals is peculiarly fitted for the vegetation of plants; no doubt this is owing to its containing a larger portion of carbonic acid.

By the analysis of soils it has been proved, that of all the substances found in the mixture of earths which constitute a soil, calcareous earth contributes most certainly to its fertilization. This probably proceeds from the carbonic acid.

Vegetables have the power to absorb oxygen from the atmosphere, and to transmit it to the absorbent vessels of the roots. It cannot be questioned but that this oxygen becomes useful in vegetation, by converting the carbon of manures into carbonic acid.

Fourcroy has remarked that "vegetables may be considered as beings intended by nature to *begin* the organization of crude matter, and to dispose the primitive materials of the earth and atmosphere in order to become the source of life, and consequently to establish

All living vegetables have the power of decomposing water, and of combining in different proportions the hydrogen of the water with the carbon of the soil, as well as with that of the carbonic acid of the atmosphere, to form the numberless productions of vegetable nature.[a]

45. If carbon and hydrogen enter into the composition of all these substances, how is it that one vegetable affords gum, another resin, another oil, &c. ?

The infinite variety which there must be in the internal organization of vegetables, to enable different orders to prepare such different substances from the same elements, renders this subject too intricate and minute for our investigation.[b]

46. Is it known what other substances are employed by nature for the formation and growth of vegetables ?

All orders of vegetables are produced from four or five natural substances, viz. caloric, light, water, air, and carbon ; caloric is necessary to enable vegetables to decompose water and air ; and light is equally requisite to give a part of the oxygen of these substances a gaseous form, and to put it in a proper state to be thrown off by the leaves. The other portion of oxygen goes to the

a communication between minerals and animals ; from whence it follows, that plants are truly chemical apparatus employed by nature to produce combinations which would not take place without them." Nature is as admirable in the simplicity of her means, as in the constancy and regularity of her operations.

[a] When we decompose water, we can do it only by abstracting its oxygen by combustible substances, and liberating the hydrogen. Vegetables effect this in a different way ; they preserve the hydrogen, and set the oxygen free.

Van Helmont planted a willow, weighing fifty pounds, in a certain quantity of earth, covered carefully with sheet lead ; he kept it in this state for five years, watering it with distilled water ; and at the end of that time the tree weighed 169 pounds three ounces; the earth in which it had vegetated, being weighed at the same time, was found to have lost only three ounces. This was repeated by Mr. Boyle with a similar result.

[b] It has been found by numerous experiments that the bases of all vegetable substances are carbon, oxygen, and hydrogen.

formation of sugar and the vegetable acids. The analysis of vegetables confirms this theory; for, however they may be examined, the result is always the production of oxygen, hydrogen, and carbon. Some plants yield also a portion of silex, and others lime; but these no doubt are taken up by the roots from the soil.

47. What is the office of carbon in the animal kingdom?

As carbon is a necessary part of sugar, of oils, &c. it consequently enters into the composition of animal milk, and of animal oils and fat; it is also found in albumen, gelatine, fibrina, and animal urine.

48. Does carbon enter into any mineral combinations?

Some metals may be combined with carbon; many of their oxides are capable of forming compounds with carbonic acid.

49. What does carbon form when combined with iron?

In one proportion it forms cast iron; in another steel; and in a third proportion plumbago; generally, though improperly, called black lead.

50. What is the proportion of carbon in cast iron?

Upon an average cast iron contains, according to the analysis of Bergman, about one forty-fifth of its weight of carbon.

51. What quantity of carbon enters into the composition of steel?

Steel is iron combined with about one part of carbon in two hundred of iron.[a]

52. How is carbon combined with iron to form plumbago?

Carburet of iron or plumbago, has been found to consist of nearly nine parts of carbon to one of iron. Plumbago, like charcoal, is indestructible by heat, unless with

[a] We shall explain the nature of these compounds in the chapter on the metals.

the presence of atmospheric air. It is therefore much used for making crucibles and portable furnaces. It protects iron from rust, and on that account is rubbed on various ornamental cast-iron works, such as the fronts of grates, &c.

53. How do you account for the production of carbonic acid gas in the process of fermentation?

In all vinous fermentations a decomposition of the saccharine matter takes place; and a part of the disengaged oxygen, uniting with a part of the carbon of the sugar, forms carbonic acid. A decomposition also of part of the water of solution perhaps promotes the process.

54. What is the cause of vinous fermentation?

The cause of vinous fermentation is not well understood; but it appears to be a spontaneous commotion that takes place on the decomposition of vegetable substances, in certain favourable circumstances of temperature and solution; and it is a process which nature employs for their destruction.

55. What circumstances are necessary to produce vinous fermentation?

The presence of vegetable matters, of water, of sugar, a certain degree of heat, and free egress for the carbonic acid to escape as it is generated.

56. Can you at all account for the change which is effected in saccharine liquors by fermentation?

By the process of fermentation the sugar, which is a vegetable oxide, parts with a portion of its oxygen to form carbonic acid, and becomes converted into alcohol by being thus partially deoxidized.

57. Does sugar then become spirit of wine, or alcohol, merely by losing a part of its oxygen?

No; it parts with a portion of its carbon at the same time, in the form of carbonic acid gas, and a new arrangement of the remaining principles, both of the sugar, and of the water in which it is dissolved, takes place, furnishing an increased proportion of hydrogen, in order to form vinous liquor.

58. Endeavour to recollect the different properties of charcoal, which you have enumerated in this chapter?

Charcoal appears to be indestructible by age; it is not in the least altered by the most intense heat, if heated in *closed* vessels; when burnt in atmospheric air it becomes converted into carbonic acid gas; it is a valuable antiseptic; it is the basis of all vegetable and animal substances; it is one of the component parts of wax, oils, gums, and resins: and from its affinity to oxygen it has the property of decomposing many substances in which oxygen constitutes a material part.

59. How did chemists become acquainted with all these properties of charcoal?

Formerly, nothing was known of charcoal but its indestructibility, and its antiseptic qualities. The other peculiar and surprising properties of charcoal were reserved for the discoveries of the present age; for these we are most especially indebted to the labours and genius of Black, Priestley, Cavendish, Gay, Lussac, and Davy, and to the gradual development of the present improved system of chemistry.

CHAPTER VII.

THE ACIDS.

1. What is an acid?[a]

Most of the acids are substances which produce that sensation on the tongue which we call sour; but some

---

[a] The acids differ from each other in their appearance and properties as much as any class of bodies we are acquainted with; it is therefore difficult to give a definition of an acid. In general they are liquids, but some of them take a solid, and others a gaseous form; some are mild, others corrosive; some are pungent and volatile, others are mild and inodorous.

substances are classed with the acids which have not this. characteristic, though they possess some of the other properties of acids.

2. What are the properties of acids?

Acids change the blue juices of most vegetables to red;[a] and combine with alkalies, earths, or metallic oxides, so as to form those compounds called salts.

3. Is the power of changing blue vegetable colours essential to acids?

Some acids, owing to their insolubility in water, have not this power, though they will combine with metallic oxides, and form salts.

4. What is the origin of acids?

Many of the acids owe their origin to the combination of certain substances with oxygen, which has been called the acidifying principle; incorrectly, however, as hydrogen forms, by combination with bases, a very extensive class of acids.

5. What are the electrical relations of the acids?

When a salt containing an acid is placed in the electrical circuit and decomposed, it is found that the acid appears at the positive pole, and the base at the negative. It follows, therefore, that the acids possess electro-negative properties.

6. How is it shown that oxygen and hydrogen, by union with bases, produce acids?

Many of the acids can be decompounded by bodies having stronger attraction for the oxygen than the acidified base by which they lose their acid properties: in a similar manner the acids of hydrogen, by separation of the hydrogen, lose their acidity—we may also, by

---

[a] This property is frequently made use of in chemistry for discovering the presence of a free acid in solution; for this purpose *test* paper, made by staining paper of a blue colour with an infusion of litmus or turnsole, are employed; the colour of which is immediately changed to red by an acid dissolved in water. An infusion of litmus or blue cabbage in water, is also used as a test for the presence of uncombined acid in solution.

direct combination of oxygen or hydrogen with bases, form acids.

7. Do acids always result from the union of oxygen with bases?

By no means; alkalies, earths, and metallic oxides, are all compounds of oxygen with bases; and these do not possess acid properties.

8. Do the same bases always combine with an equal portion of oxygen?

No; some acidifiable bases combine with different proportions of oxygen, producing different states of acidity.[a]

9. How do chemists distinguish this difference?

When two acids have the same basis, but contain different quantities of oxygen, they are distinguished by their termination. The name of that which contains most oxygen ends in ic, the other in ous. Thus we have *sulphuric* acid, and *sulphurous* acid; *phosphoric* acid, and *phosphorous* acid.

10. How are the acids classed by chemists?

The acids were formerly divided into three classes, viz. the mineral, the vegetable, and the animal acids; but the more useful and scientific way of dividing the acids is into two classes only.

11. How are the acids now divided?

Those acids which are formed with two principles only, are comprised in the first class; while those acids which are formed with more than two principles compose the second class.[b]

---

[a] The first portion of oxygen converts some bodies into oxides; the second, into that class of acids, of which the specific names drawn from their particular bases terminate in *ous*, as the sulphurous acid; the third degree of oxygenisement changes some of these into that division of acids which are distinguished by the termination in *ic*, as the sulphuric acid.

[b] Those acids of the first class, which are formed with two principles only, are composed of oxygen and some other substance which is called their base. The acids of the second class are composed chiefly of oxygen, hydrogen, and carbon; though some of them contain nitrogen, as mentioned in a former note.

12. Can you enumerate the principal acids of the first class ?

The sulphuric and sulphurous acids ; hydrosulphuric or sulphuretted hydrogen, the chloric, and bromic, the muriatic acids; the nitric, the carbonic, the hydriodic, the phosphoric and phosphorous, the fluoric, the boracic, the arsenious and arsenic, the tungstic, the molybdic, the titanic, and the chromic acids.

13. Enumerate the most important acids of the second class.

The acetic, the oxalic, the tartaric, the citric, the malic, the lactic, the gallic, the benzoic, the succinic, the camphoric, the suberic, the lactic, the prussic, or hydrocyanic, the ferrocyanic or ferroprussic, the sebacic, the uric, and the amniotic acids.

14. What is the sulphuric acid?

The sulphuric acid is a combination of sulphur and oxygen. It is commonly called oil of vitriol, from its having been formerly distilled from green vitriol (sulphate of iron) and from its great density.

15. How is the sulphuric acid obtained?

Sulphuric acid is procured by burning sulphur mixed with nitrate of potash, in contact with air and moisture ; by which process the sulphur combines with the oxygen of the nitrate of potash and the air, and becomes acidi-fied.[a]

---

[a] In this country sulphuric acid is prepared by burning sulphur mixed with nitrate of potash in a leaden chamber, the floor of which is covered some inches deep with water ; several complicated changes take place during this process, by which the sulphurous acid is by the joint action of the water, and nitrous acid evolved from the nitre, converted into sulphuric acid, with which the water becomes gradually charged.   This is drawn off, and concentrated by boiling in glass or platina vessels, after which it forms the dense sulphuric acid, or oil of vitriol of commerce.   In this state it is always combined with a certain quantity of water, forming a chemical compound with it. Anhy-drous sulphuric acid, or acid without water, is prepared at Nordhausen in Germany from the green sulphate of iron ; and in this state it forms a white crystalline solid.—ED.

16. What are the properties of sulphuric acid?

The sulphuric is a very ponderous,[a] corrosive acid, destitute of colour and smell, and has a very strong acid taste. It has a great attraction for water,[b] and, when combined with the alkalies, the earths, or the metallic oxides, forms with them those salts called sulphates. It may be at once discovered in solution by a salt of baryta with which it forms an insoluble white precipitate.

17. Does sulphur form with oxygen another acid?

Yes; the sulphurous acid is formed whenever sulphur is burned in contact with oxygen gas; it may also be formed by the action of substances having a strong attraction for oxygen upon sulphuric acid; by heating, for example, charcoal or copper. in sulphuric acid this air is decomposed, part of its oxygen unites with the charcoal or metal, and sulphurous acid is set free.

18. What are the properties of sulphurous acid?

Sulphurous acid in the gaseous state is invisible like air, but of a strong, suffocating smell. It is readily absorbed by water, and then forms liquid sulphurous acid. It is capable of uniting with various bases, and forms the salts named sulphites. It has alsothe property of destroying certain vegetable colours, and is on this account used in certain cases for bleaching.[c]

---

[a] The specific of sulphuric acid is about 1·8, or nearly twice as heavy as water.

[b] Sulphuric acid has a great affinity to water; they combine so intimately that the new compound gives out a large portion of caloric, and becomes very much condensed. Four pounds of this acid mixed with one pound of water will raise the thermometer to 300°.

The sulphuric acid of commerce is never perfectly pure—it always contains a portion of sulphate of lead and sulphate of potash. The former comes from a partial solution of the lead of the chamber in which it is made, and the latter from the nitre which is always used in the process.

[c] By means of pressure and reduced temperature, this gas may be condensed into a fluid; in this state by diminution of pressure and increase of temperature, it rapidly again assumes the gaseous form, and absorbs so much heat during the change, that mercury may be frozen by means of the evaporation of the liquid gas.—ED.

19. What is the difference between these two acids?

Sulphurous acid is found to consist of one atom or equivalent of sulphur united to two of oxygen, or 16 of sulphur to 16 oxygen. Sulphuric acid consists of three atoms of oxygen united to one of sulphur, or 24 to 16. The representative numbers of these acids will be 32 and 40.

20. What is the muriatic acid?

The muriatic is a peculiar acid obtained from sea-salt. In its pure state it exists as a gas, and when combined with water forms the liquid muriatic or hydrochloric acid: water when saturated with this gas acquired about the specific gravity 1·196.

21. What method is made use of to collect and preserve the muriatic acid?

Muriatic acid is distilled from common salt by means of sulphuric acid, and collected in appropriate receivers, where it is condensed in water, for which it has a powerfull affinity.

22. What are the properties of muriatic acid?

This acid in the gaseous[a] state is invisible like air; has a pungent suffocating smell. With water it forms the liquid muriatic acid, which preserves the smell of the gas, and gives out white fumes when exposed to the atmosphere. This acid is much employed in the arts, and in chemical laboratories. With various bases it forms the salts called *muriates*.

23. What is the composition of muriatic acid?

It is composed of equal volumes of chlorine and hydrogen: which when mixed together and heated or exposed to the sun's light combine with explosion and form this

---

[a] Muriatic acid gas may be obtained for chemical experiments, by pouring one part of sulphuric acid upon two parts of dry muriate of soda in a tubulated retort, and collecting the gas, as it becomes disengaged, over mercury in a pneumatic apparatus. This gas may also be collected by heating the muriatic acid of commerce in a glass retort.

gas. It is by decomposition of this gas that we obtain chlorine for chemical experiments.

24. Does chlorine form an acid with oxygen as well as with hydrogen?

Yes; with oxygen chlorine forms the chloric and perchloric acids: the former of these, by combination with potash, forms the salt called chlorate of potash, now so extensively employed in the preparation of different kinds of matches, which take fire by friction or dipping the match in sulphuric acid.

25. What are the properties of chloric acid?

The chloric acid has an acid reaction, unites with alkaline and earthy bases to form the class of salts called chlorates. When concentrated it has a yellow tint, and acts strongly on combustible substances, setting them on fire; by different substances having an attraction for oxygen it is readily decomposed: it consists of five atoms of oxygen and one of chlorine.

26. What are the properties of perchloric acid?

Perchloric acid when concentrated, has a sp. gr. 1·65; it has acid reaction; it does not inflame organic substances; and emits white fumes when exposed to air; it may, by certain means, be obtained in a solid form: it forms with bases salts possessing little solubility in water.

27. What is euchlorine?

Euchlorine, or protoxide of chlorine, is a gaseous substance, first discovered by Sir H. Davy, and obtained by the action of muriatic acid on the salt of chloric acid and potash. When these substances are heated together a gas of a deep, yellowish green colour, and having the smell of burnt sugar, is disengaged by the mutual reaction of the muriatic and chloric acids—the hydrogen of the muriatic acid uniting with some of the oxygen of the chloric acid, and the remaining oxygen combining with the chlorine of the muriatic acid to form protoxide of chlorine.

28. What are the properties of this gas?

It is much heavier than atmospheric air; it does not,

like chlorine, set fire to metallic foils. At a temperature a little above that of boiling water it explodes, and is resolved into oxygen and chlorine gases.

29. What is nitric acid or aqua fortis ?[a]

Nitric acid is one of the constituent parts of nitre or saltpetre. It is a composition of oxygen and nitrogen, in the proportion of about 14 parts by weight of the latter, to about 40 of the former.[b]

30. How is nitric acid obtained ?

Nitric acid is obtained by distilling two parts of nitre and one part of sulphuric acid in a glass retort, and collecting the gas in proper receivers. This acid, which at first contains nitrous gas, is in a great measure deprived of it, and rendered transparent and colourless by the application of heat in a subsequent process.

31. What are the properties of nitric acid ?

Nitric acid is clear and colourless, like water; its smell is sharp and pungent, its taste exceedingly acid, and its action on animal substances very corrosive. It has the property of staining the skin yellow; which colour does not disappear until the cuticle is separated. It has a great affinity for water; is capable of oxidizing most of the metals;[c] and with various bases forms the salts called *nitrates*.

[a] Nitric acid was known to Raymond Lully in the thirteenth century; but it was Mr. Cavendish who discovered its component parts, in the year 1785. See his paper in the Philosophical Transactions for that year.

[b] If a proper mixture of these gases be made in a glass tube, and a number of electric explosions passed through the mixture, the gases will unite, and nitric acid will be the product. As nitric acid is formed of the same substances as atmospheric air, we have no difficulty in accounting for the natural production of saltpetre.

[c] Nitric acid is very easily decomposed by any body having a strong attraction for oxygen; most of the metals readily decompound it. Charcoal also, from its attraction for oxygen, will decompose this acid very rapidly. If the charcoal be dry and finely powdered, and the acid strong, and allowed to run down the inner side of the

32. What is nitrous acid?

Nitrous acid is a compound of four atoms of oxygen and one of nitrogen.

33. What are the properties of nitrous acid?

Nitrous acid is an extremely volatile fluid, being converted into vapour at the temperature of the human body: for this reason, it generally exists in the state of orange red vapour; it is readily formed by the action of oxygen gas or nitric oxide gas, or by the decomposition of nitrate of lead. It is this gas which gives a colour to the nitric acid of commerce, which is for this reason often called nitrous acid, though it may readily be freed from the nitrous acid vapour by heat.

34. What other compounds does oxygen form with nitrogen?

It forms hyponitrous acid, nitric oxide, and nitrous oxide gases.

35. The hyponitrous acid being of little importance, we need not inquire its properties; what are the properties of nitric oxide gas?

This gas is formed by taking away a portion of oxygen from nitric acid; if, for example, we dissolve in a glass matrass, (see fig. p. 86,) copper wire in nitric acid, a large quantity of gas is disengaged, which forms orange fumes by contact with air or oxygen gas. If we collect this gas in a glass bell over water, we find it colourless and transparent.

36. What are the most remarkable properties of this gas?

It is not acid; when oxygen gas is mixed with it, it is at once converted into nitrous acid gas; it does not support flame, but phosphorus inflamed and plunged into it, will continue to burn brilliantly in consequence of the gas being decompounded and its oxygen uniting

vessel to mix with the charcoal, it will burn rapidly, giving out a beautiful flame, and throwing up the powder so as to resemble a brilliant fire-work.

with the phosphorus. This gas is composed of 14 parts
of nitrogen and 16 of oxygen.

37. What are the properties of nitrous oxide gas ?

This gas has neither acid nor alkaline properties; it
supports combustion better than atmospheric air; it is not
decompounded by oxygen or nitric oxide gas, and it can
be respired with safety; the respiration of this gas is
attended by very remarkable effects on the person who
inhales it, resembling intoxication : in consequence of the
pleasurable sensation it excites it has been called laugh-
ing gas.

38. How is this gas procured ?

By the action of heat upon the salt called nitrate of
ammonia. When this salt is heated the nitric acid and
ammonia are both decomposed, giving rise to the production of water and nitrous oxide gas.*

39. What is the composition of this gas ? .

It consists of one atom of oxygen and one of nitrogen
or 8 parts of oxygen by weight to 14 of nitrogen.

40. What is nitromuriatic acid or *aqua regia ?*

This name is given to the mixture of the nitric and
muriatic acid which is used as a solvent for gold, platina,
and other metals, which cannot be dissolved in any of the
simple acids; it is made by mixing together one part of
strong nitric acid with two of strong muriatic acid. It is
generally supposed that its power of dissolving gold depends on chlorine being evolved by the reaction of these
acids on each other.

41. What is carbonic acid ?

Carbonic acid is a combination of carbon and oxygen.

It was formerly called fixed air, on account of its being
found in chalk, limestone, magnesia, &c.

42. What are the properties of carbonic acid ?

Carbonic acid is invisible when in the state of gas,

* This process may be better explained when we come to speak
of this salt, in a subsequent chapter.

and unfit for combustion, or respiration. Water, by pressure, may be made to absorb three times its bulk of this gas: by which it acquires an agreeable acidulous taste.[a] Carbonic acid enters into combination with the alkalies, with earths, and metallic oxides; and forms with them those salts called *carbonates*.

43. How can you show that this gas extinguishes flame?

If this gas be poured from a wide-mouthed jar upon a lighted candle, it will be as effectually extinguished as by water. Its superior gravity to atmospheric air, and its unfitness for supporting combustion, may also be shown by pouring a common glassful of this gas into another tall glass, containing a short taper burning within it.

44. What is the composition of carbonic acid?

Carbonic acid is found to consist of 6 parts by weight of carbon united with 16 parts of oxygen, and it is formed whenever charcoal is burned in an atmosphere of oxygen gas, the specific gravity of which is greatly increased by union with carbon.

45. In what states does carbonic acid exist in nature?

Carbonic acid is found in nature in three different states, viz. in gas, in mixture, and in chemical combination; it is perhaps the most abundant of all the native acids.

46. What instances are there of its natural existence in the state of gas?

It is found in small proportion in atmospheric air; also in caverns and mines, where it is called the choke damp.[b]

[a] Carbonic acid gas is found in abundance in many natural waters. Those of Pyrmont, Spa, and Seltzer, are instances; the last particularly, is highly impregnated with this acid. These waters are so pleasant and salutary, that various imitations of them, made in this country, are sold under the names of single and double soda water.

[b] The floor of the Grotto del Cane, in Italy, is lower than the door and this hollow is always filled with fixed air, which can rise no higher than the threshold, but there flows out like water. It has been

47. What instances are there of carbonic acid being found mixed with fluids?

It is abundant in Spa-water, and in some other acidulous waters.

48. In what substances is carbonic acid found chemically combined?

Carbonic acid is found in all parts of the world in great plenty, in combination with the alkalies, in earths, and in stones; particularly in chalk, limestone, and marble.

49. What is the effect of the combination of carbonic acid?

Carbonic acid renders mild and salutary some of the most acrid and destructive of all known substances.

50. How is the carbonic acid separated from alkalies and earths?

Carbonic acid may be disengaged by all the other acids; but it is usually separated from alkalies by the

a common practice to drive dogs into this cavern, where they suffer a temporary death, for the entertainment of the passengers; but a man enters with safety, because his mouth is far above the surface of this deleterious air. From the loss of so many dogs in this cavern it acquired the name of the Grotto del Cane. The lake of Averno, which Virgil supposed to be the entrance to the infernal regions, evolves so large a quantity of this gas, that birds flying over it drop with suffocation. Fatal accidents have happened to persons who have incautiously descended into brewers' vats, and into wells, before they been purified from this gas.

Carbonic acid gas so often occupies the bottoms of wells, that workmen ought never to venture into such places without previously letting down a lighted candle. If the candle burns, they may enter it with safety; if not a quantity of *quick lime* should be let down in buckets, and gradually sprinkled with water. As the lime slakes it will absorb the carbonic acid gas, and the workmen may afterwards descend in safety.

Fatal accidents often happen from burning charcoal in chambers; as whenever charcoal is burned this gas is formed. Workmen have also lost their lives by sleeping too near limekilns, where this gas is extricated in abundance. It is surprising that no advantage has been taken of the vast quantities of carbonic acid gas, which are perpetually escaping from the vats of the large breweries in this metropolis. It might surely be collected, and applied to many useful purposes. The benefit which is derived from *yeast* in putrid diseases, is perhaps due to its carbonic acid.

addition of quick-lime, which absorbs this acid, and thus is converted into carbonate of lime.

51. How is carbonic acid usually procured for chemical purposes?

Carbonic acid gas may be collected in abundance from the surface of fermenting liquors; but it is more commonly obtained by pouring sulphuric acid upon a mixture of chalk, or marble and water.

52. What is phosphoric acid?

Phosphoric acid is a compound of oxygen and phosphorus.

53. How is phosphoric acid procured?

Formerly phosphoric acid was procured only by burning phosphorus in oxygen gas; but, since it is known that this acid is a component part of animal bones, we now procure it at a much cheaper rate.

54. What are the properties of phosphoric acid?

Phosphoric acid, deprived of water, is solid and transparent;[a] when liquid, it has a thick oily appearance, is of considerable gravity, and very acid to the taste. It forms by its union with earthy, alkaline, and metallic bases, that variety of salts which we call *phosphates.*

55. What is the phosphorous acid?

This acid contains a smaller proportion of oxygen than the phosphoric acid. It is procured by the *slow* combustion of phosphorus; for when phosphorus is heated it burns *rapidly,* and the product is phosphoric acid.[b]

56. What are the properties of phosphorous acid?

---

[a] If phosphoric acid be exposed to heat it gradually becomes thick and glutinous; and if the heat be continued it acquires more consistence, and at last melts into a solid transparent glass. This phosphoric glass must be preserved from the action of the atmosphere, or it will be gradually dissolved again into liquid phosphoric acid. If the phosphoric acid has been fused in an earthen crucible, it will not be deliquescent nor soluble in water.

[b] The compounds of oxygen and phosphorus are not as yet perfectly understood. It is supposed that by combination these substances form four distinct compounds or oxides, and three acids, the

Phosphorous acid is a dense, viscid liquid, with an acid taste, and emits the smell of garlic when heated. Like the phosphoric, this acid may be decomposed by charcoal, but cannot be obtained in a concrete state. It has not yet been applied to any use. The salts formed with it are called *phosphites*.

57. How is phosphorous acid procured?

Phosphorous acid is generally prepared by exposing sticks of phosphorus to the action of atmospheric air, in a glass funnel, and receiving the acid, as it forms, in a bottle placed underneath. Two or three pieces of broken glass placed in the neck of the funnel to support the phosphorus, and a small quantity of distilled water put into the receiving bottle, complete this simple apparatus. The pieces of phosphorus should be placed so as not to touch each other.

58. What is fluoric acid?

The fluoric is an acid of a very peculiar nature, found in the fluor spar. This mineral is a natural production, composed of fluoric acid and lime.

59. What are the properties of fluoric acid?

In the state of gas it is invisible, like air. Water rapidly absorbs it, and forms liquid fluoric acid. It has an acid taste, and the peculiar property of dissolving silex. Its base is not yet known.

60. What is the use of fluoric acid?

Fluoric acid has not been used except for etching upon glass.[a] It appears that it was first employed for this purpose in the seventeenth century.

---

hypophosphorous, phosphorous, and phosphoric acids; the last of these is supposed to consist of two atoms of phosphorus and five of oxygen. Other compounds of phosphorus are also described, the para-phosphoric, and metaphosphoric acids, which are considered as identical in composition with the phosphoric acid, and can only be distinguished from it by certain compounds which they form with metallic oxides. —ED.

[a] This acid acts so powerfully on silex, that it is impossible to use glass vessels for its distillation. A glass retort would be destroyed

61. How is fluoric acid procured?

Fluoric acid is obtained by pouring sulphuric acid upon the powdered fluor spar in a leaden or silver retort, and applying a gentle heat. The sulphuric acid unites with the lime forming sulphate of lime, and the fluoric acid is disengaged.

62. What is the composition of this acid?

It is supposed to consist of a peculiar base to which the name fluorine has been given united to hydrogen; the decomposition of this acid has, however, never been effected.

63. What is boracic acid?

The boracic acid is obtained from the substance called borax. It consists of boron united to oxygen.—(*Vide* ch. vi. 20.)

64. What are the properties of boracic acid?

Boracic acid is in the form of thin scales, slightly acid, and unalterable in the air. It forms the variety of salts called *borates*, when combined with the alkalies, some earths, and some of the metallic oxides. One of the peculiar properties of this acid is, that it imparts a green colour to burning bodies. If a small quantity be mixed with spirit of wine and the spirit inflamed, a fine green tinge will be given by the boracic acid to the flame.

65. What is arsenic acid?

Arsenic acid is a compound of arsenic and oxygen. It is a heavy, thick, incrystallizable mass: very soluble in hot water; of an acid taste, and poisonous. With different bases it forms the salts called *arseniates*. .

66. What is arsenious acid?

---

before the gas could be obtained. It combines with the siliceous earth of the glass, and carries it over with it in distillation.

Its action on glass may be shown by strewing a little powered fluor spar on the surface of a pain of glass, and pouring a little sulphuric acid upon it. The sulphuric acid will disengage the fluoric acid from the spar, which will act upon the glass as it becomes disengaged.

Arsenious acid is the compound of oxygen and arsenic, in the lower state of oxidation; the common white arsenic of commerce consists entirely of this acid.

67. What is tungstic acid?

The tungstic acid is a tasteless yellow powder, composed of oxygen and tungsten. It is insoluble in water, and forms the salts, called *tungstates*, by its union with alkalies, earths, and metallic oxides.

68. How is tungstic acid obtained?

Tungstic acid is found native in wolfram (which is a tungstate of iron and manganese) and other minerals. It may be obtained from wolfram by boiling three parts of muriatic acid on one part of the mineral. The acid is to be decanted off in about half an hour, and allowed to settle: the powder which precipitates is to be dissolved in ammonia; the solution evaporated to dryness, and the dry mass kept for some time in a red heat. It then forms tungstic acid in a state of purity.

69. What is molybdic acid?

Molybdic acid is a white powder, composed of molybdenum and oxygen. It requires a large quantity of water to dissolve it. When combined with salifiable bases, the compounds are called *molybdates*.[a]

70. What is chromic acid?

Chromic acid is a dark red powder, composed of 32 parts chromium and 20 parts oxygen. It has an acrid metallic taste, is very soluble in water, and crystallizable. When mixed with different saline solutions it assumes a variety of beautiful colours; it also forms with the earths and alkalies various salts, called *chromates*.

71. How is this acid obtained?

---

[a] Molybdic acid was discovered by Scheele in 1778. It is procured from the sulphuret of molybdenum by distilling nitric acid off it repeatedly, till the sulphur and metal are both acidified; which is known by the conversion of the whole into a white mass. Hot water carries off the sulphuric acid, and leaves the molybdic in a state of purity.

G

It exists in nature, combined with lead; it may be procured by decompounding fluochromic by water, or the bichromate of potash of commerce by means of fluosilic acid, which separates the potash, and leaves the acid in a pure state.

72. What is the acetic acid?

Acetic acid is principally obtained from saccharine liquors which have undergone the vinous fermentation.[a]

73. What are the properties of acetic acid?

Acetic acid, as it is usually prepared, is the well known fluid vinegar. When distilled it is colourless as water, and of an agreeable odour. When concentrated it has a strong sharp acid taste, and pungent smell. With the different bases it forms the class of salts called acetates.

74. What is oxalic acid?

The oxalic is a peculiar acid found in the juice of some species of sorrel, in combination with potash. It may be prepared artificially by the decomposition of some vegetable substances. If sugar be heated with nitric acid it will be converted into the oxalic acid. It crystallizes in four-sided prisms, has a very acid taste, and is soluble in water. It is composed of oxygen, hydrogen, and carbon.

75. What are the uses of oxalic acid?

Oxalic acid is of great use to us in detecting the presence of lime in solution.[b] It is also become an article of great consumption with the calico-printers, both in a state of purity and in combination with potash.

[a] It was formerly imagined that acetic acid could be prepared only from vinous liquors; but it is not an indispensable condition that it shall have been preceded by the vinous fermentation. This acid may be prepared from wood by the destructive distillation. There are at present many extensive manufactories of this acid in Great Britain, where the wood is burnt in large iron cylinders. This acid, which is called the *pyroligneous*, is chiefly used in making acetate of iron and acetate of alumine for the calico-printers.

[b] The oxalic has a greater affinity for lime than any other acid; and as it forms with it an insoluble substance, it is the most proper test for discovering this earth. Thus, if a few drops of the solution of oxalic acid be dropped into a neutral solution of muriate of lime,

76. What is tartaric acid?

Tartaric acid is found in the cream of tartar of commerce. It is capable of crystallization, and easily soluble in water. It is used by calico-printers to discharge false prints. The salts formed with it are called *tartrates*.

77. How is tartaric acid prepared?

By decomposing the tartrate of lime or potash by means of sulphuric acid which unites with the base, and leaves the acid in solution; from which it may be obtained in a pure state by crystallization.

Cream of tartar (bitartrate of potash) is procured from vessels in which wine has been kept. The tartaric acid appears to be a necessary substance in all wine; for it seems from some late experiments that *must* will not ferment if all the tartaric acid be taken from it.

78. What is citric acid?

Citric acid is found in the juice of lemons and several other fruits. It crystallizes in beautiful rhomboidal prisms; is extremely acid to the taste, and very soluble in water. It is used in various ways for domestic purposes, for medicine, and in the arts. The salts formed with it are called *citrates*.[a]

79. What is malic acid?

Malic acid is obtained from the juice of apples, in which it exists ready formed. It is a very acid, reddish-coloured liquid, composed, like the other vegetable acids, of oxygen, hydrogen, and carbon. It is incapable of crystallization, and has not yet been brought into any use except as a chemical test.[b] Its salts are called *malates*.

an abundant precipitate of insoluble oxalate of lime will appear. In consequence of the solubility of the oxalate of lime in muriatic acid, oxalate of ammonia is preferred as a test for the presence of lime.

[a] In consequence of its great solubility in water citric acid is extensively used in calico printing.

[b] Malic acid is of use in the analyses of earths for separating alumine from magnesia, as it forms with the former an insoluble salt; which precipitates, leaving malate of magnesia in solution.

80. What is lactic acid?

Lactic acid is prepared from milk after the curd has been separated; it has also been discovered by Gay-Lussac and Pelouze in considerable quantities in the beet root. It is incapable of crystallization. The salts formed with it are called *lactates*.

81. What is gallic acid?

Gallic acid is found in the galls of commerce, and in most astringent vegetable substances. It is obtained in thin transparent plates, and in minute needle-shaped crystals, of an acid taste. It has the property of precipitating the persalts of iron, from their solution in acids, of a *black* colour. Its salts are called *gallates*.

82. How is this acid prepared?

By infusing gall nuts in water we may obtain an impure solution of this acid; this may be purified by long exposure to air, evaporating the liquor nearly to dryness and then dissolving the acid in water and boiling it with charcoal.

83. What is tannic acid?

Tannic acid also exists in gall nuts, in oak bark and different astringent vegetables; by digesting gall nuts in ether and evaporating the solution at a low temperature we obtain tannic acid in the form of a white spongy mass.

84. What are the properties of this acid?

It has a bitter taste, is soluble in water, and with solution of iron gives a deep purple precipitate; with gelatine it forms an insoluble precipitate, for which property it owes its value in the process of tanning which consists in uniting this acid with the gelatine of leather. This acid has been made artificially by the action of nitric acid on charcoal.

85. What are the principal uses of gallic and tannic acids?

They are both extensively used in dying black and purple, and also in the preparation of ink, by combining hem with peroxide of iron; the tannic acid that exists in oak bark is employed in tanning.

86. What is mucic acid?

Mucic, or saccholactic acid, as it has been called, is obtained by nitric acid from gum arabic, and other muci-laginous substances. It is in the form of a white gritty powder, with a slightly acid taste. Its salts are called *mucites*.

87. What is benzoic acid?

Benzoic acid is prepared from a vegetable resin called benzoin.[a] It is a light whitish powder, with a peculiar and aromatic odour. Its taste is acrid and bitter. It is unalterable in the air, insoluble in cold, but soluble in boiling water. It is used in medicine under the name of flowers of benjamin. Its salts are called *benzoates*.

88. How may benzoic acid be prepared?

Benzoic acid may be procured by boiling the resin with carbonate of soda, and adding to the filtered solution diluted muriatic acid as long as it produces any precipitation. The precipitate which forms, is the benzoic acid. It may also be procured, but not in a pure form, by sublimation of benzoin.

89. What is succinic acid?

Succinic acid is prepared from amber.[b] It takes the form of shining white crystals, of a slight acid taste. It sublimes by a strong heat. It is soluble in hot, but dis-

---

[a] Benzoin is a resin procured from a tree which grows in the island of Sumatra. The acid procured from this resin has been known for 200 years. It is obtained from benzoin, in the form of flowers, by sublimation.

This acid is found also in balsam of Tolu, Peruvian balsam, liquid storax, and other similar substances. It has been likewise discovered in the urine of children, and of graminivorous animals; in blood; and in some of the species of fungi.

[b] Amber is a transparent combustible substance, dug out of the earth, or found upon the sea coast. It manifests electricity by friction, and was much admired by the ancients as an ornament of dress. The amber-pits of Prussia are said to afford the king a revenue of 26,000 dollars annually.

solves in small quantities in cold water. It is useful as a re-agent, but of no use in the arts. Its salts are called *succinates*.

90. How is this acid procured?

If we fill a retort half way with equal parts of powdered amber, and dry sand, lute on a receiver, and distil in a sand-bath with a gentle heat, the succinic acid will attach itself to the neck of the retort. It is generally coloured by a portion of oil which comes over in distillation; but it may be purified by pouring nitric acid upon it, and then expelling the nitrous acid by a heat not sufficient to drive off the succinic acid.[a]

91. What is camphoric acid?

Camphoric acid is prepared from camphor by means of nitric acid. It is in very white crystals, which have a slightly acid, bitter taste, and a smell like saffron. It is very insoluble, requiring nearly 200 times its weight of water to dissolve it. With salifiable bases it forms *camphorates*.

92. What is suberic acid?

Suberic acid is prepared from cork, by means of nitric acid. Its taste is acid; it is generally seen in the state of powder, and is not crystallizable. Boiling water dissolves half its weight, but it is very insoluble in cold water. Its salts are called *suberates*.

93. What it prussic or hydrocyanic acid?

The prussic is a peculiar acid, composed of hydrogen united to cyanogen. It is a colourless liquid like water, has a bitter taste, resembling bitter almonds, and is highly poisonous—laurel water owes its poisonous property to this acid. It is prepared from the bicyanide of mercury, by decomposing this salt by muriatic acid or sulphuretted hydrogen.

---

[a] When combined with ammonia this acid becomes a valuable re-agent, by the property of separating iron from its solutions, and not operating upon other metals. Thus, if a little of this succinate of ammonia be added to a solution of sulphate of iron, succinate of the metal will be precipitated.

94. What is cyanogen?

Cyanogen is a gaseous compound of carbon and nitrogen; it may be procured by heating strongly in a glass retort bicyanide of mercury, when a gas passes over, characterized by its pungent smell, and its burning with a fine purple flame: this gas consists of two atoms of carbon and one of nitrogen, or 12 parts by weight of carbon to 14 of nitrogen.

95. What is the composition of the salt called in commerce prussiate of potash?

This salt consists of iron, cyanogen, and potash; the iron united with the cyanogen to form ferrocyanic acid, and this combined with cyanuret of potash to form ferrocyanuret of potassium, or prussiate of potash.

96. What are the properties of this compound?

It forms with most of the metals precipitates insoluble in water. With iron it forms the deep blue compound called prussian blue, with copper a reddish yellow, and with manganese a white precipitate.

97. How is the prussiate of potash prepared?

By heating strongly together animal matters, such as blood or pieces of leather, with carbonate of potash and sulphate of iron, and after complete decomposition of the animal matter, lixiviating the residue and crystallizing: the prussiate of potash forms in large lemon-coloured crystals.

98. What is sebacic acid?

Sebacic acid is procured from animal fat or tallow. It has an acid, sharp, bitterish taste. It combines with alkalies, earths, and metallic oxides, and forms the salts called *sebates*.

99. What is uric acid?

The uric or lithic acid is found in human urine. Some of the human calculi are composed entirely of this acid. It has neither taste nor smell, but it reddens vegetable blues, and combines with alkalies and earths.

100. What is amniotic acid ?[a]

Amniotic acid is obtained from the liquor of the amnios of the cow. It is slightly acid; it reddens the tincture of turnsole; and may be obtained in white crystals.

101. What are the uses of these various acids ?[b]

The uses of the acids are so many and important, that it is impossible to enumerate them. They are indispensable to various arts and manufactures; are employed for culinary purposes, and for medicine : they act an important part in the great laboratory of nature; produce that numerous class of bodies called salts; and form many of the rocky and mountainous parts of the globe we inhabit.

102. Do you recollect any instances of acids entering into the composition of rocks and mountains?

The vast masses of limestone, chalk, and marble, which are found in every part of the world, are combinations of lime and carbonic acid : the mountains of gypsum in the vicinity of Paris and elsewhere, are com-

---

[a] The amniotic acid was discovered by Vauquelin and Buniva. It dissolves readily in hot water, and but slowly and sparingly in cold. In order to obtain it, nothing more is necessary than to evaporate the liquor of the amnios of the cow to one-fourth, and leave the remainder to cool, which will be found to contain the acid in crystals.

We have omitted many of the acids which, from their rarity and the complexity of their composition, would have but little interest for the elementary student.

[b] The acids are such powerful agents in a variety of chemical changes which take place in nature and in the arts, that it is of the utmost importance to acquire a knowledge of the modes in which they operate. Let it be recollected then, that there are two ways in which the acids produce changes in the substances with which they are brought into contact. In some cases they effect an union with these substances, and become a part of the new compound, without having themselves undergone any decomposition. In others they become partially decomposed, by affording a part of their oxygen to the bodies on which they operate. The formation of common salt by the union of muriatic acid with soda, is an instance of the first of these cases, and the action of nitrous acid on iron will exemplify the latter.

binations of lime and the sulphuric acid. And the masses of silicious rocks, which form so large a portion of the solid crust of the globe, are composed chiefly of silicic acid united with earthy bases.

103. Do acids exist also in the vegetable kingdom?

Yes; in the processes of nature acids are continually being produced or undergoing decomposition, by the vital action of vegetable substances, and there is hardly a plant that grows which does not contain either a free or combined acid in its structure.

CHAPTER VIII.

THE ALKALIES.

1. What is the nature of an alkali?

The alkalies have a sharp acrid taste; they change the blue juices of vegetables to a green,[a] and have the property of rendering oils miscible with water. They are incombustible, but may be rendered volatile by a great heat. They are soluble in water; form various salts by combination with acids; and act as powerful caustics when applied to the flesh of animals.

2. How many alkalies are there?

There are four alkalies; three of which have been called *fixed* alkalies, the other has long been known by the name of *volatile* alkali.

3. Have we any historical account of these substances?

[a] The tests used for discovering the presence of free alkalies are either blue cabbage infusion, which is changed to green by them, or infusion of turmeric or rhubarb, which is changed to reddish brown. Litmus, though it gives a blue infusion, is not affected by alkalies. It may, however, be used as a test by slightly reddening it; by means of a weak acid, its blue colour will be restored by an alkali. Reddened litmus paper, and turmeric paper, both serve as good tests for alkalies.

Potash was known to the ancient Gauls and Germans ;[a] and soda was familiar to the Greeks and Hebrews. This latter substance was known to these ancients by the name of nitrum. [b] Ammonia and lithia owe their discovery to modern research.

4. Which are the fixed alkalies?

The fixed alkalies are potash, soda, and lithia.

5. Why have they been called *fixed* alkalies?

Because they will endure a great heat without change.[c]

6. What substances enter into the composition of these alkalies?

The fixed alkalies were formerly considered *simple* substances, but they are now known to be compound bodies.

7. What is the composition of the fixed alkalies?

They consist of a metallic base united to oxygen.

8. How is this proved?

Sir H. Davy shewed that the alkalies, potash and soda, when subjected to the action of a strong electric current, are decomposed, oxygen appearing at the positive, and the metallic base at the negative pole of the galvanic battery ; he also reproduced the alkalies by uniting their metallic bases with oxygen, and thereby proved the composition of these substances.

9. What is the composition of potash?

It consists of the metal potassium united to oxygen in the proportion of 40 potassium to 8 oxygen.

[a] These people were probably the *inventors* of soap, as we are told by Pliny, that they made soap with the ashes of vegetables and tallow. A soap-boiler's shop with soap in it was discovered in the city of Pompeii, overwhelmed by Vesuvius, A.D. 79.— See "*Miss Starke's Letters from Italy.*

[b] This substance is found native in Egypt, and is there called *natron ;* a name not much unlike that which it bore among the Jews and Greeks.

[c] The fixed alkalies are volatilized by a very strong heat ; however, the difference in volatility between them and ammonia renders the name *fixed* appropriate.

10. How is potassium procured?

Davy procured it by decomposing potash by means of electricity; this process is, however, difficult and expensive; it is now obtained in large quantities by strongly heating iron or charcoal in contact with potash, which is decomposed by these substances, and the metal potassium is set free, and being volatile is collected in the cool part of the apparatus.

11. What are the properties of potassium?

This metal is lighter than water; it is of a silvery white colour; when heated in air or oxygen gas it takes fire, burns with flame, and is converted into pure potash; when thrown upon water it remains upon its surface, decomposes the water, and is converted into potash by uniting with its oxygen. The disengaged hydrogen takes fire and burns with a beautiful violet-coloured flame on the surface of the water.

12. What is the origin of potash?

Potash is chiefly procured by lixiviation from the ashes of burnt wood, and other vegetable substances;[a] it was for this reason formerly named vegetable alkali, but as it exists in minerals and earths,[b] there is reason to believe that plants receive it from the earth during vegetation.

13. What is the origin of soda?

Soda is generally produced from the ashes of *marine* plants;[c] but its great depository is the ocean, which contains it in union with muriatic acid.

[a] Potash is prepared in large quantities in wine countries, by the incineration of wine-lees and must. This article is known in France by the name of *cendres gravelées*. The cream of tartar of commerce yields a very pure salt of potash by incineration.

[b] Potash has been discovered in the pumice-stone, in the zeolite, and in the leucite, an earth of the siliceous kind; also in felspar and some other minerals.

[c] Soda is obtained by burning sea weed and maritime plants of different kinds, which afford the stony masses known in commerce by the names of kelp and barilla, from which carbonate of soda is procured by lixiviation. It is also obtained by the decomposition of sea-weed by means of carbonate of lime.

14. How is it that marine plants give out soda, while those which grow in the interior of the country afford potash ?

This can only be accounted for by supposing that vege- tables have the power, during vegetation, of decomposing sea-salt, and retaining the soda in their constitution.

15. Is soda found in any other state ?

Yes : soda is found in great plenty combined with car- bonic acid in the natron beds of Egypt,[a] and in the East Indies : also in various parts of the world, united with other acids.

16. Are the potash and soda prepared by these pro- cesses in a pure state ?

No : the salts commonly called potash and soda consist of these alkalies united to carbonic acid ; from this acid they may be separated by means of lime, which unites with the carbonic acid and leaves the soda and potash in a pure state.

- 17. What is the composition of soda ?

Sir H. Davy by the same means by which he proved potash to be a compound of oxygen and a metal, proved that soda also consisted of a metal which he named sodium, united to oxygen in the proportion of 32 to 8.

18. What are the properties of sodium ?

Like potassium, it is lighter than water ; it is of a silver white colour, and is rapidly converted into soda by ex- posure to oxygen or water, which it rapidly decompounds : there is one striking difference, however, between the

---

[a] The natron lakes of Egypt annually produce a large quantity of soda. It probably arises from the decomposition of muriate of soda, by means of carbonate of lime, assisted by the heat of the climate. In summer the water of these lakes is evaporated by the sun, which leaves a bed of natron generally two feet thick ; and this is broken up by wedges, and packed for the European markets.

Berthollet formed an *artificial* natron bed in one of the gardens of the National Institute, by the mixture of carbonate of lime, silex, and muriate of soda. After a time, a partial decomposition was effected, which was evident from the incrustation on the surface changing the colour of test paper.

appearances attending the decomposition of water by potassium and sodium; when the latter is thrown upon the surface of water the extricated hydrogen is not inflamed.

19. What are the distinguishing properties of potash and soda?

The fixed alkalies are very similar in their general properties; but are easily distinguished by the variety of salts which they form with the acids;[a] and by potash being more deliquescent than soda.

20. Is there any chemical test by which you can distinguish these two alkalies?

The following are the best tests to distinguish these alkalies from each other; the tartaric acid, with potash, forms a salt very little soluble in water but with soda a very soluble salt; the terchloride of platina also forms an insoluble triple salt with potash, but not with soda; the salts of potash give to flame a violet tinge; the salts of soda give a greenish yellow tinge to flame.

21. What are the chief uses of these alkalies?

The fixed alkalies have various uses in surgery and medicine; they are the bases of several salts; are employed much in the arts;[b] and are also of great use to the analytical chemist.

22. How are the fixed alkalies employed in the arts?

[a] When the fixed alkalies are in a state of purity, it is impossible by inspection to distinguish them from each other; and yet they form by union with the *same* acid, salts very opposite in their saline properties and appearance. Thus the sulphuric acid and soda form a salt very soluble in water, which crystallizes in long separate six-sided prisms, effloresces in the air, and undergoes a watery fusion by the action of heat; whereas, the same acid and potash form a salt extremely difficult of solution, which crystallizes in hexahedral pyramids, or in short prisms, crossing each other at right angles, is not affected by the action of the air, and decrepitates in the fire.

[b] The greatest consumption of the alkalies in this country is in the manufacture of soap. They are also largely employed in bleaching and in the manufacture of glass. Soda and potash are both used in washing, and for other domestic purposes; as they powerfully unite with all greasy substances, which they render soluble in water.

The fixed alkalies are used in large quantities by the glass-maker, the dyer, the soap-maker, the colour-maker, and by various other manufacturers.

23. To what uses are the alkalies applied in dying?

The alkalies are known to have the property of altering the hue of most colours: they are therefore employed with this view by the persons who are engaged in this trade.

24. Why are the alkalies employed in making soap?

An alkali is an essential ingredient in all soaps, as it is capable of readily converting tallow or oil into a saponacious substance and enabling it to combine with water.[a]

25. Why are the fixed alkalies employed in making colours?

[a] The following is the process usually employed in this country for the manufacture of soap: barilla or kelp is broken in pieces, or coarsely ground by a horse mill; and, when mixed with a sufficient quantity of quick-lime to absorb the carbonic acid, the whole is thrown into large wooden or iron vats, and covered with water. In large works, these vats are generally of cast iron, and sufficiently capacious to hold 3 or 4 tons of alkaline ashes. At a proper time the water, impregnated with the caustic alkali, is let off into iron receivers below, and the vats are covered again with water, which, after standing a sufficient time, is let off as before. This liquor is called soap-boilers' ley. When a sufficient quantity of this is prepared, Russian or English tallow is put into a large iron boiler, and melted with a portion of the above-mentioned alkaline ley. At first the tallow appears liquid like oil, but during its boiling it acquires by degrees consistence as it saponifies. When the alkali is uniformly combined with the tallow, the weak liquor is pumped from beneath the soap, and fresh leys are added in their stead. These are boiled as before, till the soap exhibits certain appearances well known to the manufacturer: it is then cooled down, and poured into deep wooden frames 15 inches wide and 45 inches long; where it remains till it has acquired a sufficient degree of solidity to be cut up for sale. It is the *alkali* which gives soap its detergent quality, and which renders it soluble in water. The tallow serves to moderate the sharpness of the alkali, and to prevent its injuring the hands of those who use it.

In making yellow soap, resin is used in the proportion of about 1 part to 3 or 4 parts of tallow. The resin makes the soap more detersive, and enables the manufacturer to sell it cheaper. Common fish oil, when its price permits, is also used in yellow soap.

Many colours now manufactured in this country cannot be made without an alkali: thus, animal matters are incinerated with an alkali to form Prussian blue; a fixed alkali is also employed as a flux in the formation of mineral blue from cobalt. The rich colours made from chromic acid are also formed by combining the acid with potash before producing the metallic chromates; there are many other colours also formed by means of the alkalies.

26. What are the other uses of these alkalies?

They are employed in making alum, in bleaching, &c. &c.

27. From whence is this country supplied with these alkalies?

The greatest part of the potash used in this country comes from America and Russia; but the *kelp* of our own coasts, and the *barilla* of Spain and Sicily furnish us with most of our soda.[a]

28. Are these alkalies sold in a state of purity?

No: both potash and soda always contain a quantity of carbonic acid and water; and are often contaminated with various earths, and sometimes with a portion of sulphur.[b]

29. Have alkalies any peculiar affinity for sulphur?

Both potash and soda have a strong affinity for sulphur; they combine by trituration or heat, and form *sulphuret*

---

[a] The soda of Spain is procured from the *salsola sodæ*, and also from the *basis maritima*. The Sicilian barilla which is imported into this country, is chiefly made by the incineration of the *zostrea maritima*. These plants contain much more alkaline salt than the different species of *fuci*.

[b] An ash which contains 20 per cent. of pure alkali, is capable of taking up 15 parts of sulphur. Such ashes may be desulphurated by three processes; by calcining them in an open furnace, exposed to a rapid blast of air; by saturating them with any vegetable acid; or by exposing them in a situation to imbibe carbonic acid. See a paper on this subject in the Transactions of the Royal Irish Academy for 1789.

of the metallic base, formerly called *hepar sulphuris*, " liver of sulphur."

30. What is the nature of sulphuret of an alkaline base?

Its colour is similar to that of the liver of animals; its taste is acrid and bitter; and it has the property of decomposing water, being changed into hydrosulphuret of the alkali.

31. How are the alkalies of commerce purified for the use of the chemist or manufacturer?

Potash or soda is generally mixed with a portion of quick-lime, to divest it of carbonic acid, and then lixiviated in proper vessels, to obtain a solution of the caustic alkali, free from other impurities. When it is required *perfectly* pure for nice purposes, the alkali is dissolved in alcohol, and purified by evaporation.

32. Are the fixed alkalies ever used in a state of combination with carbonic acid?

Carbonic acid gives potash and soda the property of crystallizing readily : it also renders them mild,[a] and fit for purposes in which caustic alkali would be improper ; hence, carbonate of potash is employed in medicine, and carbonate of soda for washing and other domestic uses.

33. What is lithia?

Lithia is an alkali, found in the rare minerals spodumene and petalite; like potash and soda, it consists of a metal (named lithium) united to oxygen. It is characterized by giving a red tinge to flame.

34. What is ammonia?

Ammonia, or the volatile alkali, as it is sometimes called, exists in its pure state as a gas ; it is characterized by its strong alkaline properties, though it is not corrosive as the other alkalies ; by its sharp pungent smell, and its levity, being much lighter than atmospheric air.

---

[a] Caustic soda is so corrosive that it will affect glass vessels in which it is kept, and render them brittle, like earthenware half burnt.

35. As this alkali is a gaseous substance, how is it applied in the arts?

Ammonia has an affinity for water, by which it is rapidly absorbed, and forms *liquid* ammonia, in which state it is generally used; and it is remarkable that the specific gravity of water is diminished, in proportion to the quantity of this gas combined with it.

36. What is the composition of ammonia?

Ammonia is a compound of hydrogen and nitrogen, in the proportion of about three parts of the former, and fourteen of the latter.

37. Can we form this gas by directly combining hydrogen and nitrogen?

No, we cannot; but by presenting these gases to each other, in what is named their *nascent* state, or at the instant of their extrication from substances containing them we can form ammonia. If we take some filings of tin or zinc, pour on them some moderately dilute nitric acid, and after a short time stir into the mixture some quicklime, or caustic alkali, a very strong pungent smell of ammonia will be produced. In this, the hydrogen evolved from the water, meeting with the nitrogen of the nitric acid, and both being in their *nascent* state, form ammonia, which unites with the free acid, from which it is separated by the lime.

38. Is this alkali capable of being decomposed?

Yes: ammonia may be decomposed by the electric spark, or by a strong heat. If ammoniacal gas be passed through a porcelain tube heated strongly, it is resolved with its elements hydrogen and nitrogen, or if it be subjected to electrization it will be likewise decomposed.

39. How do we obtain ammoniacal gas?

If we mix together muriate of ammonia and quicklime, and apply heat to the mixture, ammoniacal gas will be disengaged; the quicklime abstracting the muriatic acid from the ammonia, and the gas being extricated. This must be received in vessels filled with mercury, and inverted in that fluid, the gas being, as already mentioned, rapidly absorbed by water.

40. What are the principal salts formed by ammonia and the acids ?

The most important salts are the carbonate, muriate, and sulphate of ammonia.

41. How is carbonate of ammonia procured ?

All animal and vegetable substances will furnish ammonia when in a state of putrefaction; this salt is, however, generally procured in England by a dry distillation of bones, horns, and other animal substances ; and may also be procured by distillation of muriate of ammonia, and carbonate of soda or lime, or by the direct combination of ammoniacal and carbonic acid gases, when solid carbonate of ammonia will be obtained.

42. What are the uses of ammonia?

In a liquid state ammonia has various uses in our manufactories,[a] and in medicine; it is a valuable re-agent to the chemist ; and when combined with carbonic acid it takes a concrete form and a beautiful white colour, being then the article known in commerce by the name of *volatile salts*.

43. Are there any other uses to which ammonia is applied ?

Ammonia is serviceable in dyeing, and in staining ivory; but its principal use is in making the muriate of ammonia, of which it is the basis.

44. How is muriate of ammonia formed ?

Muriate of ammonia is formed by combining ammonia with muriatic acid. It is known in commerce by the name of *sal-ammoniac*. It is prepared in commerce by lixiviating soot, which contains a large quantity of sulphate

[a] Ammonia is of use in making archil, an article in great demand with dyers. A Florentine merchant about the year 1300, having accidentally observed that putrid urine, which contains ammonia, imparted a very fine colour to a certain species of moss, he made experiments, and learned to prepare archil.

of ammonia, and mixing the salt obtained by evaporation
of the liquor with muriate of soda, and heating the mixed
salts in earthen vessels to which covers are luted; by
double exchange of principles muriate of ammonia is
formed and passes from the hotter to the colder part of
the vessels, where it forms into large cakes; it is also
formed from gas liquor by saturating the carbonate of
ammonia it contains with sulphuric acid, and then treating
the sulphate of ammonia in the manner mentioned above.[a]

45. Muriate of ammonia being formed by two gaseous
substances, how does it acquire solidity?

It may appear surprising that the union of two gases
should produce a hard, ponderous body; but this may be
attributed to their loss of caloric. The bases of these
gases having a greater affinity for each other than they
have for caloric, they combine intimately whenever they
come in contact; and the compound having less occasion
for caloric than the separate ingredients, the caloric is
given out, and a solid is produced.[b]

46. What are the uses of muriate of ammonia?

Muriate of ammonia or sal-ammoniac is used in many
of our manufactories, particularly by dyers, to give a
brightness to certain colours; also by braziers, and tin-
plate workers, for the different kinds of soldering. It

[a] Sal-ammoniac is made in France by a distillation of animal substances, and mixing the aqueous product with the mother-waters of
the saline springs of La Meurth, Mount Blanc, &c. which contain
muriate of lime and muriate of magnesia. By this mixture a double
decomposition takes place; and the carbonate of lime and magnesia,
being insoluble, precipitate, while the muriate of ammonia remains
dissolved. The latter solution is then evaporated to dryness, and the
salt sublimed for sale.

[b] This mixture may be considered one of the most striking chemical combinations with which we are acquainted. Ammoniacal gas,
and muriatic acid gas, are two of the most pungent and volatile substances known; they are so volatile and gaseous, that when in a state
of purity neither of them can be condensed; and yet these gases are
no sooner thrown together than they form a solid and inodorous
substance, void of volatility, and of little taste.

is the salt generally employed for the preparation of pure ammonia or its solution, and is frequently employed for the purposes of preparing artificial freezing mixtures in consequence of the large quantity of heat it absorbs when dissolved in water.

47. From whence was sal-ammoniac procured before it was made in this country?

Sal-ammoniac was formerly brought from Egypt in suffi‐cient quantity for the supply of all Europe.[a]

48. Is ammonia capable of entering into any other combinations?

Yes; ammonia is capable of forming salts with most if not all of the acids.

49. Can you recapitulate the origin of the different alkalies?

Ammonia is procured from bones and other animal matters, and also from soot and the liquid produced in the manufacture of coal gas; potash, from the ashes of weeds and burnt wood; soda, from the ashes of some marine plants, also from sea salt; and lithia, from the minerals spodumene and petalite. Ammonia is at once recognized by its volatility; potash, by the salts it forms with sulphuric and tartaric acids, and the chloride of platina; soda by its not giving a precipitate with the two latter, and forming a very soluble salt with sulphuric acid; and lithia by the colour which it gives to flame.

[a] Sal-ammoniac acquired its name from the Temple of Jupiter Ammon, it being first made in the neighbourhood of that temple. According to Pliny, there were large inns in the vicinity of this famous temple, where the pilgrims, who came to worship, lodged; and who usually travelled on camels. The proprietors of these stables had some contrivance for preserving and concentrating the urine of these beasts, and the salts which it produced were afterwards sublimed in glass vessels for sale.—PLINY, lib. xxxi. c. 7.

CHAPTER IX.

THE EARTHS.

1. What are the principal characters of the earths?

The earths in general are incombustible and unalterable in the fire; when combined with carbonic acid they are insoluble in water, or nearly so; and of a specific gravity seldom exceeding five times that of water.

2. How many earths are there?

There are known at present ten substances to which the name of earths has been given, baryta, strontia, lime, magnesia, silica, alumina, glucine, yttria, zircon, and thorina.

3. How can we recognize an earth in solution?

By its not giving a coloured precipitate with the ferro-prussiate of potash or tincture of galls, and forming with the alkaline carbonates a precipitate insoluble in water.

4. Are these earths simple bodies?

The earths were formerly supposed to be simple bodies, or *elements*. They are now known to be compounds of oxygen with different metals. Baryta, consisting of the metal barium and oxygen, strontia, of strontium and oxygen, &c.

5. Why are some of these earths called alkaline earths?

Barytes, strontia, and lime, are called alkaline, because they agree with alkalies in taste, causticity, solubility in water, and in their effect on vegetable colours. Magnesia also slightly affects vegetable colours. They can at once be distinguished from the alkalies by their infusibility by fire, by forming insoluble compounds with carbonic acid, and by being insoluble in alcohol.

6. What are the chief properties of silex, or silica?

Silex, or pure flint, is insoluble in water,[a] and in every acid except the fluoric; it endures a very strong heat without alteration, but may be fused by means of the oxyhydrogen blowpipe; when mixed with soda or potass, becomes fusible in a strong fire into glass. Its specific gravity is 2·65.

7. How do you procure silica in a pure state?

Should pure silex be wanted for chemical experiment, it may be procured by fusing common flint stones with three or four times their weight of potash, dissolving the product in water, and then taking up the alkali by the addition of an acid, which will precipitate the silex, which is to be well washed for use. The siliceous stones should be previously heated red in a crucible, and plunged in that state into cold water. This will render them brittle, so that they may easily be reduced to powder before they are mixed with potash.

8. To what class of bodies does silica seem properly to belong?

Silica, properly speaking, is an acid; though it has not an acid reaction on test paper in consequence of its insolubility in water, yet from the readiness with which it combines with the alkalies and some of the earths, it seems properly to belong to this class. It also, at a high temperature, displaces carbonic acid from its combination with the alkalies with effervescence.

9. In what state is silex found native?

Silica, or siliceous earth, is found in quartz, in rock crystal, gravel, sand, and most of the precious stones. It is also the chief ingredient of those stones which seem

---

[a] We cannot by any means dissolve silex in water. Nature, however, by some wonderful and unknown process, contrives to dissolve it, even copiously, so as to form stalactites and other incrustations. In Iceland there is a boiling fountain which spouts water 90 feet in the air, and deposits in falling so great a quantity of siliceous earth, that it forms around its base a sort of solid cup, which surmounts and envelops it. This earth has also been found in solution in the Bath waters, and in some other spring water.

to constitute the most bulky material of the solid parts of our globe.[a]

10. What are the chief uses of silex ?

Silex is the most durable article in the state of gravel for the formation of roads; it is a necessary ingredient in earthen-ware, porcelain, and cements; is the basis of glass,[b] and of all vitreous substances; and is an indispensable article in many of our chemical furnaces and utensils.

11. What is the use of silica in glass-making ?

Silica is the chief ingredient in glass. It is rendered fusible by a due mixture of alkali, which acts as a flux to the silica, and renders the whole transparent.[c]

---

[a] " A granite mountain, about thirty miles from the Cape of Good Hope, called the PEARL DIAMOND, rises out of the ground to the height of 400 feet, being half a mile in circumference; and formed of a single block of granite."—PARKINSON'S Organic Remains.

Silex also constitutes two-thirds of the asbestus, so valued by the ancients for wrapping up the bodies of the dead before they were committed to the funeral pile. They discovered methods of drawing the fibres of the mineral into thread, and afterwards weaving it into cloth. In consequence of its incombustibility, it preserved the ashes of the body from mixing with those of the wood, upon which it was laid to be burnt. The practice was, however, probably confined to the families of the opulent. So late as the year 1702, a funeral urn was discovered at Rome, in which were a scull and other remains of a human body wrapped in a cloth of amianthus, or flexible asbestus. The whole was deposited in the Vatican library.

[b] The manufacture of glass was known very early; but glass perfectly transparent was reckoned so valuable, that Nero is said to have given a very large sum of money for two glass cups with handles. When the excavations were made in the ancient city of Pompeii, which was buried by an eruption of Vesuvius, A. D. 79, the windows of some of the houses were found glazed with a thick kind of glass, not transparent. In others mica was substituted, split into thin plates. —MISS STARKE'S Letters from Italy.

[c] Glass cannot be made without great heat, as the alkali strongly retains the last portions of carbonic acid and water, and it is only at a very high temperature that the alkali fuses, and then it prefers the silex; for it is one of the laws of nature, (to which there are few exceptions,) that, in order that two bodies may become *chemically* united, one of them must be in a state of fluidity.

12. Are these the only articles necessary to form glass?

In Holland, and some other parts of Europe, glass is manufactured with alkali and sand only; but in England, flint-glass is made by a mixture of red lead[a] with those substances; which gives the glass great weight, and makes it more useful for all common purposes.

13. What are the chief properties of alumina?

Alumina, or pure clay, is soft to the touch; adhesive to the tongue; emits a peculiar odour when moistened; forms a paste with water; will unite with most acids; and acquires great hardness, and contracts in the fire. Its specific gravity is 2.

14. In what state is alumina found native?

This earth acquired its name from its being the basis of alum; it has also been called *argil*, as it is the principal part of all clays; it is found in a state of crystallization in the sapphire, and is united to the oxides of iron in the ochres; and also forms a part of many precious stones.

15. How may we obtain pure alumina?

By decomposing the salt called alum, which is a sulphate of alumina and potash by ammonia, which unites with the acid and the alumina is precipitated.

16. What are the chief uses to which alumina has been applied?

---

[a] Some metallic oxides have the property of making glass more fusible. The oxide of lead is serviceable in this way when mixed with glass.

The common bottle-glass is made with a large portion of the ashes of vegetables, or soap-boilers' waste ashes, instead of pure alkali. The portion of iron, which is generally found in vegetable substances, gives it the green colour.

For the best flint-glass, rather more alkali is used than is necessary to flux the sand; and, when the whole is in fusion, the fire is continued so as to volatilize the superabundant quantity. If an excess of alkali be left in the glass, it will attract water from the atmosphere, and in time assume the fluid state.

Alumina in the state of *common clay*[a] is employed for various purposes, on account of its aptitude for moulding into different forms, and its property of hardening in the fire; such as for making bricks, earthenware, porcelain,[b] crucibles, &c. Its uses are so various and important, that we cannot conceive how man could have attained his present degree of civilization, if this earth had not been given him in abundance by nature.

17. Is alumina employed in forming any chemical combinations?

Aluminous earth is employed in different combinations by the dyer and the calico-printer, as a mordant for fixing various colours; and upon the continent it is artificially combined with sulphuric acid, in order to form alum, though we possess the compound ready formed in its native state.[c]

[a] Common clay is a mixture of alumina and silex. It frequently contains metallic oxides, chalk and other earths. Alumina united to the oxides of iron, is found in Staffordshire and Derbyshire; in which state it is called raddle, an article very useful in colour-making. Fullers' earth is alumina combined with very fine silex. It is owing to the affinity which alumina has for greasy substances, that this article is so useful in scouring cloth. Hence pipe-clay is frequently used for the same purpose.

[b] Earthenware, according to the Old Testament, was known at an early period to the Jews; and the potter's wheel, there spoken of, was probably the same simple machine as is used at the present day to form round vessels with plain surfaces. The making of porcelain has long been known in China and Japan; but it was accidentally discovered in Europe by a chemist, in the beginning of the 18th century. It was so esteemed by the Romans, that, after the taking of Alexandria, a porcelain vessel was the only part of the spoil retained by Augustus.

[c] In England alum is procured from alum-slate. This is found on the sea coast of the north-east part of Yorkshire, from Whitby to Stockton, a distance of about 50 miles. The slate, when procured, is broken to pieces by the aid of fire, and afterwards further acidified, by being frequently moistened, and by exposure to the air. When the efflorescence has taken place, it is put into lixiviating vessels for the extraction of the salt. The saline liquor is then boiled down to the proper strength for crystallization; previous to which is added a

H

18. Why do potters employ a mixture of alumina and silex for earthenware?

In making earthenware a due proportion of both these earths is necessary; for if alumina alone were used, the ware could not be sufficiently burnt without shrinking too much, and perhaps cracking; and a great excess of silex would lessen the tenacity, and render the ware brittle.[a]

19. What is zirconia?

Zirconia is a peculiar earth, found only in the gems called zircon and the hyacinth of the island of Ceylon. It was

portion of alkali, to saturate the superabundant acid, and to favour the crystallization. Indeed, alum cannot be made without a portion of ammonia or potash, as it is a triple salt. All alum is either a sulphate of alumina and potash, or a sulphate of alumina and ammonia. Urine is generally used in Scotland, and sulphate of potash in Yorkshire.

The first English alum-work was established at Gisborough in Yorkshire, in the reign of Queen Elizabeth, by Sir Thomas Chaloner, who engaged workmen from the Pope's alum-works to superintend it; and kept those workmen till his manufacture was brought to perfection, notwithstanding the bulls and anathemas which his Holiness issued in abundance against him.

One of the most ancient manufactures of alum was at Roche, a city of Syria; whence the name of Roche-alum.

[a] For making pottery, or earthenware, the clay is beaten in water; by which the fine parts are suspended in the fluid, while the coarser sink to the bottom of the vessel. The thick liquid is further purified by passing it through hair and lawn sieves of different degrees of fineness; and is afterwards mixed with another liquor of about the same density, consisting of ground flints. This was the composition of the *white stone ware*, about 40 years ago the staple manufacture of the potteries of this kingdom; and it is also that of the finer earthenwares at present in use, though in different proportions, and with various improvements, introduced by the ingenuity of succeeding manufacturers. This mixture is then dried in a kiln, and after being beaten to a proper consistence, becomes fit for being formed by the workman into dishes, plates, bowls, &c. The fine white and cream-coloured earthenwares now made in England are fired twice: the first time to give them the requisite hardness; and in that state they are called *biscuit*: they are then dipped in a vitreous composition, and being subjected to a second burning, acquire a coating of true glass, thence called a glaze. If they are finished with painting in enamel, it is necessary to pass them a third time through the fire. The different colours are given to porcelain by means of different metallic oxides.

discovered by Klaproth, in the year 1793. The stone from which he procured it came from Ceylon: but the same stone has since been found in various parts of Europe.

A mineral from Greenland, called *compact* hyacinth, has been lately analysed, and found to contain 10 per cent. of zirconia.

20. What are the properties of zirconia?

Zirconia, when separated from the precious stones in which it is found, has the form of a fine white powder, destitute of taste and smell. It is soluble in the acids and the alkaline carbonates, but differs from all the other earths in not being soluble in pure alkalies. Its present scarcity prevents our employing it to any useful purpose.

21. Whence do we procure glucine?

The peculiar earth called glucine has been found only in the emerald and beryl, precious stones procured from Peru and from the mountains of Siberia.

22. What are the properties of glucine?

Glucine, when separated from the stones which contain it, is a soft, light white powder, without taste and smell; adhesive to the tongue like alumina; infusible by heat; but soluble in the acids, with which it forms soluble sweet-tasted salts, (from whence its name from the Greek word γλυκυς, sweet,) slightly astringent. This earth is not very plentiful, nor has it yet been employed in the arts.

23. What is the origin of yttria?

Yttria is a peculiar earth which was discovered by Gadolin, in a mineral named Gadolinite, found in Yetterby in Sweden, which also contains iron, manganese, lime, and silex.

24. How is yttria to be distinguished?

Yttria, when separated from the mineral, is in the form of a fine, insipid, white powder. It forms sweet and coloured salts with the acids, is insoluble in the caustic alkalies, but easily dissolved in a solution of carbonate of ammonia.

25. What is the origin of baryta ?

Baryta was discovered by Scheele in combination with sulphuric acid, in a mineral called ponderous spar, afterwards terra ponderosa. It is chiefly found in this state in England, and in other parts of the globe.

26. Is this earth found in any other states ?

Yes: it occurs in Northumberland, Cumberland, and Lancashire, in large masses combined with carbonic acid; and also in France in combination with the oxide of manganese.

27. How may we procure pure baryta ?

We may obtain this earth pure for chemical purposes, by dissolving the carbonate of barytes in very weak nitric acid, by which means the carbonic acid will be expelled, and then in the usual way, by proper evaporation, crystals of nitrate of baryta will be formed. By exposing this salt to a strong heat, the nitric acid will be expelled, and pure baryta will be left in the crucible. We can also obtain it by decomposing the sulphate of baryta, by mixing it in fine powder with charcoal, and exposing the mixture to a strong heat: by this means we decompose the sulphuric acid and convert the sulphate of baryta into sulphuret of barium; if we dissolve this in water we can obtain nitrate of baryta by decomposing it by nitric acid, and from the nitrate obtain the pure earth by heat.

28. What are the properties of baryta ?

Baryta is of a greyish-white colour; when fresh prepared it slakes like quicklime, if water be poured upon it, and forms a hydrate. It changes the vegetable blues like alkalies, has a pungent, caustic taste, and is a violent poison. It may be known from the other earths by its solubility in water,[a] by its forming an insoluble compound with sulphuric acid, and by its tingeing flame green. Its specific gravity is 4.00.

[a] Boiling water will dissolve half its weight of this earth, part of which will crystallize on cooling.

29. What are the uses of baryta?

Baryta forms some of the most useful chemical tests for sulphuric acids, which it separates from all other bases and forms an insoluble compound with it, whether in its pure state dissolved in water, or combined with particular acids: in muriatic acid also it is employed as a medicine. It is capable of making a very tenacious cement, but has not been applied to any use in the arts, though sometimes employed in the form of sulphate as a white paint.

30. What is the origin of strontia?

Strontia was first discovered about the year 1787, in a mineral brought from the lead-mine of Strontian in Argyleshire, by Professor Hope. That mineral is a *carbonate* of strontian, and has been since found in Braunsdorf in Saxony, and also in Peru.

31. Is this earth found in any other state?

Strontia, combined with sulphuric acid, has been found in various parts of the world, particularly near Bristol, where it exists in such abundance as to be employed in the repairs of the neighbouring roads.

32. What are the properties of strontia?

Strontia, in its pure state, is like baryta, soluble in water; it is of a greyish-white colour; its taste is acrid and alkaline, but less so than baryta or the alkalies. It is not poisonous; and its solution in water is capable of crystallization. It gives a carmine tinge to flame, which is the chief characteristic that distinguishes it from baryta. If we mix some of the muriate of strontia with spirit of wine, and inflame it, the spirit will be tinged of a rich carmine red colour.

33. How do we obtain pure strontia?

It may be obtained from the native carbonate, and sulphate, by precisely the same process as that directed for the preparation of baryta.

34. What are the uses of strontia?

Strontia, though it combines readily with all the acids,

and possesses alkaline properties, has not hitherto been employed except as a chemical test and in the manufacture of artificial fire-works.[a]

35. What are the properties of lime?

Lime is a solid substance, of a white colour; of a hot caustic taste; it dissolves in about 800 times its weight of *cold* water, in which it is more soluble than in hot; it changes vegetable blue colours to green, and unites with acids; is incapable of fusion, except at a very high temperature; slaked or combined with water it gives out a great quantity of caloric, and forms a hydrate, and it absorbs carbonic acid when exposed to atmospheric air.[b]

36. In what state is lime found in nature?

Pure lime is never found native; it is always in a state of combination, generally with an acid, and most frequently with carbonic acid, as in chalk, marble, limestone, &c. It is found also combined with sulphuric acid in gypsum, or plaster of Paris. It exists in some vegetables, in sea and river water, the shells of fishes, and the bones of animals.[c]

37. How is pure lime procured?

Carbonate of lime, by whatever name it is called,

[a] If we mix together nitrate of strontia, sulphur, chlorate of potash, and charcoal, the mixture will show the fine colour imparted to flame by this earth.

[b] It is for this reason that lime-water, when exposed to the air, is quickly covered with a thin pellicle. This is carbonate of lime, formed by the combination of the carbonic acid of the air with the lime.

[c] It may be remarked, that while *testaceous* shells are formed with carbonate of lime, the shells of *crustaceous* animals, and the shells of birds' eggs, contain also a portion of phosphate of lime. Its use in the former is not known; but the design of Nature in furnishing shells of eggs with phosphoric acid is very apparent. The body of the egg contains neither phosphoric acid nor lime: it was necessary, therefore, that Nature should provide means of furnishing both these substances, which it does at the expense of the shell; which becomes thinner and thinner during the whole time of incubation, till the living embryo has appropriated a sufficient quantity for the formation of its bones. Part of the albumen for this purpose combines with the shell, and another portion forms feathers, &c.

whether chalk, marble, limestone, &c. is to be broken into convenient pieces, and piled with coal, stratum super stratum, in kilns, where it is kept for a considerable time at a strong heat. By this means the carbonic acid and water are driven off, and tolerably pure lime is the product.

38. What are the chief uses of lime?

Lime, united with the acids, is applied to various useful purposes, and forms a large portion of the solid fabric of the globe. In a *separate* state it is used in many of the arts, particularly in making mortar for buildings. Also by farmers as a manure; by bleachers,[a] tanners, sugar-bakers, soap-boilers, iron-masters,[b] and others, in their several manufactories, and in medicine.

39. How do you explain the operation of lime in forming mortar and cements?

Pure lime has, when united to a certain portion of water, a very strong affinity for silex, another most essential ingredient in mortar and cements; for without this it never hardens; but when mixed in proper proportions, the whole crystallizes as it gradually imbibes carbonic acid from the atmosphere, and thus in a series of years becomes as hard as unburnt limestone.[c]

[a] Combined with chlorine it forms the salt so extensively used in bleaching. It was by the ancients used for bleaching in its pure state. Therphrastus, the disciple of Aristotle, who wrote more than 300 years before Christ, speaks of it in this connection. He relates an instance of a ship which was loaded in part with linen, and in part with quicklime, having been set on fire by water that was accidentally thrown over the latter, which fired the linen, and occasioned the destruction of the vessel.

[b] The iron ores that are wrought in this country contain a large portion of alumina and silica. In order, therefore, to flux these earths, and more effectually separate the iron, a quantity of lime is usually mixed with the ore in the furnace; lime having the property of rendering the other earths more fusible.

[c] When lime is made into mortar, it takes a long time in acquiring the portion of carbonic acid which it possessed in the quarry; but the mortar hardens as this absorption takes place. This accounts for the great strength of some ancient buildings, in which the mortar is found to have a greater degree of firmness than even limestone itself.

40. How does lime act so as to be of use as a manure for land?

The use of lime in agriculture may be attributed to a property of hastening the dissolution and putrefaction of all animal and vegetable matters, and of imparting to the soil a power of retaining a quantity of moisture necessary for the nourishment and vigorous growth of plants, corn, &c.;[a] but there is no good soil that does not contain a certain portion of lime, though always without exception, combined with carbonic acid.

41. What is the use of lime in the operation of tanning leather?

Lime is used by the tanner in a state of a solution; in this the hides are immersed in order to dissolve the sebaceous part of the skin, and to facilitate the removal of the hair.

42. How is lime used in refining sugar?

By boiling the sugar in lime-water the manufacturer deprives it of the free acid that may exist in it, which would interfere with its crystallization.

43. What is the use of lime in the manufacture of soap?

Lime is mixed with the alkali in order to deprive it of

[a] Hence lime and chalk are found to be particularly useful on sandy soils. Marle is a mixture of carbonate of lime and clay. Marles are useful in agriculture only in proportion to the calcareous earth they contain. Unless they contain more than 30 per cent. of lime, they are of no value to the farmer. Of all the modes of trial, the one best suited to the unlearned farmer is, to observe how much *fixed air* the marle gives out; and this he will learn by dissolving a little of it in diluted muriatic acid, and observing what portion of its weight it loses by the escape of this air. Thus, if an ounce loses only 40 grains, he may conclude that the ounce of marle contained only 100 grains of calcareous earth, and that it would be his interest to pay seven times as much for a load of lime as he must pay for a load of marle at the same distance.

Every farmer should ascertain the nature of his lime before he uses it in agriculture, as there are many extensive districts in England where the lime is contaminated by magnesia, which renders it injurious to the growth of vegetables.

carbonic acid, lime having a stronger attraction for carbonic acid than the alkalies have. The alkali is thus
rendered what is called *caustic*, and in this state combines
with the oil or tallow which is to be converted into
soap.

44. Does lime exist in nature in combination with
other acids, besides those already mentioned?

Lime is found also combined with phosphoric and
fluoric acids. The Derbyshire spar consists entirely of
fluoric acid and lime.

45. What is magnesia?

Magnesia is a soft, white, light earth, with little taste
or smell; unalterable in the fire, and almost insoluble in
water—its solution having a very slight action upon
vegetable infusions; and when combined with sulphuric
acid forms a purgative salt very easy of solution.

46. How is magnesia procured?

Magnesia is never found in a state of purity, but is
generally procured from sulphate of magnesia (Epsom
salt), which exists with the muriate of this earth in sea
water and in many springs: it is also found in many
mineral substances.[a]

47. What are the uses of magnesia?

Pure magnesia, as well as the sulphate and carbonate,
has important uses in medicine. It is also required in
some chemical processes, and is employed by the manufacturers of enamels and porcelain. It is the most effectual antidote in case of poison by the mineral acids.

48. How do we discover the presence of magnesia in
solution?

We can at once discover magnesia in solution by means
of ammonia and phosphoric acid, magnesia forming with
them a triple salt; the phosphate of magnesia and am-

---

[a] Magnesia is found in talc, steatites, potstone, asbestus, fossil cork,
and other minerals. The stones which contain a large portion of this
earth have generally an unctuous feel, a fibrous texture, and a silky
lustre.

H 2

monia, which being nearly insoluble, is precipitated from the solution.

49. What is thorina?

Thorina was discovered by Berzelius, some years since, in a rare mineral named thorite; it is a white substance, soluble in sulphuric acid, and precipitated from its solution by the caustic alkalies, in excess of which it is insoluble. It is precipitated from its solution by ferro-prussiate of potash.

50. Are there not instances in nature of the earths entering into combination with each other?

Yes; minerals are found, in which the earths are combined in different proportions by processes unknown to us, which nature employs to produce that endless variety of what, in common language, we call rocks, stones, gems, &c.[a]

51. You have enumerated the separate uses of most of the earths;—can you recollect the collective advantages which arise from this class of bodies?

The uses of many of these earths are not yet discovered; but the benefits which we derive from lime, clay, silex, and magnesia, are various and important. Lime has an extensive and important use in agriculture; it is employed in building, &c. and adds much both to the neatness and durability of our dwellings. Silica is the basis of all mortar and cements, and is a necessary ingredient in earthenware, porcelain, and glass. Baryta is employed in chemical laboratories as a re-agent, and for the formation of salts. Magnesia, besides being the basis of several salts, is of great use in medicine; and

[a] Potter's clay is a mixture chiefly of silex and alumina; the colouring earths used as pigments are mixtures either of clay and the oxides of iron, or clay and charcoal; garden mould is a mixture extremely various, sometimes containing silex, alumina, magnesia, iron, lime, and carbon; the common millstone is generally composed of alumina and silex; and the crumbling sandstone is a mixture of iron and silex.

alumina, by a due mixture with silex, is capable of forming vessels for chemists that will resist the action of the most concentrated acids; it is the material of which the bricks are formed which construct the walls of our habitations, and is also spread out in strata within our hills and mountains, to arrest the progress of subterraneous waters, and to produce those springs that fertilize the valleys, and which take such diversified courses upon the surface of the globe.

CHAPTER X.

SALTS.

1. What is a salt?

When an acid is combined with an alkali, an earth, or a metallic oxide, it forms what is called a salt. There is another class of salts formed by the union of chlorine, iodine, bromine, and sulphur with metallic bases; to this class belongs common salt, and all other metallic chlorides,[a] iodides and bromides.

2. How many salts are there?

As the acids are capable of forming various combinations with the different earthy, alkaline, and metallic bases, the precise number of the salts is not known. Probably they amount to some thousands.[b]

[a] To give the pupil a clear idea of this class of bodies, it may be advisable to set him to form some of the salts from their component parts. He might be directed to pour a little sulphuric acid into a solution of soda in water, to evaporate the superfluous water, and then to notice the crystallization of the new-formed salt: if the liquor be allowed to stand quietly for a few hours in a cool place, he may observe the salt shoot into beautiful crystals of sulphate of soda.

[b] Should any one express his surprise that the number of one class of bodies should be so great, he may be told that nature seems to aim at variety in all her productions. Saint Pierre informs us that there

3. What method has been taken to distinguish the different salts?

Modern chemists have adopted a new nomenclature for this purpose, which is simple, ingenious, and useful.

4. How are the salts distinguished by this nomenclature?

Every salt has a double name, one part of which indicates its acid, and the other its base; so that, in a collection of many hundred different salts, the composition of each is immediately known by its appellation.[a]

5. Can you explain the manner in which this is effected?

All substances which are compounds of metallic oxides, earths, or alkalies with the sulphuric acid, are called *sulphates*; with the muriatic acid, *muriates*; with the nitric acid, *nitrates*; with the carbonic acid, *carbonates*, &c. &c.[b]

6. Do the advantages which we derive from the nomenclature compensate for the inconvenience of changing the names of so many substances?

The new nomenclature, by its scientific classification of bodies, gives such a facility to the acquisition of chemical knowledge, that this alone would have been sufficient to have justified chemists in adopting it; but its

are 6,000 species of flies, and 760 different butterflies. Ray computed the number of species of insects at ten thousand. There are above 1,000 different species of beetles in Great Britain.

[a] Fourcroy has well remarked, that if this arrangement had not been made, it would have been absolutely impossible to know the characters of the numerous salts which have been discovered, and the science of chemistry would then have been confined to the very few men who are capable of extraordinary efforts of memory.

[b] These are the terms generally made use of in chemical language; but sometimes, in order to prevent monotony, we give an adjective termination to the word which expresses the base of the acid. Thus we say calcareous salts, instead of acid of lime; ammoniacal salts, instead of salts of ammonia; aluminous salt, instead of salt of alumina; and with the same design, the terms barytic, magnesian, and the like, are used.

contrivance for pointing out the nature of the substances bearing the new names, gives it advantages far surpassing every inconvenience attending the alteration.[a]

7. Describe the nature of some of these advantages?

The saline compound, formerly called *Glauber's* salt, is now called sulphate of soda, for it is a combination of sulphuric acid and soda; what was called *gypsum*, or plaster of Paris, a compound of lime and sulphuric acid, is now called sulphate of lime; in like manner what was called *green copperas*, is now sulphate of iron, that substance being a compound, not of copper, as the old name seemed to import, but of oxide of iron and sulphuric acid.[b]

8. Have the framers of this nomenclature been equally happy in the choice of names for the salts which are composed with the other acids?

Yes; the principle upon which the nomenclature is formed is such, that the composition of every salt is designated by an appropriate name with the utmost perspicuity.

9. According to the new nomenclature, what is the common culinary salt called?

Common salt was called by the framers of the new nomenclature muriate of soda, on the supposition of its consisting of muriatic acid and soda; it is now more correctly named chloride of sodium, as it consists, in its dry state,[c] of these elements alone.

[a] As the boundaries of chemical science have been extended, the number of known salts has been surprisingly increased; so much so, that it would have been impossible to recollect the nature of each, without the assistance of a nomenclature of this kind.

[b] It is necessary to remark, that when an acid is combined with two bases, the names of both are subjoined to that of the acid. Thus we say sulphate of alumina and potash, and tartrate of potash and soda.

[c] Formerly the word SALT was confined to muriate of soda. No other substance was then known as a salt. Afterwards the acids and alkalies were called salts also. There are innumerable proofs of this in the old chemical writings.

10. What do you call saltpetre?

Saltpetre is called *nitrate of potash;* it being composed of potash and nitric acid.

11. What is chalk now called?

Chalk being a compound of lime and carbonic acid, is called *carbonate of lime.*

12. These bodies were formerly called neutral **salts,** why is not that term now applied as before?

No salt can strictly be called *neutral* except such in which the acid is completely neutralized by the base, and the base by the acid, so as to be mutually saturated by each other.[*]

13. Is not that the case with all saline compounds?

No: some have an excess of acid, as cream of tartar; and other salts have an excess of base, as common borax.

14. How are such salts distinguished?

When a salt is found to contain an excess of acid, the preposition SUPER is sometimes prefixed to its name; but when it does not contain a sufficiency of acid to saturate the base, the preposition SUB is added; as super-tartrate of potash, and sub-borate of soda. It is, however, better to name the lowest combination of an acid with a base, by the generic names of each, and to express the other combinations of an acid with the same base by the prefixes *bi, tri,* &c.; thus we have the sulphate and bisulphate of potash; where there is a combination consisting of an acid and base united in the proportion of one to one and a half atoms, we will express it by the prefix *sesqui,* thus we have the carbonate and sesqui-carbonate of ammonia.

15. Some salts are formed with acids not fully oxy-

---

[*] The propriety of restricting the use of the term *neutral* will appear, if we consider that we have some bases that combine with more than one dose of acid, and thereby form salts which differ in their appearance and properties. Thus we have sulphate of potash, and bi-sulphate of potash. The one is a neutral salt, the other a salt with excess of acid.

genized, as the sulphurous and phosphorous acids : how are such salts distinguished ?

All salts composed with acids ending in *ous*, take an ending in *ite*, instead of *ate*. Thus we say *sulphite* of lime, or *phosphite* of potash.

16. Having shown the nature of the present chemical nomenclature as far as respects the salts, it will now be necessary to enter on the consideration of each genus separately. Therefore, what are the generic characters of the sulphates ?

The sulphates[a] have generally a bitter taste; are precipitable from fluids by a solution of baryta; and afford sulphurets when heated red-hot with charcoal.

17. Can you enumerate a few of the principal sulphuric salts ?

Among the principal of them are sulphate of baryta,[b] sulphate of strontia, sulphate of potash, sulphate of soda, sulphate of lime,[c] sulphate of magnesia, sulphate of

---

[a] The quantity of sulphuric acid contained in any of the sulphuric salts may be known by means of baryta. For, if any of the solutions of this earth be added to a solution containing sulphuric acid, a sulphate of barytes will instantly be formed and precipitated. When this precipitate is dried, every hundred and seventeen grains of it will contain 40 grains of sulphuric acid.

[b] Sulphate of baryta, or *ponderous spar*, as it has been called, is abundant in different parts of the earth. Sulphate of strontia is found in Scotland and elsewhere in abundance. Sulphate of potash, sulphate of soda, and sulphate of ammonia are prepared by chemical manufacturers in many of their processes. Sulphate of lime, sulphate of magnesia, and sulphate of alumina are native productions. Sulphate of ammonia, it has been said, has been found native in the neighbourhood of volcanos.

[c] Sulphate of lime is found in abundance in Staffordshire, Derbyshire, and other counties of England. The hills around Paris are composed entirely of this earthy salt; hence its name *plaster of Paris*. When burnt and ground it is miscible with water, for which it has so great an affinity that it becomes solid almost immediately. This property renders it an excellent substance for forming busts, cornices, &c. which are very durable, if protected from the weather, and not exposed in damp situations.

ammonia, sulphate of alumina, and sulphate of alumina and potash.

18. What are the generic characteristics of the sulphites?

The sulphites have always a disagreeable sulphurous taste; they are decomposed by the nitric, muriatic, and some other acids which do not affect *sulphates;* if exposed to fire they yield sulphur, and become sulphates; and are converted into sulphates even by exposure to the action of the atmosphere.

19. Can you enumerate some of the sulphurous salts?

The principal are, the sulphites of baryta, of lime, of potash, of soda, of ammonia, of magnesia, and of alumina.

20. What are the generic characteristics of the muriates or hydrochlorates?

The muriates, when acted upon by concentrated sulphuric acid, yield muriatic acid in the form of gas; and when by the nitric acid, chlorine gas. Some of them are the most volatile, and yet the least decomposable by fire, of all the salts; not being perceptibly altered by being heated with combustible substances.

21. Can you enumerate the chief of the muriatic salts?

The principal of the muriatic salts are the muriates of baryta, of potash, of soda,[a] of strontia, of lime, of

---

[a] Muriate of soda is the salt which has been longest known. It is our common culinary salt, and is supposed to furnish the necessary supply of soda to preserve the bile in an alkaline and antiseptic condition.

This salt is of great use to the animal creation; horses are very fond of it; and cows give more milk when supplied with it. Dr. Mitchill relates, that in the back settlements of America, wherever this salt abounds, thither the wild beasts of the forests assemble to regale themselves; and that some of these places are so much frequented, that the ground is trodden to mud by them. The natives call these spots *licks,* or licking places. In some parts of Africa, large herds of cattle travel from great distances at stated seasons to enjoy the marine plants which grow on the coast, and are saturated with sea-salt. The fattening property of our own salt marshes is well known to graziers and farmers.

ammonia, and muriate of magnesia,[a] these may however be all, with the exception of muriate of ammonia, considered as chlorides ‘or compounds of chlorine, with the metallic bases of the several alkalies or earths.

22. What are the generic characteristics of the chlorates?

The chlorates yield very pure oxygen gas by the action of heat, and are thus converted to chlorides, and muriatic acid when heated with these salts decomposes them, and euchlorine gas is given off, (see chap. vii. 30.) When mixed with combustible substances, they detonate with great violence, by mere friction or percussion, and sometimes spontaneously.[b]

23. Can you enumerate the chlorates?

The chief are; the chlorates of potash,[c] of soda, of barytes, of strontia, and of lime.

24. What are the generic characteristics of the nitrates?

The nitrates yield oxygen gas mixed with nitrogen gas by the action of heat; they give out white vapours of nitric acid when acted on by concentrated sulphuric

[a] Muriate of potash has been found native in the bogs of Picardy: this salt was formerly, and is still, much used by some alum-makers to procure the crystallization of alum. Muriate of ammonia is the common sal-ammoniac of commerce. Muriate of barytes and strontian are both artificial salts. Muriate of lime is found native in various states; it is also furnished in abundance by the makers of carbonate of ammonia.

[b] By gently triturating 3 grains of this salt and one of sulphur in a mortar with a metallic pestle, a series of detonations will take place resembling the cracks of a whip. If struck on an anvil, the report is as loud as a gun. But too great caution cannot be exercised in the use of this salt. Three parts of it with half a part of sulphur and half a part of charcoal produce most violent explosions.

[c] Chlorate of potash is used not only for experiment, but also in medicine. From its explosive effects Berthollet was induced to propose it as a substitute for nitre in the manufacture of gunpowder. The attempt was made; but no sooner did the workmen begin to triturate the mixture than it exploded with violence, and proved fatal to two individuals who were near it.

acid; and when mixed with combustible substances, produce at a red heat inflammation and detonation. This may be shown by heating a little nitre in a crucible, and throwing powdered charcoal upon it. The charcoal will combine with the oxygen of the nitric acid, and pass off in the state of carbonic acid gas; except the part that combines with the potash, and remains in the crucible.

25. What are the generic characteristics of the carbonates?

All the alkaline carbonates are soluble in water; those of the earths and metals are nearly insoluble, unless the acid be in excess;[a] and they all effervesce, and give out the carbonic acid, when treated with the stronger acids.

26. Endeavour to enumerate the principal carbonates, or bases combined with this acid.

The carbonates of baryta, of strontia, of lime, of potash, of soda, of magnesia, of ammonia, of iron, of lead, and of manganese, are the principal carbonates that occur. All these, except the alkaline carbonates, are found in the native state.

27. What are the generic characteristics of the phosphates?

The phosphates are fusible either into opaque or transparent glass; are phosphorescent at a high temperature; are soluble in nitric acid without effervescence; and are precipitable from their solutions by lime-water.

28. What are the chief phosphoric salts?

The phosphates of lime,[b] of soda, and of ammonia,

---

[a] It is in consequence of this property that many waters hold a large quantity of carbonate of lime in solution; and on being boiled or long exposed to the air deposite the carbonate of lime: stalactites are formed by water holding carbonate of lime, depositing it when it comes in contact with air.

[b] Phosphate of lime is found in bones, milk, and some other animal matters. It is white, tasteless, and insoluble in water. Entire mountains in Spain are formed of this salt. It is composed of phosphoric acid 8.5 parts, lime 57. It is prescribed by the French physicians as a specific in the rachitis, to diminish the effects of acids

and the phosphate of soda and ammonia, formerly called microcosmic salt.[a]

· 29. What are the generic characteristics of the phosphites?

The phosphites yield a phosphorescent flame when heated; and in a strong fire give out a portion of phosphorus, by which they become converted into phosphates. They are fusible by a violent heat into glass.

30. Endeavour to enumerate the principal phosphites.

The chief of them are; the phosphites of lime, of baryta, of potash, of soda, and of ammonia.

31. What are the generic characteristics of the fluorides.

The fluorides may be decomposed by strong sulphuric acid, when the fluoric acid in state of vapour will pass off, if the mixture be heated; this vapour corrodes glass, and when condensed in water, forms liquid fluoric acid. They are not decomposible by mere heat, nor altered by combustible substances.

32. What are the chief fluoric salts?

which soften the bones. Fourcroy, vol. iii. 356. See also Bonhomme's paper on this subject in Annales de Chimie, tome xvii.: the cases which he adduces are extremely curious.

Phosphate of lime exists also in the farina of wheat. La Grange remarks, that a person who eats a pound of farina a day will swallow 3 pounds 6 ounces 4 drams and 44 grains of phosphate of lime in the year. It is a curious fact, that the grain of wheat should contain *phosphate* of lime, while the straw which was *not* intended for our food, should contain *carbonate* of lime only.

It is remarkable, that, though phosphate of lime is always found in the urine of adults, this salt is not evacuated by infants.

[a] Phosphate of ammonia is found in urine, and is also prepared by art to be used as an ingredient in making pastes, to imitate precious stones. It is one of the best fluxes for experiments with the blowpipe.

Phosphate of soda and ammonia is found in human urine, from whence it may be procured by evaporation in the state of a triple salt.

Fluate of lime, fluate of soda, fluate of ammonia, and fluate of alumina.[a]

33. What are the generic characters of the borates?

The borates are all fusible into glass; and, with most of the metallic oxides, form glasses of different colours.[b] Concentrated solutions of some of the borates, especially that of soda, afford, by the strong acids, scaly crystals of of boracic acid.

34. Can you enumerate the boracic salts?

The principal are; the borates of lime, of magnesia,[c] and of potash; and the borate of soda,[d] which is called borax.

---

[a] Several varieties of fluate of lime have been found. They are of different colours, owing to the different degrees of oxidation of the iron which they contain. If any of these coloured fluates be pulverized, and then heated on a shovel, they will emit a violet phosphoric light, the cause of which is not known. This crystalline substance is known by the names of Derbyshire spar and Blue John; it consists almost entirely of fluate of lime. It is of various colours, and bears an excellent polish: hence it is used in making ornamental vases, &c. Where there are flaws or cracks in the mineral, I am told the workmen have an ingenious method of filling them up with lead ore, which they execute so well, that it cannot be discovered but by very close examination. Such specimens of the mineral as are not fit for ornamental work, will answer very well for the production of fluoric acid.

[b] For this reason they are frequently used as blowpipe tests, the nature of the metallic oxide to be examined by the blowpipe being ascertained by the colour it gives to the glass of borax (borate of soda). This salt is also used in the manufacture of artificial gems.

[c] Borate of magnesia has also been found near Lunenburgh. The other borates are prepared artificially.

[d] This salt, which is the common borax of commerce, was formerly called sub-borate of soda, because it contains an excess of soda. According to Bergman, it requires half its weight of boracic acid to bring it to the state of a neutral salt. Borax is generally brought from the East Indies in a state of impurity. The article is then called *tincal.* It has also been found near Lunnenburgh, in the duchy of Brunswick, in a mountain of gypsum.

Borax is likewise found at the bottom of pools of stagnant water, in the kingdom of Thibet.

Boracic acid is found dissolved in several lakes of Tuscany. In the waters of the lake Cherchiago, near Monte Rosonde, in the province of Sienna, this acid exists in sufficient abundance to be advantageously converted into borax, by soda.

35. What is the distinguishing characteristic of the arseniates ?

When heated with charcoal they are decomposed, and arsenic sublimes, which is known by its alliaceous or garlic smell.

36. Which are the chief salts formed with arsenic acid ?

The arseniates of lime, of baryta, of magnesia, of potash,[a] of soda, and of ammonia.

37. What are the characters of the tungstates ?

The salt called tungstates are combinations of the yellow acid of tungsten with the alkalies and earths. Most of them have a metallic and sharp taste.

38. Which are the principal salts formed with the tungstic acid ?

The tungstates of lime,[b] of magnesia, of potash, of soda, and of ammonia.

39. What are the generic characteristics of the acetates ?

The acetates are all very soluble in water ; are decomposed by the action of heat ; and afford acetic acid when distilled with sulphuric acid.

40. Which are the chief acetic salts ?

We have the acetates of baryta, of potash, of soda, of lime, of ammonia, of magnesia, and of alumina.[c]

41. What are the generic characteristics of the oxalates ?

The oxalates are decomposable by a red heat ; and lime-water precipitates a white powder (the oxalate of

[a] Arseniate of potash may be formed by heating in a crucible white arsenic and nitrate of potash; by this process we get a salt very soluble in water and which crystallizes in regular four-sided prisms. We shall have occasion in the next chapter to refer to this salt when we treat of the metal arsenic.

[b] This compound is formed abundantly in nature, and from it we generally obtain tungstic acid ?

[c] The acetate of lime is prepared in the preparation of pyroligneous acid ; the acetate of alumina is extensively used by calico-printers.

lime) from their neutral solutions ; which exposed to a red heat, is converted into carbonate of lime. The insoluble oxalates are soluble in an excess of the stronger acids.

42. Can you enumerate the principal oxalic salts ?

Oxalate of lime,[a] of baryta, of potash, of soda, and of ammonia.

43. What are the generic characteristics of the tartrates ?

When the tartrates are exposed to a red heat, the acid is decomposed, and the base remains. The earthy tartrates are less soluble than the alkaline, but all are capable of combining with another base, and forming triple salts.

44. Can you enumerate the principal tartaric salts ?

The principal are ; the tartrates of lime,[b] of strontia, and of potash ; and the tartrates of potash and soda, and of potash and ammonia.

45. What are the generic characteristics of the citrates ?

The citrates are decomposed by the strong mineral acids ; and the oxalic and tartaric acids also decompose

---

[a] Oxalate of lime is one of the compounds most frequently found in human calculi. Oxalate of potash and oxalate of ammonia are both very useful tests of lime. Oxalate of potash is prepared in England in considerable quantities for the calico-printers. It is found ready formed in the juice *wood-sorrel*, in the state of a binoxalate.

[b] Tartrate of lime is found in the tartar of commerce ; and it is also formed by art, by adding lime or its carbonate to a boiling solution of cream of tartar. This latter salt is merely the common tartar, or argol, purified, which adheres to the inside of wine casks, and is brought in large quantities from the wine countries. There is a considerable demand for it by the dyers and other manufacturers ; and both in the crude and refined state there is an excess of acid, therefore they are called *super*-tartrates of potash. Tartrate of potash and soda is usually called Rochelle salt, or sel de Seignette : it is formed artificially by adding soda in crystals to a solution of cream of tartar, till the excess of acid is saturated. A neutral tartrate of potash is also formed in our laboratories, called soluble tartar. The other tartrates are made without any view to their use in the arts.

them. Solutions of these salts in water when long kept undergo decomposition.

46. Which are the principal citrates?

The citrates of lime, of baryta, of potash, of soda, and of ammonia.[a]

47. What are the generic characteristics of the camphorates?

The camphorates have generally a bitterish taste; they are decomposable by heat, and burn with a blue flame.

48. Which are the principal camphorates?

The camphorates of lime, of potash, of soda, of baryta, of ammonia, of alumina, and of magnesia.

49. What are the generic characters of the suberates?

The several suberates differ so much in their properties, that it would be difficult to characterize the genus otherwise than by saying that they generally possess a bitter taste, and are decomposable by heat.

50. Which are the principal suberates?

Suberate of baryta, of potash, of lime, and of ammonia.

51. How are these different salts known from each other?

They are known by the peculiar figure of their crystals, by their taste, by their solubility in water, the nature of their acids and bases, and other distinctive or *specific* characters.

52. What is meant by the figure of their crystals?

There is a great variety in the form of crystallized salts; and each salt preserves its own peculiar form: thus common culinary salt generally crystallizes in cubes, and sulphate of soda in six-sided prisms.[b]

[a] The citrates are all formed artificially. Citrate of potash is used much in medicine, and is usually called the *saline draught*. The other citrates are not yet found to be of any use. The affinities of the citric acid are in the following order:—baryta, lime, magnesia, potash, soda, strontia, ammonia, and alumina.

[b] When, either by the diminution of the quantity of the liquid, or the reduction of the temperature, the force of cohesion causes a separation of a portion of the dissolved substance, in almost all cases

53. How is the crystallization of salts effected?[a]

When a certain portion of their solutions is evaporated, and the remainder left in a proper temperature at rest, the salts will form into crystals,[b] and will be found dispersed through the mother water at the bottom and at the sides of the vessel. In order that regular crystallization may

the parts which are separated form a regular arrangement; owing to the relation between their figure and reciprocal affinity. Hence those crystals which Nature offers in such variety, and which are produced in so great a number of chemical combinations.

The plates which continue to be added (either because the crystal acts on the dissolved substance, or because the cause of separation continues to exist in the liquid) are composed of moleculæ similar to the first, and continue to augment the bulk of the crystal, preserving its first form: nevertheless, this increase may be determined to one face in preference to another, according to the position of the crystal and the circumstances in which the solution is found.

[a] Sir Isaac Newton seems to have had a very clear idea of the cause of crystallization. "When," says he, "a liquor saturated with a salt is evaporated to a pellicle, and sufficiently cooled, the salt falls in regular crystals. Before being collected, the saline particles floated in the liquor, equally distant from each other; they acted, therefore, mutually on each other, with a force which was equal at equal distances, and unequal at unequal distances; so, in virtue of this force, they must arrange themselves in an uniform manner."—Optics, book iii.

[b] It must not be imagined that all crystallization is owing to solution in water. Melted sulphur always crystallizes on cooling, which is the case with many substances that have endured a strong heat. Many of the metals crystallize in this way, particularly tin and bismuth. Nothing can exemplify this kind of crystallization better than chloride of lead, commonly called patent yellow. It affords beautiful and regular crystals on cooling. If glass be kept in a red heat for a long time, and cooled gradually—instead of being the transparent body we generally see it—it will crystallize like metals. Dr. Garnet accounts for the origin of basaltes in this way. (See his Tour to the Western Isles.) The Giants' Causeway, in the county of Antrim in Ireland, is a most stupendous natural curiosity of this kind. It is formed of perpendicular pillars of basaltes, which stand in contact with each other. The pillars are irregular prisms of various forms, from three to nine sides; but they are principally hexagons. The appearance of the whole is as neat as it is magnificent. The columns at Fairhead are 250 feet high, arranged in the utmost regularity and order; and from the base to the level of the sea there is a precipitous declivity of at least 300 feet, making together a perpendicular height of 550 feet.

take place, it is necessary that the fluid, whether water or caloric, or both, should be subtracted gradually. This gives an opportunity for the parts of the substance to unite regularly, according to their several attractions, and to produce regular crystals, such as nature furnishes; whereas, a sudden subtraction of the fluid causes the particles often to unite in a shapeless mass.

54. What is meant by the mother water?

Mother water is the liquor which remains after a salt has combined with the portion of water necessary for its crystallization. By repeating the evaporation and cooling, the mother waters generally afford fresh portions of salt.

55. What is the cause of the crystallization of salts?

The crystallization of salts results from an attraction exerted among their molecules, which causes them to cohere in masses of determinate form; in many cases the water parts with its caloric of fluidity and takes a solid form.

56. What is the water called which combines with salts during their crystallization?

It is called the water of crystallization.

57. What quantity of water do salts combine with during their crystallization?

The quantity of water varies very much in different salts; for though some salts take up very little water, others combine with more than their own weight, which is the case with alum, carbonate of soda, and some others. The quantity of water of crystallization is, however, always fixed and determinate in the same salts; crystals of carbonate of soda, for example, always contain 62.5 per cent. of water; crystallized sulphate of soda always 46.8 per cent.

58. Are salts as unalterable in their appearances as they are in their chemical properties?

No: *crystallized* salts are liable to changes in their appearance by exposure to atmospheric air. Thus some salts deliquesce, and others effloresce, so as to lose their crystalline form entirely by such exposure.

I

59. What is meant by the deliquescence of a salt?

Some salts have so great an affinity for water, that they absorb it with rapidity from the atmosphere. Such salts thereby become moist or liquid, and are said to deliquesce, when exposed to atmospheric air.

60. What is meant by the efflorescence of a salt?

Some salts, having less affinity for water than atmospheric air has, lose their water of crystallization by exposure, and readily fall into powder; such salts are said to effloresce. Carbonate and sulphate of soda afford good examples of this property.

61. Are salts capable of any other changes besides efflorescence and deliquescence?

Yes: salts have the properties of solubility and fusibility.

62. What is meant by the solubility of a salt?

It is their capacity to unite with, and remain dissolved in water; but the different salts possess different degrees of solubility, requiring more or less of this fluid for their solution.[a]

63. What is meant by the fusibility of a salt?

Salts have not only the property of dissolving in water, but will become fluid by exposure to heat. The different salts require different degrees of heat to bring them to a state of fusion. There are two kinds of fusion, watery and igneous; the former term is applied to these salts

[a] We generally denominate all salts as insoluble, which require for sulution more than 1000 times their weight of water. The most general rule for judging of the solubility of a salt is by its taste. Those salts which have the most taste are generally the most soluble in water.

This difference in the solubility of salts is of great use in separating them from each other. The refiners of saltpetre operate entirely on this principle; for the rough petre, as it is called, is always contaminated with a portion of muriate of soda and other salts. In order to separate them they dissolve the whole in water, and then by boiling the solution to evaporate a part of the water, the muriate of soda, &c. falls down, while the saltpetre is held in solution. When the greatest part of these salts is thus separated, the remaining liquor is suffered to cool, and the nitrate of potash is obtained in crystals.

which, containing a large quantity of water of crystallization, dissolve in this water and become liquid by a
moderate heat; of this species we have examples in sulphate and carbonate of soda; salts not combined with
water of crystallization or deprived of it by heat, may be
made undergo igneous fusion by a strong heat.

64. Have the different salts any action upon each
other?

Yes: we have many instances of salts mutually decomposing each other.

65. What takes place in these decompositions?

When such salts are mixed in solution, the acid of the
first, having more attraction for the base of the *second* than
for its own base, unites itself to it, while the acid of the
second combines with the base of the first; so that two
new salts are produced, differing in appearance, and possessing properties different from those of the original salts.

66. What is the cause of this?

It is occasioned by chemical attraction, and the operation itself is called double decomposition, or the effect
of compound affinities.

67. What use is made of these decompositions?

By these means many valuable salts are procured for
the use of the chemist and the manufacturer, which can
be formed in no other way.

68. What knowledge have we attained respecting the
native salts?

Many of the salts are found native; and since the
science of mineralogy has been so much cultivated, great
attention has been paid to these natural productions.

69. What salts are furnished by nature in the greatest
abundance?

The carbonates, the sulphates, and the muriates, are
most abundant; but some of the nitrates, borates, &c.
are also found native.

70. Which of the carbonates have been found native?

Of carbonate of lime, (known by the names chalk, limestone, marble, and calcareous spar,) there are immense mountains in most parts of the world; carbonate of baryta has been found in Lancashire and elsewhere; carbonate of strontia, at Strontian, in Scotland; carbonate of soda, in the natron beds of Egypt, and in the East Indies; and carbonate of potash, as well as the carbonate of soda, has been discovered in some spring waters.

71. What sulphuric salts are found native?

Sulphate of soda is found in sea-water and in salt springs; sulphate of magnesia, in spring water;[a] sulphate of alumina, in abundance at Whitby; sulphate of baryta, in Derbyshire, and other parts of the world; sulphate of strontia, in the neighbourhood of Bristol; and sulphate of lime is an abundant mineral in the vicinity of Paris, and in several of the counties of England.[b]

---

[a] Sulphate of magnesia and sulphate of lime are both very common in our spring waters; the last salt and carbonate of lime are the chief causes of what we call *hard* waters, which are very unwholesome and unfit for washing. When soap is used with these waters a double decomposition takes place; the sulphuric acid of the sulphate unites with the alkali of the soap and forms sulphate of potash, or sulphate of soda, which remains in solution, while the magnesia or lime unites with the tallow, and forms an insoluble compound which swims upon the surface of the water like curds. In this way hard waters require much more soap for any given purpose than rain water, or waters which do not contain these earthy salts. Such waters are also unfit for boiling any esculent vegetable; but they may be rendered soft by adding to them a very little carbonate of soda, or carbonate of potash, 24 hours previous to their use. By this addition, a double decomposition will be effected, and the carbonate of lime, a very insoluble salt, precipitated.

The property which sulphate of lime has of setting into a compact mass when mixed with water was well known to the ancients. Herodotus informs us of a curious method by which the inhabitants of Ethiopia preserved the remembrance of their deceased relatives. They had the custom, he says, of drying the body in the sun, then covering it with a paste of gypsum, and afterwards painting the portrait of the deceased upon the plaster covering that which encrusted the real body.

[b] Sulphate of lime is obtained in great abundance at Chelaston, near Derby, and Beacon Hill, near Newark. This mineral is much used

72. What native salts of muriatic acid are there ?

Muriate of lime and muriate of magnesia are found in abundance in sea-water;[a] muriate of ammonia appears in the neighbourhood of volcanos ; and muriate of soda not only exists in immense quantities in the ocean,[b] but vast mountains in different parts of the world are entirely formed of this salt.

73. Which of the nitric salts are found native?

Nitrate of potash is collected in various parts of the globe ; nitrate of magnesia sometimes occurs in combination with that salt, and nitrate of lime is found also in the same combination, and likewise in calcareous stones,

---

in Derbyshire for making the floors of cheese-chambers, store-rooms, granaries, &c. They burn the gypsum, grind it to powder, and then mix it with water. In this state it is laid upon the floors about 2½ inches thick, and when dry is a smooth and durable flooring. Gypsum is also found in most of the cliffs of the Severn, especially at the Old Passage near Bristol.

[a] The magnesia of commerce is generally procured from this source. It is prepared in great quantities in the island of Guernsey, and elsewhere.

[b] In the south of France large trenches are cut near the sea, which fill with sea-water at high tide ; the water being confined there by flood-gates, the sun evaporates it and leaves the salt in the trenches, from whence it is laid up to dry for use.

Dr. Shaw gives an account of salt works on the coast of Syria, where the rocks on the sea shore have been hollowed into salt pans two or three yards long. By continually throwing in sea water, as the aqueous part evaporates a large quantity of salt gradually forms at the bottom.

In Sweden they freeze the sea water, throw away the ice, and boil down the remainder to salt.

In the landgravate of Thuringia in Saxony, a new method has been adopted in the manufacture of salt. A number of vessels of wood are placed firm upon posts six feet from the ground, which may be covered or uncovered in an instant by a moveable roof, accordingly as the weather is dry or rainy. In this manner salt is obtained by the mere heat of the sun, and such salt is much purer than that which is procured by evaporation in boilers.

and in mineral springs :—these are the only nitric salts that have been found native in any large quantities.[a]

74. Are any other of the salts found native?

Yes: vast rocks in Derbyshire and elsewhere are formed of fluate of lime; borate of soda is found in a crystallized state in the kingdom of Thibet; and phosphate of lime, which is the basis of all animal bones, exists native in Hungary, and composes several entire mountains in Spain.

75. How do you imagine these immense masses of salts have been formed by nature?

The vast mountains of salts which occur in various parts of the earth were probably formed in very remote ages, and by processes of which we can form no idea. It may be supposed that these changes have been slow and gradual, as several of the native salts exhibit marks of regularity and beauty in their crystallization, which cannot be imitated by art.[b]

---

[a] The salt mines near Cracow in Poland, which have been worked ever since the middle of the thirteenth century, contain an immense store of muriate of soda. The excavations have been made with so much regularity and beauty, that these mines are visited by travellers as one of the greatest curiosities in the world. Eight hundred workmen are employed in them, who raise 168,000 quintals of salt annually.

[b] Some of the saltpetre grounds are now much more productive than formerly, owing to a knowledge of the circumstance, that carbonate of potash will decompose nitrate of lime. The saltpetre-makers, in lixiviating the earths, now add a portion of wood ashes, and hence their produce of nitre is much more abundant.

CHAPTER XI.

METALS.

1. What are the characters of the metals?

The general characters of the metals are, combustibility, lustre, opacity, fusibility, and the power of conducting electricity.

2. Are not malleability, ductility, and great density, essential characters of metals?

They were formerly considered so: but there are several metals which are neither malleable nor ductile, and some which have less specific gravity than water; for example, the metallic bases of the fixed alkalies.

3. How are the metals procured?

They are generally found in the earth,[a] in a state of combination either with other metals, with sulphur, oxygen, chlorine, or with acids, though a few of them have occasionally been found in a state of purity.[b]

4. By what methods are metals purified from these substances?

The metals are purified from their ores by various means; such as washing, roasting, fusion, &c.; but the

[a] Metals are generally found in mountainous countries, in such as form a continued chain: but the metallic part of a mountain usually bears but a small proportion to its whole contents. Granite rocks seldom contain any metallic ores.

It is deserving of notice, that if minerals had been placed on the *surface* of the globe, they would have occupied the greatest part of the earth, and would have prevented its cultivation.

[b] Gold, silver, platina, and mercury, are generally found in a state of purity, or in the *native* state.

method must always be regulated by the nature of the ore to be assayed.[a]

5. How many metals are there?

There are forty-two distinct metals, which possess properties very different and distinct from each other.[b]

6. How are the metals classed by chemists?

They were formerly divided into two classes. The one containing the malleable, the other the brittle metals. This last class was sometimes subdivided into two others, viz. those which are easily and those which are difficultly fused. This classification is however abandoned as imperfect; they are now divided into two classes, 1st, those which by union with oxygen produce earths and alkalies, (*Vide* pp. 130, 141.) 2nd. those which by union with oxygen produce neither alkalies nor earths.

7. What are the chemical characters of the metals?

They are all electro-positive bodies; most of them have

---

[a] The analysis of metallic ores on a large scale is always performed by fire, and this is called the *dry* way; but the more accurate analysis is effected by means of various chemical re-agents which modern chemistry has applied to that purpose, and is termed the *moist* way. Before the time of Bergman, every kind of analysis of minerals was conducted by fire: he was the first chemist who resorted to the method of solution in acids, which is easy, simple, and effectual.

[b] For a knowledge of most of the metals, we are indebted to the more perfect modes of analysis which modern chemistry has afforded. The ancients were acquainted with only seven of these metals. The properties of these were tolerably well known to the early chemists, who acquired their knowledge from the alchemists. These infatuated people tortured silver, mercury, copper, iron, tin, and lead, in every way they could devise, in order to convert them into gold. Alchemy was probably introduced into Europe by the crusaders, whose minds were prepared for the reception of any delusion. In all likelihood they picked up the idea of the transmutation of metals on their return from Palestine; and as error generally operates more powerfully than truth with such fanatics, they deluged their native country with these absurdities. The vain and conceited Paracelsus, a Swiss physician, was one of the last of the alchemists. He announced to the world that he had discovered a medicine, which would render man immortal: but, worn out by his debaucheries and excesses, he gave the lie to this assertion; for he himself died in the year 1534, at the age of 41.

a strong tendency to combine with oxygen, chlorine, iodine, and bromine, and also with sulphur and phosphorus; and their union with these substances is often attended with extrication of heat and light or combustion.

8. As we have already considered the properties of the metals of the first class, will you enumerate the metals of the second order?

There are in this class 28 metals.

1. GOLD.	15. COBALT.
2. PLATINA.	16. MANGANESE.
3. SILVER.	17. TUNGSTEN.
4. MERCURY.	18. MOLYBDENUM.
5. COPPER.	19. URANIUM.
6. IRON.	20. TITANIUM.
7. TIN.	21. CHROMIUM.
8. LEAD.	22. COLUMBIUM.
9. NICKEL.	23. PALLADIUM.
10. ZINC.	24. RHODIUM.
11. BISMUTH.	25. IRIDIUM.
12. ANTIMONY.	26. OSMIUM.
13. TELLURIUM.	27. CERIUM.
14. ARSENIC.	28. VANADIUM.[a]

9. It will be necessary to consider each of these metals separately; what is the nature of gold?

Gold is the heaviest of all the metals, except platina, its specific gravity being 19.3; it is not very elastic, nor very hard; but it is so malleable and ductile, that it may be drawn into very fine wire, or beaten out into leaves thin enough to be carried away by the slightest wind.[b]

[a] Of these metals, the three first have been called noble or perfect metals; because they stand the most intense heat of our furnaces, without suffering oxidizement, or any diminution in their weights.

[b] Dr. Black has calculated, that it would take fourteen millions of films of gold, such as is on some fine gilt wire, to make up the thickness of one inch; whereas fourteen million leaves of common printing paper make up near ¾ of a mile. According to Fourcroy, the ductility of gold is such, that one ounce of it is sufficient to gild a silver wire, more than thirteen hundred miles long.

Such is the tenacity of gold, that a wire one-tenth of an inch in

I 2

10. Where is gold found?

Gold is found in Peru and in some other parts of the world. It generally occurs in a metallic state, and most commonly in the form of grains.[a]

11. What are the effects of oxygen upon gold?

Gold has so little affinity for oxygen, that its oxides may be reduced to the metallic state by heat alone ; there are supposed to be three oxides of gold, the peroxide

diameter, will support a weight of five hundred pounds without breaking.

Gold becomes much harder by union with a small quantity of copper.

Fulminating gold is made by diluting a saturated solution of gold with three times its measure of distilled water, and precipitating the oxide by solution of ammonia *gradually* added. The precipitate, when dried on a filter, forms this fulminating powder, which detonates by heat or friction. A shocking accident is related by Macquer, of a person losing both eyes, by the bursting of a phial containing fulminating gold, at the house of Baumé, and which exploded by the friction of the glass stopper against a minute quantity that adhered unobserved to the neck of the bottle.

[a] Gold frequently occurs in the ores of other metals, but it is chiefly found in the warmer regions of the earth. It abounds in the sands of many African rivers, in South America, and in India. Several of the rivers in France contain gold in their sands. It has also been discovered in Hungary, Sweden, Norway, and Ireland. Near Pamplona, in South America, single labourers have collected upwards of £200 worth of wash-gold in a day. In the province of Sonora, the Spaniards discovered a plain fourteen leagues in extent, in which they found wash-gold at the depth of only sixteen inches; the grains were of such a size that some of them weighed 72 ounces, and in such quantities, that in a short time, with a few labourers, they collected 1000 marks, (equal in value to £31,219 10s. sterling,) even without taking time to wash the earth that had been dug. They found one mass which weighed 132 ounces. This is deposited in the Royal Cabinet at Madrid, and is worth £500.

The native gold found in Ireland was in grains, from the smallest size up to between two and three ounces. Only two pieces were found of greater weight, one of which weighed five, and the other 22 ounces.

Gold mines were formerly worked in Scotland ; and indeed now grains of this metal are often found in brooks in that kingdom, after a great flood. It has been said, that, at the nuptials of James V. covered dishes, filled with coins of *Scotch gold*, were presented to the guests by way of dessert.

is the only one, the properties of which are well known; it is found as a yellow powder by precipitation of the solution of gold in *aqua regia* by means of an alkali.

12. What salts of gold are there?

There is only one salt of this metal that is much known to chemists, viz. the muriate or terchloride of gold, which is obtained in small crystals by dissolving gold in *aqua regia*, and evaporating the solution; it is very soluble in water. We may precipitate the metallic gold from this solution by means of green sulphate of iron or the oxide of gold by means of an alkali.

13. What are the uses of gold?

Gold is used for jewellery, for plate, and for current coin : but for these purposes it is generally alloyed with $\frac{1}{12}$th of copper. It is employed in various ways in the arts.[a] Gold is also used to be spread over other metals to preserve them from tarnishing or rusting, as gold does not become oxidized by exposure to atmospheric air.

14. What is the origin of silver?

Silver is found in various parts of the world in a metallic state; also in the states of a sulphuret, a chloride, and an oxide.

17. What are the properties of silver?[b]

---

[a] Gold is also used in a state of solution, for staining ivory and ornamental feathers. It gives a beautiful purple red, which cannot be effaced; even marble may be stained with it. The nitro-muriatic acid is the menstruum used for this purpose. The potters dissolve gold in this way, to be applied to the common kinds of porcelain. Bismuth or zinc will precipitate gold from this solution. Tin will precipitate it of a beautiful purple, called the *purple precipitate of Cassius*. This also is used by the potters in printing on porcelain. Sulphuret of potash will likewise dissolve gold. Some have thought that Moses made use of this process to render the calf of gold, adored by the Israelites, soluble in water. Stahl wrote a long dissertation in order to prove that this was the case.

[b] Ores of silver occur in the silver-mines of South America, Germany, Hungary, Saxony, and Siberia. Silver has also been found in the copper-mines in Cornwall. Most of our lead-mines also afford it, particularly some of the lead-mines in Scotland and

. Silver is a sonorous, brilliant, white metal; exceedingly ductile, and of great malleability and tenacity, having, when pure, the specific gravity of 10.5. It possesses these latter properties in so great a degree, that it may be beaten into leaves much thinner than any paper;[a] or drawn out into wire as fine as a hair, without breaking.

16. What is the effect of oxygen upon silver?

Silver cannot be oxidized by atmospheric air, unless it be exposed to an intense heat; but the oxide of silver may be procured by dissolving the metal in an acid, and then precipitating it by an alkali or an alkaline earth.

17. Does silver combine with chlorine?

Silver has so strong an attraction for chlorine that it will take it from most other substances; if we pour a solution of any chloride or muriatic acid, into a solution

Ireland. " In the museum of the Academy of Sciences at Petersburg, is a piece of *native* silver from China, of such firmness, that coins have been struck from it, without its having passed through the crucible."

By the silver which was procured from the lead-mines in Cardiganshire, Sir Hugh Middleton is said to have cleared two thousand pounds a month, and that this enabled him to undertake the great work of bringing the New River from Ware to London. In 1637, a mint was established at Aberystwith for coining Welsh silver.— *Bishop Watson.*

Aristotle says, that some shepherds discovered the method of working the silver-mines of Spain; for, having occasion to clear a quantity of land by burning down the wood, they found fused silver produced by the operation of the fires.

. [a] Fifty square inches of silver leaf weigh not more than a grain. The silver wire used by astronomers is no more than half as thick as a fine human hair.

. Silver melts at 28° of Wedgwood. In a temperature much higher it becomes volatilized.

Silver readily combines with sulphur. According to Mr. Hatchett, those who rob the public, by diminishing the current silver coin, make use of the following method. " They expose the coin to the fumes of burning sulphur, by which a black crust of sulphuretted silver is soon formed, which, by a slight but quick blow, comes off like a scale, leaving the coin so little affected, that the operation may sometimes be repeated twice or thrice, without much hazard of detection."

of a salt of silver, an immediate precipitate of the chloride of silver will be formed, and may be recognized by the remarkable property of its colour being changed by exposure to light from white to pearl grey; it is from this property of silver that it may be easily ascertained whether an ore contains silver, by pulverizing it and dissolving it in nitric acid, and afterwards adding a little muriatic acid. Should it contain any silver, the chlorine of the acid will instantly combine with the whole of it, and precipitate it from the nitric solution in white flakes of chloride of silver. In order to know the proportion of silver in any given quantity of ore, collect this precipitate on a filter, heat it red, and weigh it accurately. Every 143 parts of this chloride of silver indicate 108 of pure silver.

18. What salts are there of silver?

The nitrate of silver[a] is best known; but in analysis the sulphate of silver is also a most useful test: many other salts of this metal may likewise be formed. The chloride and the carbonate of silver are both found native.[b]

19. What are the uses of silver?

Silver is used chiefly for ornamental work, for domestic

[a] This salt is kept in chemical laboratories as a test for the muriatic acid. When melted, and run in moulds, it forms the lunar caustic of the apothecary. When dissolved in water and left at rest, it crystallizes in brilliant transparent plates of different forms. Though the solution is as pale as pure water, it will stain the skin and other animal substances of an indelible black. It is employed to dye human hair; for staining marbles and jaspars; and for silvering ornamental work. This salt is the most powerful antiseptic known. One ounce of it dissolved in 12,000 ounces of water, will preserve the water from putrefaction for ever, and it may be separated therefrom in a few minutes, by adding a small lump of common salt.

A solution of nitrate of silver mixed with a little gum water forms the *indelible ink* used in marking linen.

[b] Chloride of silver has been found crystallized in Saxony, and in South America. Carbonate of silver has been found in masses in Suabia.

utensils, and for current coin; but for these purposes it is generally alloyed with copper, without which it would not have sufficient hardness.

20. How is platina procured?

Platina is found in grains, in a metallic state, at St. Domingo, and at Santa Fé in Peru; it is also found in considerable quantity in the Ural Mountains in Russia.[a]

21. What is the nature of platina?

[a] Charles Wood was the first person who brought any of this metal to England. He brought it from Jamaica, in the year 1741; and published an account of his experiments upon it in the Phil. Trans. for 1749 and 1750. Platina, in the language of Peru, means *little silver*.

Platina has lately been discovered in an ore of silver found in Estremadura. It exists in this ore in its metallic form, and as none of the new metals found with the South American platina are here present, the platina may be obtained from this ore at a trifling expense.

The ore of platina contains no less than nine different substances, viz. silex, iron, lead, copper, platina; and four new metals, which are called iridium, osmium, rhodium, and palladium. The properties of these new metals have as yet been but little investigated. For the methods of analysing the ore of platina, consult Dr. Wollaston's and Mr. Tenant's papers in the Philosophical Transactions, which are the best treatises on this metal.

Platina may be distinguished from all other metals by adding a solution of muriate of ammonia to a solution of the metal in nitro-muriatic acid, when a red-coloured precipitate will instantly appear. This is the only means yet known to discover when gold has been alloyed with this metal. Gold is generally known, if weighed hydrostatically, by its specific gravity; but if it be alloyed with platina some other test is necessary, as platina has a greater specific gravity than gold.

The specific gravity of hammered platina is 23.66, which is more than double that of lead. It may always be known from other metals by this superior specific gravity, it being the heaviest body in nature.

The strongest of the pure mineral acids has no effect upon this metal, if employed separately; neither has the strongest fire, unless it be urged by a stream of oxygen gas. It may, however, be melted by a burning lens, or dissolved in a solution of chlorine or nitro-muriatic acid. If mixed with arsenic, and then exposed to a great heat, it fuses readily. If a platina wire be introduced into the flame produced by the combustion of mixed hydrogen and oxygen gases, it will burn with all the brilliancy of iron wire, and emit sparks in abundance.

. Platina is the heaviest of all the metals; is nearly as white as silver; and is difficultly fusible; but by great labour it way be rendered malleable, so as to be wrought into utensils like other metals. It will resist the strongest heat of our fires without melting; and, like iron, is capable of being welded when properly heated.

22. What is the effect of oxygen upon platina?

The oxygen in atmospheric air has no effect upon platina, unless when assisted by an intense heat; but the oxide may be procured by dissolving the metal in nitro-muriatic acid, and precipitating it by an alkali.

23. What salts are there of platina?

A variety of salts may be formed with the oxide of this metal; but none of them have yet been brought into much use. No salt of platina has yet been found native.

24. What are the uses of platina?

Platina has hitherto been chiefly used for chemical apparatus, such as crucibles, spoons, and for the evaporating vessels used in the manufacture of sulphuric acid;[a]

[a] Platina vessels are very valuable to the experimental and manufacturing chemist, on account of their infusibility by ordinary heat, and their not being acted upon by the common acids. They cannot, however, be employed in any examination of the fusible metals, lead, antimony, arsenic, &c. as all these metals will readily alloy with platina at their fusing points.

A very neat method to cover other metals with platina was discovered by Mr. Stodart, who found that, like gold, it may be taken up from its solution by sulphuric ether. Where the expense of ether would be an objection to its use, good oil of turpentine may be employed in its stead. M. Strauss succeeded in applying platina to the coating of copper with as much ease as the common operation of tinning. The durability of this metal, and its resistance to acids and saline matters, renders this a most valuable application of the metal.

Platina alloyed with copper and silver affords a compound that is acted upon but little by muriatic or nitric acid, and which when drawn into wire is highly elastic, and very useful for springs that are designed to be exposed to the action of the atmosphere.

By melting 15 parts of gold with one part of purified platina, Mr. Hatchett produced a yellowish white alloy, extremely ductile, and very elastic.

it is also employed for coinage in Russia, for which purpose it is well adapted, owing to the difficulty of debasing it. When drawn into wires, it is applied to various purposes in the arts, and in thin leaves has sometimes been applied to porcelain, in the same manner as gold. In the form of fine powder, or spongy platina, procured by precipitating it by muriate of ammonia, it is employed in Doebereiner's lamps, to procure instantaneous light.

25. What is the construction of these lamps?

It is found that when a stream of hydrogen gas, mixed with oxygen or atmospheric air, is directed upon spongy platina, the metal becomes so hot, that the hydrogen is inflamed; this phenomenon will occur any number of times with the same portion of platina.

26. How is this phenomenon explained?

It is supposed to arise in consequence of the strong cohesive attraction exerted by the platina on the particles of the gases, which brings them within the limits at which they mutually combine to form water, and overcomes the repulsive force exerted among their particles.

27. Where is mercury found?

Mercury is brought to Europe from the East Indies, and from Peru;[a] it is found in great abundance at Almaden in Spain. The quicksilver mines of Idria, a town in Hungary, have constantly been wrought for 300 years, and are thought, upon an average, to yield above 100 tons of quicksilver annually. It is also found in China. It is sometimes obtained in the native state, but more frequently combined with sulphur, with which it forms the

---

[a] The quicksilver mine of Guanca Velica, in Peru, is 170 fathoms in circumference, and 480 deep. In this profound abyss are seen streets, squares, and a chapel, where religious mysteries on all festivals are celebrated. Millions of flambeaux are continually burning to enlighten it. Mercury is raised in such abundance in Spain, that in the year 1717 there remained above 1200 tons of it in the magazines at Almaden, after the necessary quantity had been exported to Peru for the use of the silver mines there.

ore of mercury called cinnabar. It is obtained from this in the pure state by distillation, the cinnabar being previously mixed with lime or iron.

28. What are the general properties of mercury?

Mercury, at the ordinary temperature of our atmosphere, is a fluid metal,[a] having the appearance of melted silver : in this state it is neither ductile nor malleable; it is volatile when heated,[b] and the heaviest of all the metals except platina and gold. It readily combines with several of the other metals, and forms with them what are called amalgams.

29. What effect has oxygen upon mercury?

Mercury does not combine with oxygen in the ordinary temperature of the atmosphere, even when an extended surface is exposed; but if heated to about 600° of Fahr. it gradually becomes oxidized, and is converted into red or deutoxide of mercury. It also forms with oxygen a protoxide which may be prepared by the action of an alkali, on calomel, or protochloride of mercury.

[a] We see mercury always in a fluid state, because it is so very fusible that a small portion of caloric is always able to keep it in a state of fluidity; but it is as perfectly opaque as other metals. All metals require different portions of heat to fuse them. Tin melts with a degree of heat not sufficient to char paper, whereas platina cannot be fused by the strongest heat of the best furnaces. Mercury, when submitted to a sufficient degree of cold, is similar in appearance to other metals, and may be beaten out into plates. It has been determined that 39 degrees below zero of Fahrenheit's thermometer is the point at which the congelation of mercury takes place.

At Hudson's Bay, frozen mercury has been reduced to sheets as thin as paper, by beating it upon an anvil that had previously been reduced to the same temperature. On plunging a mass of this frozen quicksilver into a glass of warm water, the former became fluid, and the latter was immediately frozen.

[b] Mercury, heated to the temperature of 600 degrees of Fahrenheit, may be distilled like water. It is sometimes purified in this way from a mixture of other metals, it being often adulterated with lead and bismuth. It is also so elastic when in a state of vapour, that it is capable of bursting the strongest vessels. There is no better way of ascertaining the purity of mercury than by mixing it with an equal weight of iron-filings, and submitting it to distillation.

30. Does mercury combine with the other simple non-metallic substances?

Yes; it combines readily with chlorine, iodine, bromine, and sulphur. With chlorine it combines in two proportions to form calomel or protochloride of mercury,[a] and corrosive sublimate or the bichloride of mercury. The latter may be formed by heating mercury in chlorine gas, when it takes fire, unites with the chlorine, and forms the bichloride of mercury. With sulphur, mercury forms the well-known substance vermillion, or bisulphuret of mercury, and Ethiop's minerals which is a protosulphuret.

31. What other salts are there of mercury?

There is a great variety of mercurial salts; but the acetate, the sulphate, and the nitrate of mercury are best known.

32. What are the uses of mercury?

Mercury is used in large quantities for silvering mirrors, for water gilding, for making barometers and thermometers, and in the manufacture of vermillion. It has also various and important uses in medicine.[b]

33. How is copper procured?

Copper is found in several parts of England, particularly in Cornwall, in Ireland, and in the isles of Man and

[a] Calomel is made by triturating fluid mercury with corrosive sublimate, and then submitting the mixture to sublimation. As this medicine is much used in private families, and as dreadful consequences might ensue if it were improperly prepared, it ought to be generally known, that if it be not perfectly insipid to the taste, and insoluble by long boiling in water, it contains a portion of bichloride of mercury, or corrosive sublimate, and is consequently poisonous.

[b] In South America mercury is used to separate gold and silver from the extraneous matter found with those metals. By triturating the mass with mercury, the gold and silver become amalgamated with it; and afterwards this amalgam is submitted to heat, when the mercury sublimes, and the metals are left in a state of purity.
Several of the uses of mercury were known to the ancients. Theophrastus, an ancient Greek philosopher, who wrote about 300 years before Christ, was acquainted with it, and knew how to work it so as to form vermillion.

Anglesea. It is an abundant metal, and has been raised in various other parts of the world. Its specific gravity is 8·66.[a]

34. What are the general properties of copper ?

Copper is of a red colour, very sonorous and elastic, and the most ductile of all the metals, except gold.

35. What are the effects of oxygen upon copper ?

Copper will in some measure become oxidized by long exposure to atmospheric air, in which case its surface will be covered with the green carbonate of copper.[b] It is susceptible of three degrees of oxidation.

[a] Copper mines have been worked in China, Japan, Sumatra, and in the north of Africa. Native copper is found in Siberia crystallized in cubes. The copper pyrites found in Cornwall and upon several parts of the English coast are sulphurets of copper. Anglesea formerly yielded more than twenty thousand tons of copper annually.

In the museum of the Academy of Sciences at Petersburgh is a piece of native malleable copper of extraordinary magnitude, found on the copper island lying to the east of Kamtschatka.

Native oxides of copper are found in Cornwall and in South America. Carbonate of copper occurs as a natural production in two varieties called malachite and blue carbonate of copper.

In several copper mines, as those of Connecticut in America, and Ballymurtagh in Ireland, the water which flows from the mines is strongly impregnated with sulphate of copper, and is separated from the acid by immersing pieces of iron in tanks filled with the solution, which after some time precipitate the whole of the copper in the metallic state.

[b] In domestic economy the necessity of keeping copper vessels always clean is generally acknowledged; but it may not perhaps be generally known, that fat and oily substances, and vegetable acids, do not attack copper while hot; and, therefore, that if no liquid be ever suffered to grow cold in copper vessels, these utensils may be used for every culinary purpose with perfect safety.

Dr. Johnstone relates the shocking case of three men who died, after excruciating sufferings, in consequence of eating some victuals prepared in an unclean copper, on board the Cyclops frigate. Thirty-three other men became ill, and were put upon the sick list, at the same time and from the same cause.

Dr. Percival gives an account of a young lady who amused herself while her hair was dressing, with eating samphire pickle impregnated with copper. She soon complained of pain in the stomach, and in five days vomiting commenced, which was incessant for two days. After this her stomach became prodigiously distended; and in nine

36. What salts of copper are there?

There are a great many salts of copper; but those most used are, sulphate of copper, acetate of copper; nitrate, muriate, and arseniate of copper; besides these, which are generally formed by art, the carbonate, the arseniate, the muriate, the phosphate, and the sulphate of copper are found in the native state.[a]

37. How may we detect copper in solution?

Solutions of copper may be known by the following properties: they are generally of a blue or green colour; they give with sulphuretted hydrogen a black precipitate. A clean plate of iron is immediately covered with metallic copper if dipped into a solution containing this metal. Potash precipitates the oxide of copper, of a rich, blue colour, which becomes black on being heated; and ammonia produces with salts of copper a deep blue solution, which consists of oxide of copper dissolved by the alkali.

38. What are the uses of copper?

The uses of this metal are too various to be enumerated. Besides its employment to make vessels for domestic and other purposes, and to sheathe the bottoms of ships, it is alloyed with zinc to make brass,[b] and with

days after eating the pickle, death relieved her from her sufferings. The best antidote in case of poisoning by copper, is the white of egg, which forms an inert compound with the oxide of copper.

[a] Verdigris is an acetate of copper. Blue verditer, much used in staining paper for hanging rooms, is a carbonate of copper combined with carbonate of lime. The beautiful grass green colour of the shops called mineral green, is precipitated in a peculiar way from sulphate of copper, by means of caustic potash. The colour known by the name of Scheele's green is an arseniate of copper.

[b] Brass is never made with pure zinc, but generally with alumina, which is a native oxide, or, rather, carbonate of zinc. Bishop Watson is of opinion that the orichalcum of the ancients was the same as our brass. Pliny says that the best mirrors were anciently made with a mixture of copper and tin; but that in his time those of silver were so common, that they were used even by the maid servants. These metallic mirrors were very much in request among the ancient nations. The Egyptian women, whenever they went to their temples, carried one of these mirrors in their left hand.

tin to form bell metal, bronze and gun metal, and when combined with sulphuric acid forms Roman vitriol.[a] Its oxides are employed in enamel painting, and in the manufacture of several colours.

39. What is the origin of iron?

Iron is plentifully and universally diffused throughout nature, pervading almost every thing, and is the chief cause of colour in earths and stones. It may be detected in plants and in animal fluids. It is found in great masses, and in various states, in the bowels of the earth in most parts of the world.[b]

40. What are the general properties of iron?

[a] In order to make Roman vitriol, plates of copper are heated red hot in an oven, by which means they become quickly covered with a crust of oxide, which separates as the plates cool; this oxide is then boiled in sulphuric acid, and when it is dissolved and the solution is become of a proper strength, the whole is poured into leaden vessels to cool and crystallize.

Oxide of copper is used by the coloured-glass-makers. It forms a beautiful bluish-green glass.

[b] Iron is found in greater abundance than any other metal. In the northern parts of the world whole mountains are formed of iron ore, and many of these ores are magnetic. Of the English ores, the common Lancashire hematite and the Cumberland iron stone produce the best iron.

In the great iron works, the ore, broken into small pieces and mixed with substances to promote its fusion, is thrown into the furnace; and baskets of charcoal or coke, in due proportion, are thrown in along with it. A part of the bottom of the furnace is filled with fuel only. This being kindled, the blast of the great bellows is directed on it, and soon raises the whole to a most intense heat; this melts the ore immediately above it, and the reduced metal drops down through the fuel and collects at the bottom. The rest sinks down, to fill up the void left by the consumed fuel and metal: this, in its turn, comes next in the way of the bellows, and is also reduced. More ore and fuel are supplied above, and the operation goes on till the melted metal at the bottom, increasing in quantity, rises almost to the aperture of the blast: it is let out by piercing a hole in the side of the furnace, and then forms what are called *pigs* of cast iron.

Pure iron is soft and ductile,[a] and when dissolved has a sweet and styptic taste, and emits a peculiar smell when rubbed. It is attracted by the magnet, and has the property of becoming itself magnetic. It may be fused by a very intense heat little inferior to that required to fuse platina.

41. Is iron always used in the state in which it is procured from the ore?

No; iron is employed in three states; viz. that of *cast* iron,[b] *wrought* iron,[c] and *steel;* each of which is of a different quality, and used for different purposes.

42. What constitutes the difference in these three kinds of iron?

Cast iron is the metal in its first state, rendered fusible

---

[a] An iron wire, only one-tenth of an inch in diameter, will carry 450 pounds without breaking. A wire of tempered steel of the same size will carry near 900 pounds.—BLACK.

Iron is of a livid bluish colour, very hard, and the most elastic of all the metals. Its specific gravity varies from 7.6 to 7.8.

Iron becomes soft by heat, and has the capability of being welded to another piece of iron, both being sufficiently heated, so as to form one entire mass. No other metal possesses this singular property, except platina. Notwithstanding this, pure iron is nearly infusible. In order to effect the fusion of this metal, it is necessary to surround it with the fuel, and to urge the fire to the utmost degree of heat. Crude or pig iron is fused readily: hence, it may be cast into any form, and is employed in the fabrication of a vast variety of machinery and utensils.

[b] To convert *cast* iron into *wrought* iron, the former is kept in a state of fusion for a considerable time, and, by repeated stirring in the furnace, the oxygen and carbon which it contains form an union, and rise from the mass in the state of carbonic acid gas. As the carbon and oxygen thus go off, the iron becomes more infusible; it gets thick or stiff in the furnace; and the workmen know by this appearance that this is the time to remove it from the fire, and to submit it to the action of the hammer, or the regular pressure of large steel rollers, by which the remaining impurities are forced out, and the metal is rendered malleable, ductile, and totally infusible. In this state it is known in commerce by the name of bar iron. A considerable loss in weight, however, is sustained by this process; not only from the impurities, but from the surface of the iron oxidizing and falling off in scales while hammering.

[c] In purchasing wrought iron, the workmen distinguish two kinds

by the combination of carbon and oxygen.[a] *Wrought* iron differs from the former, in being deprived of this carbon and oxygen, by continued heat and repeated hammering, which render the metal malleable. *Steel* is made of wrought iron, by various processes, whereby the metal resumes a small portion of carbon, and acquires a capacity to receive different degrees of hardness.[b]

which are both of very inferior value. They are called *hot-short* and *cold-short* iron. The former is a fusible metal, which possesses ductility when *cold*, but is so brittle when *heated*, that it will not bear the stroke of the hammer. The cause of this variety is not known. The latter kind is very malleable and ductile while hot, but the utensils made with it are as brittle as cast iron when cold. Such iron contains a portion of *phosphuret of iron*, which Bergman believed to be a new metal, and called it *siderite*.

[a] Cast iron, which breaks of a *white* colour, should be refused, as it contains a portion of phosphuret of iron.

[b] Steel, like cast iron, contains carbon; but it is divested of oxygen, which is always combined with the latter.

If a slender rod of wrought iron be plunged into cast iron in fusion, it will absorb part of the carbon, and become steel. What is called *case-hardening* is a conversion of the surface of iron into steel.

M. Morveau exposed a diamond to intense heat, shut up in a small cavity in a piece of tough iron. When he opened the cavity he found the diamond entirely gone, and the iron around it converted into steel.—Annales de Chimie, tom. xxxi. 328. This is one proof that the diamond is carbon, and shows that it is *pure* carbon, which combines with iron to form steel. The peculiar hardness of steel is to be ascribed to its union with a proportion of pure carbon or *diamond*.

A steel instrument may be known from one of iron thus:—If a drop of nitric acid be let fall upon it, it will occasion a black spot if it be steel, but will not have this effect if it be wrought iron. The blackness is owing to the acid oxidizing the carbon of the steel, and converting it into charcoal.

Cast steel is manufactured in some parts of this kingdom with great secrecy; but it is now known that it may be made merely by fusing iron in an intense heat with carbonate of lime. Cast steel contains more carbon, and is more fusible than common steel.

As different tempers are given to all kinds of edge-tools, by the different degrees of heat to which they are submitted, what is now a very precarious operation, might be reduced to a certainty by means of a metallic bath of fusible metals, containing a thermometer, to show the degrees of temperature. A mixture of bismuth, lead, and tin will afford a compound that will continue fusible with the heat of boiling water.

43. What are the effects of oxygen and chlorine upon iron ?

Iron has such an affinity for oxygen, that it will become oxidized merely by exposure to the air. The oxides of iron are found in great abundance ready formed in the earth. This metal forms with oxygen two oxides, the protoxide, which is the base of the green salts of iron, and the peroxide, which forms the bases of the red salts of iron; the black oxide is supposed to be a compound of these two oxides. Chlorine forms with iron also two salts, the protochloride and the perchloride of iron; the first of these is procured by the action of muriatic acid upon iron.

44. What salts of iron are there ?

The most useful salts of iron are those composed with the sulphuric,[a] the nitric, the muriatic, and acetic acids; and these with some others are very essential to our manufactures. The arseniate, sulphate, phosphate, chromate, and tungstate of iron have all been found native.[b]

---

[a] The sulphate is prepared in commerce by decomposing the bi-sulphuret of iron or martial pyrites, which is found native in great abundance. The sulphuret of iron in this mineral is converted into *sulphate* of iron at the great copperas works, by exposing the pyrites to the air and rain, for several months, in large beds prepared for the purpose. The sulphur decomposes the water which falls upon the beds, and is itself converted thereby into sulphuric acid, which combining with the oxide of iron forms the salt in question. This is afterwards extracted from the mass by lixiviation and crystallization, and is extensively used in dyeing black.

[b] The native arseniate of iron is found in Cornwall; native sulphate of iron occurs frequently with pyrites; *phosphate of iron* ready formed is seen frequently in bogs,—it is called native Prussian blue; chromate of iron has been found in France and in Siberia; and tungstate of iron exists native in a mineral, found in Britain and elsewhere, called wolfram. The sparry iron ore is a carbonate of iron.

Carbonate of iron is commonly found in solution in chalybeate waters: such waters may be known by the dark, orange-coloured film which generally appears upon their surface: the oxide of iron is rendered soluble by an excess of carbonic acid. This may be shown by adding a few grains of quick-lime to a small quantity of such water;

45. What are the uses of iron?

The uses of iron are innumerable; every thing we possess is manufactured by its means; it is the most useful of all known substances.[a] When converted into steel, it is employed in various ways,[b] especially for edge-tools; which are all formed in part with this metal, from the ponderous pit-saw to the finest lancet.[c] Its oxides are used in painting, enamelling, dyeing, and in medicine.

46. How may we detect iron in solution?

the lime will combine with the carbonic acid, and the oxide of iron will be precipitated.

Besides the above, *carburet* of iron (usually called *black lead*) is found in several parts of the world. A combination of iron and silex also occurs native, and forms what is called *emery ;* a substance very useful in the arts; and of which large quantities are found in the island of Jersey. It is employed by lapidaries, and by glass-cutters to cut glass and to stopper bottles for chemical and other purposes.

Some of the ores of iron are used in their native state; such as the hæmatite, which is made into burnishers, &c.

[a] The property of *welding*, which, except platina, no other metal possesses, renders iron the most suitable of all others for every common purpose. It becomes soft by heat, and thus may be moulded by the hammer into any form, and united in as many parts as the workman pleases, without rivets or without solder.

Were it not for this peculiar quality of iron, many works of the utmost importance could never have been executed. The stupendous fabrics, the Chinese *bridge of chains*, hung over a dreadful precipice in the neighbourhood of Kingtung, to connect two high mountains, and at Menai in Wales, are formed by means of *welded* iron. The chains of the former are twenty-one in number, stretched over the valley, and bound together by other cross chains, so as to form a perfect road from the summit of one immense mountain to that of the other.

Fourcroy says, iron is the only metal which is not noxious, and whose effects are not to be feared. Indeed its effects on the animal economy are evidently beneficial.

[b] Good steel is much more ductile than iron; hence very minute instruments are generally made with it. A finer wire may be drawn from it, than from any other metal.

[c] The excellence of edge-tools depends upon the temper given to them by heat. This requires great skill and peculiar management. The reader will find a full and detailed account of the manufactures in iron and in steel in Lardner's Cabinet Cyclopedia.

K

The salts of iron may be recognized by the following properties : they are generally when fresh prepared of a green colour, (those salts containing the protoxide of iron,) and give with potash a greenish white precipitate, which by exposure to air becomes red ; with alkaline carbonates they give a dark green precipitate ; they also precipitate gold, silver, and platina, from their solutions. The salts of the peroxide of iron give with ferro-prussiate of potash deep blue precipitates, with tincture of galls, dark purple or black precipitates, and with the hydrosulphurets of the alkalies black precipitates.[a]

47. Where is tin procured ?[b]

Tin is found in Germany, in Saxony, in South America, and in the East Indies; but in England it is chiefly procured from Cornwall, and Devonshire.[c] Tin occurs

---

[a] Sulphate of iron is not only used by hatters and dyers, but also in making ink, in the manufacture of Prussian blue, in preparing leather, and in forming colcothar for painters. Colcothar is nothing more than sulphate of iron calcined to redness. It not only makes an useful pigment, but is employed in polishing different kinds of metals. It is from the iron which it contains that a piece of an old hat is useful for the same purpose. The oxide of iron imparts its colour to a great variety of natural substances. It is the cause of the redness of common bricks; it gives colour to the carnelian, the oriental ruby, the garnet and other precious stones. With different proportions of oxygen it imparts other and different colours. Thus it gives the blue to the lapis lazuli, the yellow to the topaz, &c.

[b] Tin must have been known very early, as it is mentioned in the books of Moses. The edge-tools of the ancients, and their coins, were made with mixtures of copper and this metal.

[c] According to Aristotle, the tin mines of Cornwall were known and worked in his time. Diodorus Siculus, who wrote about forty years before Christ, gives an account of the method of working these mines : he says that their produce was conveyed to Gaul, and from thence to different parts of Italy. The miners of Cornwall were so celebrated for their knowledge of working metals, that about the middle of the seventeenth century the renowned Becher, a physician of Spire, and tutor of Stahl, came to this country on purpose to visit them ; and it is reported of him that, when he had seen them, he exclaimed, that " he who was a *teacher* at home, was a *learner* when he came here."

only in the primitive mountains. Its ores are found most frequently in granite. Above 3,000 tons weight of tin are furnished annually in Cornwall, which has been celebrated for its tin mines from the earliest times.

48. What is the nature of tin?

Tin is a white metal, of little elasticity, and but little taste. It is one of the lightest of the metals, and so exceedingly soft and ductile that it may be beaten out into leaves thinner than paper. Its specific gravity is 7.9, and it fuses at the temperature of 442° of Fahrenheit.

49. What is the effect of oxygen upon tin?

Tin unites in different proportions with oxygen, and forms three distinct compounds, the protoxide, sesquioxide, and peroxide of tin.[a]

50. What salts of tin are there?

The chloride, the nitro-muriate, and the sulphate of tin are most known; but many other salts may be formed with this metal. None of the salts of tin have been found native.

51. What are the uses of tin?

Tin is consumed in large quantities by the dyers; it is used also for covering sheet iron to prevent its rusting, and in forming plumbers' solder, speculum metal, pewter, and some other alloys. Its oxides are used in polishing

---

[a] A *yellow* oxide of tin may be procured by dissolving granulated tin in very dilute nitric acid, and precipitating it from the solution by an alkali: by pouring very strong nitric acid on granulated tin, a *white* oxide may be prepared, which precipitates in a pulverulent form, and is to be washed and dried for use.

The yellow oxide of tin found in commerce is called putty; but what is sold generally contains also oxide of lead. It is employed in polishing fine steel goods, and the best kinds of ornamental glass.

Oxide of tin is used to form the opake kind of glass called enamel. This composition is made by calcining 100 parts of lead and 30 parts of tin in a furnace, and then fluxing these oxides with 100 parts of sand, and 20 of potash. To this enamel every kind of colour may be given by metallic oxides.

glass, in glazing some kinds of earthenware, and for various other purposes.[a]

52. What is the use of tin to the dyers?

Tin is employed by the dyers to give a brightness to cochineal, archil, and other articles used in forming reds and scarlets; and to precipitate the colouring matter of other dyes.[b] For these purposes it is previously dissolved in *aqua-regia*.

[a] The consumption of tin for covering thin rolled iron, and forming what are improperly called sheets of tin, is very considerable: besides this, tin is used for coating the inside of iron and copper utensils, brass and iron pins, &c.

The use of tin was known to the Grecians. Homer mentions it in the Iliad. Pliny says, the Romans learnt the method of tinning their culinary vessels from the Gauls. They used tin also to alloy copper for making those elastic plates which they employed in shooting darts from their warlike machines.

Tin is employed to form bell-metal, bronze, brass for cannon, and a variety of other compounds. The addition of tin renders copper more fluid, and disposes it to assume all the impressions of the mould. With this view it was probably used by the ancient Romans in their coinage. Many of the imperial *large brass*, as they are called, are found to consist of copper and tin alone. Coins also frequently occur which are undoubtedly antique, that contain a very large proportion of tin made by the forgers, in the different reigns, in imitation of the silver currency. There are coins of Nero of a most debased and brittle bronze.

A combination of tin with sulphur forms *aurum musivum* (mosaic gold,) an article used by artists to give a beautiful colour to bronze. I suspect that the change produced in tin by this process gave rise to the idea of the transmutation of metals. If the alchemists were acquainted with this compound substance, no wonder that they should indulge the hope of being able to form gold. An experimentalist without theory is the dupe of every illusion.

[b] Several of the colouring substances which produced to the ancients only faint and fleeting colours, give us such as are brilliant and durable by the use of this metallic solution. A considerable degree of nicety and judgment is however requisite for its preparation. The difficulty is in a great measure owing to the nature of the acid that is used; as those makers of aquafortis who know but little of chemical affinities, or of the nature and operation of this invaluable mordant, often furnish the dyers with an article which is unfit for their use. Few arts have received such improvements from chemistry as the art of dying; for even cochineal gave but a dull kind of *crimson* till a chemist of the name of Kuster, who settled at

53. How may we recognize tin in solution?

Tin may, when recently dissolved in muriatic acid, be recognized by its property of giving with an alkaline, hydro-sulphuret, a black precipitate of the proto-sulphuret of tin, and precipitating the powder known by the name of the purple of Cassius from a solution of gold: it also changes the colour of a solution of platina to red.

54. What are the general properties of lead?

Lead is a heavy metal of the specific gravity of 11.35, of a pale, livid, white colour; slightly sonorous; has scarcely any taste; and emits a peculiar smell on friction. It has little elasticity, and yields readily to the hammer, being the softest of all metals. It generally contains a small portion of silver, and sometimes of mercury.[a]

Bow, near London, about the middle of the sixteenth century, discovered the use of tin in dying, and the mode of preparing by means of it and cochineal a brilliant and durable scarlet.

[a] Lead may be mixed with gold and silver in a moderate heat, but when the heat is much increased the lead rises to the surface combined with all heterogeneous matters. The art of refining the precious metals is built upon this property of lead.

Lead when dissolved in acids, has the property of imparting a saccharine taste to substances with which it may be mixed. The ancients knew that this metal rendered harsh wine milder, but they did not suppose that it was poisonous. According to Pliny, the Greeks and Romans proved the quality of their wines by dipping a plate of lead in them. Lead will not only correct the acidity of wines, but it will also take off the rancidity of oils. With this intention, I have been informed, it is often used to make inferior olive oil pass for good.

Vats of lead have been used in some cyder countries, which have produced incalculable mischief. What is called the Devonshire colic is occasioned by this practice, and is identified, by its effects on the system, with the colic of the plumbers, the painters, and the white-lead-makers.

"Lead, in its metallic state, like all the other metals, is probably inert: but it is so easily acted upon by the weakest acids and alkalies, that it cannot be taken even in this form without the most imminent danger."

Sir George Baker has carefully investigated the effects of lead on the animal œconomy, and in the 1st vol. of the Medical Transactions has fully described the *peculiar kind* of colic produced by it.

55. Where is lead procured ?

Lead ore is very abundant in Scotland and Ireland, and in the western parts of Northumberland and Durham ; it is also procured in large quantities in Spain.[a]

56. What combinations does lead form with oxygen ?

Lead combines with oxygen to form four distinct compounds : the first oxide of lead, which contains the smallest proportion of oxygen, is formed by decomposing dry oxalate of lead in a glass tube ; the second oxide, is formed when we melt lead in contact with air, the gray film which forms on its surface being a combination of lead and oxygen, and when fused forming the litharge and massicot of commerce ; the third oxide is the minium or red lead of commerce, and the peroxide or puce coloured oxide is formed by heating nitric acid on minium, by the action of which the red oxide is turned into the peroxide of lead.[b]

[a] Lead ore is generally found in veins, both in siliceous and calcareous rocks. Galena, or sulphuret of lead, is very common both in masses and crystallized. Lead is also found combined with silver, antimony, sulphur, and bismuth. Oxides of lead combined with various earths also occur in mining countries. Lead ochre is a native oxide of lead.

Lead was in common use among the ancients. The Romans sheathed the bottoms of their ships with this metal, fastened by nails made of bronze. During the first century, lead at Rome was twenty-four times as dear as it is now in Europe ; whereas tin was only eight times its present price.

Lead in the state of ceruse, was in great request among the Roman ladies as a cosmetic. Plautus introduces a waiting-woman refusing to give her mistress either ceruse or rouge, because, forsooth, in the true spirit of a flattering Abigail, she thought her quite handsome enough without them.—BISHOP WATSON.

The lead ores which are found in the primitive slate mountains contain much silver, sometimes 8 or 9 per cent.

[b] All the oxides of lead may be reduced to metallic lead by heating them with a mixture of tallow and charcoal, or any substance that will decompose the oxide. This may readily be shown by placing a few grains of red lead upon a piece of charcoal, and fusing it with a blow-pipe. Even the oxide of lead which is combined with flint-glass may be reduced by melting the glass with any carbonaceous substance.

57. What salts of lead are there?

The salts of lead are very numerous, but the chloride, sulphate, carbonate, acetate, and chromate of lead are those most known. The carbonate, sulphate, phosphate, molybdate, arseniate, and chromate of lead are native productions.

58. What are the uses of lead?

Lead is employed to cover buildings, to form water-pipes, to make a great variety of vessels for economical and chemical purposes ;[a] and in refining gold and silver.[b] Its oxides are used in dying and calico-printing ; in the manufacture of glass, earthenware, and porcelain ; and in the preparation of various pigments.

59. How can we discover the presence of lead in a solution?

Fourcroy says that all the oxides of lead have the property of absorbing carbonic acid from the atmosphere, and that if an oxide of lead be required in a state of purity, it ought to be defended from the access of air.

[a] Sheet lead is made by suffering the melted metal to run out of a box through a long horizontal slit upon a table prepared for the purpose, while the box is drawn by appropriate ropes and pulleys along the table, leaving the melted lead behind it in the desired form to congeal.

An alloy of this metal with tin forms pewter, and in different proportions soft solder. It enters likewise into the composition of other useful alloys, especially one that is employed in the manufacture of white metal buttons ; for it has lately been discovered that a certain proportion of lead may be mixed with the metal formerly used, without injuring the appearance of the button : thus affording a very considerable profit to the manufacturer. There is also a large consumption of lead in making shot.

[b] Litharge of lead is often used in the analysis of the ores of what are called the *perfect* metals. It has the property of combining with all the other metallic oxides, and of forming with these fusible compound which are absorbed by the earthy support during the cupellation; while it separates them from those metals which do not become oxidized by heat only.

Lead is used in the finer kind of glass, in order to make it bear sudden changes of heat and cold better, also to give it a proper degree of weight, a susceptibility of its being cut without breaking, a greater power of refracting the rays of light, and a capacity to bear a higher polish.

The best test for the presence of lead in solution is sulphuretted hydrogen, which precipitates it in the form of a black sulphuret; the minutest portion of lead may be detected in a solution by passing a stream of sulphuretted hydrogen through it, or applying to it a solution of this gas in water. Sulphuric acid may also be applied as a test; it precipitates the lead in the form of sulphate of lead of a white colour. Hydriodate of potash and bichromate of potash, when applied to solutions of salts of lead give precipitates of a bright yellow colour.

60. What are the properties of nickel?

Nickel is a metal of a white colour, ductile and malleable, but of difficult fusion. It is attracted by the magnet, and capable of being converted into a magnet. Its specific gravity when pure is about 9.[a]

61. Where, and in what state, is nickel found?

The ore of nickel is very similar to that of copper, and is procured from various parts of Germany; it is also found with cobalt; but the nickel of commerce is always impure.[b]

62. What compounds does nickel form with oxygen?

Nickel combines with two proportions of oxygen to

[a] As common nickel generally contains iron, the iron disguises its properties, and prevents its nature being exactly known. This metal dissolves readily in several of the acids, and communicates to them a green colour; but sulphuric acid acts very slowly upon it, even with the assistance of heat. Nitric acid dissolves it more readily.

[b] The most abundant ore of this metal is a sulphuret of nickel, called *kupfernickel*, which is generally a compound of nickel, arsenic, and sulphuret of iron.

It is a curious circumstance, that all the specimens that have been examined of the stones which are known to have fallen from the atmosphere contain iron alloyed with nickel. These stones, which have at different periods been seen to fall on every quarter of the earth, are supposed by many to be cast from a volcano in the moon. In the year 1803 a shower of them fell in Normandy, which covered an extent of three quarters of a league long, and half a league broad. Several dissertations on this curious subject may be seen in the latter volumes of the Philosophical Magazine; Nicholson's Journal; and other periodical and scientific works.

form a protoxide and a peroxide. The former is of a dusky gray colour, the latter of a black colour. The protoxide forms green salts with the acids and is precipitated from its solutions of a light green colour by the alkalies.

63. What salts of nickel are there?

Numerous salts have been formed with nickel, but none of them have hitherto been brought into any use. A native arseniuret of this metal has been found.

64. What are the uses of nickel?

Nickel is employed by the Chinese in making their *white* copper, which is a beautiful metallic compound; it is also much used at present for the manufacture of German silver, which is an alloy of this metal with copper; its oxide is also employed in the manufacture of porcelain to give a light green colour.

65. What is the nature of zinc?.

Zinc is a very combustible metal, possessing but a small degree of malleability and ductility, except under certain circumstances.[a] When broken, it appears of a shining blueish white; and when exposed to the air, it becomes covered with a pellicle, in consequence of its affinity for oxygen; its specific gravity is about 6.8.

66. How is zinc procured?

Zinc, generally called by the artists *spelter*, is not found native;[b] but in England and elsewhere, is

[a] At the ordinary temperature of the air zinc is neither malleable nor ductile, but if it be heated to a temperature between 200 and 300 of Fahrenheit it may then be rolled into very thin sheets and drawn into wire. Zinc is at present much used in the state of sheets for roofing houses, &c. instead of lead, and also for domestic utensils, for which it is well adapted on account of its lower specific gravity and its salts not being poisonous.

[b] Some mineralogists consider zinc to be the most abundant metal in nature, excepting iron. Calamine, or lapis calaminaris, is found both in masses and in a crystallized state, and is generally combined with a large portion of silex. Calamine is a *native oxide* of zinc, combined with carbonic acid. Zinc is found also in an ore called *blend*. In this state it is combined with sulphur. Workmen call it

extracted from calamine and other ores, by distillation.[a]

67. What is the effect of oxygen upon zinc?

Zinc is readily oxidized when it is heated; at a high temperature, when exposed to the air, zinc takes fire and burns with a brilliant bluish white flame, and forms a white oxide which has been named flowers of zinc; it may also be oxidized by acids.

68. What salts of zinc are there?

A great number of salts[b] have been formed with this metal; but the carbonate, the sulphate, and the acetate of zinc[c] are most known; the two first are found in a native state.

Black Jack—a mineral employed till lately in Wales for mending the roads.

In China there is a great abundance of zinc:—it is used in that country for current coin, and for that purpose is employed in the utmost purity. These coins have frequently Tartar characters on one side and Chinese characters on the other. They have generally a square hole in the centre, that they may be carried on strings and more readily counted.

[a] Metallic zinc is procured from calamine by distillation *per descensum*. The calamine is pounded, and with powdered charcoal put into large pots, which are placed in a furnace like a common oven. These pots have tubes fixed in their bottoms, which pass through the bottom of the furnace into a vessel of water. After the tops of the pots are covered, and rammed close with clay a strong fire is made around them, so that the metallic zinc, being separated from the ore, and being of a volatile nature, is forced to rise to the upper entrance of the tubes, and thence passes downwards into the water.

[b] Zinc has so great an affinity for oxygen, and its salts are so permanent, that none of the metals, except manganese, will precipitate it from its solutions in a metallic form.

[c] Sulphate of zinc, formerly called *white vitriol*, is usually formed in Germany from an ore called *blende*, which is a sulphuret of zinc. By the agency of fire and the access of atmospheric air, the sulphur is converted into sulphuric acid, and by means of proper evaporation and cooling, the salt is obtained in a crystallized mass. The white vitriol of commerce ought never be administered in medicine without previous purification; for it frequently contains copper as well as iron. Sulphate of zinc occurs in some mineral waters.

69. What are the uses of zinc?

Zinc, when combined with copper or tin, in various proportions, constitutes some of the most useful compound metals or alloys; it is also used in medicine; it is the base of white vitriol.[a]

70. What are the principal alloys of zinc and copper?

Three parts of copper and one of zinc constitute *brass;* five or six of copper and one of zinc form *pinchbeck. Tombac* has still more copper, and is of a deeper red than pinchbeck. *Prince's metal* is a similar compound, excepting that it contains more zinc than either of the former. A mixture of tin and copper with zinc forms *bronze.* To make *brass,* the calamine is previously roasted; it is then mixed with charcoal and grain copper, and put into large crucibles, which are kept for a considerable time in a heat that will not melt the copper; after a time, the heat is raised so as to fuse it, and the compound metal is then run into ingots. Brass is a valuable alloy on many accounts, especially the superior brightness of its colour, in its not being so liable to tarnish by exposure to the air as copper, and in its being more readily melted, and more malleable when cold. Sieves of extreme fineness are made with brass wire, after the manner of cambrick weaving, which could not possibly be made with copper wire.

71. How may we detect zinc in solution?

By its affording with an alkali a white precipitate which

Acetate of zinc has been recommended by Dr. Henry to be applied in cases of inflammation. This salt is easily formed by dissolving oxide of zinc in acetic acid.

[a] Zinc, in fine filings, is used to mix with gunpowder, to produce those brilliant stars and spangles which are seen in the best artificial fire-works.

Zinc is generally one of the metals employed to form Galvanic batteries.

An amalgam of zinc is used to rub upon the cushions of electrical machines. It is very conveniently amalgamated, by melting it in a bowl of a tobacco-pipe, and pouring it while hot into the mercury.

is soluble in an excess of the alkali; with hydrosulphuret of ammonia and the fixed alkaline carbonates permanent white precipitates.

72. What are the general properties of cadmium?

Cadmium is a metal of a white colour resembling tin very malleable and ductile; it melts at about the temperature of 400° of Fahrenheit, and is very volatile; it becomes tarnished by exposure to air in consequence of absorbing oxygen, and is very soluble in nitric acid, from which it may be precipitated as oxide of cadmium of a white colour which dissolves readily in ammonia.

73. How is cadmium obtained?

Cadmium was found by Stromeyer in oxide of zinc, and it generally accompanies that metal. It is procured from the chimneys of manufactories where zinc is melted in considerable quantity, where it has collected during the preparation of that metal.

74. What compounds does this metal form with oxygen and chlorine?

It forms with oxygen a white oxide and with chlorine a compound soluble in water and volatile at a high temperature.

75. How do we discover cadmium in solution?

Cadmium may be detected in solution by the following properties: it is precipitated from its solution as a white powder by ammonia, in excess of which it is redissolved, but when precipitated by soda or potash it is not redissolved by excess of either; by sulphuretted hydrogen it is precipitated as a bright yellow sulphuret, which is neither volatile nor soluble in solution of potash.

76. What are the properties of antimony?

Antimony is a brilliant, brittle metal; of a. white colour, and is destitute of ductility and malleability, having the specific gravity of 6.8.

77. How is antimony procured?

Antimony is procured from an ore which is found chiefly in Hungary and Norway, and which consists of

sulphur united to this metal; it may be obtained in a pure
state by heating together in a crucible the sulphuret with
iron filings, or with a mixture of nitre and bitartrate of
potash. By either of these processes the sulphur is separated from the antimony and the metal left in the pure
state.

Native antimony, alloyed with a small portion of silver
and iron, has been found in Sweden.[a]

78. What are the effects of oxygen upon this metal?

Antimony is susceptible of three degrees of oxidation; the first is the sesquioxide of antimony, which
contains 125 parts of antimony to 24 of oxygen, the
second containing 125 of antimony to 32 of oxygen,
and the third containing 125 of antimony to 40 oxygen;
the two latter seem to have the properties of acids.

79. What salts of antimony are there?

Many different salts have been formed with the oxides
of this metal; but those most known are the chloride of
antimony, and the tartrate of potash and antimony, or
emetic tartar. The first has been found native.[b]

80. How may the chloride of antimony be procured?

If antimony be ground fine, and thrown into a dry
glass jar filled with chlorine gas, it will inflame immediately, and continue to burn with great rapidity and
with a brilliant white flame, forming the chloride of antimony, or what was formerly known by the name of the

---

[a] There are several ores of antimony, but the gray is the only one
which is found in sufficient quantity for the manufacturer; it is a
sulphuret of antimony. This ore is purified by exposure to a strong
heat in a reverberatory furnace. By this process, the pure sulphuret
runs from the earthy matter: this is afterwards remelted, and cast
into cakes for sale. This sulphuret may be divested of nearly all its
sulphur by long roasting, leaving the metal in a state of almost a
pure oxide.

[b] The well-known medicine *emetic tartar* is a tartrate of potash
and antimony, composed of about 56 parts tartrate of antimony, 36
tartrate of potash, and 8 of water. *James' powder* also consists
principally of the oxide of antimony.

butter of antimony. This substance is found native in Bohemia.

81. What are the uses of antimony?

Antimony is combined with some other metals in making printers' types, and specula for telescopes. Its oxides are employed in medicine[a] and in colouring glass. In times of remote antiquity its sulphuret was used by females as a black pigment, for staining the eye-lashes.

82. What are the properties of bismuth?[b]

Bismuth is of a yellowish white colour, of a lamellated texture, and moderately hard, but not malleable. It is so brittle that it breaks readily under the hammer, and may be reduced even to powder. Bismuth has the singular property of *expanding* as it cools; hence its use in the metallic composition for printers' types; as from this expansive property are obtained the most perfect impressions of the moulds in which the letters are cast. In manufactories this metal is known to the workmen by the name of *tin-glass*. Its specific gravity is 9.8.

83. How is bismuth procured?

Bismuth is generally found with cobalt in the cobaltic ores of Saxony and England. Native bismuth and sulphuret of bismuth are also found upon the continent; but this is not an abundant metal.

84. What are the effects of oxygen and chlorine upon bismuth?

---

[a] *Kermes mineral,* and what was called *golden sulphur* of antimony, are both made from the sulphuret of this metal, by means of potash. The first took its name from its resemblance in colour to the kermes insect, used in dyeing. The sulphuret, and some other preparations of antimony, are given to horses and cattle, more than any other medicines. They act as alteratives, and are generally to be depended upon for the certainty of their effects.

[b] If water be added to a solution of bismuth in nitric acid, the oxide will be precipitated of a pure *white* colour; but if a little tincture of galls be poured into a similar solution, a *brown* precipitate will be produced. This is the distinctive characteristic of this metal.

Bismuth is gradually oxidized by fusion in atmospheric air ; and may be thus converted into the white or protoxide ; by solution in nitric acid, and pouring the solution into water we get a white powder which is a peroxide of this metal.[a] When bismuth in fine powder is thrown into chlorine gas it takes fire and burns, forming the chloride of bismuth.

85. What salts are there of bismuth?

Several salts of bismuth have been formed, but their properties have not been much examined by chemists. The nitrate[b] and chloride of bismuth are occasionally prepared, but no salts of this metal have been found in a native state.

86. What are the uses of bismuth?

Bismuth is used with other metals to form printers' types, to make pewter,[c] and for some other compounds.

---

[a] Pearl-white is an oxide, or rather a sub-salt, of this metal. Ladies use it for painting the skin, to which it imparts a beautiful white ; but it has the inconvenience of becoming black by the contact of sulphuretted hydrogen gas, or the fumes of fetid substances. The gas which arises from the burning of a mineral coal will have the same effect. It is related of a lady of fashion, who had incautiously seated herself too near the fire at a quadrille table, that her countenance changed on a sudden from a delicate white to a dark tawny, as though by magic. The surprise and confusion of the whole party had such an effect upon the disfigured fair-one, that she was actually dying with apprehension, when the physician dispelled their fears by informing his patient that nothing more was necessary than for her to wash her face, to abstain from the use of mineral cosmetics, and to trust in future to those charms which nature had bestowed upon her.

Some of the French chemists recommend the use of the oxides of bismuth for dyeing, to fix some particular colours. Pomatum prepared with the oxide of bismuth turns the hair black.

[b] Nitrate of bismuth does not dissolve in water like other metallic salts, but becomes decomposed, forming one of the most delicate white precipitates : hence, this metal is readily distinguished from most others. This precipitate, washed and dried, is what has been called *magistery* of bismuth, or pearl-white.

[c] The common mixture for pewter is 112 pounds of tin, 15 pounds of lead, and 6 pounds of brass ; but many manufacturers use also bismuth and antimony to compose this metal. Bismuth is likewise

It remarkably contributes to the fusibility of some alloys; hence, it is employed to make solder.[a] Bismuth is also given in medicine, though very rarely.

87. What are the general characters of arsenic?

Arsenic is generally found in combination with sulphur, oxygen, or metals. When reduced to its pure metallic state, it is a friable, brilliant metal, of a blueish white colour, easily tarnishing, that is, oxidizing, by exposure to the air. It may be recognized by its being volatilized by a moderate heat, and its fumes having the smell of garlic. Its sp. gr. is 8·310. In all its states of combination it is highly poisonous.

88. Where is arsenic found?

Arsenic is found in Bohemia, Hungary, Saxony, and other places on the continent.[b] It is united with, and contaminates, many of our metallic ores in England.

89. What are the effects of oxygen and chlorine upon arsenic?

generally mixed with tin for vessels of capacity, &c. as it gives to that metal a greater degree of brilliancy and hardness. From its property of rendering lead more fusible, it is too often employed with that metal to adulterate quicksilver.

[a] If eight parts of bismuth, five of lead, and three of tin, be melted together, the mixed metal will fuse at a heat no greater than 212°. Tea-spoons made with this alloy are sold in London, to surprise those who are unacquainted with their nature. They have the appearance of common tea-spoons, but melt as soon as they are put into hot tea. A composition of lead, zinc, and bismuth, in equal parts, will melt with so small a portion of caloric, that it may be kept in fusion upon paper over a lamp.

[b] The arsenic of commerce is prepared in Saxony in the operation of roasting the cobalt ores for the manufacture of zaffre. The reverberatory furnace in which the ores are roasted terminates in a long horizontal chimney; and in this chimney the arsenical vapours are condensed, forming a crust, which at stated times is cleared off by criminals, who are condemned to this work for crimes for which they would otherwise have suffered death. Pure arsenic is prepared by mixing the common orpiment with potash, and submitting it to sublimation. By this process the arsenic is separated, and sublimed, leaving its sulphur behind, united to the potash.

Arsenic has a great affinity for oxygen, with which it combines in two proportions to form arsenious and arsenic acids. The former consists of 75.4 parts of arsenic and 24 of oxygen; the latter of 75.4 parts of arsenic and 40 of oxygen. 'The arsenious acid, or white arsenic of commerce, is a permanent solid compound, and may be formed by burning arsenic in atmospheric air or oxygen gas; the arsenic acid is formed by heating the arsenious acid with nitric acid, which imparts its oxygen to it, and converts it into arsenic acid, which is a very deliquescent substance. Chlorine also readily combines with this metal, and forms the *butter* of arsenic, or chloride of arsenic.

90. What are the salts formed with arsenic ?

The arsenious and arsenic acids both form salts with metallic oxides. The former with bases forming the class of salts named arsenites, the latter the arseniates.[a]

91. Does arsenic combine with sulphur ?

Yes; arsenic combines in two proportions with sulphur, and forms orpiment and realgar, which are both sulphurets of arsenic. Realgar is a dark orange or scarlet, the other a beautiful lemon colour. They are both much used in dyeing and calico printing ; and have been found native. Orpiment, or bisulphuret of arsenic, may be readily formed by passing a stream of sulphuretted hydrogen through arsenite of potash ; the solution, however, must be neutralized with an acid, as orpiment is soluble in the alkalies.

92. How may we discover the presence of arsenic in any compound?

Arsenic may at once be recognized by the following properties :—if, in the *metallic* state it be exposed to a moderate heat, it sublimes with a smell of garlic ; if it be strongly heated in contact with oxygen gas, it takes fire

[a] Though there are no native salts in which arsenic forms the base, yet we are acquainted with several in which it is combined as an acid ; such are the arseniates of lime, copper, iron, cobalt, &c.

and burns, and is converted into white arsenic or arsenious acid: from the state of arsenious acid, or sulphuret of arsenic it may be readily changed into the metallic state by exposure to a strong heat in contact with charcoal and an alkali. If it exists in solution, as an alkaline arsenite, it will be precipitated by a solution of copper, as a green arsenite of copper, (Scheele's green,) and by oxide of silver in solution as a yellow arsenite of silver, and by sulphuretted hydrogen as the yellow sulphuret.

93. How can we distinguish the arsenites from the arseniates?

The arsenites give with salts of copper green precipitates; the arseniates produce with salts of copper blue precipitates; with salts of silver yellow precipitates are given by the arsenites and by the arseniates brick-red precipitates.

94. What are the uses of arsenic?

Arsenic, in its metallic state, is used to whiten copper, and it enters into the composition of several compounds for metallic specula, and is also used to give hardness to lead in the manufacture of shot.[a] Its acids are employed in many processes of the dyer; and also as fluxes for glass, and in several of the arts. The sulphurets of arsenic form valuable pigments of different colours.

[a] In melting the lead a small quantity of arsenic is added, which disposes it to run into spherical drops. When melted, it is poured into a cylinder whose circumference is pierced with holes. The lead streaming through the holes, soon divides into drops, which fall into water, where they congeal. They are not all spherical; therefore, those that are must be separated, which is done by an ingenious contrivance. The whole is sifted on the upper end of a long, smooth, inclined plane, and the grains roll down to the lower end. But the pear-like shape of the bad grains makes them roll down irregularly, and roll off from the sides of the plane; while the round ones run straight down, and are afterwards sorted into sizes by sieves. The manufacturers of the patent shot have fixed their furnace, for melting the metal, at the top of a tower 100 feet high, and procure a much greater number of spherical grains, by letting the melted lead fall into water from this height, as the shot is gradually cooled before it reaches the water.

95. What are the properties of cobalt?

Cobalt is a whitish-grey, brittle metal, nearly resembling fine hardened steel. It is difficult of fusion and oxidation, and is magnetic. Its sp. gr. is 7·8.

96. How is cobalt procured?

Formerly all our cobalt came from Saxony; but it is now found abundantly in the Mendip hills in Somersetshire, and in a mine near Penzance in Cornwall.

97. What is the effect of oxygen on this metal?

Cobalt may be oxidized by an intense heat. The oxygen converts it into that beautiful blue colour which is seen on earthenware and porcelain.[a] There are at least three different oxides of cobalt,[b] the protoxide, dentoxide, and peroxide, which are known to chemists.

98. What salts are there of cobalt?

A great variety of salts have been formed with the oxides of this metal; but the muriate of cobalt is that which has, perhaps, been longest known. A solution of this salt much diluted, has been long used in forming Hellot's sympathetic ink. Whatever is written on paper with this ink remains invisible, while it is cold; but if the paper be gently warmed, the letters will appear of a beautiful blue colour:—thus, by warming or cooling the paper, the writing may be made to appear and disappear at pleasure. It is, however, from some iron or nickel generally found in cobalt that the muriate forms a green ink; for, if it be perfectly pure, it is always blue. The muriate of cobalt in the dry state is blue but its solution

[a] The oxide of cobalt forms the most permanent blue colour that we are acquainted with. La Grange says that the old painters used this oxide mixed with oil in their paintings; which is the reason why the sky and drapery in some old pictures are of so durable a blue.

[b] Zaffre, which we have long imported from Saxony, is an oxide of cobalt, mixed with three times its weight of ground silex. There are the black, the brown, and the yellow cobalt ores, all which are oxides of this metal. The white cobalt ore is a sulphuret of cobalt.

is of a light pink colour. An arseniate and a sulphate of cobalt have been found native.

99. What is the use of cobalt?

Cobalt has hitherto been chiefly used for making the different kinds of smalts for painting and enamelling.[a] It is extremely valuable to the manufacturers of porcelain, as it not only produces a beautiful colour, but endures the intense heat of their furnaces without any deterioration. It is also used for staining glass of a blue colour, but its principal use is in the porcelain manufacture.[b]

100. What is the nature of manganese?

Manganese is a brilliant metal, of a dark grey colour, of considerable hardness, and one of the most infusible of the metals. It is very brittle, and when pure it is not attracted by the magnet. Exposed to the air its surface rapidly tarnishes in consequence of its strong attraction for oxygen. It can consequently be preserved only by keeping it under naphtha or strong alcohol: its specific gravity is 8.

101. Where is manganese found?

The manganese, which we use in this country, is obtained in the state of black oxide, from the Mendip hills in Somersetshire, and at Upton-Pyne, three miles from

[a] The *strewing-smalt*, an article used by sign-painters, is made by melting the oxide of cobalt with flint-glass, and grinding the whole to a coarse powder. The same composition reduced to an impalpable powder forms the smalt, sold under the name of powder blue; which is now not only used by laundresses, but is made the basis of several pigments. It has also been much employed by paper-manufacturers to give a blue tinge to writing and printing papers.

[b] In the fifteenth century cobalt was employed to colour glass, and yet till lately but small quantities of it have been used. Formerly the miners threw it aside as useless. They considered it so troublesome when they found it among other ores, that a prayer was used in the German church that God would preserve miners from *cobalt*, and from *spirits*.—Beckmann's History of inventions, vol. ii. 363. Other ancient uses of this metal, as a colour, may be seen in the same work.

Exeter. It is also found in abundance in America, and
on various parts of the continent. Pure manganese is
never found native.

102. What are the effects of oxygen upon manganese ?

This metal will become oxidized by mere exposure to
the air ; it is supposed to form by union with oxygen
four oxides and two acids.

103. What are the properties of these oxides ?

The protoxide is a substance of a light green colour,
it forms the base of most of the salts of manganese. The
sequi-oxide of manganese is sometimes found native, and
it constitutes the principal part of the residue after the
preparation of oxygen gas from the black oxides of manganese. The peroxide is the native black oxide which is
found abundantly in nature, and which is so extensively
employed in the manufacture of bleaching salt and in
the preparations of oxygen gas.

104. What are the acids formed by union of manganese with oxygen ?

Manganese forms with oxygen the manganic and per-
manganic acids. The first of these forms with alkaline
bases the chameleon mineral, which is prepared by fusing
nitrate of potash with black oxide of manganese. The
manganese is oxidized by the nitric acid of the nitre and
converted into an acid which combines with the potash,
and forms the dark green manganate of potash.

105. What are the properties of this salt ?

When dissolved in water it forms a solution of a dark
green colour which speedily changes to blue, then to
purple, and lastly becomes red, hence the name chameleon
mineral. This property of manganese is frequently had
recourse to in an analysis to discover the presence of
manganese.

106. What salts are there of manganese ?

A variety of salts have been made with the oxides of
this metal ; and when dissolved in water may be recognised
b y giving with pure prussiate of potash white precipi-

tates, with ammonia or potash white precipitates which speedily change to brown, and with alkaline carbonates also white precipitates. A carbonate of manganese is found native in Norway and Sweden.

107. What are the uses of manganese?

The oxides of manganese are used in the preparation of bleaching salt, in glazing black earthenware, and in purifying glass. In consequence of its readily parting with oxygen at a red heat, any carbonaceous matter which may be mixed with the melted glass undergoes combustion and passes off in the form of carbonic acid, and leaves the glass colourless. Too much manganese must not, however, be employed or the glass will acquire a purple colour.[a]

108. What is the nature of tungsten?

Tungsten is a heavy metal, of a greyish-white colour, very hard and of great infusibility: its specific gravity is 17.

109. How is tungsten procured?

It exists in the native tungstate of lime, and also in the mineral called wolfram as an acid in combination in the former with the lime, and in the latter with iron and manganese. The acid may be separated from them by processes already described (chap. vii. 68); and from this the metals may be procured by passing a stream of hydrogen gas over it when heated to redness, or by heating it intensely in contact with charcoal.

---

[a] The *rubelite* and the *amethyst* owe their colours to the *red* oxide of manganese. A *violet* colour may be given to flint glass by melting it with a large portion of the *black* oxide of this metal.

There is a peculiarity attending the salts of manganese, that, when dissolved in water, the manganese cannot be precipitated from its solution, in a metallic state, by any of the other metals. The reason is, that, in respect to all other metals, manganese has a superior attraction for oxygen.

Its use in making white flint glass may be seen in Berthollet's Treatise on Dyeing, vol. i. 8. It was employed for this purpose more than two thousand years ago.

110. How is molybdenum obtained?

Molybdenum exists in nature in combination with sulphur, and also in combination with lead. From the former compound it may be obtained by digesting the sulphuret with strong nitric acid, and by this means converting it into molybdic acid, and reducing this in the manner already mentioned for obtaining tungsten.

111. How is columbium obtained?

Columbium exists in the rare minerals tantalite and yttrotantalite. It is a metal of an iron-gray colour, exceedingly infusible, and forming, by union with oxygen, an acid.

112. What are the general properties of chromium?

Chromium, in its pure state, is a brittle metal, fusible only by the most intense heat, and with little disposition to unite with oxygen. Its sp. gr. is 5·9.

113. How is chromium obtained?

Chromium exists in nature combined with lead and iron. It was discovered by Vauquelin, in a rare mineral from Siberia, which is a native bichromate of lead, and is also found abundantly combined with iron at Baltimore in North America, and in the Shetland islands.

114. What compounds does chromium form with oxygen?

Chromium forms with oxygen two compounds, the oxide of chromium and chromic acid. The former of these may be prepared by boiling the bichromate of potash with muriatic acid until the acid is reduced to the state of oxide, and then precipitating by means of an alkali; and the chromic acid may be prepared from the same salt by the addition of fluosilic acid, which precipitates the potash and leaves the chromic acid in a pure state; or by mixing fluor spar with chromate of lead and strong sulphuric acid, and applying heat; by this process we obtain a gas which, on being passed into water and the solution then evaporated to dryness, affords pure chromic acid.

115. What are the principal salts of chromic acid ?

The most important salt of chromic acid is the bichromate of potash, which is used in large quantities in the arts, and the chromate of lead, which is much used as a pigment.

116. What are the uses of chromic acid ?

Chromic acid is extensively used by calico printers in combination with potash for printing yellow and orange colours. The chromic acid is also much used in combination with lead as a yellow pigment, for which it is much preferable to orpiment, in consequence of its not having the noxious properties of this substance.

117. How is uranium obtained?

Uranium was discovered by Klaproth, in a mineral named pechblend; it also exists in different varieties of mica, to which it imparts a green colour.

118. How is titanium procured?

Titanium exists in considerable abundance in the state of an acid, combined with the oxide of iron; from this it may be procured by converting the titanic acid into chloride of titanium, and heating this strongly in contact with ammoniacal gas. It has also been discovered in the metallic state in the slags of several iron foundries. In these slags it is found in minute cubical crystals of a red colour, of extreme hardness and infusibility. Its specific gravity is 5·3. The oxide of titanium is sometimes employed for giving a brown colour to porcelain.

119. What are the properties of tellurium?

Tellurium is a brittle metal, of a grayish-white colour: it is fused at a very low temperature, and may be volatilized by an increase of heat. It is found only in the gold mines of Transylvania. Its specific gravity is 6.

120. What are the properties of palladium ?

Palladium is a metal of a white colour, resembling platina, in the ores of which it is found; when pure it is ductile and malleable; and when dissolved in the acids it gives red salts on crystallization: its specific gravity is 11·8.

121. What are the properties of rhodium ?

Rhodium was also discovered by Dr. Wollaston in the ores of platina; it is a brittle metal of a white colour, and great hardness : its specific gravity is 11. Alloyed with steel it forms a very hard compound.

122. What are the properties of osmium ?

Osmium is procured from the ores of platina. It is characterized by its peroxide being volatile, and having a sharp and pungent smell, something resembling chlorine, and when dissolved in water giving a purple solution, which changes rapidly to blue.

123. What are the properties of iridium ?

Iridium is one of the most infusible metals known. It is found to exist in the ores of platina: it is with difficulty dissolved in *aqua regia*. It may be procured by heating the chloride of iridium to redness : its specific gravity is stated to be, when fused, 18.6.

124. Endeavour to recapitulate the general properties of this class of bodies.

The metals are simple substances,[a] distinguishable from all other bodies by their lustre, by their great specific gravity, by their perfect opacity, and by their power of conducting electricity.

125. What are the obvious advantages which we derive from these bodies ?

The metals are the great agents by which we are enabled to explore the bowels of the earth, and to examine the recesses of nature ; their uses are so multiplied, that they are become of the greatest importance in every occupation of life. They are the instruments of all our improvements, of civilization itself, and are even subservient in the progress of the human mind towards perfection.

---

[a] The ancient chemists supposed the metals were compound bodies. They were probably led to this by observing the pulverulent nature of the metallic oxides. Their undecompounded nature was first suspected by Mayow.

126. You can doubtless offer some reasons why one metal possesses such opposite and specific differences from another.

This variety is not to be attributed to chance, but must certainly be the effect of consummate wisdom and contrivance. These metals differ so much from each other in their degrees of hardness, lustre, colour, elasticity, fusibility, weight, malleability, ductility, and tenacity, that Nature seems to have had in view all the necessities of man, in order that she might suit every possible purpose his ingenuity can invent, or his wants require.

127. By what means are these bodies rendered so important to us ?

We not only receive this great variety from the hand of Nature, but these metals are rendered infinitely valuable by various other properties they possess. By their combustibility,[a] their solubility in fluids, their combinations with phosphorus, sulphur, and carbon, and by their union with each other ;[b] whereby compounds or alloys are formed, extremely useful in a variety of arts, manufactures, and other requisites of life.

128. By what other means does Nature render these bodies subservient to our wants, and capable of ministering to our comfort and gratification ?

_____

[a] Some of the metals are so combustible that they will burn before they acquire a heat sufficient to fuse them. This is the case with iron and zinc. A thin shaving of zinc, as we before noticed, will burn without melting, if held in the flame of a candle. The combustion of iron in oxygen gas is an interesting and beautiful experiment.—See an account of the method of managing it in the chapter on combustion.

[b] Several of the metals have a very strong affinity for each other, as may be shown by experiment. Mercury will dissolve lead, bismuth, zinc, and other metals. If a piece of lead and a piece of bismuth, each alloyed with mercury, be melted together, they form, when cold, a solid metallic mass; but from their affinity for mercury they have acquired so much fusibility that they will melt by the heat of boiling water.

Nature has furnished us with acids, whereby the most
refractory metals may be dissolved and purified, and thus
rendered fit for a variety of purposes, to which they could
not otherwise be applied. By combining the metals with
oxygen[a] we can invest them with *new* properties, and are
enabled to employ these to promote the progress of the
fine arts, by imitating the masterpieces of creation, in the
production of artificial salts, spars, and gems, of every
colour, and of every shade.[b]

CHAPTER XII.

OXIDES.

1. What is an oxide?

Any one or more of the simple substances, when united
to a less quantity of oxygen than is necessary to form an
acid, is called an *oxide.*

2. What substances are capable of forming oxides?

The mineral, the animal, and the vegetable kingdoms,
all furnish matters which are convertible into oxides by
union with oxygen.[c]

[a] This is exemplified in a striking manner by the metal called
chromium. When acidified and combined with lead, the metallic salt
that results is of a beautiful orange yellow; whereas chromate of
mercury is of the colour of vermillion; chromate of silver, of a
carmine red; chromate of zinc and bismuth, a bright yellow.

[b] If phosphoric acid be united with silex by fusion, artificial precious stones may be prepared with the compound, which may be
coloured to imitate any particular kind, by one or other of the metallic
oxides.

[c] The oxides appear to range themselves into two classes. There
are oxides which are permanently such, so long as they retain the
oxygen which enters into their formation; and there are others which
seem to possess only a kind of intermediate state between combustibles and acids, being convertible into acids by a further portion
of oxygen. This will appear as we proceed.

According to the old theory, metals were supposed to be oxidized

3. In what way do metals become united to oxygen ?

There are several ways in which metallic oxides are formed, the chief of which are by the access of atmospheric air, by the decomposition of water, and by the decomposition of acids.

4. Will all metals become oxidized by exposure to the air ?

No: gold, silver, and platina, cannot be oxidized, unless in a very high temperature; though iron,[a] copper, and lead, by long exposure to the air, will become oxidized in the coldest atmosphere. Manganese, by such exposure, will in a few hours be converted into a perfect oxide.

5. Are metals ever exposed to the air with the design of converting them into oxides?

The common red lead of the shops, which is an oxide of lead, is made by melting that metal in ovens so constructed as to have a free access of atmospheric air. Some metallic solutions cannot be formed but in contact with atmospheric air or oxygen. Thus, copper or lead, placed in acetic acid, and excluded from the air, do not form any solution; but if the mixture be exposed, oxygen is absorbed, and the solution takes place.

by the loss of phlogiston; and when these oxides were reduced to a metallic state, it was imagined that they recovered their phlogiston from the carbonaceous matter employed in their reduction. Those persons who have not been in the habit of reading the works of the older chemists may understand their phraseology by attending to the following particulars:—In most cases, all that is necessary is to substitute the word *oxygen* for *phlogiston*, with a slight inversion of the language. For, the effects which they attributed to the combination of phlogiston, appear to be due to the extrication of oxygen; and what they supposed to be owing to the loss of phlogiston, was really occasioned by the absorption of oxygen.

[a] Metals not only become oxidized by atmospheric air, but sometimes, by exposure to its action, pass from a lower to a higher degree of oxidation. Thus, if a solution of the common sulphate of iron be exposed to the atmosphere, it acquires a further dose of oxygen, and by degrees a portion of the metal, in a higher state of oxidation, is precipitated.

· 6. How is it known that the change of common lead to red lead is caused by the absorption of oxygen?

This is known by the increase of weight which the metal acquires during the operation;[a] and to confirm the fact, the oxide may be again reduced, and the original quantity of metal left unaltered.

7. Do all metals increase equally when converted into oxides?

No: each metal has its extremes, between which it absorbs oxygen in various proportions; and one metal may not only have a greater or less capacity, but also a greater or less attraction for oxygen than another; so that one will often deprive the other of it, thus reducing the oxide to its primitive metallic form.[b] Zinc, for example, by its powerful attraction for oxygen, decomposes a great number of salts and metallic solutions, and precipitates the metal from them in a metallic form, or in the state of oxides, less oxidized than they were before. This

[a] The following account of the manufacture of red lead, from Watson's Chemical Essays, will be a satisfactory proof of this doctrine. In the manufactories of red lead in Derbyshire, the melted lead is exposed to atmospheric air; the surface soon becomes covered with a dusky pellicle; this pellicle being removed, another is formed; and thus, by removing the pellicle as fast as it forms, the greater part of the lead is changed into a yellowish green powder. This powder is then ground very fine in a mill, and, when washed and properly dried, is thrown back into the furnace, and by constant stirring for 48 hours, so as to expose every part to the action of the air, it becomes red lead, and is taken out for use. Twenty cwt. of lead generally give 22 cwt of red lead; so that 2 cwt. of oxygen is absorbed from the atmosphere during the process.

[b] This may be shewn by keeping a given weight of ironwire red hot for some time in the bowl of a common tobacco-pipe, and weighing the iron before and after it has been submitted to the experiment.

The pin-manufacturers whiten their pins on the same principle. They fill a pan with alternate layers of pins and grain tin, into which they pour a solution of super-tartrate of potash, and then boil the whole for four or five hours. In this process, the tartaric acid first dissolves the tin, and then gradually deposits it on the surface of the pins, in consequence of its greater affinity for the zinc, of which the *brass* wire is composed.

may be exemplified by the experiment of the metallic tree, which is formed by suspending a piece of zinc in a solution of oxide of lead in an acid. After a short time the whole of the lead is precipitated in the form of a tree, and in the metallic state, in consequence of the zinc depriving it of its oxygen.

8. What metals are oxidized by the decomposition of water?

Iron, zinc, tin, and antimony decompose water, and become oxidized by the process. The rust which forms upon polished iron is occasioned by the iron imbibing the oxygen of the water which it decomposes,[a] as it meets it in the atmosphere. This metal, when heated, decomposes water with great rapidity.

9. How do these metals operate in thus decomposing water?

This effect, like most of the operations of nature, depends on chemical affinity. These metals have a greater affinity for oxygen than oxygen has for hydrogen; the oxygen of the water, therefore, unites with the metal, to form a metallic oxide, while the hydrogen, the other ingredient of the water, escapes in the form of gas.

10. Is it known what proportion of oxygen each metal requires, in order to its being converted to an oxide?

Most of the metals are capable of combining with different proportions of oxygen, according to the mode by which they are oxidized.[b]

---

[a] An increase of near 30 per cent. may be given to iron, by heating it red hot, and passing a continued stream of the vapour of water over it, when in that state. This increase of weight arises from its decomposing the water, and combining with its oxygen.

[b] In the oxidation of metals by acids, though there be no oxygen gas sensibly present by which it is effected, oxygen exists in the acids, also in the water with which the acids are diluted; and the effect is owing to the passage of a portion of oxygen from one of these substances to the metal; and the increase in weight, which the metal acquires, is always equal to the weight of the oxygen absorbed. Whenever a metallic oxide dissolves in an acid, it causes most or all of the

11. In what instances are acids used to oxidize metals?

Many instances of this mode of forming metallic oxides might be adduced: thus, common white lead is made by exposing sheet lead to the fumes of acetic acid;[a] and the oxide of tin, by submitting that metal to the action of the nitric acid.

12. What are the properties of metallic oxides?

They are in general friable and pulverulent; are heavier than the primitive metal; and with the different acids form metallic salts. The nature of the combination of oxygen with a metal, the subsequent solution of the metal in an acid, and its reproduction, may be shown in a satisfactory manner by the following experiment:—take a quantity of copper filings, boil them in concentrated sulphuric acid (common oil of vitriol) with a small portion of nitric acid; and when the copper is dissolved dilute the solution with water, and set it aside to crystallize. The crystals thus produced will be sulphate of copper, and will exemplify the formation of a metallic salt. If these crystals be now dissolved in a little water, and the polished blade of a knife be immersed in the solution, the copper will be reduced, and appear of its natural colour upon the knife. The oxygen, having a greater affinity for the iron than the copper, passes to the iron, by which the copper becomes deoxidized, and

acid properties to disappear exactly as if an alkali had been employed; and saturates corresponding quantities of the different acids.—BERTHOLLET.

[a] The manufacture of white lead is conducted in the following manner:—a number of earthen crucibles, holding from 3 to 6 quarts each, and nearly filled with vinegar, are placed in hot-beds of tan; upon these crucibles thin sheets of lead, rolled up in coils, are placed, one coil over each crucible. The heat of the bed occasions the vinegar to rise in vapour, which attaches itself to the lead, and oxidizes its surface to a considerable depth. At a certain time the oxide which has been thus formed is scraped off, and the coils of the lead replaced: in this manner the operation is repeated, till the whole of the metal is oxidized. This oxide, which contains a portion of carbonic acid, is afterwards washed, and ground for sale.

consequently insoluble in the acid: it is therefore precipitated from the solution, and attaches itself to the knife in a metallic form. In the formation of sulphate of copper, the oxidation of the metal, and its solution in the acid, seem to be only one operation; but the metal is undoubtedly *first* oxidized by the oxygen of the nitric acid, and *then* becomes soluble in the sulphuric acid.

13. Is it necessary to oxidize the metals that are intended to be formed into metallic salts?

All metals are incapable of dissolving in most of the acids, until they are combined with oxygen.[a] This is a fact of great importance to be remembered; and it is for this reason that many metals will dissolve but slowly in strong acids which will yet rapidly be acted upon by diluted acids. Zinc, for instance, is but slightly acted upon by strong sulphuric acid; but if the acid be diluted with water a rapid action takes place, and hydrogen gas is disengaged in consequence of the oxygen of the water uniting with the zinc to form oxide of zinc which is immediately dissolved in the acid, and the hydrogen is disengaged. The action of diluted nitric acid on iron or tin affords an example of the same fact.

14. Is there any instance of the stronger acids being made use of by manufacturers to dissolve metals?

Yes: the manufacturers of sulphate of copper, commonly called makers of Roman vitriol, boil the oxide of copper in strong sulphuric acid, and dissolve it by that operation.

15. What other instances are there of manufacturers using the mineral acids for dissolving metals?

Silver is dissolved in nitric acid, by the refiners, in the business of parting; gold is dissolved in nitro-muriatic

[a] When metals are dissolved in the muriatic or hydriodic acids, it is not necessary to suppose that they are first oxidized, as in these cases the metals form soluble chloride or iodides, and the hydrogen of the acid is set free.

acid, for painting china; and the dyers use large quantities of tin dissolved in nitro-muriatic acid.

16. Is it possible to recover metals which have been dissolved in acids?

The attraction of the different metals for oxygen is so various, that several of them, when dissolved, may be precipitated even in a metallic form, by the addition of metals that have a greater affinity for oxygen than the dissolved metal.[a]

17. What is the usual mode of reducing metallic oxides?

Charcoal is the agent usually employed, on account of its superior affinity for oxygen.[b] Hydrogen gas may also be employed for the same purpose, for from its great attraction for oxygen it will separate this gas from a great number of oxides, if they be exposed to heat and a current of hydrogen passed over them.

18. Are you acquainted with any other agent which is equal to the de-oxidizement of a metal?

Yes: some metals have so loose an attraction for oxygen, that even light will separate it, and reduce the oxide to its original metallic state. Sennebier first pointed out the fact that the violet rays of the solar spectrum have the greatest power of reducing metallic oxides. It was afterwards shown by Wollaston and Ritter that the de-

[a] This is exemplified by the refiners in their operations. When the silver is dissolved in aqua-fortis, they recover it by placing plates of copper in the solution. The copper absorbs oxygen from the silver, and the latter is precipitated in a metallic state. All metals have the power of de-oxidizing gold and silver; copper will take oxygen from mercury; and iron will reduce an oxide of copper. The degree of attraction for oxygen, which the different metals possess, seems to be in the following order:—manganese, zinc, iron, tin, copper, mercury, silver, gold.

[b] The usual mode of procedure is to mix a quantity of charcoal with the metallic oxide, and subject the mixture to an intense heat in crucibles. The oxygen combines with the charcoal, and with a portion of caloric, and goes off in carbonic acid gas; the metal then falls to the bottom of the crucible, and runs into a solid mass.

L 2

oxidizing or chemical rays of the spectrum actually exist beyond the limits of the violet rays, and that there are some invisible rays in the spectrum which possess the chemical effects of decomposing solutions of gold and silver; heat will also decompound the oxides of gold, silver, and platina.

19. What oxides are there besides metallic oxides?

We are acquainted with oxides of each of the simple combustibles, phosphorus, hydrogen, carbon, and with several of nitrogen.

20. What is the origin of the oxide of phosphorus?

If phosphorus be not preserved entirely from the access of air and light, it soon becomes first white and then of a dark brown colour, by its union with oxygen. In this state it is *oxide* of phosphorus.

21. What is the nature of the oxide of hydrogen?

Hydrogen combined with one proportion of oxygen, or one part by weight of hydrogen combined with eight parts by weight of oxygen, forms the well-known substance water.

22. Does hydrogen form any other compound with oxygen?

Thenard succeeded in producing a compound consisting of one part of hydrogen and 16 of oxygen, which he named peroxide of hydrogen. This compound is a fluid having the specific gravity 1.4. of a sharp acrid taste, and readily decomposed by heat, long exposure to air, or by the action of many metals.

23. What is the nature of the oxides of carbon?

The first degree of oxidation of carbon produces *carbonic* oxide; a further degree of oxidation produces *carbonic* acid gas.

24. How is carbonic oxide prepared?

Carbonic oxide, which was one of the last discoveries of Dr. Priestly, is procured by heating charcoal with metallic oxides, or earthy carbonates, or by the means mentioned in a preceding chapter.

25. What is the difference in the composition of carbonic oxide and carbonic acid?

Carbonic oxide contains 8 parts by weight of oxygen to 6 of carbon, and carbonic acid 16 of oxygen to 6 of carbon.

26. What are the properties of carbonic oxide?

Carbonic oxide, like most other gases, is invisible and elastic; its specific gravity is somewhat less than that of atmospheric air; it is highly combustible; but it is a gas that will not itself support combustion; neither is it fit for animal respiration.

27. What are the oxides of nitrogen?

The first degree of oxidation produces nitrous oxide; a further portion of oxygen forms nitric oxide. Both these oxides are in the state of gas.

28. What is the origin of nitrous oxide; and how is it procured?

Nitrous oxide is another of the gases discovered by Dr. Priestley. It is readily procured by exposing crystals of nitrate of ammonia in a retort, to the heat of a lamp; by which means the ammoniacal salt is decomposed, and this gas evolved.

29. What are the properties of nitrous oxide gas?

This gas bears the nearest resemblance of any other to atmospheric air. It will support combustion even better than common air, and is respirable; it is in a slight degree absorbed by water, to which it imparts a sweetish taste.

30. How do you explain the changes which take place when nitrous oxide gas is produced from nitrate of ammonia?

When nitrate of ammonia is heated strongly the only products which arise from its decomposition are nitrous oxide gas and water; the nitrate of ammonia consists of nitric acid, which is composed of five equivalents or atoms of oxygen to one of nitrogen, and ammonia, which consists of three equivalents of hydrogen and one of nitrogen; the three equivalents of hydrogen of the ammonia unite with three equivalents of the oxygen of the nitric acid to form water, and the remaining two equivalents of oxygen of the acid unite with the two equivalents of nitrogen to form nitrous oxide gas.

31. How is nitric oxide procured?

Nitric oxide, or nitrous gas, as it has usually been called, was also discovered by Dr. Priestley, during some of his first experiments on air. It is procured by digesting copper or mercury in diluted nitric acid, and collecting the gas which rises during the solution.

32. What are the properties of nitric oxide?

Nitric oxide is an invisible gas, which assumes an orange colour whenever it comes in contact with atmospheric, or any other air that contains oxygen, in consequence of the production of nitrous acid.

33. How has this gas been applied to the purpose of eudiometry?

In consequence of the property which this gas has of being decomposed by oxygen gas, Dr. Priestley proposed to apply it to the purposes of eudiometry, by using it to deprive air of its oxygen, which it immediately combines with, forming nitrous acid, which may be absorbed by water, and thus the whole of the oxygen is separated from atmospheric air. However, the use of nitric oxide gas for this purpose is much restricted by the number of the precautions necessary to be observed, and the modes of analyzing atmospheric air already mentioned are generally preferred.

34. What are the general properties of the chlorides?

Like oxygen, chlorine has a strong attraction for bases, and in general a stronger attraction than this substance, which it will displace from most of its compounds. It also forms with bases, acids and salts, resembling oxides in their composition; the general properties of the chlorides are, they are solid, crystalline substances, having solubility in water not decomposable by the strongest heat; many of them are volatile, and they may in general, like the oxides, be decompounded by the action of hydrogen gas,—and when in solution they may be all decompounded by a solution of silver which takes chlorine from all its combinations.

CHAPTER XIII.

COMBUSTION.

1. What is combustion?

Combustion[a] was formerly considered a process by which combustible bodies decomposed oxygen gas, absorbed its base, and suffered its caloric to escape in the state of sensible heat. As we are now acquainted with many chemical combinations which are attended with combustion (or the extrication of heat and light) in which no oxygen is present, we must define combustion to be the union of substances having strong attraction for each other, and which during their combination evolve heat and light.

2. Can you give any examples of combustion in which oxygen does not bear a part?

The combustion of phosphorus and metals in chlorine gas afford examples of this, and of copper in the vapour of sulphur; potassium also undergoes combustion in chlorine and in the vapour of iodine.

---

[a] Lavoisier and other French chemists defined combustion to be the combination of any body with oxygen. This definition, however, has very properly been objected to; for there are many instances of oxygen combining with a body without producing combustion. Indeed, this union is sometimes effected when no combustion can possibly take place. Oxygen often combines with bodies without any sensible extrication of heat or light; but we never, in common language, give the name of combustion to any operation in which heat and light are not liberated.

3. Are all substances capable of being burnt ?

No: some substances are combustible, others incombustible.

4. What do you mean by simple combustibles ?

Those combustible substances that have resisted every attempt to decompose them are called simple combustibles.

5. Endeavour to enumerate the simple combustibles ?

The simple combustibles with which we are acquainted are hydrogen, sulphur, phosphorus, selenium, carbon, and the metals.

6. How can you prove that the· metals are combustible ?

If we pass some copper foil into a bottle containing chlorine gas the copper will take fire and burn ; the same will happen with zinc, tin, antimony, &c. &c. This may also be proved by the following experiment of Dr. Ingenhouz with respect to oxygen. " Twist a small iron wire into the form of a corkscrew, by rolling it round a small stick; fix one end of it into a cork (which will fit a glass jar previously filled with oxygen gas,) and lap round the other end a small bit of cotton thread dipped in melted tallow. Set fire to the cotton and immediately plunge the whole into the jar of oxygen gas. The wire will take fire from the cotton, and burn with great brilliancy, throwing out very vivid sparks in all directions. During the combustion, the iron combines with the oxygen, in the jar, and is converted into an oxide, with an augmentation of its weight.[a]

7. What substances are there which are incombustible ?

We are acquainted with thirteen incombustible sub-

[a] Mr. Accum says, that a thick piece of iron or steel, such as a file, may be burned in oxygen gas, if it be made very sharp-pointed, and a small piece of wood be stuck upon its extremity and set fire to previous to its being immersed in the gas. ·

stances; viz. nitrogen, the three alkalies, and the nine earths.

8. What is the nature of combustion?

Combustion was formerly considered to be a double decomposition, in which the combustible and the supporter of combustion divided themselves each into two portions, which combined in pairs; the one forming the product, the other the fire which escapes. It is now considered that combustion arises from the union of bodies in opposite electrical states, the heat and light disengaged being probably due to the union of the two electricities.

9. What do you mean by supporters of combustion?

The substances which are called supporters of combustion are not of themselves combustible, but are necessary to the process; that is, no combustion can ever take place without one or other of the supporters of combustion being present.

10. What substances are deemed supporters of combustion?

Oxygen, chlorine, iodine, and bromine, are all supporters of combustion; to these may, perhaps, be added, fluorine. It is in consequence of the existence of oxygen in atmospheric air that the combustion of candles, fuel, &c. takes place, the oxygen uniting with the carbon and hydrogen of the burning body forming water and carbonic acid gas.[a]

[a] Dr. Thomson's account of combustion will convey to the reader a clear idea of this natural phænomenon.—" When a stone, or brick, is heated, it undergoes no change except an augmentation of temperature, and when left to itself it soon cools again, and becomes as at first. But with combustible bodies the case is very different. When heated to a certain degree in the open air, they suddenly become much hotter of themselves, continue for a considerable time intensely hot, sending out a copious stream of caloric and light. This emission after a certain period begins to diminish; and at last ceases altogether. The combustible body has now undergone a most complete change; it is converted into a substance possessing very different properties, and no longer capable of combustion. The product is incombustible, because its base being already saturated with oxygen cannot combine with any more."

11. Is it known how oxygen supports combustion ?

The agency of oxygen in combustion is attributable to its affinity for combustible bodies. For, whenever such bodies are ignited in circumstances favourable to combustion, they absorb oxygen from the air, or other contiguous substances, till the combustible is converted to an incombustible body.

12. From whence proceeds the heat which we observe during combustion ?

Formerly the heat produced by combustion was supposed to arise from the oxygen gas of the atmosphere[a] giving out its latent heat by changing from a rarer to a denser state: this, however, cannot be considered as the true explanation, as in many cases the density of the product of combustion is less than the mean density of the oxygen and the combustible.

13. Can you explain this operation with more precision?

The act of combustion effects a real analysis of atmospheric air; for while the oxygen combines with the combustible, the caloric, in the form of sensible heat, is thrown off in every direction.[b]

14. Does this account for the long continued heat which we experience in every common combustion?

Whenever we burn a combustible body in order to procure heat, a continued stream of atmospheric air flows towards the fireplace[c] to occupy the vacancy left by the

---

[a] Though every case of combustion requires that heat should be evolved, yet this heat process proceeds very differently in different circumstances. Hence the terms *ignition, inflammation, detonation,* &c. &c.

[b] The rapid combustion that is occasioned by inflaming combustible substances, mixed with chlorate of potash, is owing to the large quantity of oxygen contained in that salt, and which it holds by a weak affinity.

[c] On some parts of the continent rooms are warmed by stoves that have ash-pits without ; so that the combustion is kept up by air which has no connection with the air of the room ; consequently there is no current, nor is the air of the room contaminated ; and the persons

air that has undergone decomposition, and which in its turn becomes decomposed also.[a]   Hence a supply of caloric is furnished, without intermission, till the whole of the combustible is combined with oxygen.

15. Is the presence of atmospheric air necessary in all the *ordinary* cases of combustion, such as of fuel, candles, &c.

Combustion cannot take place in a vacuum : no combustible body can burn without atmospheric air, or at least without oxygen, which is a component part of the atmosphere.   This may be demonstrated by placing a lighted candle under a glass jar, inverted upon a plate of water. It will be seen that the candle will go out as soon as it has consumed all the oxygen contained in the included air.

16. In what do combustible bodies differ from each other?

Combustible bodies differ from each other principally in the rapidity with which they absorb oxygen, and in the proportion of it which they[b] can take up, to form the new compound.

who occupy them are not subject to the inconvenience of those cold draughts of air which render some of our rooms that have large fireplaces dangerous and unhealthy.

   [a] Argand's lamp is constructed upon this principle, that a current of air hastens combustion : for in consequence of this perpetual supply of oxygen the air is renewed every moment, and produces heat sufficient to burn the smoke as it is formed.   The smoke which arises from a common fire is chiefly water in the state of vapour, with a mixture of carburetted hydrogen and bituminous substances ; part of the water comes from the moisture of the fuel; the other part is formed during combustion, by the union of the hydrogen of the combustible with the oxygen of the atmosphere.   What takes place in a common fire would furnish an intelligent parent or preceptor with matter for several interesting conversations, which could not fail to rouse the curiosity and contemplation of the pupil.

   [b] Almost all the simple substances are capable of combining with various doses of oxygen.   Thus sulphur forms with oxygen sulphurous acid and sulphuric acid ; phosphorus forms oxide of phosphorus, phosphorous acid, and phosphoric acid ; carbon also unites with different portions of oxygen, and forms carbonic oxide, and carbonic acid.

17. How is it known that oxygen unites with the combustible body in the act of burning?

If a combustible substance be burnt in a sufficient quantity of vital air in a close vessel, and the product preserved, the whole will be found to be increased in weight[a] exactly in proportion to the oxygen gas consumed; and the combustible body will then have become incombustible.

18. What is the cause of a body becoming thus incombustible?

Because when a body is fully burnt it is saturated with oxygen; at least as far as combustion can saturate it; it, therefore, cannot combine with any more: but some bodies may be rendered combustible again by depriving them of the oxygen which they absorbed in their former combustion.[b]

19. In the decomposition of atmospheric air by combustion, what becomes of the nitrogen gas?

As the oxygen becomes fixed in the combustible body, its caloric is disengaged; part of which combines with the nitrogen, and carries it off in the form of rarefied nitrogen gas.

20. What chemical name is given to burnt bodies?

Such substances are said to be *oxygenized*, or *oxidized*; that is, changed into acids or oxides.

---

[a] Phosphorus is an eminent instance of this increase by combustion. If an ounce of phosphorus be properly inflamed, it will produce more than two ounces of phosphoric acid; the increase in weight arises from its absorption of oxygen.

[b] " This view of combustion authorises us to divide almost all the productions of nature into two grand classes; one of *combustible* bodies, the other of bodies already *burnt:* in the masses and action of the former we discern the causes of inflammable meteors, the perpetual alteration of the surface of the earth, volcanos, &c.; in the existence of the latter we perceive the source of the number and diversity of acids, saline compounds, oxides, and metallic salts, which vary in a thousand ways the appearances of ores, &c. &c."— FOURCROY.

21. Does the oxygen become fixed in all combustible bodies when burnt?

It is a characteristic property of a combustible body to form a chemical combination with the oxygen, which is furnished by the supporters of combustion. The oxygen acquires such density by this process, that it is often extremely difficult to separate it again from the oxide.

22. Is it possible to separate entirely the oxygen from burnt bodies?

Yes: bodies may be deoxidized in various ways;[a] and in some cases the oxygen may be transferred from the burnt body to a fresh combustible body, and be made the means of producing a fresh combustion; or it may in many cases be completely separated, and shown in its primitive or gaseous state.[b]

23. What part of bodies is it which is destroyed by combustion?

No part that we know of. We have reason to think that every particle of matter is indestructible, and that the process of combustion[c] merely decomposes the body,

[a] Water, as we have shown, is a product of combustion, and its base is hydrogen, the most combustible substance we are acquainted with. To restore the combustibility of the hydrogen, we have only to abstract its oxygen; which may readily be done by mixing iron or zinc filings and sulphuric acid with the water; by which means the metal becomes oxidized, and the hydrogen gas is evolved as combustible as ever. This may be adduced to show that the simple substances cannot be divested of their own peculiar properties by any of our mixtures, or even chemical combinations.

[b] This is frequently done for the purpose of procuring oxygen gas. The oxide of manganese, or of mercury, is exposed to a proper degree of heat, and the gas received in a suitable apparatus, as it is extricated.

[c] The following concise account of the theory of combustion I copy from Berthollet:—" When bodies are burnt, none of their principles are destroyed; they had previously formed together one kind of compound, and they now separate from each other, at the high temperature to which they are exposed, in order to form others with the vital air in contact with them: such of the principles as cannot unite with the vital air, that is the earth, some saline and some

and sets its several component parts at liberty to separate from each other, and to form new and varied combinations.

24. What is the nature of flame which appears in many cases of combustion?

Flame is gas or vapour heated to a sufficiently high temperature to become luminous, and this temperature is beyond that of solid bodies heated to whiteness.

25. How can this be proved?

If we hold a platina wire in the flame of hydrogen or of burning spirits of wine, we find that the wire will become white hot, even at some distance above the actual flame. We may also prove this by applying an iron heated to low redness to a jet of coal gas, when we will find that the gas will not be inflamed, but will be immediately inflamed by applying to it the metal at a white heat, or the flame of any combustible substance. We also find that by cooling flame it may be extinguished; if, for example, we surround a very small flame of a taper or lamp, with a ring of cold metal, or immerse it in a jar surrounded by a freezing mixture, the flame will be immediately extinguished.

26. Can you adduce any experiments to prove that the light of flame is due to the quantity of solid disengaged in it?

Sir H. Davy proved that the light of carburetted hydrogen was due to the quantity of solid matter disengaged in it by placing in the central part of the flame a piece of wire gauze, which immediately became coated with charcoal, which would therefore seem to be disengaged there and be the cause of the intensity of the light of that portion of the flame; if the wire gauze be placed

metallic particles, compose the cinder. The new compounds formed, are carbonic acid, or fixed air and water; the proportion of these varies according to the proportion of the carbonic particles, and of the hydrogen that had been contained in the inflammable body."— Vol. i. p. 163.

at the upper or lower extremity of the flame, no charcoal is deposited, because in the former case, it has undergone complete combustion, and has been converted into carbonic acid, and in the latter, the charcoal has not been separated by the decomposition of the gas. The flame of the oxy-hydrogen blowpipe, though producing the most intense heat that can be formed artificially, burns with a light hardly perceptible, but if a solid substance, such as lime or alumina, be introduced into it, the light becomes most brilliant.

27. How is the different quantity of light given out during the combustion of different gases accounted for?

Sir H. Davy accounted for this by saying, that the brilliancy of the flame is " proportional to the quantity of solid matter first deposited and afterwards burnt ;" that in the different kinds of carburetted hydrogen, the light emitted during their combustion is due to the quantity of solid charcoal which they contain, which is deposited in the flame during the combustion, and then intensely ignited previous to its change into carbonic acid gas ; in general it seems probable, that the intenseness of a flame depends on the quantity of solid matter which undergoes combustion in the given vapour or gas.

28. What practical use has been made by Sir H. Davy of this discovery of the nature of flame?

The knowledge of this fact, relative to flame, led to the discovery of the safety lamp ; Sir H. Davy having found that flame was gaseous matter at a most intense degree of temperature, and having observed, that flame would not pass through very small tubes, in consequence of its being cooled down below the temperature necessary for its combustion, was led to infer, that by surrounding the flame of a candle with wire gauze, (which may be considered as consisting of a collection of small tubes,) it would prevent flame from being communicated to the explosive mixtures which exist in many coal mines, (and are called by the miners the fire-damp,) which had previously frequently caused by their explosion great injury and loss of life.

29. What is the construction of the safety lamp?

It consists of a small oil lamp C, to which is screwed a cylindrical piece of fine wire gauze A B, which completely surrounds the flame, so that there is no communication with the external air, except through the meshes of the wire gauze. In some of these lamps the lower part of the cylinder consists of a double fold of wire gauze, and in others the gauze is made of copper instead of iron wire; externally are placed three strong iron wires attached to an iron ring, by which the lamp may be carried in the hand and which also serve to protect the iron gauze from injury.

30. How does this prove a means of protection against the explosion of the fire-damp?

When this lamp is brought into a mixture of the explosive gas, the explosive mixture will burn inside the lamp, but the flame cannot be communicated to the gas external to the lamp, in consequence of its being cooled down below the temperature at which combustion takes place, in passing through the meshes of the wire gauze.

This fact can also easily be proved experimentally, by holding a piece of fine wire gauze in the flame of a common candle or spirit lamp, when we find that the wire gauze, while it allows free passage to the gas which is disengaged in the combustion, will in these cases completely intercept the flame.[a]

[a] Notwithstanding the admirable discovery of the safety lamp many accidents have lately occurred in mines from the explosion of the fire damp : this, however, does not in any degree diminish the claim which its illustrious discoverer has upon our gratitude, as in all cases in which accidents have occurred it has been proved that they were solely

31. What is the cause of the light emitted in all cases of combustion?

It is supposed to arise either from the separation of a peculiar imponderable substance from the burning body or the body entering into combination with it, or from a vibratory motion communicated to a subtile elastic ether supposed to pervade all space.

owing to the ignorance or carelessness of the workmen using the safety lamp; which is rendered inefficient from causes pointed out by Sir H. Davy, in his work on Flame, the principal of which the reader will find in the following extract.

"Single iron wire gauze of the kind used in the common miner's lamp is impermeable to the flame of all currents of fire-damp, *as long as it is not heated above redness:* but if the iron wire be made to burn, as at a strong welding heat, of course it can be no longer safe; and though such a circumstance can perhaps never happen in a colliery, yet it ought to be known and guarded against. I had an excellent opportunity of making experiments on a most violent blower (jet of inflammable air) in a mine belonging to J. C. Lambton, Esq. This blower is walled off and carried to the surface, where it is discharged with great force. It is made to pass through a leather pipe, so as to give a stream, of which the force was felt at about two feet from the aperture. The common single and double gauze lamps were brought upon this current, both in the free atmosphere and in a confined air. The gas fired in the lamps, but did not heat them above dull redness, and when they were brought far into the stream they were extinguished. A brass pipe was now fixed upon the blower-tube, so as to make the whole stream pass through an aperture of less than half an inch in diameter, which formed a blowpipe, from which the fire-damp issued with great violence, making a flame of the length of five feet. The blowpipe was exposed at right angles to a strong wind and double gauze lamps and single lamps successively placed in it. The double gauze lamps soon became red hot at the point of action of the two currents; but the wire did not communicate explosion. The single gauze lamp did not communicate explosion as long as it was red hot, and slowly moved through the currents; but when fixed at the point of most intense combustion it reached a welding heat; the iron wire began to burn with sparks and the explosion passed.

"If a workman having only a common single lamp finds the temperature of the wire increasing rapidly in an explosive mixture near a blower, he can easily diminish the heat by turning his back upon the current and keeping it from playing upon the lamp, by means of his clothes or his body; or by bringing the lamp nearer the orifice from which the fire-damp issues, he may extinguish it: and there never can be occasion for him to place his lamp in the exact point where two currents, one of fresh air and one of fire-damp, meet each other."

32. What are the two theories respecting the nature of light?

According to Sir I. Newton, light is a material imponderable substance given out by all luminous bodies, of which the sun is the principal source, its particles moving with the velocity of 190,000 miles in a second of time; according to Huygens (whose theory is most generally adopted at the present day) light is supposed to consist in the vibrations of an elastic ether which pervades all space, which is put in motion by the particles of the luminous body, this motion being transmitted from particle to particle of this ethereal medium, thereby conveying to our senses from the illuminated body the sensation of light.

33. How has the velocity with which light moves been ascertained?

It was first ascertained by observing the difference of time at which the eclipses of the satellites of Jupiter took place, when the planet was nearest and most distant from the earth, or in opposition and conjunction : it was found that in the latter case the eclipse occurred 16 minutes 25 seconds later than it should have done according to calculation; it was therefore justly inferred that this difference was owing to the light from the planet having in the latter case to travel a distance equal to the diameter of the earth's orbit, or 190,000,000 miles ; this supposition was afterwards fully confirmed by other observations.

34. What are the principal chemical properties of light?

We have already mentioned the property which the solar rays possess of deoxidizing certain metallic compounds : light also, exercises some degree of action on the crystallization of bodies ; its effects upon the growth of animals and vegetables, which may be to a certain degree considered chemical processes, are too well known to require mention ; in fact, in the changes taking place around us, the presence of this agent seems essential, for without its influence the earth would be altogether unfit for animal or vegetable existence.

APPENDIX.

APPENDIX.

SPECIFIC GRAVITY.

Vide p. 29.

THE common method of taking the specific gravity of the metals, or of any solid body, is by comparing the difference which there is in their weight when weighed in air and in water; that is, to divide the *absolute* weight by the *loss*, and the quotient is the specific gravity. Thus, if a mineral which weighs three ounces in air, weighs only two ounces when weighed in water, the specific gravity of such mineral is 3; that is, if water, as it generally is, be called 1,000, the substance now examined is 3,000; or, to make it plain to the young student, if a pint of water weigh *one* pound, the same *bulk* of the mineral will weigh three pounds.

A more ready way to determine the specific gravity of solids is to fill a phial with water, and note the weight of the whole accurately in grains. Then weigh 100 grains of the mineral or other substance to be examined and drop it gradually into the phial of water. The difference of weight of the bottle with its contents now, and when it was filled with water only, will give the specific gravity of the matter under examination. For example, if the bottle weighs 50 grains more than it did when it was filled with water only, it shows that 100 grains of the mineral displace only 50 grains of water, and consequently that it is twice the specific gravity of water. This method is said to have been discovered by Archimedes.

The specific gravity of fluids is generally determined by an areometer, which is a graduated glass tube with a bulb, so contrived that it may swim in the fluid in a perpendicular position. The specific gravity is shown by the degree to which this instrument sinks in the fluid to be examined, and this will consequently always be lower in proportion as the liquid is lighter.

The specific gravity of ardent spirits is generally ascertained by means of a hydrometer, of which various kinds are sold by the mathematical instrument-makers.

By the following method, which was contrived by Dr. Lewis, the specific gravity of a liquor is estimated from the excess of the weight of a certain measure of it above that of an equal measure of distilled water. A set of weights is made for this purpose, called *carats*, or *cadukes*, in the following manner:—

A convenient bottle being procured, the tare of the bottle is first taken; it is then completely filled with distilled water; the weight of the water is accurately divided-into two equal parts, and a weight made equal to one of these parts is marked 64; by continuing the division, are obtained the weights 32, 16, 8, 4, 2, 1, carats; so that a carat is the 128th part of the weight of the water. Another weight is then made which counterpoises the bottle when filled with water; and so many carats as the bottle filled with an alkaline ley, or any other liquor, weighs more than this counterpoise, so many carats strong is the liquor said to be.

In taking the specific gravity of bodies attention should always be paid to their temperature, as the specific gravity of a body when expanded by caloric will always be less than it is when at a low temperature.

PYROMETERS.
Vide p. 40.

THE instruments noticed in the text are inapplicable to very high temperatures, or to ascertain the heat of closed fire-places; an object, in many processes in the arts, of the utmost importance. To supply this deficiency, our celebrated Wedgwood took advantage of the property which clay has of *contracting by heat*, and remaining afterwards in that state of contraction. This property is not, strictly speaking, an exception to the general law of expansion by increase of temperature; clay is not a homogeneous body, but a mechanical mixture of alumina and silex, which by the influence of heat are brought into more intimate union, and therefore diminish in bulk: until a temperature sufficiently high to melt them, that is, to convert them into a homogeneous mass, is applied; after which the product obeys the general law of expansion by heat. Availing himself of this property, Mr. Wedgwood employed as *pyrometric pieces* cylinders of fine porcelain clay slightly flattened on one side, formed by pressing the clay into an iron tube, and baked in a potter's furnace. It was found, after repeated trials, that the pieces of clay contracted more and more in an uniform ratio to the degree of heat communicated to them, and permanently retained this contraction; so that by applying them when cold to a scale, an indication of the degree of heat was obtained.

The scale employed by Wedgwood consisted of two brass rods $\frac{1}{4}$ inch square, and two feet in length, fixed on a brass plate *convergingly*, so that they were distant at one end just 0.5, and at the other 0.3 inch. For convenience the rods are usually divided, forming two nearly parallel grooves. With the above stated convergence the whole groove is divided into inches and tenths, making 240 degrees in the whole scale; and the higher the temperature to which the pyrometric piece has been exposed, the further will it slide up the scale.

In order to compare his scale with Fahrenheit's mercurial thermometer, which cannot measure a temperature much beyond 600°, Mr. Wedgwood was compelled to make use of the *expansions* of a pyrometric piece of fine silver, applied to a gauge on the same principle as that above described. By this, the expansions of the silver for 50° and 212° Fahrenheit were first noted; and then the silver and clay pyrometric pieces were compared at the same temperature. By such means Wedgwood estimated the value of each degree of his scale at 130° of Fahrenheit; and he reckoned that the 0_o of his scale corresponded with the 1077°.5 of the common scale. On this principle comparative tables of the two thermometers have been constructed; but their accuracy depends on two circumstances which have not been determined to the satisfaction of the philosophic world. Clay being a heterogeneous mixture, it by no means follows that its contractions are equable at different temperatures; and even were this ascertained, there is great doubt how far the means employed by Wedgwood did accurately estimate the degree of Fahrenheit at which his scale commences.

There is still another serious objection to the general use of such an instrument. It occurred to the ingenious inventor, that different portions of clay would possess different degrees of contractibility; and he endeavoured to secure uniformity, to a certain extent, by laying in a large stock of Cornish clay, which he hoped would supply innumerable pyrometric pieces of the same quality. It was found, however, that spontaneous changes take place in such clay, which render its indications liable to variation at distant intervals; or pieces, now formed of the same clay, will not give the same indication with pieces baked several years ago. Attempts were made to remedy this inconvenience by forming a clay of uniform quality of fixed proportions of silex and alumina. Fine cornish clay yielded, on analysis, two parts of silex and three of alumina; and such a mixture made into a paste with $\frac{3}{4}$ths their weight of water, has been recommended for the fabrication of pyrometric pieces. The method detailed by Wedgwood should then be followed in moulding them. The paste is first to be rammed into a metallic mould 0.6 inch wide, 0.4 deep, and 1 inch long: they should be dried in the air, and when quite desiccated, Wedgwood gauged them in another mould exactly 0.5 of an inch wide. Before they are baked they will, of course, just enter the widest end of the scale, resting at 0°. When contracted by baking to ⅟₈th of their bulk, they will pass to the 120°; and when reduced to ⅜ths, they would pass to the 240°, or the extremity of the scale; but Mr. Wedgwood never did obtain a higher temperature than 160°. From these proportions each degree of Wedgwood's scale is equivalent to a contraction of ₆₀₀th part of the pyrometric piece.

The difficulty of obtaining clay of an uniform quality, and not liable to spontaneous change, has lately given rise to a suggestion of employing pyrometric pieces formed of Chinese agalmatolite; a suggestion of Mr. Sivright of Meggetland, well worthy of attention.

A more formidable objection was started by some foreign chemists to Wedgwood's scale: one, indeed, that would have overturned the theory of the instrument. It was alleged, that the effect of a long continued, or often repeated, exposure to even *inferior degrees of heat*, would cause contraction of the clay, after it had undergone the action of a higher temperature. This point has been examined with much care by Guyton de Morveau, who has shown, in his valuable essay, the inaccuracy of this opinion: although he contends that Wedgwood has greatly erred in the attempts to convert his scale into degrees of Fahrenheit's thermometer, as we shall immediately notice.

On the whole, the pyrometer of Wedgwood is an instrument well adapted to the purposes of the potter, or to convey some idea of the relative heat of furnaces; but we cannot regard the determination of the celebrated inventor as giving even a tolerable approximation to relative degrees of high temperatures by other scales. As, however, Mr. Wedgwood's tables of temperature are often quoted, we shall here subjoin them, with the corresponding degrees of Fahrenheit according to his calculation.

	W.		F.
Red heat in full day-light	0°	=	1077°
Enamel heat	6	=	1857
Brass melts	21	=	3807
Swedish copper melts	27	=	4587
Fine silver melts	28	=	4717
Settling heat of flint glass	29	=	4847
Fine gold melts	32	=	5237
Delft ware baked	41	=	6407
Working heat of plate glass	57	=	8487

	W.	F.
Flint glass furnace, low heat................	70	= 10,177
Cream-coloured ware baked.................	86	= 12,257
Welding heat of iron, least.....	90	=.12,777
Ditto ditto greatest..............	95	=.13,427
Stone ware, baked..........................	102	= 14,337
Derby China vitrefies......................	112	= 15,637
Flint glass furnace, high heat..............	114	= 15,697
Inferior Chinese porcelain softened..........	120	= 16,677
Bow porcelain vetrefied.....................	121	= 16,807
Plate glass furnace, greatest heat..........	124	= 17,197
Smith's forge, greatest heat................	125	= 17,327
Cast iron begins to melt.....................	130	= 17,977
Bristol porcelain vitrefies..................	135	= 18,627
Hessian crucible melted.....................	150	= 20,577
Cast iron thoroughly melted................	150	= 20,577
Chinese porcelain, best sort softened.........	156	= 21,557
Greatest heat of an air furnace eight inches in diameter...............................	160	= 21,877
Extremity of Wedgwood's scale..............	240	= 32,277

These results are rendered doubtful by the causes already noticed ; and the experiments of Morveau and Daniell, with pyrometers of platina, lead to very different results.

· ·The pyrometer of Mr. Daniell was first described in Brande's Quarterly Journal. The moving power is a rod or wire of platina 10.2 inches in length, and 0.14 inch in diameter, fixed in a tube of blacklead ware $a, b, c,$ by a flanch within and a nut and screw without the tube at a. This tube has a shoulder moulded on it at b, for the convenience of always inserting it into the furnace, or muffle, to the same depth. From the extremity of the platina rod at b proceeds a fine wire of the same

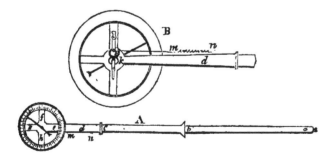

metal, $\frac{1}{100}$ inch in diameter, which comes out of a brass ferrule d, and passes two or three times round the axis of the wheel i, B. It then bends back, and is attached to a slender spring m n, which is fixed by one end to the pin at n, on the outside of the ferrule.

The substitution of a silk string for that part of the platina wire lapped round the wheel and connecting it with the spring, has rendered the motions of the index more sensible. The axis of i is $=$ 0.062 inch, and the diameter of the wheel one inch ; its teeth play in the teeth of another wheel just one-third of its diameter, by which the wheel k has three times the movement of i ; and the index on the axis of k moves therefore three times round for every revolution of i. The action of the spiral spring m draws round the wheel i and the index, when the expansion of the platina rod permits it to act. The dial is divided into 360 degrees. By experiment, Daniell ascertained that each degree of his scale $=$ 7 degrees of Fahrenheit's : and he has published an account of some well-conducted experiments on the fusing points of some of the metals with this instrument, which very widely differ from the results obtained by Wedgwood, but nearly agree with those of Morveau. Mr. Daniell found, that after being exposed to high temperatures the pyrometer did not fall to the point from which it set out ; a circumstance which he attributes, with justice, to changes in the form of the tube induced by a high temperature. This is certainly an imperfection in the principle of the instrument : but if the degrees of heat be marked by the ascending series its indications seem tolerably correct, and, although perhaps little to be depended on in nice investigations, it may become an useful instrument to manufacturers who make use of high temperatures. The tube should not be exposed to a naked fire, except it be of wood charcoal : because the foreign ingredients of fossil coal will adhere or incorporate with the black lead ware of the tube.

The following table exhibits some of Daniell's comparative results.

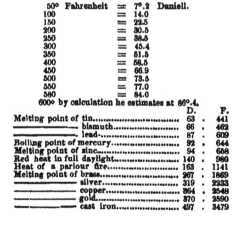

Fahrenheit		Daniell
50°	$=$	7°.2
100	$=$	14.0
150	$=$	22.5
200	$=$	30.5
250	$=$	38.5
300	$=$	45.4
350	$=$	51.5
400	$=$	58.5
450	$=$	66.9
500	$=$	73.5
550	$=$	77.0
580	$=$	84.0

600° by calculation he estimates at 86°.4.

	D.	F.
Melting point of tin	63 .	441
———— bismuth	66 .	462
———— lead	87 .	609
Boiling point of mercury	92 .	644
Melting point of zinc	94 .	658
Red heat in full daylight	140 .	980
Heat of a parlour fire	163 .	1141
Melting point of brass	267 .	1869
———— silver	319 .	2233
———— copper	364 .	2548
———— gold	370 .	2590
———— cast iron	497 .	3479

THEORIES OF HEAT.

Two different hypotheses have been proposed respecting the nature of heat. In the first, it is regarded as a material substance *sui generis*, which pervades all nature, and is capable of combination with other bodies, and by such combination, produces the various effects attributed to heat. In the other, heat is regarded not as a material substance, but as a quality of matter. A body when heated is supposed to be put in a certain state in which its constituent molecules, or the molecules of some subtle fluid which pervades it, are put into a state of vibration ; and this vibration is considered as the cause of heat.

The vibratory hypothesis has been maintained in different senses by different philosophers. By some, the vibration is attributed to the constituent molecules of the body which manifests the quality of heat. Others suppose, that a certain subtle fluid pervades all nature, which is highly elastic, and susceptible of vibration ; that it not only fills the abysses of space, but is diffused through the dimensions of all bodies, whether in the gaseous, liquid, or solid form ; that this subtle fluid is capable of being put into a state of vibration ; and that such vibrations are the cause of heat, and probably, in another degree, the cause of light. Leslie attributes these vibrations to the *air*.

According to the material hypothesis, the expansion produced, when the temperature of the body is raised, is owing the calorific fluid which penetrates its dimensions, and increases its bulk ; and the more of this fluid is added, the greater will be the increase of bulk.

Different bodies are differently enlarged by the addition of this fluid, according to the nature of their powers, and to the degree of attraction which their molecules have for the molecules of heat. If there be a slight attraction, then the increase of dimension by the infusion of the particles of heat is considerable. If, on the contrary, there be a strong affinity, then the molecules coalescing into a smaller capacity, produce a less degree of expansion ; and hence the phenomena of specific heat are attempted to be explained.

In some cases an actual chemical combination takes place between the molecules of heat and those of the body by which the form of the body is totally changed, and by which the molecules of heat lose their characteristic property. These circumstances are derived, by an obvious analogy, from the ordinary phenomena of chemical combination, in which the component parts often lose their peculiar qualities by combination ; and the more frequently they do so the more

M 2

powerful the affinity by which the combination is produced. When the molecules of heat thus intimately combine with the molecules of the solid, the solid becomes a liquid, and the heat loses its ordinary quality of raising the temperature of the body. In order to awaken this affinity, and give efficacy to it, it is necessary that the body should previously be raised to a certain temperature. Hence the melting point of each body is fixed. When the liquefaction is completed, the affinity is satisfied, and the body is so far saturated with heat. A similar combination is adduced in explanation of the transition of a body from the liquid to the vaporous form. According to this hypothesis, the condensation of the vapour and the congelation of the liquid, are instances of a decomposition, in which the matter of heat is separated from them. Bodies, when they radiate heat, dismiss the particles of caloric, which pass through the space with a force proportional to that with which they are emitted, and, encountering other bodies, are absorbed or reflected in a greater or a less degree, according to the affinities of the particles occupying the surface of these bodies for them.

The fact that heat is transmitted through a vacuum, is also generally adduced in support of this hypothesis, in opposition to the vibratory theory. If heat be admitted to be a material substance, it is easily conceivable that it may pass through a glass receiver, and, penetrating the vacuum, affect the thermometer placed in it.

Such are the leading arguments by which the material hypothesis is supported; and are, indeed, the facts on which it was probably formed.

The fact that certain liquids expand in freezing, although, at first, it appears at variance with this hypothesis, may, perhaps, admit of explanation, on the supposition that the extrication of heat calls into existence among the particles forces which cause their mutual separation. The expansion of water between 39° and the freezing point, might be conceived to be explained in the same way. It is difficult, however, to reconcile this theory with the phenomena of ignition and combustion ; and these phenomena are, accordingly, by some philosophers, considered to be utterly inconsistent with the material hypothesis.

If it be admitted that heat is a material substance *sui generis*, we might naturally expect that a body would increase in weight in proportion as heat is added to it. Thus, a given weight of water, at 212°, when converted into steam, receives 1000° of heat, and should, therefore, be heavier, when in the form of steam, by the weight of the heat added to it. Accordingly, many philosophers have attempted to test the material theory by this fact. Dr. Fordyce put about 1700 grains of water into a glass vessel, and sealed it hermetically. Its temperature was reduced to 32° by a freezing mixture. It was carefully weighed, and again exposed to the action of cold, by which a considerable portion of the water it contained was frozen. This water then dismissed 140° of heat; and it was expected, in conformity with the material theory, that a loss of weight would have ensued. On the contrary, it was found, by weighing the vessel, that the weight was increased by the sixtieth part of a grain. Similar experiments, however, were subsequently made by other philosophers; and there is reason to conclude that no actual change of weight takes place in a body by any change of temperature, or by the extrication of heat in the processes either of condensation or liquefaction. It must hence be admitted, that, if heat be a material substance, it is one which either does not possess the property of gravitation, or possesses it in so small a degree as to be inappreciable by any means which we possess of measuring it.

An ingenious experiment, instituted by Count Rumford, with a view to determine this point, may be here mentioned. He suspended equal weights of water and quicksilver, inclosed in two bottles, from the arms of a highly sensible balance. The liquids in this case had the temperature of the apartment in which the experiment took place, which was 61°. He then exposed them, for twenty-four hours, to an atmosphere of 34°; the weight, however, remained precisely the same. Now, from the respective specific heats of these two liquids, it is certain that, in descending from the temperature of 61° to 34°, the water must have parted with at least thirty times as much heat as the mercury.

Besides the defect in the material theory of failing to explain these phenomena in which heat is evolved, together with light, this theory contains an inherent vice, by assuming the existence of a body which has never been obtained in a separate form,—a body also, which, so far as all means of practical investigation afford any evidence, is destitute of the leading material character of gravitation. In this respect, the theory is in the predicament of the exploded phlogistic theory of Stahl, in which the only evidence of the existence of such a substance as phlogiston, was the convenience it afforded, in explaining the phenomena of combustion.

The advocates for the vibratory theory contend, that the material hypothesis, besides totally failing to explain an extensive and striking class of the phenomena of heat, is involved in a contradiction, by the result of the experiment of Count Rumford, in which heat is evolved by friction. In this experiment no source can be assigned from which the material fluid, to which heat is ascribed, could be derived. It was not in any change of capacity, for the borings had the same specific heat as the metal from which they were abraded. That the oxygen of the atmosphere, or the atmosphere in any manner, might not be supposed to influence the experiment, it was performed, as has been already described, in water. The water underwent no chemical change, dismissed no constituent part, and yet it received so great a quantity of heat that it boiled. Now, it appears, from these experiments, that heat may be derived from a body, without any limit whatsoever, by the continued application of friction. Two bodies rubbed together for all eternity will still continue to give out the matter of heat, yet they will still contain as much heat as they did at the commencement; a conclusion which implies a manifest contradiction in terms. Hence it is argued, that whatever heat may be, it cannot be material.

To this Dr. Thomson replies, by denying the alleged fact, that the specific heat of the cylinder remains the same. He considers that a diminution of specific heat has taken place, and ascribes the evolution of heat to this cause. This being a matter of fact into which it does not appear that Dr. Thomson has experimentally inquired, and into which it is certain that Count Rumford did experimentally inquire, we must, at present, rather incline to admit the force of Count Rumford's reasoning until his facts are disproved.

To ascertain whether the heat produced by friction depended on the presence of any body, besides the body under examination, an experiment of this nature was performed in an exhausted receiver by Boyle, Pictet, and, more lately, by Sir Humphry Davy. In all cases heat was developed by the rubbing surfaces. Sir Humphry Davy caused two pieces of ice to melt each other by the heat developed by their mutual friction in a vacuum. It is argued that the heat devolved in this experiment could not arise from any diminution of specific heat in the bodies under examination, because the specific heat of water is greater than that of ice. The pieces of ice used in this experiment, also, were intercepted from all communication with objects, from which they might derive heat, by being placed on a plate of ice under the receiver.

Sir Humphry Davy argues, that the immediate cause of the phenomena of heat is motion; "that the laws of its communication are precisely the same as the laws of motion. Since all matter may be made to fill a smaller volume by cooling, it is evident that its particles must have space between them, and since every body can communicate the power of expansion to a body of lower temperature, that is, can give an expansive motion to its particles, it is a probable inference that its own particles are possessed of the same motion; but if there is no change in the position of its parts as long as its temperature is uniform, the motion, if it exists, must be a vibratory or undulatory motion, or a motion of the particles round their axes, or a motion of particles round each other.

" It seems possible to account for all the phenomena of heat, if it be supposed that, in solids, the particles are in a constant state of vibratory motion, the particles of the hottest body moving with the greatest velocity, and through the greatest space; that, in liquids and elastic fluids, besides the vibratory motion, which must be conceived greatest in the last, the particles have a motion round their own axes, with different velocities, the particles of elastic fluids moving with the greatest quickness; and that, in ethereal substances, the particles move round their own axes, and separate from each other, penetrating in right lines through space. Temperature may be conceived to be dependent on the velocity of the vibrations; increase of capacity on the motion being performed in greater space; and the diminution of the temperature, during the conversion of solids into liquids or gases, may be explained on the idea of the loss of vibratory motion, in consequence of the revolution of particles round their axes, at the moment when the body becomes liquid or aëriform, or from the loss of rapidity of vibration in consequence of the motion of the particles through greater space."

The material theory has the advantage of offering an easy intelligible explanation of the phenomena of heat, so far as it is at all applicable or satisfactory. On the other hand, the vibratory theory is involved in the difficulty of requiring more acute powers of mind to apprehend its force, or even to understand any of its applications. Indeed, it would scarcely admit of full exposition without the use of the language of symbols of the higher mathematics; but, perhaps, the strongest support which the vibratory theory can derive, is from the facts which render it probable that heat and light are identical.

The rays of light differ from each other in refrangibility, in colour, in their chemical influence, and in their calorific power. It is, therefore, probable, that they may also differ extensively in their power of acting on the retina and on the thermometer. It has been already observed, that our organs of sensation possess a sensibility confined within certain limits; and this observation is not less true of the eye than of the other organs. It is, therefore, probable, that the sight may be sensible only to rays of light limited by certain degrees of refrangibility, and that too great or too small a degree of refrangibility may render the rays incapable of producing sensation. Certainly some, and probably all, those rays which are invisible to us, are visible to other animals. The chemical rays which are situate at the top of the spectrum, beyond the violate rays, may also have the calorific power, though in so slight a degree as not to affect the thermometer. It is, in fact, easy to conceive, that the caloric, chemical, and luminous property, may belong to every part of the spectrum, including even the invisible rays at both its extremities, but that these principles may vary according to different laws, the one decreasing as the other increases, so that one may be insensible to our powers of observation while another is in the full intensity of its action. Such an hypothesis is nothing more than a simple expression of the phenomena. If all the rays which produce invisible heat and chemical effects are assumed equally to be rays of light, it will follow that they will be all reflected by the same surfaces; and, according to the same law, of the equality of the angle of incidence and reflection. Hence it will follow, that they will be all concentrated and dispersed similarly by concave or convex reflectors. It follows, also, that they will be all polarised when transmitted through double refracting crystals, or when reflected at a particular angle by glass, and when they have received these modifications they will be susceptible of reflection by the glass when placed on two opposite sides, while they are incapable, by a similar reflection, by a glass similarly placed on two sides at right angles to these.

On the other hand, if the chemical and calorific rays be another principle, distinct from the luminous rays, there will be no reason to expect that these invisible rays will be reflected at all.

Since, therefore, all these complicated effects produced on the luminous rays are equally produced on nonluminous rays, it follows, that the fact of their being invisible is only relative to the peculiar degree of sensibility of our eyes, and has no connection with the nature of the rays themselves. According to the experiment of De la Hire, the invisible calorific rays, emitted by the body when gradually heated, assume the property and quality which the luminous calorific rays possess. It may, therefore, be inferred, that, when the rays emitted begin to be visible, they might be expected to be analogous to the least calorific part of the spectrum, which is its violet extremity, and this, in fact, is exhibited in all flames. If the flame of a candle be examined, it will be found to exhibit a blue or a violet colour, at the lowest point where it emanates from the wick, and this colour increases to whiteness where the flame attains its greatest degree of intensity.

Nevertheless, these circumstances, while they indicate the state of progression, do not exclude the peculiar property which may belong exclusively to the successive phases of that progression. Thus, the calorific emanations of different temperatures, and the luminous emanations of different colours, may differ from each other in their power of producing vision, heat, and chemical action; in their power of being transmitted; in their power of penetrating transparent bodies; and, perhaps, in many other characters, which philosophers have not yet examined.

If the identity of heat and light be admitted, then the question of the nature of heat is removed to that of light. Respecting light, two theories have been proposed, precisely similar to those of heat; viz. the corpuscular and the undulatory theories. Both of these theories serve to explain the great bulk of optical phenomena; but some effects, discovered by modern investigations in physical optics, are considered to be more satisfactorily explained by the undulatory theory. The question, however, still continues unsettled.

If, on a question of this nature, authorities be considered to be entitled to any weight, the vibratory theory would seem to have the strongest support. This theory was first suggested by Bacon, and, after him, adopted successively by Boyle, Newton, Cavendish, Rumford, Davy, Young, and a host of modern philosophers. On the other hand, some distinguished chemists, among whom may be mentioned Thomson and Murray, incline to the material theory.

Dr. Young, whose optical discoveries, more perhaps than those of any other philosopher, have countenanced the vibratory theory of light, is one of the strongest advocates for the adoption of the same theory in heat. "The nature of heat," he says, "is a subject upon which the popular opinion seems to have been lately led away by very superficial considerations. The facility with which the mind conceives the existence of an independent substance, liable to no material variations, except those of its quantity and distribution, especially when an appropriate name, and a place in the order of the simplest elements, has been bestowed on it, appears to have caused the most eminent chemical philosophers to overlook some insuperable difficulties attending the hypothesis of caloric. Caloric has been considered as a peculiar elastic or ethereal fluid, pervading the substance or the pores of all bodies, in different quantities, according to their different capacities for heat, and according to their actual temperatures; and being transferred from one body to another, upon any change of capacity, or upon any other disturbance of the equilibrium of temperature; it has also been commonly supposed to be

the general principle or cause of repulsion ; and in its passage from
one body to another, by radiation, it has been imagined by some
to flow in a continual stream ; and, by others, in the form of separate
particles, moving, with inconceivable velocity, at great distances from
each other.

  " The circumstances which have been already stated, respecting
the production of heat by friction, appear to afford an unanswerable
confutation of the whole of this doctrine.   If the heat is neither received from the surrounding bodies, which it cannot be without a
depression of their temperature, nor derived from the quantity already
accumulated in the bodies themselves, which it could not be, even if
their capacities were diminished in any imaginable degree, there is
no alternative but to allow that heat must be actually generated by
friction ; and if it is generated out of nothing, it cannot be matter,
nor even an immaterial or semi-material substance.   The collateral
parts of the theory have also their separate difficulties : thus, if heat
were the general principle of repulsion, its augmentation could not
diminish the elasticity of solids and of fluids ; if it constituted a continued fluid, it could not radiate freely through the same space in
different directions ; and if its repulsive particles followed each other
at a distance, they would still approach near enough to each other,
in the focus of a burning glass, to have their motions deflected from
a rectilinear direction.

  " If heat is not a substance, it must be a quality ; and this quality
can only be motion.   It was Newton's opinion, that heat consists in
a minute vibratory motion of the particles of bodies, and that this
motion is communicated through an apparent vacuum, by the undulations of an elastic medium, which is also concerned in the phenomena of light.   If the arguments which have been lately advanced
in favour of the undulatory nature of light be deemed valid, there
will be still stronger reasons for admitting this doctrine respecting
heat ; and it will only be necessary to suppose the vibrations and undulations, principally constituting it, to be larger and stronger than
those of light ; while, at the same time, the smaller vibrations of
light, and even the blackening rays derived from still more minute
vibrations, may, perhaps, when sufficiently condensed, concur in
producing the effects of heat.   These effects, beginning from the
blackening rays, which are invisible, are a little more perceptible in
the violet, which still possess but a faint power of illumination ; the
yellow-green afford the most light ; the red give less light, but much
more heat ; while the still larger and less frequent vibrations, which

have no effect on the sense of sight, may be supposed to give rise to the least refrangible rays, and to constitute invisible heat.

" It is easy to imagine that such vibrations may be excited in the component parts of bodies by percussion, by friction, or by the destruction of the equilibrium of cohesion and repulsion, and by a change of the conditions on which it may be restored, in consequence of combustion, or of any other chemical change. It is remarkable that the particles of fluids, which are incapable of any material change of temperature from mutual friction, have also very little power of communicating heat to each other by their immediate action, so that there may be some analogy, in this respect, between the communication of heat and its mechanical excitation."—LARDNER.

GUNPOWDER.

THIS explosive substance consists of an intimate mixture, in determinate proportions, of saltpetre, charcoal, and sulphur; and is better in proportion, every thing else being equal, to the quality of these ingredients. The nitre, in particular, ought to be perfectly refined by successive crystallizations, and finally freed from adhering water by proper drying, or by fusion in iron pots at a regulated heat. Nothing can surpass in these respects the nitre prepared in the Government Powder-works at Waltham Abbey. It is tested by adding to its solution in distilled water, nitrate of silver, with which it occasions no perceptible opalescence. The sulphur ought also to be of the finest quality, and purified by skimming or even sublimation, if at all necessary. The charcoal should be newly made; it should burn without having any sensible residuum, be dry, sonorous, light, and easily pulverized. The charcoal for gunpowder is made either of alder, willow, or dogwood, the latter being preferred, which are cut into lengths, and ignited in iron cylinders. It deserves notice, that the proportion of powder used for the several pieces of ordnance by the navy, &c. has been reduced one-third in consequence of the increased strength of the composition into which this cylinder charcoal enters, compared with that made formerly from charcoal made in pits. The wood, before charring, is carefully stripped of its bark.

The three ingredients being thus prepared, are ready for manufacturing into gunpowder. They are, 1st, Separately ground to a fine powder, which is passed through proper sieves or bolting machines. 2dly, They are mixed together in the proper proportions. These do not seem to be definitely determined, for they differ in different establishments of great respectability, as is shown in the following table :—

	Nitre.	Charcoal.	Sulphur.
Royal mills at Waltham Abbey,	75	15	10
French, for war, - - -	75	12.5	12.5
for sportsmen, - -	78	12	10
for mining, - -	65	15	20
Chaptal's proportions, - -	77	14	9
Chinese do. - -	75.7	14.4	9.9
Mr. Napier's do. - -	80	15	5

3d, The composition is then sent to the gunpowder mill, which consists of two edgestones of a calcareous nature, turning by means of a shaft on a bedstone of the same nature, which gives no sparks, as sandstones would be apt to do. On this bedstone the composition is spread, and moistened with as small a quantity of water as will, in conjunction with the weight of the revolving stones, bring it into a proper body of *cake*, but not of *paste*. The line of contact of the edgestone is constantly preceded by a scraper, which goes round with the wheel, constantly scraping up the cake, and turning it into the track of the stone. From 50 to 60 pounds are usually worked at once in each mill-wheel. When the cake has been thoroughly incorporated, it is sent to the corning-house, where a separate mill is employed to form the cake into grains or corns. 4. Here it is first pressed into a hard firm mass, then broken into small lumps; after which the graining is executed, by placing these lumps in sieves, on each of which is laid a disc of *lignum vitæ*. The sieves are made of parchment skins, perforated with a multitude of round holes. Several such sieves are fixed in a frame, which by proper machinery has such a motion given to it as to make the *lignum vitæ* runner in each sieve move round with considerable velocity, so as to break the lumps of cake and force the substance through the sieves, forming grains of several sizes. These granular particles are afterwards separated from the finer dust by proper sieves and reels. 5. The corned powder is next hardened, and the rougher edges taken off, by being revolved in a close reel or cask turning rapidly on its axis. This vessel somewhat resembles a barrel churn; it should be only half full at each operation; and has frequently square bars inside parallel to its axis, to aid the polish by attrition. 6. The gunpowder is now dried, which is done generally by a steam heat; or by transmitting a body of air, slightly heated in another chamber, over canvass shelves, covered with the damp gunpowder.

Mr. Coleman considers, that the strength of gunpowder depends very materially on the purity of the carbon employed.

After describing briefly the composition and preparation of gunpowder, we must inquire into the products of its detonation or instantaneous combustion. Of these products some are gaseous, and others solid. The first class consist of much carbonic acid, of a large quantity of nitrogen, a little oxide of carbon, steam of water, with carburetted and sulphuretted hydrogen. The second class of products are, sulphate of potash, sulphuret of potassium, and some traces of carbon. If the powder, instead of burning instantaneously, goes off slowly like a fusee, there would result besides, deutoxide of nitrogen, and even, according to Proust, nitrous acid, some hyponitrite of potash, and cyanide of potassium. It is easy, at any rate, to conceive the origin of all these products, by reflecting that common charcoal is always hydrogenated, and that cyanogen is a true carburetted nitrogen.

It is easy also to collect all the gases, so as to be able to examine them. To procure those springing from the slow combustion, it is merely necessary to fill with pulverized and hard pressed gunpowder, a small, narrow, and pretty long copper tube, shut at one end; to kindle the powder at the other end, plunging the tube under a bell glass filled with mercury. The solid products are easily collected.—URE.

SULPHURIC ACID.

Vide p. 109.

SULPHURIC acid was formerly obtained in this country by distillation from sulphate of iron, as it still is in many parts abroad. The fluid that is thus obtained is the German sulphuric acid, of which Bernhardt got sixty-four pounds from six hundred weight of vitriol; and on the other hand, when no water had been previously poured into the receiver, fifty-two pounds only of a dry concrete acid. This acid was formerly called *glacial oil of vitriol.*

It was shown by Fogel, that when this fuming acid is put into a glass retort, and distilled by a moderate heat into a receiver cooled with ice, the fuming portion comes over first, and may be obtained in a solid state by stopping the distillation in time. This constitutes absolute sulphuric acid, or acid entirely void of water. It is in silky filaments, tough, difficult to cut, and somewhat like asbestos. Exposed to the air it fumes strongly, and gradually evaporates. It does not act on the skin so rapidly as concentrated oil of vitriol. Up to 66° it continues solid, but at temperatures above this it becomes a colourless vapour, which whitens on contact with air. Dropped into water in small quantities, it excites a hissing noise, as if it were red hot iron ; in larger quantities it produces a species of explosion. It is convertible into ordinary sulphuric acid, by the addition of water. It dissolves sulphur and assumes a blue, green, or brown colour, according to the proportion of sulphur dissolved. The specific gravity of the black fuming sulphuric acid, prepared in large quantities from copperas at Nordhausen, is 1.896.

The ordinary liquid acid of Nordhausen is brown, of variable density, and boils at 100° or 120° F. One part of it evaporates in dense fumes, and the remainder is found to be common oil of vitriol. The above solid anhydrous acid has a specific gravity of 1.97 at 68° F. ; at 77° it remains fluid, and is less viscid than oil of vitriol. There is a little sulphurous acid present in that of Nordhausen, but it is accidental, and not essential to its constitution. The anhydrous acid makes a red solution of indigo. In the Journal of Science, xix. 62, I published the result of some experiments which I made to determine the nature of the solid acid. The brown liquid acid had a specific gravity of 1.842. When distilled from a retort into a globe surrounded with ice, a white solid sublimate was received. When this sublimate was exposed to the air, it emitted copious fumes of sulphuric (not sulphurous) acid. It burned holes in paper with the rapidity of a red-hot iron. By dropping a bit of it into a poised phial containing water, and stoppering instantly, to prevent the ejection of liquid by the explosive ebullition that ensues, I got a dilute acid containing a known portion of the solid acid, from the specific gravity of which, as well as its saturating power, I determined the constitution of the solid acid to be the anhydrous sulphuric ; or a compound of two by weight of sulphur, and three of oxygen. M. Gmelin states, in the Annales de Chimie et de Physique for June 1826, that on distilling sulphuric acid, if we change the receiver at the instant when it is filled with opaque vapours, and cover the new receiver with ice, we shall obtain anhydrous sulphuric acid, which is deposited in crystals on the inside of the vessel, and a less dense liquid acid which remains in the retort. He supposes, that during the distillation the sulphuric acid is divided into two portions, one of which gives up its water to the other.

The sulphuric acid made in Great Britain is produced by the combustion of sulphur in contact with a little nitre.

The following ingenious theory of its formation, was first given by MM. Clement and Desormes. The burning sulphur, or sulphurous acid, taking from the nitre a portion of its oxygen, forms sulphuric acid, which unites with the potash, and displaces a little nitrous and nitric acids in vapour. These vapours are decomposed by the sulphurous acid nitrous gas, or deutoxide of azote. This gas, naturally little denser than air, and now expanded by the heat, suddenly rises to the roof of the chamber; and might be expected to escape at the aperture there, which manufacturers were always obliged to leave open, otherwise they found the acidification would not proceed. But the instant that nitrous gas comes in contact with atmospherical oxygen, nitrous acid vapour is formed, which being a very heavy aëriform body, immediately precipitates on the sulphurous flame, and converts it into sulphuric acid ; while itself, resuming the state of nitrous gas, re-ascends for a new charge of oxygen, again to redescend and transfer it to the flaming sulphur. Thus we see, that a small volume of nitrous vapour, by its alternate metamorphoses into the states of oxide and acid, and its consequent interchanges, may be capable of acidifying a great quantity of sulphur.

This beautiful theory received a modification from Sir H. Davy. He found that nitrous gas had no action on sulphurous gas, to convert it into sulphuric acid, unless water be present. With a *small* proportion of water, 4 volumes of sulphurous acid gas, and 3 of nitrous gas, are condensed into a crystalline solid, which is instantly decomposed by *abundance* of water: oil of vitriol is formed, and nitrous gas given off, which with contact of air becomes nitrous acid gas, as above described. The process continues, according to the same principle of combination and decomposition, till the water at the bottom of the chamber is become strongly acid. It is first concentrated in large leaden pans, and afterwards in glass retorts heated in a sand bath. Platinum alembics, placed within pots of cast-iron of a corresponding shape and capacity, have been lately substituted in many manufactories for glass, and have been found to save fuel, and quicken the process of concentration.

Dr. Henry describes a peculiar substance, produced, during very cold weather, in the leaden pipe by which the foul air of a sulphuric acid chamber was carried away. It was a solid resembling borax. It became soft and pasty in a warm room, and gradually a thick liquid of sp. gr. 1.831 floated over the solid part. The crystalline part Dr. Henry considers as probably the same compound as MM. Clement and Desormes obtained by mingling sulphurous acid, nitrous

gas, atmospheric air, and aqueous vapour; and he thinks its constitution is probably

5 atoms sulphuric acid,	-	-	25.00
1 atom hyponitrous acid,	-	-	4.75
5 atoms water, -	-	-	5.625

$$35.375$$

Ann of Phil. xi. 368.

The proper mode of burning the sulphur with the nitre, so as to
produce the greatest quantity of oil of vitriol, is a problem, concerning
which chemists hold a variety of opinions. M. Thenard describes
the following as the best. Near one of the sides of the leaden
chamber, and about a foot above its bottom, an iron plate, furnished
with an upright border, is placed horizontally over a furnace, whose
chimney passes across, under the bottom of the chamber, without
having any connexion with it. On this plate, which is enclosed in a
little chamber, the mixture of sulphur and nitre is laid. The whole
being shut up, and the bottom of the large chamber covered with
water, a gentle fire is kindled in the furnace. The sulphur soon takes
fire, and gives birth to the products described. When the combustion is finished, which is seen through a little pane adapted to the
trapdoor of the chamber, this is opened, the sulphate of potash is
withdrawn, and is replaced by a mixture of sulphur and nitre. The
air in the great chamber is meanwhile renewed by opening its lateral
door, and a valve in its opposite side. Then, after closing these
openings, the furnace is lighted anew. Successive mixtures are
thus burned till the acid acquires a specific gravity of about 1.390,
taking care never to put at once more sulphur on the plate than the
air of the chamber can acidify. The acid is then withdrawn by stop-
cocks, and concentrated.

The ordinary form of a sulphuric acid lead chamber is the paral-
lelopiped; and its dimensions about seventy feet long, ten or twelve
high, and sixteen wide. At the middle height of one end a small
oven is built up, with a cast-iron sole, having a large lead pipe, ten
or twelve inches diameter, proceeding from its arched top into the
end of the lead chamber. On the sole the sulphur is burned, the
combustion being aided, when necessary, by heat applied from a
little furnace below it. Above the flaming sulphur a cast-iron basin
is supported in an iron frame, into which the nitre, equal to one-
tenth of the sulphur, is put, with a little sulphuric acid. The combustion of the sulphur is regulated by a sliding door on the oven. In

the roof of the remote end of the large chamber, a small orifice is left for the escape of the atmospherical azote, and other incondensable gases. This apparatus is used for the continuous process. But there is another, or that of the *intermitting* combustion, which is worthy of notice. Large flat trays, containing the sulphur and nitre, are introduced into the interior of the chamber, or into the oven, and fire is applied to the materials. When the sulphur is burned, and the chamber is replete with sulphurous and nitrous acids, the steam of water is thrown in, in determinate quantity, by a small pipe at the side. This causes a tumultuous motion among the gases and the atmospheric oxygen, which favours the mutual reaction. As the steam condenses, the sulphuric acid falls with it. After some time, the chamber is aired by opening valves of communication with the external atmosphere. The operation is then commenced anew.

Instead of using nitre, nitrous gas, disengaged from nitric acid by sugar or sawdust, is introduced into the chamber containing the fumes of burning sulphur, whereby the chemical reaction above described is produced; and then steam is thrown in to complete the process, and condense the sulphuric acid.

The bottom of the lead chamber should never be covered with pure water, but even in the first operation with a dilute acid, introduced on purpose. When nitrous acid comes into contact with water and an excess of atmospheric oxygen, it is converted into nitric acid and nitrous gas. This aëriform body gets more oxygen, and changes to nitrous acid, and thereafter to nitric. Hence, a chamber with its bottom covered with water, will, in some cases, fail in producing any sulphuric acid at all. Water, moderately charged with sulphuric and sulphurous acids, prevents the transition of the nitrous into nitric acid, and allows the progress of acidification of the sulphur to go on freely.

MM. Payen and Cartier disengage the nitrous gas in the midst of the burning sulphur, from a mixture of nitric acid and starch contained in platinum basins. The main objection to this process, is the difficulty of finding a market for the oxalic acid produced.

Other chemists find that it answers to introduce the vapour of nitric acid into the fumes of the burning sulphur, which converts it to nitrous acid; but the simplest mode of effecting this object is by the cast-iron basin placed over the burning sulphur, as already described.

In burning the sulphur, care should be taken that it does not rise in flowers by mere sublimation; to prevent which, the ingress of air should be proportional to the heat of the oven plate in the continuous process. The presence of sulphur in the acid would occasion great losses, were it not allowed to subside by repose; for in the con-centration of the sulphuric acid by heat, the sulphur would convert it into the sulphurous acid, which would be dissipated in the air.

The following form of apparatus, as used by MM. Payen and Cartier, has been lately described in the *Annales de l'Industrie*, t. i. It consists of a combustion oven, which communicates with a first chamber; this sends forward its gases into a second, which leads to a third, and this to a fourth, when necessary. But the fourth chamber does not immediately support the chimney, but communi-cates with it by a long sloping canal. In the first chamber the acid is kept up at about 1·500; in the second at 1·370; and in the third at 1·130. The floors of the several chambers rise in succession, so that, by means of syphons, a portion of the acid may be drawn from the second to the first, and from the third to the second, in propor-tion as the acid is let off out of the first for the purpose of concen-tration. Steam is also injected constantly into the terminal canal, and occasionally into each of the chambers, to facilitate the conden-sation of acid.

In comparing this and other forms of continuous apparatus, with those where the combustion is made to intermit, it obviously presents decided advantages. Each chamber is thus maintained at a tem-perature nearly uniform, which saves the injuries often done to the plates of lead, by the too frequent and abrupt expansions and con-tractions in the intermitting plan. The nitre basins and trays are, for the same reason, not so rapidly wasted. The quantity of acid obtained is greater, by nearly a third, in a given time, with an equal capacity of chambers. The wages of labour is also less, as well as the fuel requisite for burning the sulphur. Indeed the sul-phur-pan, or sole, needs heating only at the commencement. The dose of nitre is reduced to 8 per cent.

But nothing is easier than to combine the two systems, and to render these chambers intermittent, by gradually obstructing the in-gress of air into the combustion oven, then intercepting it altogether, and throwing in steam, condensing the acid vapours, and thereafter ventilating the air of the chambers.—URE.

BLEACHING.

THE chemical art by which the various articles used for clothing are deprived of their natural dark colour and rendered white.

The colouring principle of silk is undoubtedly resinous. Hence M. Baumé proposed the following process, as the best mode of bleaching it. On six pounds of yellow raw silk, disposed in an earthen pot, 48 pounds of alcohol, sp. gr. 0.867, mixed with 12 oz. muriatic acid, sp. gr. 1.100, are to be poured. After a days' digestion, the liquid passes from a fine green colour to a dusky brown. The silk is then to be drained, and washed with alcohol. A second infusion with the above acidulated alcohol is then made, for four or six days, after which the silk is drained and washed with alcohol. The spirit may be recovered by saturating the mingled acid with alkali or lime, and distilling. M. Baumé says, that silk may thus be made to rival or surpass in whiteness and lustre the finest specimens from Nankin. But the ordinary method of bleaching silk is the following :—The silk, being still raw, is put into a bag of thin linen, and thrown into a vessel of boiling river water, in which has been dissolved good Genoa or Toulon soap.

After the silk has boiled two or three hours in that water, the bag being frequently turned, it is taken out to be beaten, and is then washed in cold water. When it has been thus thoroughly washed and beaten, they wring it slightly, and put it for the second time into the boiling vessel, filled with cold water, mixed with soap and a little indigo; which gives it that bluish cast commonly observed in white silk.

When the silk is taken out of this second water, they wring it hard with a wooden peg, to press out all the water and soap; after which they shake it, to untwist it, and separate the threads. Then they suspend it in a kind of stove constructed for that purpose, where they burn sulphur; the vapour of which gives the last degree of whiteness to the silk.

The method of bleaching woollen stuffs.—There are three ways of doing this :—The first is with water and soap; the second, with the vapour of sulphur; and the third, with chalk, indigo, and the vapour of sulphur.

Bleaching with soap and water.—After the stuffs are taken out of the fuller's mill, they are put into soap and water, a little warm, in which they are again worked by the strength of the arms over a

N

wooden bench: this finishes giving them the whitening which the fuller's mill had only begun. When they have been sufficiently worked with the hands, they are washed in clear water and put to dry.

This method of bleaching woollen stuffs is called the Natural Method.

Bleaching with sulphur.—They begin with washing and cleansing the stuffs thoroughly in river water; then they put them to dry upon poles or perches. When they are half dry, they stretch them out in a very close stove, in which they burn sulphur; the vapour of which diffusing itself, adheres by degrees to the whole stuff, and gives it a fine whitening: this is commonly called Bleaching by the Flower, or Bleaching of Paris, because they use this method in that city more than any where else.

The colouring matter of linen and cotton is also probably resinous; at least the experiments of Mr. Kirwan on alkaline lixivia saturated with the dark colouring matter, lead to that conclusion. By neutralising the alkali with dilute muriatic acid, a precipitate resembling lac was obtained, soluble in alcohol, in solutions of alkalis, and alkaline sulphurets.

The first step towards freeing vegetable yarn or cloth from their native colour, is fermentation. The raw goods are put into a large wooden tub, with a quantity of used alkaline lixivium in an acescent state, heated to about the hundredth degree of Fahr. It would be better to use some uncoloured fermentable matter, such as soured bran or potato paste, along with *clean* warm water. In a short time an intestine motion arises, air bubbles escape, and the goods swell, raising up the loaded board which is used to press them into the liquor. At the end of from 18 to 48 hours, according to the quality of the stuffs, the fermentation ceases, when the goods are to be immediately withdrawn and washed. Much advantage may be derived by the skilful bleacher, from conducting the acetous fermentation completely to a close, without incurring the risk of injuring the fibre by the putrefactive fermentation.

The goods are next exposed to the action of hot alkaline lixivia, by bucking or boiling, or both. The former operation consists in pouring boiling hot ley on the cloth placed in a tub; after a short time drawing off the cooled liquid below, and replacing it above by hot lixivium. The most convenient arrangement of apparatus is the following:—Into the mouth of an egg-shaped iron boiler the bottom of a large tub is fixed air-tight. The tub is furnished with a false bottom pierced with holes, a few inches above the real bottom. In the latter, a valve is placed, opening downwards, but which may be readily closed by the upward pressure of steam. From the side of the iron boiler, a little above its bottom, a pipe issues, which, turning at right angles upwards, rises parallel to the outside of the bucking tub, to a foot or two above its summit. The vertical part of this pipe forms the cylinder of a sucking pump, and has a piston and rod adapted to it. At a few inches above the level of the mouth of the tub, the vertical pipe sends off a lateral branch, which terminates in a bent down nozzle, over a hole in the centre of the lid of the tub. Under the nozzle, and immediately within the lid, is a metallic circular disc. The boiler being charged with lixivium, and the tub with the washed goods, a moderate fire is kindled. At the same time the pump is set agoing, either by the hand of a workman or by machinery. Thus the lixivium, in its progressively heating state, is made to circulate continually down through the stuffs. But when it finally attains the boiling temperature, the piston rod and piston are removed, and the pressure of the included steam alone forces the liquid up the vertical pipe, and along the horizontal one in an uninterrupted stream. The valve at the bottom of the tube, yielding to the accumulated weight of the liquid, opens from time to time, and replaces the lixivium in the boiler.

This ingenious self-acting apparatus was invented by Mr. John Laurie of Glasgow, and a representation of it accompanies Mr. Ramsay's excellent article, Bleaching, in the Edinburgh Encyclopædia. By its means, labour is spared, the negligence of servants is guarded against, and fully one-fourth of alkali saved.

It is of great consequence to heat the liquid very slowly at first. Hasty boiling is incompatible with good bleaching. When the ley seems to be impregnated with colouring matter, the fire is lowered, and the liquid drawn off by a stopcock; at the same time that water, at first hot and then cold, is run in at top, to separate all the dark-coloured lixivium. The goods are then taken out and well washed, either by the hand with the wash-stocks, or by the rotary wooden wheel with hollow compartments, called the dashwheel. The strength of the alkaline lixivium is varied by different bleachers. A solution of potash, rendered caustic by lime, of the specific gravity 1.014, or containing a little more than 1 per cent of pure potash, is used by many bleachers. The Irish bleachers use barilla lixivium chiefly, and of inferior alkaline power. The routine of operations may be conveniently presented in a tabular form.

A parcel of goods consists of 360 pieces of those linens which are called Britannias. Each piece is 35 yards long, weighing on an average 10 pounds. Hence the weight of the whole is 3600 pounds avoirdupois. These linens are first washed, and then subjected to the acetous fermentation, as above described. They then undergo the following operations :—

1. Bucked with 60 lbs. pearl ashes, washed and exposed on the field.
2. Ditto with 80 lbs.   ditto.   ditto.
3. Ditto   90   potashes   ditto.
4. Ditto   80   ditto   ditto.
5. Ditto   80   ditto   ditto.
6. Ditto   50   ditto   ditto.
7. Ditto   70   ditto   ditto.
8. Ditto   70   ditto   ditto.
9. Soured one night in dilute sulphuric acid.
10. Bucked with 50 lbs. pearl ashes, washed and exposed.
11. Immersed in the oxymuriate of potash for 12 hours.
12. Boiled with 30 lbs. pearl ashes, washed and exposed.
13. Ditto   30   ditto   ditto.
14. Soured and washed.

The linens are then taken to the rubbing board, and well rubbed with a strong lather of black soap, after which they are well washed in pure spring water. At this period they are carefully examined, and those which are fully bleached are laid aside to be blued and made up for the market. Those which are not fully white, are returned to be boiled and steeped in the oxymuriate of potash, and soured until they are fully white. By the above process, 690 lbs. of commercial alkali are used in bleaching 360 pieces of linen, each measuring 35 yards. Hence, the expenditure of alkali would be a little under 2 lbs. a-piece, were it not that some part of the above linens may not be thoroughly whitened. It will, therefore, be a fair average to allow 2 lbs. for each piece of such goods.

On the above process we may remark, that many enlightened bleachers have found it advantageous to apply the souring at a more early period, as well as the oxymuriate solution. According to Dr. Stephenson, in his elaborate paper on the linen and hempen manufactures, published by the Belfast Literary Society, 10 naggins, or quarter pints, of oil of vitriol, are sufficient to make 200 gallons of souring. This gives the proportion, by measure, of 640 water to 1 of acid. Mr. Parkes, in describing the bleaching of calicoes in his Chemical Essays, says, that throughout Lancashire one *measure* of sulphuric acid is used with 46 of water, or one *pound* of the acid to 25 pounds of water; and he states, that a scientific calico printer in Scotland makes his sours to have the specific gravity 1.0254 at 110.

of Fahrenheit; which dilute acid contains at least 1-25th of oil of
vitriol. Five or six hours' immersion is employed.

In a note Mr. Parkes adds, that in bleaching common goods, and
such as are not designed for the best printing, the specific gravity of
the sours is varied from 1.0146 to 1.0238, if taken at the atmospheric
temperature. Most bleachers use the strongest alkaline lixiviums at
first, and the weaker afterwards. As to the strength of the oxymuriate steeps, as the bleacher terms them, it is difficult to give
certain data, from the variableness of the chlorides of potash and
lime.

Mr. Parkes, in giving the process of the Scotch bleacher, says,
that after the calicoes have been singed, steeped and squeezed, they
are boiled four successive times, for 10 or 12 hours each, in a solution
of caustic potash of a specific gravity from 1.0127 to 1,0156, and
washed thoroughly between each boiling. " They are then immersed
in a solution of the oxymuriate of potash, originally of the strength
of 1-0625, and afterwards reduced with 24 times its measure of
water. In this preparation they are suffered to remain 12 hours."
Dr. Stephenson says, that, for coarse linens, the steep is made by
dissolving 1 lb. of oxymuriate of lime in 3 gallons of water, and
afterwards diluting with 25 additional gallons. The ordinary specific
gravity of the oxymuriate of lime steeps, by Mr. Ramsay, is 1.005.
But from these *data* little can be learned; because oxymuriate of
lime is always more or less mixed with common muriate of lime, or
chloride of calcium, a little of which has a great effect on the
hydrometric indications. The period of immersion is 10 or 12
hours. Many bleachers employ gentle and long continued boiling
without bucking. The operation of souring was long ago effected
by butter-milk, but it is more safely and advantageously performed by
the dilute sulphuric acid uniformly combined with the water by much
agitation.

Mr. Tennent's ingenious mode of uniting chlorine with pulverulent lime, was one of the greatest improvements in practical
bleaching. When this chloride is well prepared and properly applied, it will not injure the most delicate muslin. Magnesia has been
suggested as a substitute for lime; but the high price of this alkaline
earth must be a bar to its general employment. The muriate of
lime solution resulting from the action of unbleached cloth on that
of the oxymuriate, if too strong, or too long applied, would weaken
the texture of the cloth, as Sir H. Davy has shewn. But the
bleacher is on his guard against this accident; and the process of

scouring, which follows most commonly the oxymuriatic steep, thoroughly removes the adhering particles of lime.

Mr. Parke informs us, that calicoes for madder work, or resist work, or for the fine pale blue dipping, cannot without injury be bleached with oxymuriate of lime. They require, he says, oxymuriate of potash. I believe this to be a mistake. Test liquors, made by dissolving indigo in sulphuric acid, and then diluting the sulphate with water, or with infusion of cochineal, are employed to measure the blanching power of the oxymuriatic or chloridic solutions. But they are all more or less uncertain, from the changeableness of these colouring matters. I have met with indigo of apparently excellent quality, of which four parts were required to saturate the same weight of oxymuriate of lime, as was saturated by three parts of another indigo. Such coloured liquors, however, though they give no absolute measure of chlorine, afford useful means of comparison to the bleacher.

Some writers have recommended lime and sulphuret of lime as detergent substances instead of alkali; but I believe no practical bleacher of respectability would trust to them alone. Lime should always be employed, however, to make the alkalies caustic; in which state their detergent powers are generally increased.

The coarser kinds of muslin are bleached by steeping, washing, and then boiling them in a weak solution of pot and pearl ashes. They are next washed, and afterwards boiled in soap alone, and then soured in very dilute (sulphuric acid. After being washed from the sour, they are boiled with soap, washed, and immersed in the solution of chloride of lime and potash. The boiling in soap, and immersion in the oxymuriate, is repeated, until the muslin is of a pure white colour. It is finally soured and washed in pure spring water. The same series of operations is used in bleaching fine muslins, only soap is used in the boilings commonly to the exclusion of pearl ash. Fast coloured cottons are bleached in the following way:—After the starch or dressing is well removed by cold water, they are gently boiled with soap, washed and immersed in a moderately strong solution of oxymuriate of potash or lime. This process is repeated till the white parts of the cloth are sufficiently pure. They are then soured in dilute sulphuric acid. If these operations be well conducted, the colours, instead of being impaired, will be greatly improved, having acquired a delicacy of tint which no other process can impart.

After immersing cloth or yarn in alkaline ley, if it be exposed to the action of steam heated to 222° in a strong vessel, it will be in a great measure bleached.

This operation is admirably adapted to the cleansing of hospital linen.

The following is the practice followed by a very skilful bleacher of muslins near Glasgow :—

" In fermenting muslin goods, we surround them with our spent leys, from the temperature of 100° to 150° F., according to the weather, and allow them to ferment for 36 hours. In boiling 112 lbs. = 112 pieces of yard-wide muslin, we use 6 or 7 lbs. of ashes and 2 lbs. of soft soap, with 360 gallons of water, and allow them to boil for 6 hours ; then wash them and boil them again with 5 lbs. of ashes, and 2 lbs. of soft soap, and allow them to boil 3 hours ; then wash them with water, and immerse them into the solution of oxymuriate of lime, at 5 on the test tube, and allow them to remain from 6 to 12 hours; next wash them, and immerse them into diluted sulphuric acid at the specific gravity of $3\frac{1}{2}$ on Twaddle's hydrometer = 1.0175, and allow them to remain an hour. They are now well washed, and boiled with $2\frac{1}{2}$ lbs. of ashes and 2 lbs. soap, for half an hour ; afterwards washed and immersed into the oxymuriate of lime as before, at the strength of 3 on the test tube, which is stronger than the former, and allowed to remain for 6 hours. They are again washed, and immersed into diluted sulphuric acid at the specific gravity of 3 on Twaddle's hydrometer = 1.015. If the goods be strong, they will require another boil, steep and sour. At any rate, the sulphuric acid is well washed out before they receive the finishing operation with starch.

" With regard to the lime, which some use instead of alkali immediately after fermenting, the same weight of it is employed as of ashes. The goods are allowed to boil in it for 15 minutes, but not longer, otherwise the lime will injure the fabric."

The alkali may be recovered from the brown lixivia, by evaporating them to dryness, and gentle ignition of the residuum. But in most situations the expense of fuel would exceed the value of the recovered alkali. A simple mode is to boil the foul lixivium with quicklime, and a little pipeclay and bullock's blood. After skimming, and subsidence, a tolerably pure ley is obtained.

PORCELAIN.

Vide p. 145.

THE two principal substances which enter into the composition of porcelain are alumina, or pure clay; silica, or pure flint, which forms the second material in the composition of pottery, has been considered as a primitive earth. It is of very common occurrence in most parts of the world, in primitive mountains. It is frequently found in great abundance imbedded in chalk. In Scotland and Ireland it occurs in secondary limestone. Flint abounds in alluvial districts in the form of gravel: an inexhaustible supply of excellent quality might be collected on some parts of the sea-coast of England, and particularly at and near Brighton, where there is enough of this material, known under the name of shingle, to serve the whole manufacturing wants of England for ages to come, while its removal would be attended with advantage to the place whence it should be taken. Flint is silica in a state nearly approaching to purity, its constituents being

Silica	.	98·
Lime	.	0·50
Alumina	.	0·25
Oxide of iron	.	0·25
Loss	.	1·
		———
		100·

It is usually gray, with occasional striped delineations occurring in its substance. It is obtained generally in rolled pieces, but often occurs in irregular shapes. It has internally a glimmering lustre; its fracture is conchoidal, and its fragments are sharp-edged. It is translucent. When two pieces are rubbed together in the dark, they emit phosphorescent light, and give off a peculiar smell. We are unable to dissolve silex in water. This process is, however, constantly performed by nature. The investigations of Klaproth enabled him to detect 25 grains of silex in 1000 ounces of the principal mineral spring at Carlsbad, in Bohemia; and the celebrated boiling fountain at Rykum, in Iceland, deposits so considerable a quantity of silicious earth, that a solid cup has been formed around it, rising to a considerable height. This solution of silica is probably owing, in both these cases, to the solvent power of soda; which is also present in the water. The water from the spring at Rykum used formerly to be projected into the air to the perpendicular height of 60 or 70 feet; but the overthrow of a mass of rock having since partially covered its orifice, the stream spouts out laterally to a distance of 50 or 60 feet. The heat of the liquid, after it has reached the surface, is sufficient to raise the thermometer to the boiling point of water; and there is little doubt that the fluid must have parted with some portion of its heat on emerging into the atmosphere. The capability of water, in its dense or liquid state, to assume, under these circumstances, a higher degree of heat than that at which it boils under ordinary atmospheric pressure, may be partly attributable to the depth from which it is brought, influenced by the same law that occasions fluids to boil at lower temperatures on the tops of high mountains. Silica is also found existing in solution in the Bath waters.

The best flints are of a dark grey colour, approaching to black, and having a considerable degree of transparency. Those which exhibit brown or yellow spots on their interior surfaces should be rejected, on account of the ferruginous particles which they contain, and which would occasion blemishes in the ware. Those larger masses of flint are always most preferred by the potter, which, being dark and clear within, are covered with a white crust externally. The rolled pieces which are taken from chalk pits are mostly of this description.

De Saussure asserts that pure silex may be fused at a heat equal to 4043 degrees of Wedgwood's pyrometer; a degree so far beyond any that has yet been observed, that one is at a loss to know upon what data the assertion is founded.

The clay principally used in the potteries of Staffordshire is brought to them from Dorsetshire and Devonshire. These earths are both of excellent quality, and, being free from any impregnation of iron, are valuable for the great whiteness which they exhibit when burnt. The Dorsetshire clay is brought from the Isle of Purbeck. It is of two kinds, distinguished as brown clay and blue clay: that from Devonshire comes from the southern part of the county, and is also of two distinct qualities, which are known as black clay and cracking clay. The clay from Dorsetshire is considered preferable to that from Devonshire for the potter's use.; so that it commands a price in the potteries equal to one-eighth more than the latter.

The good qualities of brown clay are, that it burns of an excellent white, and is not liable to crack during the process of burning. On the other hand, it is subject to the considerable imperfection of *crazing,*—an evil which induces some manufacturers to discard it

N 2

altogether from their works. Crazing is a technical phrase, used to denote the cracking of the glaze, which is believed to arise from the imperfect manner in which this is capable of uniting itself with the clay composing the body of the vessel. This defect of crazing is not, however, always referable to the cause here assigned, but may be owing equally to the faulty nature of the glaze, which may not be capable of perfect fusion in the heat of the kiln; or it may result from the error of the workmen in withdrawing the wares from the kiln at too early a period, and before they are properly cooled; the glaze, which is in fact glass, requiring great carefulness in this respect for its proper annealing, and being, without it, very liable to crack with every material variation of temperature to which it may be suddenly exposed.

Blue clay combines the greatest number of good qualities, and is the most generally esteemed, of all the four descriptions here mentioned. It burns exceedingly white, forms a very solid quality of ware, and is capable of being advantageously combined with a greater quantity of silicious earth, or flint, than any of the other kinds; a quality which is desirable, because the greater the proportion of silica that is used, the whiter will prove the ware; the limit to the use of flint being the inability of the clay to bear it in combination beyond a certain proportion without cracking. Both these descriptions of clay are much used as ingredients in the manufacture of porcelain.

Black clay owes its distinctive colour to the quantity of coaly or bituminous matter which it holds in combination, but which is entirely consumed and dissipated when the clay is submitted to the heat of the oven, leaving the articles of which it is composed of a very good white; and which is, indeed, found to be the more perfect in proportion as the clay has originally been blacker. Cracking clay has acquired its name from an evil property of occasioning the ware to crack while undergoing the first application of fire. To compensate in some degree for this evil, the goods in which it is employed prove of an extreme whiteness. Much judgment and experience must be brought to the employment of this clay, that its tendency to cracking may be as much as possible corrected by a proportionate admixture. If clay of any description were dried without the addition of any other body, after being made sufficiently plastic to be modelled on the potter's wheel, it must inevitably crack, as the evaporation of its water will occasion it to shrink in the proportion of one part in twelve during the drying.

Another description of clay much prized for the manufacture of finer kinds of earthenware and porcelain, was found in Cornwall by Mr. Cookworthy, and is commonly denominated China clay. This is very white and unctuous to the touch, and is obviously formed by the gradual disintegration of the felspar or Granite. There are found in Cornwall large mountains of this mineral, some of which are thus partially decomposed; this China clay proves, on examination, to be identical with the kao-lin of the Chinese. It was found by Mr. Gerhard in the course of some experiments upon granite (which is a compound of quartz, felspar, and mica,) that the felspar was melted into a transparent glass, that the mica was found lying under it in the form of a black slag, while the quartz remained unaltered.

The China clay of Cornwall is prepared by the clay merchants on the spot where it is found. The stone is broken up into pieces of a small size, and then cast into a running stream: there the light argillaceous parts are washed off and held suspended in the water, while the more ponderous mica and quartz remain at the bottom of the stream. At the end of the rivulet the water is stopped by a dam, and the pure clay gradually subsides. When this deposit is completed, the clear water is drawn off, and the solid matter dug out in square blocks, which are placed on shelves, and exposed to a continued current of air until sufficiently dry to be packed in casks for shipment. This clay, which is then in the state of a fine powder, is very smooth, and of an extreme whiteness. Mr. Wedgwood found by analysis that it contains sixty parts of alumina and twenty parts of silica. The manufacturers are required to pay a much higher price for this than for any other of our native earths, but for some finer purposes it is altogether indispensable.

A portion of undecomposed Cornish felspar is often added to the clay, on account of its fusibility and tenaciousness, by which it binds, as it were, the whole ingredients more closely together. The fusible quality of felspar is owing to the presence of about an eighth part of potass. If this alkaline substance be separated by decomposition, as is the case with the China clay above described, the fusibility no longer exists, and the body remains unaltered in the greatest heat of a porcelain furnace. The use of this material has of late been very much increased in our porcelain works. It is a curious and very useful fact, that although neither clay, flint, nor lime can be separately melted, yet when mixed together in due proportions, the mass is fused without difficulty, the one mineral acting as a flux to the other.

Steatite, or soapstone, has of late years been very much employed in the composition of porcelain. When present, in even a small proportion, it limits the contraction of the ware in the furnace. Steatite is a sub-species of mica, which is found abundantly in Cornwall, and is met with also in the Island of Anglesea. The mineral which forms the porcelain earth of Baudissero, was long considered to be a superior kind of clay, until it was discovered by M. Geobert that it contains not a particle of alumina in its composition. This chemist, on endeavouring to convert the substance into alum, found, to his great surprise, that he obtained only crystals of sulphate of magnesia (Epsom salts.) Proceeding thence to analyse it carefully, he ascertained its composition to be, magnesia 68, carbonic acid, 12, silica 15.6, sulphate of lime 1.6, water 2.8. The soapstone of Cornwall differs from this substance, yielding on analysis, magnesia 44, silica, 44, alumina, 2, iron 7.3, magnesia 1.5, chrome 1.2. It also contains traces of lime and muriatic acid.

In a published letter addressed by M. Proust to M. Vauquelin from Madrid, mention is made of a beautiful kind of porcelain produced in that city, and which is described to be of a texture even harder than the porcelain of France. Instead of employing kao-lin, the body of the ware is made with spuma maris, a species of pot-stone found in the neighbourhood of Madrid, and the glaze is composed of felspar brought from Gallicia. The pot-stone when taken from the quarry is sufficiently soft to admit of its being cut with a knife like soap. Besides magnesia, silex, and some particles of argil and lime, it contains a portion of potass, the presence of which, in the competent opinion of M. Proust, contributes not a little to the superior quality of the manufacture.

PAINTING ON PORCELAIN.

THE art of painting on earthenware, although of comparatively recent introduction into England, is by no means a modern invention. It is well known that the ancients manufactured coloured enamels; and some specimens of the art, performed by the Egyptians more than three thousand years ago, have been preserved to the present day, which is an evidence of this fact; showing us at the same time, that, in so remote an age, the artists of Egypt were possessed of sufficient practical knowledge of chemistry, to avail themselves of processes which have been brought to light anew by scientific investigators of more modern times.

Recently, the art has been carried to an admirable degree of

perfection in Europe. Some specimens are preserved in the porcelain
works at Sévres, of which the French artists are justly proud; while
the performances in our own potteries at Worcester, in Staffordshire,
at Derby, and yet more recently in Yorkshire, are such as entitle
them to be placed in an equal rank with those of our continental
neighbours.

When about seventy years ago, Mr. Wedgwood commenced the
series of improvements, by which his name has been rendered so
deservedly celebrated throughout Europe, no attempts at embellishment had been made in the English potteries; and if ornamented
services of porcelain were seen on the tables of the wealthy, they
were always of foreign, and generally of oriental production. So
soon, however, as, by the intrinsic merit of his wares, this enterprising
manufacturer had secured not only the patronage of royalty, but the
more solid support of his countrymen in general, he called into action
the crucible of the chemist, and the pencil of the artist, and led the
way in bestowing that degree of outward embellishment on his productions, which converted them into objects of elegance, and at once
encouraged and gratified the growing taste for luxury among the
higher classes in this country.

The system of mystery still preserved in the English potteries, in
all that respects the composition and glazing of wares, was likewise
long practised with regard to the preparation of colours. If, at any
time, a manufacturer had found out a preparation more advantageous
than that in use before, he always endeavoured to limit the benefit of
the discovery to his own works; a desire more easy of accomplish-
ment formerly than it has become since the more general diffusion of
the light of science. M. Brongniart, at one time director of the
national manufactory of porcelain at Sévres, has the merit of being
the first who published a correct statement of the most approved plans
for preparing and combining the metallic oxides used in colouring
porcelain and glass. The employment of these substances for such
purposes had been long known before and commonly practised, and the
art was even carried by some of its professors to a high degree of perfection; but, as M. Brongniart observes, no attempt had been made
at the time his essay was written (1801,) to apply to it the principles
of chemical science; and such pretended descriptions as had then
been published contained no theory, and consequently no general
principles. Where even the authors did offer explanations, these
were founded upon the most ridiculous hypotheses; so that all improvements were rather the offspring of chance than the result of
systematic inquiry.

It would afford but little satisfaction, or information, to relate by what steps the art now under consideration was reduced into a system, and thus became, in some measure, deserving of the name of a science. It will be sufficient to state the means by which that art is now rendered available in the best conducted porcelain works. In a great part of the following description, the lucid statements given by M. Brongniart in his essay will be closely followed; since with scarcely any variation, the same processes have been used in both the French and English establishments to the present day.

In this branch of the art there are various objects to be considered, a proper acquaintance with which is necessary to success. Such are, the composition of colours; the fluxes which are necessary to render these fusible, which unite them to the wares, and in many cases impart brilliancy to their tints; the vehicle employed in laying on the colours, and the course to be pursued in fixing them on the porcelain by means of heat.

Metallic oxides form the bases of all vitrifiable colours, but every metallic oxide is not proper for being employed in decorating porcelain. Some are highly volatile, as the oxides of mercury and of arsenic. Others part so freely with the oxygen they hold in combination, that their colour proves uncertain, and varies with every application of heat; such are the puce-coloured and red oxides of lead, and the yellow oxide of gold. Oxides which are susceptible of great variations are very seldom employed. Black oxide of iron is not used alone for producing that colour on porcelain; and the green oxide of copper, as formerly prepared, was so uncertain that it was very rarely employed; but this evil has, since the time of M. Brongniart, been greatly remedied.

Oxides uncombined with other substances are not susceptible of fusion; and although they may be attached in thin strata to vitrifiable bodies by a very violent heat, yet their colours, with the exception of lead and bismuth, would, in such case, become dull, and possibly be even destroyed. In order to promote their fusion, a flux is therefore added, the composition of which varies according to the means employed for diluting the colours at the time they are used. Where a volatile oil is chosen for this dilution, a flux composed of glass, nitre, and borax is most proper; but when, as in the Sèvres manufactory, gum-water is substituted for this volatile oil, the flux must be varied, because borax cannot be properly diluted in gum-water. A compound of glass, lead, and silex is therefore preferred by M. Brongniart, who, however, has given no directions regarding the proportions wherein these bodies must be brought together. The other menstruum which is recommended by M. de Montamy, in his treatise on painting in enamel, is composed of

Powdered glass	-	40 parts.
Calcined borax	-	22
Refined nitre	-	44.

It is indispensable, not only that the borax and nitre be as pure as they can be rendered, but also that the glass shall not contain the smallest particle of lead in its composition. These ingredients must first be well triturated together in a glass mortar, with a pestle of the same material, during an hour, and then exposed in a crucible to the heat of a charcoal fire, until the swelling, which for a time accompanies the fusion of the mass, has ceased.

By means of this flux the colours are fixed upon the porcelain, and made to assume a resplendent appearance : the metallic oxides, being enveloped by the flux, are preserved from all contact with the air, and their colour is rendered permanent ; the fusion having been promoted at a temperature too low for their destruction.

Trial should be made of the habitudes of different colours in combination with their flux, in order to determine the exact quantity to be employed with each. Various substances vitrify with greater or less facility when thus combined, and the greatest carefulness and skill are consequently required, so to proportion the relative quantities of each, that not more of the flux shall be added than is necessary to cause a perfect vitrification. If too little were used, the colours, although they might attach themselves to the porcelain, would nevertheless be dull ; and if too much, the colours would run, their outlines would not be sufficiently decided, and all the finer touches of the artist would disappear. It has been remarked that colours which require for their fusion more than six times their weight of flux, do not flow with sufficient facility : and as they cannot be applied with a pencil so as to produce a satisfactory result, should be rejected.

Such metallic oxides as would have their colours altered by a strong or often repeated heat, are employed after being mixed with their flux, but without having been previously fused with it. In many cases metallic oxides are first fused with the requisite proportion of their flux, and are then ground for use.

Enamel is glass made opaque by the oxide of tin, and rendered fusible by the oxide of lead. All glazes that contain lead participate in the properties of enamel. Raw glazes used for covering tender porcelain are of this nature. The colours employed in painting this porcelain are those which serve for painting in enamel ; they require

less flux than others, because the surface to which they are applied
becomes soft enough to be penetrated by them.   Hard porcelain,
whose nature is identical with those of China and Saxony, has two
kinds of colours applied to it.   Those of the first kind, which are
used in the representation of different objects, are baked in a heat
much below that necessary for baking porcelain; while the other
colours, which are few in number, must be exposed to the highest
degree required for the porcelain itself.   The glaze used for hard
porcelain has little or no lead in its composition.   The Sévres manufacturers, and some few in England, employ felspar without any
mixture of lead.   This glaze, when exposed to the heat of the gloss
oven, dilates, and its pores are opened without becoming soft, so that
the colours are not absorbed by it, and do not undergo those changes
which occur when they are applied to tender porcelain, where, by
mixing with the body of the enamel, they become faint and indis-
tinct.   This effect is much increased likewise, where some particular
colours are employed, and especially the reds produced from iron,
which are exposed to the destructive action of the oxide of lead that
is contained in the glaze.   Painting on tender porcelain must, for
these reasons, be several times retouched with the pencil, in order to
give to it the distinctness and brilliancy which follow the use of the
same colours on hard porcelain, so that a high degree of ornament is
seldom or never given to any but the latter description. In the embellishment of hard porcelain, these retouchings are not required, except for the most elaborate specimens of the art, which can by such
means, however, be produced with the most admirable degree of
perfection, so as to render paintings on porcelain not distinguishable
from the finest productions of the pictorial art, without reference to
the body upon which it is performed, or to the means used for bringing out the colours; natural objects, landscapes, portraits, and even
historical pieces being represented with all the truth, as well as with
all the brilliancy of colouring, which distinguish the works of the
first masters.

One great inconvenience attends the repeated exposure to the heat
of the oven of pieces thus retouched; the colours being liable to
peel off, unless the greatest care has been used in their application.
This defect has been remedied in the Sévres works, by introducing a
calcareous flux into the felspar glaze, which softens it, without at all
affecting the body of the ware.   Soda and potash are never used as
fluxes, as their introduction causes the colours to scale; the reason
for which is, that, becoming volatile in a great heat, they abandon the
colour, which then will not adhere to the glaze.

The liquid matter which serves as a vehicle in laying on the colours, is rubbed with them upon a glass palette until the whole is intimately united. The mixture must be brought to that state of dilution which is most proper and convenient for its application with a hair pencil on the surface of the porcelain. Great care is used in the choice and management of these diluent liquids, which must always be sufficiently volatile to be entirely dissipated in the heat to which the wares are afterwards exposed. In France, the preference is given to oil of lavender as a vehicle; and in order to ensure the proper degree of fluidity, this oil is divided by distillation into two parts: that which first comes over, being the most volatile, and having the least density, is used for diluting the colours when they become too thick; and, on the other hand, the portion that remains in the retort, having the opposite qualities, is reserved for thickening them when they run too freely. Oil of turpentine which has been some time in store, is more generally used in England, and is said to answer the purpose better than any other volatile fluid.—PORCELAIN MANUFACTURE.

GLASS MANUFACTURE.

Vide p. 143.

UNDER the general name of glass, chemists comprehend all mineral substances, which, on the application of heat, pass through a state of fusion into hard and brittle masses, and which, if then broken, exhibit a lustrous fracture. Most glasses are transparent also; and the non-existence of this property is generally owing to the presence of some foreign and unessential substance.

The glass of commerce—that beautiful manufacture to which the generic name is most commonly applied—does not include so wide a range of bodies; and is always composed of some siliceous earth, the fusion and vitrification of which has been occasioned by certain alkaline earths, or salts, and sometimes with the aid of metallic oxides.

There are five different and distinct qualities of glass manufactured for domestic purposes; viz.

Flint glass, or crystal;
Crown or German sheet glass;
Broad or common window glass;
Bottle or common green glass; and
Plate glass;

the materials and the processes used in making which form the subject
of our present inquiry.

Before commencing the description of any of the manipulations
employed in this interesting manufacture, it will be better to give a
general account of the different materials used, and to point out how
the particular qualities of glass are influenced by the properties of
those various ingredients.

Each of the five descriptions contains, in common with the others,
two ingredients, which, indeed, are essential to their formation—
silex and an alkali.

The variations of quality, and distinctive differences observable in
glass, principally result from the kind of alkali employed, and its degree of purity, as well as from the addition of other accessory materials; such as nitre, oxide of lead or of manganese, white oxide of
arsenic, borax, or chalk.

Silex is not equally proper in all its forms for the composition of
glass. Sea sand, which consists of spherical grains of quartz, so minute as to be qualified for the purpose without any preparation except careful washing, is the form wherein silex is most commonly
used for the purpose in England. All sea sand is not, indeed, equally
applicable to the glass-maker's purpose. That used in this country
for making the finer descriptions of ware is usually obtained, either
from the port of Lynn, in Norfolk, or from Alum Bay, on the
western coast of the Isle of Wight.

The best glass was formerly made with common flints, calcined and ground as used in the manufacture of pottery, and
hence the name which it acquired of flint glass. The employment of silex in this form is now wholly discontinued in glass-
houses, as it is known that some qualities of sand answer the purpose
equally well, while the labour and expense of calcining and grinding
are saved by the substitution.

Both soda and potash are well adapted to the purpose of making
glass. They are used in the form of carbonates; that is, holding
carbonic acid in combination with themselves as bases. The acid
flies off during the progress of the manufacture, and the result is a
compound of silex and alkali:

As already stated, the quality of glass is influenced by the degree
of purity of the alkali. For making the finest flint glass, pearl-ash,
which is potash in a purer form, must be used. This alkali must
previously be still further purified by solution and subsidence, and
then evaporating the fluid to dryness. By this purification a loss is
sustained, amounting to between 30 and 40 per cent. in the weight

of pearl-ash. Coarser kinds of alkali, such as barilla, kelp, or wood-ashes, which are combined with many impurities, are employed for the production of inferior glass. Complete fusion and vitrification are accomplished by these means, the impurities even being of a nature to assist towards the production of these effects. The green colour imparted to glass is produced by the iron, which is present in a greater or less degree in these coarser alkaline substances. Barilla, when sufficiently cheap, is always chosen preferably to wood-ashes or kelp.

A very small proportion of nitre is used in the composition of glass, to occasion the destruction of any carbonaceous matter which may exist in the ingredients. This salt must be added previously to the fusion of the glass. At a degree of heat much below that of the furnace, nitre will decompose, giving out much oxygen, and maintaining such metallic oxides as may be present in their highest state of oxygenation. It is thus of use in fixing arsenic, the volatile property of which increases as it approaches the metallic state.

Oxide of lead, in the form of either litharge or minium, is essential to the making of flint-glass, into the composition of which it enters very largely. This metal acts, in the first place, as a most powerful flux, promoting the fusion of all vitrifiable substances at comparatively low temperatures. It is also permanently beneficial in imparting highly valuable properties to the glass, of which it forms a part. This, by its means, is rendered much more dense; has a greater power of refracting rays of light; possesses more tenacity when red-hot, causing it for that reason to be more easily worked; and is rendered more capable of bearing uninjured sudden changes of temperature. On the other hand, glass, into the composition of which much lead has entered, is so soft as to be easily scratched and injured if rubbed against hard bodies. Such glass is also improper as a recipient for many fluids which are of an acrid nature, by which it would be corroded and destroyed. Another great inconvenience attending the use of lead is this, that it does not become intimately enough united with the other components for the whole mass to assume an uniform density. It will almost always happen, that the glass at the bottom of the pot contains a larger proportion of litharge than that above. This inequality of density is continually increasing as the contents of the pot are diminished by the workman; and it is thence impossible to withdraw from it any two portions whose densities shall agree.

Monsieur Guyton Morveau has related a very curious exemplification of this fact, which once occurred to himself when experi menting in conjunction with Monsieur de Buffon in the plate-glass manufactory near Langres. Remaining in the crucible was a portion of flint-glass in fusion, composed of thirty-two parts powdered crystal, thirty-two parts minium, sixteen of soda, and one part nitre. To this was added the requisite quantity of the ingredients commonly employed for forming plate glass in the manufactory, and the whole was melted together in the furnace. When the mass was sufficiently refined it was laded into the cistern, cast on the copper table in the usual manner, and transferred to the annealing furnace. Its quality being subsequently submitted to examination, the plate was found to be composed of two distinct and perfectly level strata through the whole mass, the lower stratum occupying about one third of its thickness.

So complete an instance of the precipitation of the denser through the lighter portion is not elsewhere to be met with in the records of glass-making : its occurrence in this particular occasion should probably be referred to the active agency of some cause which escaped the observation of the two philosophers.

It is a general effect of this inequality, that the glass, when wrought, appears waved; a defect which is particularly inconvenient in that which is intended for the construction of optical instruments. Glass is also fusible at lower temperatures according to the proportion of lead which it contains. This quality, which would be mischievous for some purposes, is, on the contrary, beneficial for others. It is often essential to chemists that they shall be able, during the progress of their experiments, to bend the tubes with which they are operating.

Black oxide of manganese has long been used for clearing glass from any foul colour which it might accidentally possess through the impurity of the alkali employed, and in particular from that green tinge which marks the presence of iron. This property of manganese, when in the form of an oxide, occasioned it to be anciently known as *glass soap*, a name which very accurately describes its use. The circumstances attending the employment of this substance in glass-making are of rather a curious nature. When added in a moderate proportion to any simple glass, it imparts a purple colour; and should its quantity be much increased, this colour is deepened until the glass becomes nearly black. If, while the mass thus coloured is still in fusion, either white arsenic, or charcoal, or other carbonaceous matter be added, an effervescence is seen to follow, and the colour becomes gradually more faint until it altogether disappears, and the glass is rendered clear and transparent. Provided the green hue which it is desired to counteract be considerable, the application of a very small quantity of manganese is not followed by any sensible tinge of purple; but the moment that the proportion is more than sufficient for the purpose, this colour immediately appears, and must be corrected. This correction is performed in a very simple manner in the glasshouse, by trusting into the pot of melted glass a piece of wood, which, becoming charred by the heat, causes the purple again to vanish; while a slight effervescence, as before described, and the escape of numerous bubbles of air, are plainly perceptible. If nitre be then added, the purple colour will be restored.

The reason for these changes it is not difficult to explain. The oxide of manganese imparts a purple colour, only when in a state of high oxygination. When brought into contact with carbonaceous matter, it is partially deprived of its oxygen, and loses its colouring property. The air bubbles which escape consist of carbonic acid gas, which is disengaged by the action of the charcoal on the oxide of manganese. The effect which follows upon the introduction of nitre is of a contrary nature. When made of a red heat this substance gives out oxygen in great abundance, and the manganese being thus re-invested with the oxygen of which it was deprived by the charcoal, resumes with it the colouring property.

Another advantage attending the use of oxide of manganese results from its property of powerfully assisting in the fusion of earthy bodies. It also gives considerable density to glass, but the same dis-advantage accompanies its use as already has been noticed with regard to litharge. Having from its greater specific gravity a tendency to settle towards the bottom of the pot, the glass by this means varies in density throughout its substance; in addition to which circumstance, the manganese acts injuriously upon the pots by corroding them at the bottom.

One of the uses of white oxide of arsenic has already been described, that, namely, of correcting the colouring effects of manganese. It is also a very powerful flux, and a great temptation to its use is found in its cheapness. It should, however, be employed with moderation. If a considerable time be not allowed for its intimate incorporation with the other ingredients of the glass, this will appear clouded or milky; a fault which will afterwards increase in the lapse of time. An excessive quantity of arsenic likewise occasions the glass to become gradually soft and to decompose, for which reason the employment of drinking-vessels in this condition is unsafe.

Another, and a harmless, application of arsenic in glass-making is, when it is introduced into the fused mass in order to dissipate any carbonaceous matters which result from defects in preparing the alkali. In this case, small lumps of white arsenic are intimately blended with the mass by stirring. The great heat causes it at once to unite with and to carry off the carbon in a volatile form, leaving the glass entirely free from carbonaceous matter, and nearly so from arsenic.

Borax is used in preparing only the finest descriptions of glass : its employment is, indeed, principally confined to plate glass. It is too expensive to admit of its forming part in the composition of common descriptions, although its use in all cases would be desirable, as its efficacy in promoting the fusion of vitrifiable substances is un-rivalled. When borax has been introduced, the compound is caused by it to flow with great freedom, and to be without specks and bub-bles, which would impair both its beauty and utility. Should the alkali employed prove deficient in strength, a small portion of this salt will serve as an effectual remedy.

Lime in the form of chalk is useful as a very cheap flux. It is also beneficial in facilitating the operations of the workman in fashioning glass, and it has the property of diminishing its liability to crack on exposure to sudden and great variations of temperature. Chalk can only be used sparingly, however, in the glasshouse, as the escape of carbonic acid causes the ingredients in the pot to swell considerably during the fusion. The presence of lime in any exces-sive degree would also occasion the rapid destruction of the pots, upon the substance of which it acts with considerable energy. Glass wherein lime exists in excess is also rendered cloudy, although the mass while in fusion appears perfectly pellucid. Not more than about six per cent. of lime can be added without risking this defect.— CABINET CYCLOPÆDIA.

* —————

GOLD MINES.

Vide p. 178.

THE simplest method of obtaining gold, consists in collecting the grains or small particles from the beds of rivers, especially after rains, which bring down fresh matter from the mountains. In some instances, the skins of animals are laid in the water courses, and they retain the metallic particles : it has been supposed that the fable of the "golden fleece," so well known in classical mythology, had reference to this practice. The Brazilians used for this purpose the blankets which, on the opening of the trade to that country some

years ago, were, with other equally ill-adapted commodities sent out
by the merchants of Great Britain. The *lavras*, or gold washings
of Geraes Minas, or gold district of Brazil, are minutely described
by Dr. Walsh, who visited them in 1829. Gold, he says, was first
known to exist in the country so early as the year 1543; the Indians
made their fishing hooks of it, and from them it was discovered that
it was found in the beds of streams, brought down from the mountains. But the first ore found by a white man in that country was in
the year 1693: this discovery led to the colonization of the Minas
Geraes, and to all those evils resulting from the " cursed lust of
gold," with details of which the history of South America abounds.
Dr. Walsh mentions that, at a very early period, " two parties
meeting on the banks of the river, where S. José was afterwards
built, instead of agreeing in their objects, and pursuing together their
operations, set upon each other like famished tigers, impelled by a
hunger still more fierce—the *auri sacra fames*. A bloody encounter
ensued, in which many were killed on both sides, and the river was
from thenceforth called the Rio das Mortes, or the River of Deaths.
" The vicinity of this river," proceeds our authority, " every where
attests the extensive search for gold formerly pursued here, as it was,
for a length of time, considered one of the richest parts of Brazil, from
the profusion of the precious metal found on its surface. All the
banks of the stream are furrowed out in a most extraordinary manner,
so as to be altogether unaccountable to one unacquainted with the
cause. The whole of the vegetable mould was washed away, and
nothing remained but a red earth, cut into square channels, like
troughs, with a narrow ridge interposed between them. Above was
conducted a head stream of water, let down through these troughs,
which were all on an inclined plane. The lighter parts of the clay
were washed away, and the gold remained behind."

The operation of collecting the precious particles is described by
Dr. Walsh, as he saw it practised in the works of a gentleman, by
whom he had been invited for the purpose. " At the bottom of a
very long, shallow, sloping trench, with a flat floor and perpendicular sides, were laid green grass sods. On some occasions,
English blankets have been used; and, on others, hides, with the
hair uppermost: but sods were found, from experience, to be the
best. At the head of the trench was a large water-course. The
former collections from the cascalho were placed here, and the water
being turned through it, it dissolved the mass, and carried down the
whole of it. The lighter parts were borne away, but the heavier
subsided into the grass, which entangled the particles of gold; and

so it was in the state in which it was first found in the country, when,
by a similar process, it was washed down from the auriferous *serras*.
The leaves and roots of the grass we saw, were covered with a yellow
and black deposit; the first gold dust, the latter esmeril, or oxide of
iron, a substance which always accompanies it. Beside the long
trench was a pool, in which stood eight or ten negroes, each holding
in his hand a round flat dish. These dishes are of three sizes and
names; the first, a gamella, a very spacious bowl, eight or nine feet
in circumference; the second, smaller, and called carumbeia; the
third, called batea, of a size between both, and in the shape of a flat
cone.

" A quantity of the impregnated sods was raised in the gamella by
negro boys, and set down before the men in the pool. They took a
portion of them, and laying it in the carumbeia, they dipped it into
the water, turning it dexterously from side to side, and separating the
leaves and fibres of the grass, which were carried away by the water
with the lighter parts of the clay, and, in a short time, nothing remained but the gold and esmeril at the bottom, exhibiting clouded
shades of black and yellow. When a quantity of this impure mixture
was thus collected, it was laid in the batea, and here it was dexterously moved from side to side in a constant ablution of fresh
water, till the esmeril also passed off, and the heavier gold dust remained alone in the point of the cone. The whole of this was
finally deposited in a large copper skillet, placed over the fire on the
spot, and stirred till all the water was evaporated, and nothing remained but dry gold dust, in general of exceedingly minute particles,
but frequently appearing in small globules, some as large as a grain
of small shot. In this state a magnet was passed through it, to
which the particles of iron, still mixed with the gold, adhered; and
this was continued till the whole was abstracted. Sometimes a more
scientific process is resorted to. The mixture of dust is put into a
bowl, and two ounces of mercury added to two pounds of gold and
oxide. This mass is worked by the hand into a dough, when the
mercury takes up the gold only, which is merely entangled, but not
amalgamated with it. It is then put into a cloth, and a portion of
the mercury squeezed out; the remainder is set in a brass vessel over
a fire, and covered with green leaves, which are removed as they
become parched. They exhibit small globules of the mercury on
the surface. What remains in the vessel is pure gold."

The quantity collected at this "harvest home" of gold, as the
Doctor terms it, was about four pounds weight, which, at 4*l*. the
ounce, would give 200*l*. sterling; apparently a rich, but, as the

writer justly asserts, in reality, a very unprofitable and ruinous mode
of farming. "The proprietor had seven or eight blacks, daily
employed, for 300 days, collecting the cascalho, whom he first
bought, and then fed, clothed, and supported, which left, in the end,
but little or no real profit. But by far the most injurious effect was
that produced on his farm. As we passed through it," proceeds the
traveller, "for several hundred acres every thing green had disappeared, and left behind a red desert, of the most irksome and barren
aspect, on which nothing hereafter would be found to grow in any
given period, as no new soil is formed, and the old workings appear
as recent as those from which the vegetable mould had been washed
but yesterday; and thus, in extracting the gold from his farm, the
proprietor had extracted along with it every particle of productive
riches also." Such is the aspect, in general, of those regions where
the search for the precious metals is carried on, whether by washing
the diluvial deposits, or by subterranean excavations: to the evil in
the latter case has to be added the immense waste of negro life, as
the auriferous soils, in most tropical climates, are peculiarly unhealthy. To the sterility produced so generally, it would seem there
are some exceptions, for a traveller who, only a few years ago,
published an account of South America, says:—" It is usually
observed in those countries where great mineral riches exist, that the
soil is of a barren and unproductive nature; but Chili affords a
striking solitary exception to this rule. Streams, abounding in gold,
wander through the most luxuriant corn-fields, and the farmer and
the miner hold converse together on their banks."

The dust and grains of gold are smelted in Brazil with a flux
of muriate of mercury; the furnaces are heated with charcoal, and
the contents of the crucibles are poured into ingot moulds, holding
about 32 pounds of the metal. Very pure gold runs in about three
hours, but when it contains more foreign admixture, it is propor-
tionately refractory in the furnace, and requires more of the flux.

Gold is afterwards purified by being submitted to the process of
cupellation, parting, and quartation: by the former process the refiner gets quit of every particle of lead or other inferior metallic
alloys, and by the latter separates any portion of silver which might
remain intermixed with the gold. The cupel, in which the first
operation is performed, and which is so called from its resemblance
to a little cup, is composed of calcined bones, or in some cases with
an intermixture of fern ashes: a vessel formed of these matters, by
slightly moistening them, and forming the cupel by means of a
mould, not only resists the action of the most vehement fire, but

O

absorbs metallic bodies which are changed by heat into a fluid scoria, while it retains them so long as they continue in a metallic state. In a small vessel of this description, placed withinside a sort of bent perforated tile made of crucible earth, and surrounded with an intense charcoal fire, the gold, in little buttons, is subjected to the heat. As the heat is continued, and the process goes on, a various-coloured scum, consisting of the scoria of the lead or other metals present, rises to the top, which, liquefying, runs to the sides, and is there absorbed by the cupel. This operation is continued, until a sudden luminous appearance of the mass in fusion, shows that the last remaining portion of inferior alloy has been given out. As, however, the gold may yet retain some portion of silver, which, being nearly as difficult of oxidation as the more precious metal, is not thrown off in the cupel, the mass is next subjected to the process called parting, which consists in reducing it to the state of very thin plates by rolling: these being cut into small pieces, are digested in hot diluted nitric acid; which dissolves the silver, leaving the gold in an undissolved porous mass: this course is adequate to the attainment of the required degree of purity, when the amount of silver is so considerable in proportion to the gold as thoroughly to expose it to the action of the acid; but when the alloy of silver is very inconsiderable, a previous course is adopted, that of quartation, so called, because the mixture is composed of three parts of silver and one of gold, which on being laminated and digested in the acid, exposes every portion of the gold to the effect of the separating menstruum. In some cases, the two metals are melted together, and sulphur being thrown in combines with the silver, the gold falling to the bottom. Bergman recommended to dissolve the mass in nitromuriatic acid, by which the silver would be deposited in the form of an insoluble muriate, and the gold would fall in a fine powder by the action of the sulphate of iron.

SMELTING SILVER ORES.

SILVER is extracted from its ores, properly so called, either by smelting in a manner similar to that practised with reference to other metals, or by amalgamation,—the former being technically designated the *dry*, and the latter the *wet* method. The processes carried on with chemical exactness at the extensive amalgamation works of Freyberg, the capital of the mining district of Saxony, and where one chief

advantage of this mode over smelting is the saving of fuel, are
described with scientific minuteness by J. H. Vivian, Esq. in the
" Annals of Philosophy," vol. xxvii. The first operation at the works
is the selection of ores to form a proper mixture, with reference to
the quantity of silver and sulphur they contain: this is a most
material point. It has been observed, that the amalgamation process
succeeds best when the silver produce is about 75 ounces in the ton.
The object, therefore, is, by a selection of different ores, to bring the
whole as near to this average as can be conveniently effected; at the
same time regard being had to the proportion of sulphur contained
in them. This is estimated by the quantity of regule, or sulphuret,
found in the ore; which is ascertained by an assay in the crucible.
The standard by which they are governed is, that a proper mixture of
the different ores gives 35 per cent. of regule; about one half of
which may be sulphur. But, as the silver in the Freyberg ores is
rarely in the metallic state, at least in any quantity, it becomes
necessary to detach it from its combination with sulphur or other
substances, before subjecting it to the actual process of amalgamation,
as otherwise these substances would prevent its union with the
mercury. This is done by adding to the mixture of raw ore 10 per
cent. of common salt, by which during the operation in the furnace
that follows, a chemical change is effected. The sulphur becomes
acidified, and the acid thus formed, uniting with the base of the salt,
forms sulphate of soda; whilst the muriatic acid thus set free, combines with the silver in the ore that was not in the metallic state, and
forms muriate of silver.

In this state the ore is subjected to various mechanical operations,
with riddles, screens, mills, and sieves, until it is reduced to an impalpable powder. It is then submitted to the action of the mercury,
which is the actual process of amalgamation. This is performed in
barrels, each about 3½ feet in length, and 2 in diameter, in the
centre; and which are so arranged as to revolve on their axis. The
mixture or charge in each barrel consists of sifted calcined ore,
mercury, metallic iron, and water, in certain proportions. The ore
is composed of sulphate of soda, muriate of silver, muriate of iron,
and other metals and earthy matters. By the process of amalgamation, the barrels being made to revolve during a period of sixteen
or eighteen hours, the muriate of silver becomes decomposed by the
action of the iron on its acid, and the silver, thus reduced to the
metallic state, combines with the mercury, forming what is termed
an amalgam; whilst the sulphate of soda, the muriate of iron, and
other salts, become dissolved in water. The silver combined with the

mercury is then filtered, by which the surplus metal is separated, and
a compound remains in the cask, consisting of six parts of mercury
and one of silver. This amalgam is subjected to the action of heat
in a distilling furnace, by which the mercury is sublimed and the
silver remains. The silver is then collected, and melted in a crucible;
but as it contains a portion of other metals that were combined with
it in the ore, it is afterwards refined in a cupel or testing furnace.
Such is the general outline of the process, described with great precision of detail by Mr. Vivian in the work above named.

The method of extracting silver from lead is every where similar
in principle; it is very simple, depending upon the different essential
properties of the two metals. It is an essential property of lead,
when melted in the open air, to lose its metallic appearance, and to
burn away into a kind of earth; it is, on the other hand, an essential
property of silver, not to burn away, or to lose its metallic appearance, when exposed to the action of the strongest fire in the
open air. Hence, when a mass of metal, consisting of lead and
silver, is melted in the open air, the lead will be burned to ashes, or
into hard masses of a scaly texture, known as litharge, or silver stone,
while the silver will sink to the bottom of the vessel in which the
mass had been melted. In practice, however, and where the
operation is conducted upon a large scale, the silver is extracted
from the lead by the oxidation of the latter metal in a reverberatory
furnace of a particular construction, the process connected with the
use of which has been described as follows :—A shallow vessel, called
a cupel, is filled with prepared fern ashes rammed down, and a con-
cavity cut out for the reception of the lead, with an opening on one
side for the nozzle of the bellows, through which the air is forcibly
driven during the process. The French smelters cover the surface
of the ashes with fine hay, upon which they arrange the pieces of
lead. When the fire is lighted, and the lead is in a state of fusion
from the reverberation of the flame, the blast from the bellows is
made to play forcibly on the surface, and, in a short time, a crust of
oxide of lead, or litharge, is formed, and driven off to the side of the
cupel opposite to the mouth of the bellows, where the shallow side or
aperture is made for it to pass over; another crust of litharge is
formed and driven off, and this is repeated till nearly all the lead has
thus been scorified and blown aside. The operation continues about
forty hours, when the complete separation of the lead is indicated by
the appearance of a brilliant lustre on the convex surface of the
melted mass in the cupel, which is occasioned by the removal of the
last crust of litharge that covered the silver. The French introduce

water through a tube into the cupel, to cool the silver rapidly, and to prevent its spirting out, which it does sometimes when the refrigeration is gradual, owing, as it is supposed, to its tendency to crystallize. The silver thus extracted is not sufficiently pure; it is further refined in a reverberatory furnace, being placed in a cupel lined with bone ashes, as in the cupellation of gold, and exposed to an intense heat, so that the lead which escaped oxidation by the first process, is converted into litharge, and absorbed by the ashes of the cupel.

Native alloys of the precious metals are sometimes met with: an amalgam, consisting of about two parts of mercury and one of silver, is said to occur in Hungary and Sweden. The mineral called electrum, consisting of about 64 per cent. of gold, and 36 of silver, is found in Siberia. An alloy known to mineralogists as auriferous native silver, and composed of gold 28, and silver 72 parts, is procured in Norway.—CABINET CYCLOPÆDIA.

COPPER MINES AND SMELTING.

THE following account of the process of smelting copper is given in the very valuable work on the manufactures in metals already quoted:—

" Process I.—*Calcination of the Ore.* The copper ores, when discharged from the vessels in which they are brought from Cornwall, are wheeled into yards or plots contiguous to the works, and there deposited, one cargo over the other, so that, when cut down perpendicularly, to be carried to the furnaces, a tolerably general mixture is formed. This is always desirable in a smelting work, as the ores being of different qualities and component parts, the one acts as a flux to the other. The ore in the yard is weighed over to the calciner-men in boxes, containing each 1 cwt. These are carried on men's shoulders to the calciners, and emptied into iron bins or hoppers, formed by four plates of cast iron tapering to the bottom placed over the roof of the furnace, and supported by wrought iron frames resting on its sides: two of these bins are usually placed over each calciner, and nearly opposite the side doors, so that the charge of ore when let into the furnace may be conveniently spread, which is done by means of long iron tools, called stirring rabbles.

This charge of ore usually consists of three to three and a half tons; it is distributed equally over the bottom of the calciner, which is made of fire bricks or square tiles. The fire is then gradually increased, so that towards the end of the process, which lasts twelve hours, the charge is drawn out through holes in the bottom of the calciner, of which there is one opposite to each door; and, falling under the arch of the furnace, remains there till it is sufficiently cool to be removed, when water is thrown over it to prevent the escape of the finer metallic particles. It is then put into barrows and wheeled to the proper depots : in this state it is called calcined ore. If the process has been well conducted, the ore is black and powdery.

Process II.—*Melting of the calcined ore.* The calcined ore is delivered, as in the raw state, to the workmen, in boxes containing 1 cwt each ; the charge is deposited in the same manner in a bin placed on the top of the furnace, and from thence passed into the interior as required. When the charge is let down and spread over the bottom, the door of the furnace is put up and well luted. Some slags from the fusion of the coarse metal or sulphuret are added, not only on account of the copper they contain, but to assist the fusion of the ore, being chiefly composed of oxide of iron.

After the furnace is charged, the fire is made up, and the main object of the smelter is to bring the substances into fusion ; it is, therefore, in this respect, different from the calcining process. When the ore is melted, the door of the furnace is taken down, and the liquid mass well rabbled, or stirred, so as to allow of the complete separation of the metallic particles from the slags or earthy matters, and to get the charge clear of the bottom of the furnace, which is made of sand, and soon becomes impregnated with metal. The furnace being ready, that is, the substances being in perfect fusion, the smelter takes an iron rabble, and skims off, through the front door, the sand or slags, consisting of the earthy matters contained in the ore, and any metallic oxides that may have been formed, which being specifically lighter than the metals in the state of sulphuret, float on the surface. When the metal in the furnace is freed from slags, the smelter lets down a second charge of ore, and proceeds with it in the same manner as with the first ; and this he repeats until the metal collected in the bottom of the furnace is as high as the furnace will admit of without flowing out at the door, which is usually after the third charge ; he then opens a hole, called the tapping hole, in the side of the furnace, through which the metal flows into an adjoining pit filled with water. It thus becomes granulated, and collects in a pan at the bottom of the cistern, which is raised by means of a crane : it is then filled into barrows, and wheeled to the place appointed for its reception.

The slags, received into moulds made in sand in front of the furnaces, are removed after each charge, and wheeled out of the work to the *slag-bank*, where they are broken, and carefully examined; any pieces found to contain particles of metal, are returned to the smelter to be remelted, and unless the 'slag is very thick and tenacious, the copper which they may contain is found at the bottom: what is clean or free of metal is rejected. These slags are composed of the earthy matters contained in the ore, and the oxides of iron and other metals that were mixed with the copper. The oxide of iron gives them a black colour; the silex or quartz remains in part unfused, and gives the slags a porphyritic appearance.

In this process, the copper is concentrated, and a mass of stuff with which it was combined in the ore got rid of. The granulated metal usually contains about one third of copper; it is thus four times as rich as the ore, and must consequently have diminished in bulk in the same proportion: its chief component parts are sulphur, copper, and iron. The men work round the twenty-four hours; and commonly melt in this time five charges: under favourable circumstances, as fusible ore, strong coal, furnace in good repair, they even do six charges: they are paid by the ton.

Process III.—*Calcination of the coarse metal.* This is conducted in precisely a similar manner to the calcination of the ore; the charge is nearly of the same weight; but, as it is desirable to oxidise the iron, which is more readily effected in this process than in the ore calciners, where it is protected from the action of the air by the earthy matters with which it is combined, the charge remains twenty-four hours in the furnace, and during that time is repeatedly stirred and turned. The heat during the first six hours should be moderate, and from that time gradually increased, to the end of the operation.

Process IV.—*Melting the coarse metal after calcination.* This is performed in furnaces exactly similar to those in which the ore is first melted, and with the calcined metal are melted some slags from the last operations in the works which contain some oxide of copper, as likewise pieces of furnace bottoms impregnated with metal: the chemical effect which takes place is, that the oxide of copper in the slags becomes reduced by a portion of the sulphur, which combines with the oxygen, and passes off as sulphurous acid gas, while the metal thus reduced enters into combination with the sulphuret. That there may be a sufficient quantity of sulphur in the furnace to promote these changes, it is sometimes necessary, when the calcined metal is in a forward state, to add a small quantity of raw or uncalcined metal, so that a clean slag may be obtained; the slags from this operation are skimmed off through the front door, as in the ore furnaces. They have a high specific gravity, and should be sharp, well melted, and free from metal in the body of the slag. After the slag is skimmed off, the furnace is tapped, and the metal is suffered either to flow into water, as before, or into sand-beds, according to the modes of treatment it is to be subjected to in subsequent operations. In the granulated state, it is called fine metal; in the solid form, blue metal, from the colour of its surface. The former is practised when the metal is to be brought forward by calcination: its produce in fine copper is about sixty per cent.

Process V.—*Calcination of the fine metal.* This is performed in the same manner as the calcination of the coarse metal.

Process VI.—*Melting of the calcined fine metal.* This is performed in the same manner as the melting of the coarse metal; the resulting product is a coarse copper, of from eighty to ninety per cent. of pure metal.

Process VII.—*Roasting.* This is chiefly an oxidising process: it is performed in furnaces of the same description as the melting furnaces, although distinguished by the appellation of roasters. The pigs of coarse copper from the last process are filled into the furnace, and exposed to the action of the air, which draws through the furnace at a great heat: the temperature is gradually increased to the melting point, the expulsion of the volatile substances that remained is thus completed, and the iron or other metals still combined with the copper are oxidised. The charge is from 25 to 30 cwt.; the metal is fused toward the end of the operation, which is continued from twelve to twenty-four hours, according to the state of forwardness when filled into the furnace, and is tapped into sand-beds. The pigs are covered with black blisters, and the copper in this state is known by the name of blistered copper: in the interior of the pigs the metal has a porous honeycombed appearance, occasioned by the gas formed by the ebullition which takes place in the sand-beds on tapping. In this state it is fit for the refinery, the copper being freed from nearly all the sulphur, iron, and other substances, with which it was combined. In some works the metal is forwarded for the refinery, by repeated roastings, from the state of blue metal: this, however, is a more tedious method. The oxidising processes are greatly assisted by a contrivance, the patent for which was purchased by Messrs. Vivian of Mr. Sheffield the inventor; the object of which is, to keep a constant stream of fresh air passing over the metal by means of a channel formed in the bridge, communicating by holes with the external air, and with the interior of the furnace.

Process VIII.—*Refining and toughening.* The refining furnace is similar in construction to the melting furnaces, and differs only in the arrangement of the bottom, which is made of sand, and laid with an inclination to the front door instead of to one side, as is the case in those furnaces from which the metal flows out; the refined copper being taken out in ladles from a pool formed in the bottom near the front door. The pigs from the roasters are filled into the furnace through a large door in the side. The heat at first is moderate, so as to complete the roasting or oxidising process, should the copper not be quite fine. After the charge is run down, and there is a good heat on the furnace, the front door is taken down, and the slags skimmed off. An assay is then taken out by the refiner with a small ladle, and broken in the vice; and from the general appearance of the metal in and out of the furnace, the state of the fire, &c. he judges whether the toughening process may be proceeded with, and can form some opinion as to the quantity of poles and charcoal that will be required to render it malleable, or as it is termed, bring it to the *proper pitch.* The copper in this state is what is termed *dry.* It is brittle, is of a deep red colour inclining to purple, an open grain, and a crystalline structure. In the process of toughening, the surface of the metal in the furnace is first well covered with charcoal. A pole, commonly of birch, is then held in the liquid matter, which causes considerable ebullition, owing to the evolution of gaseous matter; and this operation of *poling* is continued, adding occasionally fresh charcoal, so that the surface of the metal may be kept covered, until, by the assays which the refiner from time to time takes, he perceives the grain, which gradually becomes finer, is perfectly closed, so as to assume even a silky polished appearance in the assays when half cut through and broken, and it becomes of a light red colour. He then makes further trial of its malleability by taking out a small quantity in a ladle, and pouring it into an iron mould; and when *set,* beating it out while hot on the anvil with a sledge hammer. If it is soft, and does not crack at the edges, he directs the men to lade it out, which they do in iron ladles coated with clay, pouring it into pots or moulds of the size required by the manufacturer. The usual size of the cakes for common purposes is twelve inches wide by eighteen in length. The operation of refining requires great care; under-poling or over-poling being found injurious to the process.

Sometimes, when copper is difficult to refine, a few pounds of pig-lead are added to the charges of copper. The lead acts as a purifier, by assisting, on being oxidised itself, the oxidation of the iron or any metal that may remain combined with the copper, and not, as may be supposed, by uniting with the copper, and thereby increasing its malleability. This is a mistaken notion: indeed the smallest portion of lead combined with copper, renders the metal difficult to *pickle* or clean from oxide, when manufactured.

Copper for making brass is granulated, that its surface may be increased, so as to combine more readily with zinc or calamine. This is effected by pouring the metal from the ladles in which it is taken out of the furnace into a large ladle, pierced in the bottom with holes, and supported over a cistern of water. The water may be either hot or cold, according to the form to be given to the metal. When warm, the copper assumes a round form, and is called *bean shot*. When a constant supply of cold water is kept up, the metal has a light ragged appearance, and is called *feathered shot*. The former is the state in which it is prepared for brass wire making. Another form into which copper is cast, chiefly for exports to the East Indies, is in pieces of the length of six inches, and weighing about eight ounces each: these are called Japan copper."

LEAD.

IN the earliest periods of the mining in Derbyshire, the ore was undoubtedly smelted on the tops or western brows of high hills, by fires made of charcoal and wood, and blown by the wind only: these ancient hearths were termed boles, and the appellation is still retained by several elevated sites in the neighbourhood of the lead districts. One of these bleak eminences, near Chesterfield, crowned with a fine plantation, and conspicuous to a great distance on the moors has been charmingly celebrated by Mr. Montgomery, in his well-known stanzas entitled "Bole Hill Trees." These very ancient boles, or wind hearths, were succeeded by slag-mills, or hearths similar to those at Mendip; being somewhat like a blacksmith's forge on a large scale, and blown by bellows worked either by men or water, and one of which still remains attached to each cupola, where there is a stream of water, for the convenience of remelting the slag, after the metal has been first drawn from the ore in the draught furnace.

The cupolas, as they are called, or those low-arched reverberating furnaces which are commonly used for smelting the lead ore in

Derbyshire are said to have been introduced from Wales, by a com-
pany of Quakers, about the year 1747. The very perfect cupolas
of Sykes, Milnes, and Co. called Stanage, in Ashover, are minutely
described in their construction and management, by Mr. Farey; the
description of this gentleman is, therefore, here adopted:—" Each
cupola here consists of a reverberatory furnace about ten feet long,
and six feet wide in the middle, inside, and two feet high in the
centre; the flame being supplied from a fire-place at the end, over a
wall of bricks, called the fire-bridge, one foot high, and reaching
within eighteen inches of the roof, which descends gradually to the
end opposite the fire-place; where it is only six inches high, and
where are two openings, separated by a triangular block of fire-stone,
which meet in the passage or flue, eighteen inches wide. This flue
curves upwards through a length of ten feet or more, and is covered
by flat stones closely joined in fire-clay, that can be removed when
the flue-glass, or vitreous scoria, requires cleansing; these flues join
by an easy curve into a tall chimney, whose top is fifty-five feet above
the ground. One side of the furnace, or cupola, is called the labourer's side; here the door is situate for supplying coals to the fire,
and also three small openings, about six inches square, into the furnace, stopped by iron plates, that can be removed when a free current
of air is required, or the furnace needs stirring. On the other side,
called the working side, are three similar openings, stopped in like
manner, by moveable iron plates, and two others below them, for
tapping the slag and the lead, as mentioned below; the ash-hole also
opens on this side, and has conveniences for raking and opening the
grate-bars from below, in case of their slagging up, so as to impede
the draft to the fire.

The floor of the furnace, which is composed of old slag, roughly
rounded, and brought to the proper form by hoes, is made up nearly
to the level of the small doors on the labourer's side, but declines so
as to be eighteen inches below the middle door on the opposite, or
working side; and here the tap-hole is situate, for letting out the lead
into a large cast-iron pan, called the lead pan, placed under it in a
niche, in the lower part of the furnace. From the lead tap-hole the
bottom rises all ways, forming thereby a receptacle of the proper size
for the lead contained in a charge of ore; level with the usual surface of which, another tap-hole is made under the door which is
farthest from the fire-place: this is for tapping or letting off the slag.
In the centre of the top of the furnace there is a small opening,
called the crown-hole, covered by a thick iron plate when the furnace
is at work; above this crown-hole is a large hopper of wood, with an

iron tube below it, reaching down almost to the plate which covers the crown-hole ; above the iron tube the hopper is furnished with a shuttle, or sliding valve, and the whole is suspended by framing from the roof of the large building, like an immense barn, in which four of the cupolas thus described are contained. Into the aforesaid hopper a charge of ore is put, at leisure times during the working of the furnace, ready to be instantly discharged into it, by removing the crown-plate and drawing the hopper-shuttle, as soon as all the lead of the previous charge has been drawn off, and the tapping-holes are stopped up by quicklime, tempered as mortar ; so that neither time nor heat is lost between the charges.

In the cupola or furnace thus constructed, the process of roasting the ore at a moderate heat, to expel or sublime the sulphur, arsenic, &c. can be performed, and afterwards an intense heat can be applied for expelling the oxygen or reducing the metal.   The ore, which is here shot down into the furnace at once, usually consists of five or six, or even seven or eight sorts, from different mines, or dressed in a different manner ; on which mixtures, in due proportions determined by experiment, the perfection of the process much depends.   Six-teen hundred weight (of 120 lbs. each) is the usual charge, which is first raked and spread over the floor of the furnace, and then the doors are closed to bring it to a red heat; when the doors are again opened, and the ore is raked and stirred about, first from one side of the furnace and then from the other, so as to expose repeatedly every part of the ore to the action of the heat and the air, during several hours ; at the end of which time the doors are again closed, and the fire increased to an intense degree, by which the reduction of the metal is effected, collecting in the bottom of the furnace, while the slag swims on the top of it, to the depth of two or three inches. The tapping of the slag is then performed, by poking out the stopping of lime, when the slag flows out like melted glass in appearance, and soon cools on the floor of the building ; in which state it is opaque, of a whitish-grey colour, and moderately heavy.   This macaroni slag, as it is called, being drawn off, the smelter immediately scatters in upon the melted lead two or three shovels-full of quicklime, in powder; which has the effect of stiffening the remaining slag, which floats on the metal, and which is carefully raked off in a semi-fluid state : this is called drawn slag, and is, when cold, of a very dark or black colour, and very heavy.

The lead-pan being cleared out, and the stopping of lime removed, the metal is suffered to run clean out of the furnace into the pan, which is then skimmed, and the dross is thrown back into the furnace, where it exhibits the most vivid and beautiful changes of colours imaginable; the lead is then taken out by ladles, and poured into seven or more cast-iron moulds with round ends, of the proper size for pieces of lead, which are placed in a row, and are there left to cool. A new charge of ore is now let down into the furnace, through the crown-hole, and the operations repeated, by means of two sets of workmen, during every seven or eight hours for the whole week. Coals are used that are a little disposed to cake or crozzle. According to the authority now quoted, 66 *per cent.* was about the average annual produce of metal from the ore smelted at the Stanage cupolas, though some choice parcels had produced 76 *per cent.*"

EXPERIMENTS.

NOTHING tends to imprint chemical facts upon the mind so much as the exhibition of interesting experiments. With this view the following selection has been made, in which such experiments as may be performed with ease and *safety*, have uniformly been preferred. The original design of the author was to have explained the cause of each result to the student, and indeed most of the experiments were written with that intention; and the rationale of each was actually drawn up to accompany them. But having since thought that this method might perhaps tend to check that spirit of inquiry which ought to be encouraged in youth, he has determined merely to give the mode of conducting each experiment, and leaves it to the pupil himself to discover the *cause* of every effect; earnestly advising him not to perform a second experiment till he has fully satisfied himself respecting the operation of the former; this he may do by referring to the proper places in the catechism, or the notes which are annexed.

1. Take a small phial about half full of cold water; grasp it gently in the left hand, and from another phial pour a little sulphuric acid very gradually into the water. A strong SENSATION OF HEAT will immediately be perceived. This, by the continued addition of the acid, may be increased to many degrees beyond that of boiling water.

2. Take a small phial, in one hand, containing some pulverized muriate of ammonia; pour a little water upon it, and shake the mixture. In this instance a SENSATION OF COLD will immediately be felt.

3. Into a teacup, placed upon a hearth, and containing about a table-spoonful of oil of turpentine, pour about half the quantity of strong nitric acid, previously mixed with a few drops of sulphuric acid. The moment the acids come in contact with the turpentine, FLAME will be produced. In performing this experiment it is advisable to mix the acids in a phial, to tie the phial to the end of a stick, and, at arm's length, to pour its contents into the oil; as the sudden combustion sometimes occasions a part of the liquids to be thrown out of the vessel.

4. Put about an ounce of marble grossly pulverized into an eight-ounce phial, with about an equal quantity of water. Pour upon it a little muriatic acid, and CARBONIC ACID GAS will be evolved.

5. Put about an ounce of iron filings into a phial, with about three or four ounces of water; pour a little sulphuric acid upon the contents, and HYDROGEN GAS will be evolved.

6. Pour water into a small glass retort so as to occupy about one third of its capacity, lute its beak into the end of a gun barrel, the middle of which must be kept red-hot in a furnace, or by a chafing-dish; then if a lamp be applied to the retort so as to cause the water to boil, the steam will pass through the red-hot iron tube, and in this case also will be decomposed; for, as the oxygen combines with the iron, the hydrogen gas will be liberated, and may be collected in the usual way.

7. Put some sulphuret of iron into a phial, pour a little diluted sulphuric acid over it, and attach a bladder, prepared as directed for experiment No. 4, to the phial. Sulphuretted hydrogen, a gas extremely fetid and disagreeable, will immediately be evolved; though the ingredients here employed were destitute of smell.

8. Put an ounce or two of the black oxide of manganese into a small glass retort, pour a little concentrated sulphuric acid upon it, and apply the heat of a lamp. Oxygen gas will be disengaged in abundance.

9. Into a small glass retort put a mixture of two parts of quick-lime, and one of muriate of ammonia, both in powder. Apply the heat of a lamp, and ammoniacal gas will come over.

10. Pour a little sulphuric acid upon a small quantity of quick-silver in a glass retort, apply heat and sulphurous acid gas may be collected.

11. Take a few shreds or filings of copper, and pour over them a little diluted nitrous acid, in the proportion of about three parts of water to one of acid. The gas evolved in this case is nitric oxide gas.

12. Upon an ounce or two of nitrate of potass in a glass retort pour some sulphuric acid; give it heat by means of a lamp, and collect nitric acid.

13. Treat muriate of soda in the same manner with sulphuric acid and muriatic acid in the gaseous form will rise from the retort.

14. Convey some muriatic acid gas into a glass jar containing a portion of the gas produced in experiment 9. From the mixture of these two invisible gases a solid substance will be produced; viz. the common sal ammoniac; this may be perceived to deposit itself upon the sides of the vessel in a neat crystallized form.

15. Convey some carbonic acid gas into a glass jar containing a portion of ammoniacal gas. The instant the two gases come into contact a great absorption will take place, and solid carbonate of ammonia will be formed on the inner surface of the jar.

16. If common Glauber's salt be dried and reduced to powder, and then dissolved in three times its weight of boiling water, it will not only be found to crystallize again on cooling, but the crystals will assume the identical forms which they exhibited before they were pulverized. This experiment is designed to show that a determinate figure has been stamped upon every individual salt.

17. Dissolve $\frac{3}{4}$ of an ounce of Glauber's salt in two ounces of boiling water, pour it while hot into a phial. In this state it will not crystallize even when perfectly cold : but if the fluid be agitated by shaking the vessel, or dropping into it any solid substance, the crystallization will be seen to commence and proceed with rapidity.

18. Repeat the experiment with a small thermometer immersed in the solution. If the solution be suffered to cool completely under these circumstances, the thermometer will be seen to rise on agitating the solution. This experiment is designed to show that saline solutions give out caloric in the act of crystallization.

19. Put about half an ounce of quicksilver into a wine-glass, and pour about an ounce of diluted nitrous acid upon it. The nitrous acid will be decomposed by the metal with astonishing rapidity; the colour of the acid will be quickly changed to a beautiful green, while its surface exhibits a dark crimson; and an effervescence indescribably vivid and pleasing will go on during the whole time the acid operates upon the quicksilver. When a part only of the metal is dissolved, a change of colour will again take place, and the acid by

degrees will become paler, till it is as pellucid as pure water. This is one instance of a metallic solution by means of an acid; in which the opacity of a metallic body is completely overcome, and the whole rendered perfectly transparent.

20. Take the metallic solution formed in the last experiment, add a little more quicksilver to saturate the acid; then place it at some distance, over the flame of a lamp, so as gently to evaporate a part of the water. The new formed salt will soon be seen to begin to shoot into needle-shaped crystals, crossing each other in every possible direction; affording an instance of the formation of a metallic salt.

21. Pour a drachm by weight of strong nitric acid into a wine-glass, add two drachms of distilled water, and, when mixed, throw a few very small pieces of granulated tin into it. A violent effervescence will take place, the lighter particles of the tin will be thrown to the top of the acid, and be seen to play up and down in the liquor for a considerable time until the whole is dissolved. This is another example of a transparent liquid holding a metal in solution.

22. Dissolve one ounce of quicksilver without heat in ¾ of an ounce of strong nitric acid, previously diluted with one ounce and a half of water. Dissolve also the same weight of quicksilver, by means of heat, in the same quantity of a similar acid, and then to each of these colourless solutions, add a colourless solution of potash. In the one case the metal will be precipitated in a black, in the other in a yellow powder, affording an example of the difference of colour of metallic oxides, arising from different degrees of oxidation.

23. Take an ounce of a solution of potash, pour upon it half an ounce of sulphuric acid; lay the mixture aside, and when cold, crystals of sulphate of potash will be formed in the liquor. Here a mild salt has been formed from a mixture of two corrosive substances.

24. Take carbonate of ammonia (the common volatile smelling salt,) and pour upon it muriatic acid so long as any effervescence continues. The produce will be a solid salt, perfectly inodorous, and of little taste.

25. Take caustic soda one ounce, pour over it one ounce of muriatic acid, both of these corrosive substances. The produce will be our common table salt.

26. Mix in a wine-glass equal quantities of a saturated solution of muriate of lime, and a saturated solution of carbonate of potash, both transparent fluids; stir the mixture, and a solid mass will be the product.

27. Take the substance produced in the foregoing experiment,

and pour a very little nitric acid upon it. The consequence will be, the solid matter will again be taken up, and the whole exhibit the appearance of one homogeneous fluid. An instance of a solid opake mass being converted by a chemical agent to a transparent liquid.

28. Take a transparent saturated solution of sulphate of magnesia, (Epsom salt,) and pour into it a like solution of caustic potash, or soda. The mixture will immediately become almost solid. This instance of the sudden conversion of two fluids to a solid, and that related in number 26, have been called chemical miracles.

29. Take a portion of dried sulphate of iron and an equal quantity of nitrate of potash, grind them together in a mortar, and put the whole into a small glass retort. Adapt a receiver to the retort with one or two bottles, according to the plan of Woulfe's apparatus, and apply the heat of an Argand lamp. After some time a gas will be disengaged, which will be condensed by the cold receivers forming the strong nitric acid. We have here a corrosive fluid produced from the mixture of two mild and solid substances.

30. Pour a little pure water into a small glass tumbler, and put one or two small pieces of phosphuret of lime into it. In a short time flashes of fire will dart from the surface of the water, and terminate in ringlets of smoke, which will ascend in regular succession.

31. Put thirty grains of phosphorus into a Florence flask with three or four ounces of water. Place the vessel over a lamp, and give it a boiling heat. Balls of fire will soon be seen to issue from the water, after the manner of an artificial firework, attended with the most beautiful coruscations. An experiment to show the extreme inflammability of phosphorus.

32. Into an eight-ounce retort pour four ounces of pure water, add a little solution of pure potash, and give it a boiling heat with a lamp. When it boils drop a small piece of phosphorus into it, and immerse the beak of the retort in a vessel of water. Bubbles of phosphuretted hydrogen gas will issue from the retort, rise through the water, and take fire the moment they come in contact with atmospheric air, somewhat similar to the appearance mentioned in experiment No. 30.

33. Fix a small piece of solid phosphorus in a quill, and write with it upon paper. If the paper be now carried into a dark room the writing will be beautifully luminous.

34. Pour a little phosphuretted ether upon a lump of sugar, and drop it into a glass of water, a little warm. The surface of the water will soon become luminous; and if it be moved by blowing

gently with the mouth, beautiful and brilliant undulations of its surface will be produced, exhibiting the appearance of a liquid combustion.

35. If any part of the body be rubbed with phosphorus dissolved in oil, or phosphuretted ether, that part, in a dark room, will appear as if it were on fire, without producing any dangerous effect, or sensation of heat.

36. Take about six grains of chlorate of potash, and three grains of sulphur; rub them together in a mortar, and a smart detonating noise will be produced. Continue to rub the mixture hard, and the reports will be frequently repeated, accompanied with vivid flashes of light. If the same mixture be wrapped in paper, laid on an anvil, and smartly struck with a hammer, the report will be as loud as what is usually produced by a pistol.

37. Take ten grains of chlorate of potash, and one grain of phosphorus. Treat this mixture as in the last experiment, and very violent detonations will be produced. It is advisable never to exceed the quantity of phosphorus that is prescribed here, and in other similar experiments.—N. B. This and the preceding experiment should be made with the greatest caution, as particles of the inflamed phosphorus are frequently thrown about by the explosion.

38. Take a similar quantity of chlorate of potash, with three or four grains of sulphur, and mix the ingredients very well on paper. If a little of this mixture be taken up on the point of a knife and dropped into a wine-glass containing some sulphuric acid, a beautiful column of flame will be perceived, the moment the powder comes in contact with the acid.

39. Put a little chlorate of potash and a bit of phosphorus into an ale-glass, pour some cold water upon them cautiously, so as not to displace the salt. Now take a small glass tube, and plunge it into some sulphuric acid: then place the thumb upon the upper orifice, and in this state withdraw the tube, which must be instantly immersed in the glass, so that, on removing the thumb, the acid may be immediately conveyed upon the ingredients. This experiment is an example of a very singular phenomenon, combustion under water.

40. Proceed in all respects as in the last experiment, and add a morsel of phosphuret of lime. Here, besides the former appearance, we shall have combustion also on the surface of the water.

41. Prepare a mixture of equal parts of lump sugar and chlorate of potash; put a small quantity of this mixture upon a plate or a tile; then dip a piece of sewing-thread into a phial of sulphuric acid,

so as to convey the smallest quantity of the acid; with this touch the powder, and an immediate burst of flame will be the consequence.

42. Mix without much friction, ten grains of chlorate of potash with one grain of phosphorus, and drop the mixture into concentrated sulphuric acid. This is an instance of detonation and flame being produced by the mixture of a powder with a cold liquid.

43. Pour boiling water upon a little red cabbage sliced, and when cold decant the clear infusion. Divide the infusion into three wine-glasses. To one add a solution of alum, to the second a little solution of potash, and to the third a few drops of muriatic acid. The liquor in the first glass will assume a purple, the second a bright green, and the third a beautiful crimson. Here is an instance of three different colours from the same vegetable infusion, merely by the addition of three colourless fluids.

44. Prepare a little tincture of litmus. Its colour will be a bright blue with a tinge of purple. Put a little of it in a phial, and add a few drops of diluted muriatic acid; its colour will change to a vivid red. Add a little solution of potash; the red will now disappear, and the blue will be restored. By these means the liquor may be changed alternately from a red to a blue, and from a blue to a red, at pleasure. An instance of the effects of acids and alkalies in changing vegetable colours.

45. Make an infusion of red roses, violets, or mallow flowers; treat it with solution of potash, and it will become green; the addition of diluted muriatic acid will convert it immediately to a red. This experiment may be frequently varied as the last, and furnishes an excellent test for acids and alkalies.

46. Add a drop or two of solution of potash to tincture of turmeric. This will change its original bright yellow colour to a dark brown; a little colourless diluted acid will restore it. By this tincture we can detect the most minute portion of any alkali in solution.

47. Into a wine-glass of water put a few drops of prussiate of potash; and a little dilute solution of sulphate of iron into another glass: by pouring these two colourless fluids together, a bright deep blue colour will be immediately produced, which is the true prussian blue.

48. Put some prussiate of potash into one glass; into another a little nitrate of bismuth. On mixing these colourless fluids, a yellow will be the product.

49. Pour a little prussiate of potash into a glass containing a colourless solution of sulphate of copper, and a reddish brown will be produced, being a true prussiate of copper.

50. Prepare a phial with pure water and a little tincture of galls; and another with a weak solution of sulphate of iron; then mix these transparent colourless fluids together, and they will instantly become black.

51. Pour a little tincture of litmus into a wine glass, and into another some diluted sulphate of indigo; pour these two blue fluids together, and the mixture will become perfectly red.

52. Drop as much nitrate of copper into water as will form a colourless solution; then add a little ammonia, equally colourless, and an intense blue colour will arise from the mixture.

53. Take water holding carbonate of iron in solution, and add some diluted prussiate of potass: prussian blue will be formed by the mixture.

54. Take some of the same water as that used in the last experiment; boil it, and now add prussiate of potash. In this case no colour will be produced.

55. Take some water impregnated with carbonic acid, and add to it a little blue tincture of litmus. The whole will be changed to a red.

56. Take some of the same carbonated water, and boil it. Then add a little tincture of litmus, and the blue colour will experience no change.

57. Take some of the black liquid described in experiment 50, add by degrees muriatic acid to it, and the colour will be discharged. Now drop in a little solution of potash, and the black colour will be restored. Some nicety is requisite in adding the acid and alkali; for if they be given in excess the effects will not be so apparent.

58. Take the blue solution formed by experiment No. 52, add a little sulphuric acid, and the colour will disappear; pour in a little solution of caustic ammonia, and the blue colour will be restored. Thus may the liquor be alternately changed at pleasure.

59. Spread a piece of tinfoil, such as is used for coating electrical jars, upon a piece of thick paper; pour a small quantity of strong solution of nitrate of copper upon it. Fold it up quickly, and wrap it round carefully with the paper, more effectually to exclude the atmospheric air. Place it then upon a tile, and in a short time combustion will commence, and the tin will inflame.

60. Take three parts of nitre, two of potash, and one of sulphur; all of these should be thoroughly dry; then mix them by rubbing them together in a warm mortar: the resulting compound is called fulminating powder. If a little of this powder be placed upon a fire-shovel over a hot fire, it gradually blackens, and at last melts. At

that instant it explodes with a violent report. Note.—This mixture is not dangerous, like the metallic fulminating powders; none of which should be intrusted in the hands of young people.

61. Whenever uncombined muriatic, or any volatile acid is suspected to be present in any chemical mixture, it may be detected by ammonia. A single drop of ammonia on a feather, or small slip of paper, held over the mixture, will immediately render the vapour visible.

62. Ammonia in solution may in like manner be detected by a single drop of muriatic, or acetic acid, which will produce very evident white fumes. This is merely the reverse of the former experiment.

63. Procure a bladder furnished with a stop-cock, fill it with hydrogen gas, and then adapt a tobacco-pipe to it. By dipping the bowl of the pipe into a lather of soap, and pressing the bladder, soap-bubbles will be formed, filled with hydrogen gas. These bubbles will rise into the atmosphere, as they are formed, and convey a good idea of the principle upon which air-balloons are inflated.

64. Procure a bladder similar to that described in the last experiment, and charge it with a mixture of oxygen and hydrogen gases. With this apparatus blow up soap-bubbles as before, and touch them with a lighted match. The bubbles as they rise will explode with a smart noise.

65. Fill a bladder, similar to that directed for experiment No. 4, with hydrogen gas; apply a lighted match to the end of the tobacco-pipe, and press the bladder gently. A pencil of flame, extremely beautiful, will be seen issuing from the pipe, till the whole of the hydrogen gas is consumed.

66. Place some *small* phials on the shelf of the pneumatic tub, filled with water, and inverted as usual for receiving gases. Now fill these with mixed oxygen and hydrogen gases from the bladder as described in experiment 64. A lighted match will cause any one of them to explode with violence. When the phials are used, it will be prudent to fold them round with a handkerchief, to prevent any injury being received from the glass, in case of bursting; but if small bladders be employed in place of the phials, this precaution will be unnecessary.

67. Pour a little lime-water into a wine-glass, and put some solution of oxalate of ammonia, equally transparent, into another glass. If the two clear liquors be poured together, a white precipitate of oxalate of lime will immediately become visible,

68. Pour a little lime-water into a phial, and throw some carbonic acid into it. The carbonic acid will unite with the lime, and precipitate it in the state of carbonate of lime.

69. Take the phial made use of in the last experiment, with its contents, and convey an additional portion of carbonic acid into it. The carbonate of lime will now be re-dissolved, and the liquor rendered transparent.

70. Take the transparent liquid produced in the last experiment, and give it heat. The earth will now be precipitated in the state of carbonate of lime, as before.

71. Pour some lime-water into a wine-glass, and a little solution of carbonate of potash into another glass. When these two transparent fluids are thrown together, an abundant precipitate of carbonate of lime will be the consequence.

72. Proceed as in the last experiment, but instead of carbonate of potash, pour a solution of epsom salt into one of the glasses. When these transparent fluids are poured together, a mixed precipitate of carbonate of magnesia, and sulphate of lime will be produced.

73. For another experiment take in the same manner, separately, lime-water, and a solution of alum. The union of these solutions will produce a mixed precipitate of alumina and sulphate of lime.

74. If a strong solution of caustic potash, and a saturated solution of epsom salt be mixed, the union of these transparent fluids will produce also an abundant precipitate. But this will consist of magnesia and sulphate of potash.

75. To a glass of water, suspected to contain carbonic acid, add a small quantity of any of the other acids. If carbonic acid be present, it will become visible by a sparkling appearance on the sides of the glass and surface of the fluid.

76. Prepare two glasses of pure water, and into one of them drop a single drop of sulphuric acid, and mix it with the water. Pour a little muriate of baryta into the other glass, and no change will be perceived; pour some of the same solution into the first glass, containing the sulphuric acid, and a white precipitate of sulphate of baryta will be produced.

77. Prepare two glasses of water as before, conduct the experiment in the same way as the last, but instead of muriate of baryta, use nitrate of lead. In this case sulphate of lead will be precipitated.

78. Prepare two glasses of rain water, and into one of them drop a single drop of sulphuric acid. Pour a little nitrate of silver into the other glass, and no change will be perceptible. Pour some of

the same solution, into the first glass, and a white precipitate of sulphate of silver will appear.

79. Prepare two glasses as in the last experiment, and into one of them put a drop or two of muriatic acid. Proceed as before, and a precipitate of chloride of silver will be produced.

80. Take two glasses, as in experiment 78, and into one of them put a drop of sulphuric acid, and a drop or two of muriatic acid: proceed as before with the nitrate of silver, and a mixed precipitate will be produced, consisting of chloride of silver, and sulphate of silver.

81. Take the glass containing the mixed precipitate of the last experiment, and give it, by means of a lamp, the heat of boiling water. The sulphate of silver, if there be a sufficiency of water, will now be re-dissolved, and the chloride of silver will remain separate at the bottom of the vessel. This experiment exhibits a method of separating these metallic salts wherever they occur in a state of mixture.

82. Mix one ounce of litharge of lead with one dram of pulverized muriate of ammonia, and submit the mixture to a red heat in a clean tobacco-pipe. The increase of temperature will separate the ammonia in the form of gas, and the muriatic acid will combine with the lead. When the compound is well melted, pour it into a metallic cup, and you will have a true muriate of lead of a bright yellow colour, the brilliancy of which may be much heightened by grinding it as usual with oil. In this state it forms the colour called patent yellow.

83. Take one ounce of red-lead, and half a dram of charcoal in powder, incorporate them well in a mortar, and then fill the bowl of a tobacco-pipe with the mixture. Submit it to an intense heat in a common fire, and, when melted, pour it out upon a slab. The result will be metallic lead.

84. Take a little red-lead, expose it to an intense heat in a crucible, and pour it out when melted. The result will be metallic glass, and will furnish an example of the vitrification of metals.

85. Pour a little solution of indigo in sulphuric acid into a glass of water, and add about an equal quantity of solution of carbonate of potash. If a piece of white cloth be dipped in this mixture, it will come out blue. If a piece of yellow cloth be dipped in it, it will become a green, or a red will be converted to a purple. A slip of blue litmus paper immersed in it will immediately become red.

86. If a little fustic, quercitron bark, or other dye, be boiled in water, the colouring matter will be extracted, and a coloured solution

formed. On adding a small quantity of dissolved alum to this decoction, the alumina, or base of the salt, will attract the colouring matter, forming an insoluble compound, which in a short time will subside, and may easily be separated.

87. Boil a little cochineal in water with a grain or two of cream of tartar, (bitartrate of potash,) and a dull kind of crimson solution will be formed. By the addition of a few drops of nitro-muriate of tin, the colouring matter will be precipitated of a beautiful scarlet. This, and some of the former instances, will give the student a tolerably correct idea of the general process of dyeing woollen cloths.

88. If a few strips of dyed linen cloth, of different colours, be dipped into a phial of chlorine, the colours will be quickly discharged; for there are few colours that can resist the energetic effect of this acid. This experiment may be considered as a complete example of the process of bleaching coloured goods.

89. Having found a piece of blue linen cloth, that will bleach in chlorine, dip the tip of the finger in a solution of muriate of tin, and press it while wet with the solution, upon a strip of this cloth. After an interval of a few minutes immerse the cloth in the phial of liquid chlorine, and when it has remained in it the usual time, it will be found that the spot which was previously wet with muriate of tin has preserved its original colour, while the rest of the cloth has become white.

90. Dip a piece of white calico in a strong solution of acetate of iron; dry it by the fire, and lay it aside for three or four days. After this, wash it well in hot water, and then dye it black, by boiling it for ten minutes in a strong decoction of Brazil wood. If the cloth be now dried, any figures printed upon it with a colourless solution of muriate of tin, will appear of a beautiful scarlet, although the ground will remain a permanent black.

91. Dissolve 4 drachms of sulphate of iron in one pint of cold water, then add about 6 drachms of lime in powder, and 2 drachms of finely pulverized indigo, stirring the mixture occasionally for 12 or 14 hours. If a piece of white calico be immersed in this solution for a few minutes, it will be dyed green; and by exposure to the atmosphere only for a few seconds, this will be converted to a permanent blue.

92. If a piece of calico be immersed in a solution of sulphate of iron, and, when dry, washed in a weak solution of carbonate of potash, a permanent colour will be produced, viz. the buff of the calico-printers.

93. Boil equal parts of arnotto and common potash in water till the whole are dissolved. This will produce the pale reddish buff so much in use, and sold under the name of nankeen dye.

94. If muriate of tin, newly made, be added to a solution of indigo in sulphuric acid, the oxygen of the indigo will be absorbed, and the solution instantly converted to a green. It is on the same principle that muriate of tin is employed in cleansing discoloured leather furniture; as it absorbs the oxygen, and the leather is restored to its natural colour.

95. Take a piece of very dark olive-coloured linen that has been dyed with fustic, quercitron bark, or weld, and spot it in several places with a colourless solution of muriate of tin. Wherever the cloth has been touched with this solution, the original colour will be discharged, and spots of a bright yellow will appear in its stead.

96. Dip a piece of white calico in a cold solution of sulphate of iron, and suffer it to become entirely dry. Then imprint any figures upon it with a strong solution of colourless citric acid, and allow this also to dry. If a piece be then well washed in pure warm water, and afterwards boiled in a decoction of logwood, the ground will be dyed either of a slate or black colour, according to the strength of the metallic solution, while the printed figures will remain beautifully white. This experiment is designed to show the effect of acids in discharging vegetable colours.

97. If lemon juice be dropped upon any kind of buff colour, the dye will be instantly discharged. The application of this acid by means of the block, is another method by which calico-printers give the white spots or figures to piece-goods. The crystallized acid in a state of solution is generally used for this purpose. These few experiments will give the student some idea of the nature of calico-printing.

98. Take a slip of blue litmus paper, dip it into acetic acid, and it will immediately become red. This is a test so delicate, that, according to Bergman, it will detect the presence of sulphuric acid, even if the water contain only one part of acid to thirty-five thousand parts of water. Litmus paper which has been thus changed by immersion in acids, is, when dried, a good test for the alkalies; for, if it be dipped in a fluid containing the smallest portion of alkali, the red will disappear, and the paper be restored to its original blue colour.

99. Take a slip of turmeric paper, and dip it into any alkaline solution; this will change the yellow to a deep brown. In many

cases turmeric is preferable to litmus paper for detecting alkali in solution, as it suffers no change from carbonate of lime, which is often found in mineral waters. This paper will detect the presence of soda, though it should amount to no more than $\frac{1}{11000}$dth part of the water. The paper thus changed by an alkali, would, if died, be /ɹ still useful as a test for acids, as these restore its original yellow.

100. Write upon paper with a diluted solution of muriate of copper; when dry it will not be visible, but on being warmed before the fire the writing will become of a beautiful yellow.

101. Write with a solution of muriate of cobalt, and the writing, while dry, will not be perceptible; but if held towards the fire, it will then gradually become visible; and if the muriate of cobalt be made in the usual way, the letters will appear of an elegant green colour.

102. Write with acetate of cobalt, or with a muriate of cobalt, previously purified from the iron which it generally contains. When the writing is become dry, these letters will also be invisible. Warm the paper a little, and the writing will be restored to a beautiful blue.

103. Draw a landscape with Indian ink, and paint the foliage of the vegetables with muriate of cobalt, the same as that used in experiment No. 101, and some of the flowers with acetate of cobalt, and others with muriate of copper. While this picture is cold it will appear to be merely an outline of a landscape, or winter scene; but when gently warmed, the trees and flowers will be displayed in their natural colours, which they will preserve only while they continue warm. This may be often repeated.

104. Write with dilute nitrate of silver, which when dry will be entirely invisible; hold the paper over a vessel containing sulphate of ammonia, and the writing will appear very distinct. The letters will shine with the metallic brilliancy of silver.

105. Write with a solution of nitrate or acetate of lead. When the writing is dry it will be invisible. Then having prepared a glass decanter with a little sulphuret of iron strewed over the bottom of it, pour a little very dilute sulphuric acid upon the sulphuret, so as not to wet the mouth of the decanter, and suspend the writing by means of the glass stopper, within the decanter. The writing on the paper will become visible by degrees, as the gas rises from the bottom of the vessel.

106. Write with a weak solution of sulphate of iron; let it dry, and it will be invisible. By dipping a feather in tincture of galls and

drawing the wet feather over the letters, the writing will be restored and appear black.

107. Write with a similar solution, and when dry wash the letters in the same way with prussiate of potash, and they will be restored of a beautiful blue.

108. Write with a solution of sulphate of copper, wash as before with prussiate of potash, and the writing will be revived of a reddish brown colour.

109. Procure a glass jar, such as is generally used for deflagrating the gases, and fill it with chlorine gas. If nickel, arsenic, or bismuth in powder be thrown into this gas, and the temperature of the atmosphere be not lower than 70°, the metal will inflame, and continue to burn with the most brilliant combustion.

110. Into a large glass jar, inverted on a flat brick tile, and containing near its top a branch of fresh rosemary, or any other such shrub, moistened with water, introduce a flat thick piece of heated iron, on which place some gum benzoin in gross powder. The benzoic acid, in consequence of the heat, will be separated, and ascend in white fumes, which will at length condense, and form a most beautiful appearance upon the leaves of the vegetable. This will serve as an example of sublimation.

111. Introduce a little carbonate of ammonia into a Florence flask, and place that part of the flask which contains the salt on the surface of a basin of boiling water : the heat will soon cause the carbonate of ammonia to rise undecomposed, and attach itself to the upper part of the vessel, affording another example of simple sublimation.

112. Fill a glass tumbler half full of lime-water; then breathe into it frequently ; at the same time stirring it with a piece of glass. The fluid, which before was perfectly transparent, will presently become quite white, and, if suffered to remain at rest, real chalk (carbonate of lime) will be deposited.

113. Mix a little acetate of lead with an equal portion of sulphate of zinc ; both in fine powder; stir them together with a piece of glass or wood, and no chemical change will be perceptible; but if they be rubbed together in a mortar, the two solids will operate upon each other ; an intimate union will take place, and a fluid will be produced.   If alum or Glauber salt be used instead of sulphate of zinc, the experiment will be equally successful.

114. If the leaves of a plant, fresh gathered, be placed in the sun, very pure oxygen gas may be collected.

115. If the student be in possession of an air pump, the following

experiment may be easily performed:—Let him fix a small tin cup of *ether* within a large watch-glass containing a little water, and place both under the receiver of the air-pump.   The exhaustion of the receiver will cause one of the fluids to boil, and the other to freeze at the same instant.

116. If a few pounds of a mixture of iron filings and sulphur be made into a paste with water, and buried in the ground for a few hours, the water will be decomposed with so much rapidity, that combustion and flame will be the consequence.

117. Put a little alcohol in a tea-cup, set it on fire, and invert a large bell glass over it.   In a short time an aqueous vapour will be seen to condense upon the inside of the bell, which, by means of a dry sponge, may be collected, and its quantity ascertained. This may be adduced as an example of the formation of water by combustion.

118. Pour a little water into a phial containing about an ounce of olive oil.   Shake the phial, and if the contents be observed we shall find that no union has taken place.   But if some solution of caustic potash be added, and the phial be then shaken, an intimate combination of the materials will be formed by the disposing affinity of the alkali, and a perfect soap produced.

119. Put a little common sulphur into an iron dish, place it under a jar of oxygen gas, and set fire to it and sulphuric acid will be formed.   This is an example of the formation of an acid by combustion.

120. Take the acid formed in the last experiment, concentrate it by boiling, mix it with a little powdered charcoal, and submit the mixture in a Florence flask to the heat of an Argand's lamp.   By this process sulphur will be regenerated, and will sublime into the neck of the flask.   An example of the decomposition of an acid.

121. Drop upon a clean plate of copper, a small quantity of solution of nitrate of silver; in a short time a metallic vegetation will be perceptible, branching out in very elegant and pleasing forms, furnishing an example of precipitation of a metal.

122. Dissolve an ounce of acetate of lead in about a quart or more of water, and filter the solution.   If this be put into a glass decanter, and a piece of zinc suspended in it by means of a brass wire, a decomposition of the salt will immediately commence, the lead will be set at liberty, and will attach itself to the remaining zinc, forming a metallic tree.

123. Place a phial of water, enclosing a thermometer, in a frigorific mixture, and by avoiding agitation cool it some degrees below

the freezing point. If it be now agitated, it immediately becomes solid, and its temperature instantly rises to 32°; an instance of a change of form occasioning an extrication of caloric.

124. Fill a small glass matrass, or flask, holding about half a pint, with any kind of coloured water, having previously put in a few teaspoonfuls of *ether*: then invert the flask in a shallow vessel of water, and by degrees pour boiling water upon its bulb. By the sudden accession of heat the ether will be changed into vapour; which will force out the coloured water, and fill the whole of the vessel. This experiment will afford an example of a liquid being converted into an elastic vapour by caloric.

125. For want of a proper glass vessel, a table spoonful of ether may be put into a moistened bladder, and the neck of the bladder closely tied. If hot water be then poured upon it, the ether will expand, and the bladder become inflated.

126. Put a small piece of phosphorus into a crucible, cover it closely with common chalk, so as to fill the crucible. Let another crucible be inverted upon it, and both subjected to the fire. When the whole has become perfectly red hot remove them from the fire, and when cold, the carbonic acid of the chalk will have been decomposed, and the black charcoal, the basis of the acid, may be easily perceived amongst the materials.

127. Place a lighted wax taper within an narrow glass jar, then take a jar or phial of carbonic acid gas, and cautiously pour it into the jar containing the taper. This being an invisible gas, the operator will appear to invert merely an empty vessel, though the taper will be as effectually and instantaneouly extinguished as if water itself had been used.

128. Make a little charcoal perfectly dry, pulverize it very fine, and put it into a warm tea-cup. If some strong nitric acid be now poured upon it, combustion and inflammation will immediately ensue.

129. If strong nitric acid be poured upon a small quantity of a mixture of chlorate of potash and phosphorus, flashes of fire will be emitted at intervals for a considerable time.

130. Put a bit of phosphorus into a small phial, then fill it one-third with boiling olive oil, and cork it close. Whenever the stopper is taken out in the night, light will be evolved sufficient to show the hour upon a watch.

131. Let sulphuric acid be poured into a saucer upon some acetate of potash. Into another saucer put a mixture of about two parts of quicklime and one of sal ammoniac, both in powder, adding to these a very small quantity of boiling water. Both saucers while

separate will yield invisible gases; but the moment they are brought close together the operator will be enveloped in very visible vapours. Muriate of soda, in this experiment, may be substituted for acetate of potash.

132. Take a glass tube with a bulb in form of a common thermometer; fill it with cold water, and suspend it by a string. If the bulb be frequently and continually moistened with pure sulphuric ether, the water will be presently frozen, even in summer.

133. Dissolve five drams of muriate of ammonia and five drams of nitre, both finely powdered, in two ounces of water. A thermometer immersed in the solution will show that the temperature is reduced below 22°. If a thermometer tube, filled with water, be now suspended within it, the water will soon be as effectually frozen as in the last experiment.

134. Procure a phial with a glass stopper accurately ground into it; introduce a few copper filings, then entirely fill it with liquid ammonia, and stop the phial so as to exclude all atmospheric air. If left in this state, no solution of copper will be effected. But if the bottle be afterwards left open for some time, and then stopped, the metal will dissolve, and the solution will be colourless. Let the stopper be now taken out, and the fluid will become blue, beginning at the surface, and spreading gradually through the whole. If this blue solution has not been too long exposed to the air, and fresh copper filings be put in, again stopping the bottle, the fluid will once more be deprived of its colour, which it will recover only by the re-admission of air. These effects may thus be repeatedly produced.

135. Pour concentrated nitric acid upon pieces of iron, and very little action will be seen: but if a few drops of water be added a most violent effervescence will immediately commence; and the acid will be decomposed with rapidity, clouds of red nitrous gas will be evolved in abundance, and a perfect solution of the metal effected.

136. Take any solution of iron, a chalybeate water for instance, and add a little succinate of ammonia; a precipitate will be immediately visible, being succinate of iron. By this test the quantity of iron in any solution may be accurately ascertained.

137. In like manner add sulphuretted hydrogen to a solution of lead, and a deep brown precipitate will be occasioned. This is an effectual mode of detecting this and some other poisonous metals.

138. Melt sulphur in a small iron ladle, and carry it into a dark room in the state of fusion. If an ounce or two of copper filings be now thrown in, light will be evolved.

139. Dissolve some quicksilver in nitric acid, and drop a little of

the solution upon a bright piece of copper. If it be then gently rubbed with a bit of cloth, the mercury will precipitate itself upon the copper, which will be completely silvered. This experiment is illustrative of the precipitation of one metal by another.

140. If a little nitro-muriate of gold be added to a fresh solution of muriate of tin, both being much diluted with water, the gold will be precipitated of a purple colour, forming that beautiful pigment called powder of cassius.

141. Take a phial with solution of sulphate of zinc, and another containing a little liquid ammonia, both transparent fluids. By mixing them, a curious phenomenon may be perceived :—the zinc will be immediately precipitated in a white mass, and, if then shaken, almost as instantly re-dissolved.

142. If a colourless solution of galls be added to a solution of bismuth in nitric acid, equally colourless, a brown precipitate will be produced. This is a distinguishing characteristic of this metal.

143. If a colourless solution of arsenic in nitric acid be poured into a solution of copper, a bluish green precipitate will be produced, forming an arsenite of copper similar to an ore found in the Cornish mines. These metals may be thus reciprocally detected.

144. If a spoonful of good alcohol and a little boracic acid be stirred together in a tea-cup, and then set on fire, they will produce a very beautiful green flame.

145. If alcohol be inflamed in like manner with a little pure strontian in powder, or any of its salts, the mixture will give a carmine flame.

146. If barytes be used instead of strontian, we shall have a brilliant yellow flame.

147. Alloy a piece of silver with a portion of lead, place the alloy upon a piece of charcoal, attach a blow-pipe to a gasometer charged with oxygen gas, light the charcoal first with a bit of paper, and keep up the heat by pressing upon the machine. When the metals get into complete fusion, the lead will begin to burn, and very soon will be all dissipated in a white smoke, leaving the silver in a state of purity. This experiment is designed to show the fixity of the noble metals.

148. Fuse a small quantity of nitre in a crucible, and, when in complete fusion, throw pulverized coal into it by small quantities at a time. The carbonaceous matter will decompose the nitric acid of the nitre, and rapidly deflagration will ensue.

149. Burn a piece of iron wire in a deflagrating jar of oxygen

gas, and suffer it to burn till it goes out of itself. If a lighted wax taper be now let down into the gas this will burn in it for some time, and then become extinguished. If ignited sulphur be now introduced, this will also burn for a limited time. Lastly, introduce a morsel of phosphorus, and combustion will also follow in like manner. These experiments show the relative combustibility of different substances.

150. If oxide of cobalt be dissolved in ammonia, a red solution will be produced, different in colour from that of all other metallic oxides.

151. If nickel be dissolved in nitric acid, a beautiful green solution will be formed. The oxide of this metal is used to give a delicate grass green to porcelain.

152. When colourless prussiate of potash is added to a solution of titanium, this metal will be precipitated also of a green colour.

153. Add a little colourless solution of galls to a clear solution of antimony in nitro-muriatic acid, and the metal will be precipitated of a pale yellow colour.

154. If a solution of tungstate of potash be poured into a solution of the green sulphate of iron, a yellow precipitate will fall down. By this experiment the distinguishing characteristic of this metal is exhibited.

155. Add a few grains of chlorate of potash to a teaspoonful or two of alcohol, drop one or two drops of sulphuric acid upon the mixture, and the whole will burst into flame, forming a very beautiful appearance.

156. A mixture of chlorate of potash and arsenic furnishes a detonating compound, which takes fire with the utmost rapidity. The salt and metal, first separately powdered, may be mixed by the gentlest possible triture, or rather by stirring them together on paper with the point of a knife. If two long trains be laid on a table, the one of gunpowder and the other of this mixture, and they be in contact with each other at one end, so that they may be fired at once, the arsenical mixture burns with the rapidity of lightning while the other burns with comparatively extreme slowness.

157. Into an ale-glass of water put a few filings of zinc, and a small bit of phosphorus; then drop a little sulphuric acid upon the mixture by means of a glass tube, as described at No. 39, and phosphuretted hydrogen will presently be disengaged, which will inflame on rising to the surface of the water.

158. Take a small piece of phosphuret of lime, a little moistened by the air, and let a single drop of concentrated muriatic acid fall upon it. In this case phosphuretted hydrogen will also be evolved

accompanied by small balls of fire darting from the mixture, and a very fetid smell.

159. If twenty grains of phosphorus, cut very small, and mixed with forty grains of finely granulated zinc, be put into four drams of water, and two drams of concentrated sulphuric acid be added thereto, bubbles of inflamed phosphuretted hydrogen gas will quickly cover the whole surface of the fluid in succession, forming a real aqueous fountain of fire.

160. If any light substance capable of conducting heat, be placed upon the surface of boiling water, and a bit of phosphorus be laid upon it, the heat of the water will be sufficient to set the phosphorus on fire.

161. If hot water be poured into a glass jar of cold water, it will remain on the surface; but if cold water be poured upon hot water, it will sink to the bottom of the vessel. This experiment may be rendered more obvious by colouring that portion of the water which is poured in. The design of this experiment is to show the change of the specific gravity of the same body, merely by the agency of caloric.

162. If a solution of the green sulphate of iron be dropped into a nitro-muriate of gold, the last metal will be immediately precipitated. In this state it is often employed in gilding china.

163. If flowers, or any other figures, be drawn upon a ribbon or silk with a solution of nitrate of silver, and the silk moistened with water, be then exposed to the action of hydrogen gas, the silver will be revived, and the figures, firmly fixed upon the silk, will become visible, and shine with metallic brilliancy.

164. By proceeding in the same manner, and using a solution of gold in nitro-muriatic acid, silks may be permanently gilt at a most insignificant expense, and will exhibit an appearance the most beautiful that can be conceived.

165. To a similar solution of gold add about a fourth part of ether; shake them together, and wait till the fluids separate; the upper stratum, or ethereal gold, is then to be carefully poured off into another vessel. If any polished steel instrument or utensil be dipped into this solution, and instantly plunged into water, the surface will have acquired a coat of pure gold, being a very elegant and economical mode of preserving polished steel from rust.

166. If terchloride of platina be mixed with a fourth part of its bulk of ether, and the mixture suffered to settle, the ethereal solution of platina may be decanted as in the preceding experiment. Polished brass, and some other metals immersed in this solution, will be covered

with a coat of platina. This process may be applied to many useful purposes.

·167. Fill a thermometer tube with tepid water, and immerse it in a glass vessel of water of the same temperature, containing a mercurial thermometer. If the whole be now placed in a bed of snow, or in a frigorific mixture, the water in the tube will suffer a progressive diminution of volume, until it arrives at about 40°; it will then begin to expand gradually until it becomes solid. This shows how ice is enabled to swim on the surface of water.

168. Another example on this subject may be shown. Fill a thermometer tube with cold water, at about 32°, and immerse it in a vessel of warm water. In this case, the water in the tube will contract in volume till it arrives at about 42°, when it will appear for a time nearly stationary. If the heat be now continued, the effect will be reversed, for the water in the tube will *expand* as its temperature is increased.

169. It is an interesting experiment to place a glow-worm within a jar of oxygen gas, in a dark room. The insect will shine with much greater brilliancy than it does in atmospheric air, and appear more alert. As the luminous appearance depends on the will of the animal, this experiment probably affords an instance of the stimulus which this gas communicates to the animal system.

170. Prepare a very dilute and colourless solution of platina by dropping a small quantity of the nitro-muriate of that metal into a glass of water. If a single drop of the solution of muriate of tin be added to this, a bright red precipitate will be instantly produced. A more delicate test than this of any metal, cannot be conceived.

171. If a morsel of the dried crystals of nitrate of silver (not the lunar caustic) be laid on a piece of burning charcoal, the metallic salt will immediately deflagrate, throw out the most beautiful scintillations that can be imagined, and the surface of the charcoal will be richly coated with metallic silver.

172. To a colourless solution of nitrate of mercury, add an equally colourless solution of sub-borate of soda. This will produce a double decomposition, and form a bright yellow precipitate of borate of mercury; giving an instance of difference of colour in metals, by their union with different acids.

173. Into a diluted solution of sulphate of copper, pour a little liquid caustic ammonia; this will precipitate the copper of a bluish white. During its examination, however, the precipitate will be re-dissolved, and a beautiful blue liquid, called aqua celestis, will be the result.

174. If one grain of dry nitrate of bismuth be previously mixed with a grain of phosphorus, and then rubbed in a metallic mortar, a loud detonation will be produced.

175. Write on paper with a solution of nitrate of bismuth; when this is dry the writing will be invisible; but if the paper be immersed in water, it will be distinctly legible.

176. A letter written with a diluted solution of bismuth, becomes, when dry, illegible; but a feather dipped in a solution of sulphate of potash, will instantly blacken the oxide, and revive the writing.

177. Drop a piece of phosphorus about the size of a pea into a tumbler of hot water, and from a bladder, furnished with a stop-cock, force a stream of oxygen gas directly upon it. This will afford the most brilliant combustion under water that can be imagined.

178. Paste a slip of litmus paper within a glass jar, near the bottom, then fill the jar with water, and invert it on the shelf of a pneumatic trough. If as much nitric oxide gas, previously well washed, be passed into the jar as will displace the water below the level of the paper, the colour of the litmus paper will still remain unaltered; but on passing up atmospheric air it will immediately be reddened; showing the formation of an acid, by the mixture of two gases.

179. Take a few grains of citric acid, and twice as much dry carbonate of potash, or of soda, both in powder; mix them, and put them into a dry glass. No chemical change will take place in either of these salts, but the moment water is poured upon them, an effervescence will ensue; affording an instance of the necessity of water to promote some chemical decompositions.

180. Dissolve a few crystals of nitro-muriate of gold in about 8 times their weight of pure water; place a thin slip of charcoal in the solution, and heat the whole by means of a sand-bath. When the solution has acquired nearly a boiling heat, the gold will precipitate itself on the charcoal, in its metallic splendour, forming a singular and beautiful appearance. This experiment is designed to show that metals become insoluble, the moment they impart their oxygen to foreign bodies.

181. Proceed as in the last experiment, and submit the vessel with its contents to the rays of the sun. Here the metal will be reduced, and the charcoal as effectually gilt as before. This is illustrative of the deoxidizing power of the sun's rays.

182. Drop a little leaf gold into nitro-muriatic acid, and it will instantly disappear. This experiment is designed to show the great solubility of the metals, when submitted to a proper menstruum.

183. Pour a little purified nitric acid into one wine-glass, and mu-

riatic acid into another; and drop a little leaf gold into each. Here neither of these corrosive acids will act at all upon the metal, the gold will remain untouched. Now pour the whole contents of the two glasses together, and the metal will disappear, and be as effectually dissolved as in the last experiment.

184. If a little metallic arsenic in powder be mixed with a few zinc filings, and then treated with diluted sulphuric acid, arseniuretted hydrogen gas may be collected, which burns with a peculiar kind of lambent white flame.

185. If a portion of this gas, issuing from a very small tube, be set on fire, and then immersed in a large glass receiver of oxygen gas, and the stream of arseniuretted hydrogen kept up by the pressure of the bladder, a blue flame of great splendour will be produced.

186. Take an amalgam of lead and mercury, and another amalgam of bismuth, let these two solid amalgams be mixed by triture, and they will instantly become fluid.

187. Charge a small glass retort with strong muriatic acid, and insert its beak into a tubulated receiver, containing a little water; then into this receiver insert two small thermometers, the one immersed in the water, the other suspended above it. By applying the heat of a lamp to the retort, muriatic acid gas will be disengaged in abundance; and if the thermometers be examined, that which is suspended in the gas will be found to have risen only a few degrees, while that which was immersed in the cold water has acquired a boiling heat.

188. Take a glass of cold water, pour a little sulphuric ether upon its surface, and inflame it by a slip of lighted paper. The ether will burn for a considerable time and produce a large volume of flame, but when it is extinguished the water will be found not to have increased in temperature. The design of this experiment is to show that water is a bad conductor of caloric, and that when we wish to heat water, the heat ought not to be applied at its surface.

189. Dip the bulb of a thermometer in melted rosin so as to coat the glass with it, and suffer it to cool completely. If the flame of a taper be now applied to the bulb so as to melt the rosin, the mercury in the thermometer will not rise at the approach of the taper, but will actually be seen to contract as the rosin becomes liquid.

190. Put into a wine-glass about a scruple of the manganesiate of potash, and an equal quantity of the same compound into another glass. On one pour hot, and on the other cold water. The hot solution will exhibit a beautiful green colour; the cold one, a deep purple.

191. If a small portion of the same compound be put into several glasses, and water at different temperatures be poured upon each, the contents of each glass will exhibit a different shade of colour. This experiment affords another instance of metals producing various colours according to their different states of oxidizement.

. 192. Into a glass of water containing a small portion of common salt, drop some of a clear solution of nitrate of silver, and an insoluble precipitate of chloride of silver will be produced. This experiment is designed to give the pupil some idea of the method of analyzing mineral waters. Every 100 grains of this precipitate, when dried, indicate about 42 grains of common salt.

. 193. Into a glass of Aix-la-Chapelle water, or water holding a small portion of potash, drop a little of the solution of nitro-muriate of platina, and an immediate yellow precipitate will be produced. This affords another instance of the nature of the means usually employed to detect whatever substances may be dissolved in mineral waters.

194. Into distilled water drop a little spirituous solution of soap, and no chemical effect will be perceived: but if some of the same solution be added to hard water, a milkiness will immediately be produced, more or less, according to the degree of its impurity. This is a good method of ascertaining the purity of spring water.

195. If a little pure white calomel be rubbed in a glass mortar with a little colourless solution of caustic ammonia, the whole will become intensely black.

196. A little of the solution of sulphate of manganese, being exposed in a glass phial to the light of the sun, its rose colour will be entirely destroyed. This is another experiment to show the deoxidizing power of the sun's rays. If the phial be removed into a darkroom, the original colour of the solution will be restored.

197. Dissolve about a drachm of pulverized sulphate of copper in a little boiling water, and an equal quantity of powdered muriate of ammonia in a separate vessel in hot water. By mixing the contents of the two glasses, a quadruple salt will be formed which gives a yellow colour to the solution while hot, and becomes green when cold.

198. Mix three grains of sulphur with nine grains of dry nitrate of silver, and lay the mixture in a small heap on an anvil, or on any piece of solid metal. If the mixture be now struck smartly with a cold hammer, the sulphur will inflame, but no detonation will ensue. This is an instance of a metallic salt being decomposed and a combustible substance inflamed by percussion.

199. If the experiment be repeated, and the mass be struck with a *hot* hammer, the mixture detonates, and the silver is reduced.

200. Pour a solution of nitrate of silver into a glass vessel, and immerse a few slips of copper in it. In a short time a portion of the copper will be dissolved, and all the silver precipitated in a metallic form. If the solution, which now contains copper, be decanted into another glass, and pieces of iron added to it, this metal will then be dissolved, and the copper precipitated, yielding a striking example of peculiar affinities.

201. Melt a portion of grain tin, and pour it into a metallic cup. Allow it to cool till it is congealed to some depth, then pierce the solid crust, and carefully pour out that portion which is still liquid. If what remains in the vessel be suffered to cool entirely, it will present rhomboidal crystals of considerable size, formed by the assemblage of a great number of small needles longitudinally united.

202. Treat silver in the same way, and we shall procure a metallic mass, crystallized in quadrangular or octahedral prisms. These two experiments will succeed better if the metal be poured into a vessel with an orifice in the bottom, which must be stopped with a proper plug, and this removed as soon as the upper crust hardens; the liquid metal will then run out, and that which is congealed will exhibit a regular crystallization.

203. Form an amalgam with four parts of silver leaf and two of mercury, and dissolve this amalgam in diluted nitric acid. Then add water to the solution, equal to 30 times the weight of the metals employed, and put the whole aside for use. If an ounce of this solution be at any time poured into a phial, and a small piece of soft amalgam of silver be dropt in, filaments of reduced silver will shoot from it, and extend upwards, in the form of a shrub. This appearance of arborescence is called the Tree of Diana.

204. If two parts of sulphate of copper, and three of carbonate of ammonia, (the one a blue, the other a white salt,) be rubbed together in a glass mortar till the carbonic acid be expelled, the mass will become soft and humid, and, when dried, forms a crystalline powder of a deep violet colour. This compound was formerly called cuprum ammoniacum.

205. If a flat bar of iron be hammered briskly on an anvil, its temperature will soon be so increased, that a piece of phosphorus laid upon it would instantly be inflamed. This experiment is designed to show that caloric may be evolved merely by percussion; and that, when evolved, it is as active and energetic as though it had never been latent.

206. If a little colourless and recently prepared muriate of tin be poured into a rich green solution of muriate of copper, the copper will be deprived of a portion of its oxygen, and a white muriate precipitated.

207. Into the phial containing the white muriate of the last experiment, pour a little muriatic acid. The precipitate will quickly be dissolved, and the solution will be colourless.

208. Procure some solution of sulphate of iron at the minimum of oxidizement, by digesting iron filings with the common sulphate. Into this, when filtered, drop a little of the solution of prussiate of potash, and a white prussiate of iron will be precipitated.

209. If a very little colourless nitric acid be added to a solution of sulphate of iron prepared as in the last experiment, the addition of the prussiate of potash will produce not the white, but the blue prussiate of iron.

210. Pour some pure nitric acid on the black oxide of manganese, and no solution will be effected; but if a little sugar be added, the sugar will abstract a part of the oxygen from the oxide of manganese, and the acid will then be enabled to dissolve the metal.

211. If a piece of bright silver be dipped in a solution of sulphate of copper, it will come out unchanged; but if the blade of a clean penknife, or any piece of polished iron, be dipped in the same solution, the iron will instantly assume the appearance of copper.

212. Take the piece of silver employed in the last experiment, hold it in contact with the iron, and then, in this situation, dip them into the same solution, and both will be covered with copper.

213. Dissolve some oxide of nickel in caustic ammonia, which will produce a solution of a rich blue colour. By exposure to the air this gradually changes to a purple, and lastly to a violet. The addition of an acid will, however, convert the whole to a green.

214. Take the green solution of the last experiment, and pour caustic ammonia upon it. The original blue colour will now be reproduced.

215. Prepare a colourless solution of tartrate of potash and antimony, (the common emetic tartar,) and pour into it a little liquid sulphuretted hydrogen. This will combine with the metal, and form an orange-coloured precipitate.

216. Melt together equal parts of copper and antimony, the one a yellow, the other a white metal, and the alloy that results from this mixture will take the colour of the violet.

217. If the grey sulphuretted oxide of antimony be fused in a

crucible we procure a beautiful transparent glass, which is called the glass of antimony. This takes the colour of the hyacinth.

218. When antimony is heated to whiteness in a crucible, and in this state agitated, in contact with the air, it inflames with a sort of explosion, and presents while burning a very singular kind of white flame, forming what have been formerly called argentine flowers.

219. When antimony is well fused upon charcoal, and if, at the moment when its surface is not covered with any particle of oxide, we throw it suddenly upon the ground, the globules, into which it divides in its fall, burn with a very lively flame, throwing out on all sides brilliant sparks, different from that of any other metal.

220. Mix five or six grains of sulphuret of antimony with half its weight of chlorate of potash, and then, if a sudden stroke be given to the mixture upon a steel anvil, it fulminates with a loud report, emitting, according to Fourcroy, a flame as brilliant and rapid as lightning.

221. If alcohol contains muriate of magnesia, it has the property of burning with a reddish yellow flame.

222. Evaporate to dryness a solution of gold, made with nitro-muriatic acid, and dissolve the crystals in a sufficiency of pure water, to prevent the crystallization of the metallic salt. Thoroughly moisten a little magnesia with this aqueous solution, and place the mixture in the sun's rays. A change of colour will soon be apparent. It will first take a faint violet hue, and in a few hours the whole will have acquired a very deep purple.

223. Moisten a little magnesia with some of the solution as before, and then dry the mixture in the *dark*. If it be then submitted to the action of the sun's rays, it will acquire only a faint violet, even by several hours' exposure.

224. If the mixture employed in the last experiment be now thoroughly wetted with pure water, and again placed within the rays of the sun, its colour will rapidly change, and will acquire a deep purple approaching a crimson.

225. Moisten a piece of white ribbon with the aqueous solution of gold, described at No. 222, and dry it thoroughly in the dark : then suspend it in a clean, dry, transparent phial, and cork it close with a dry cork. Expose the ribbon, thus secured, to the strong light of a bright sun, for half an hour, and only a faint appearance of change of colour will be perceived.

226. Take the ribbon out of the phial that was employed in the last experiment, and wet it well with distilled water. If it be now

exposed to the sun's rays, it will instantly change colour, and will quickly be stained of an indelible purple.

227. Dissolve dry nitrate of silver in pure water; add a little oil of turpentine, shake the mixture, and cork it close. Submit the phial with its contents to the heat of boiling water for an hour, when the metal will be revived, and the inside of the phial, where the oil reposed on the aqueous solution, will be beautifully silvered, the reduced metal forming a metallic ring, extending quite round the phial.

228. Immerse a slip of white silk in a solution of nitro-muriate of gold in distilled water, and dry it in the air. Silk thus prepared will not be altered by hydrogen gas; but if another piece of silk be dipped in the solution and exposed while wet to the same current of hydrogen gas, instant signs of metallic reduction will appear; the colour will change from yellow to green, and a brilliant film of reduced gold will soon glitter on its surface.

229. If a piece of silk be immersed in a solution of nitrate of silver and dried in a dark place, and then submitted to hydrogen gas, the silver will not be reduced; but if exposed while wet to a stream of the same gas, the surface will quickly be coated with reduced silver; various colours, such as blue, purple, red, orange, and yellow, will accompany the reduction, and the threads of the silk will look like silver wire. During these experiments the silk should be constantly kept wet with distilled water.

230. Dissolve some crystals of muriate of tin in distilled water, then dip a piece of white silk in the solution, and dry it in the air. If this be now immersed in hydrogen gas, no change will be observed; but if it be exposed while wet to the same current of gas, the reduction will soon commence, attended with a great variety of beautiful colours, as red, yellow, orange, green, and blue, variously intermixed.

231. Prepare a strong solution of phosphorus in sulphuric ether, and dip a piece of white silk in the solution; then, when the ether has evaporated, and the phosphorus begins to fume, apply a solution of nitro-muriate of gold, made by dissolving the crystals of that salt in distilled water; the silk will in an instant be covered with a splendid coat of metallic gold.

232. Proceed as in the last experiment, and instead of the solution of gold, apply, with a camel's-hair pencil, a solution of nitrate of silver. Here the silver will instantly be restored to its metallic brilliancy, and frequently attended by spangles of a beautiful blue.

233. If a bit of white silk be immersed in an ethereal solution of

gold, and dried, the application of phosphorized ether will only im-part a brown colour to the silk; but if, as soon as the phosphorus begins to fume, it be placed on the palm of the hand, and breathed on for a considerable time, the brown will be succeeded by a purple tinge, and the metallic lustre of the gold will soon begin to appear.

234. If a stick of phosphorus be suspended in an aqueous solution of nitromuriate of gold, in a few minutes the phosphorus will become covered with pure gold.

235. If a piece of white silk be dipped in an aqueous solution of nitro-muriate of gold, and exposed while wet to sulphurous acid gas, the whole piece will in a few seconds be covered with a coat of re-duced gold, which remains permanent.

236. If a piece of white silk be immersed in an aqueous solution of nitrate of silver, thoroughly dried in the dark, and then exposed to sulphurous acid vapours, it will suffer no change; nor, if it be wetted with alcohol and then replaced in the vapour, will any sign of reduction appear; but if it be wetted with pure water, and then ex-posed to the vapour, metallic silver will immediately be seen on its surface.

A glass funnel is a convenient apparatus for these experiments. The silk may be suspended by a thread passed through it, and made fast to the funnel with a cork. The funnel is then to be placed on a table, and by moving it a little over the edge of the table, a lighted match may be readily introduced, and when the glass is full of vapour the match may be withdrawn. The vapour is confined by sliding the funnel back upon the table; and thus the phænomena of the experi-ment may be easily observed.

237. If a bit of silk be immersed in diluted acetate of lead, and exposed while wet to a stream of sulphuretted hydrogen gas, a brown tinge will instantly diffuse itself over the whole surface of the silk, accompanied with a bright coat of sulphuret of lead.

238. If a piece of silk be immersed in an aqueous solution of muriate of tin, and exposed while wet to a stream of the same gas, reduced tin of great brightness will immediately cover the surface, and in a little time this will be accompanied by various colours, such as blue, orange, and purple.

239. A piece of silk, treated in the same way, but dipped in an aqueous solution of chloride of arsenic, will be covered with re-splendent metallic arsenic, attended with a citron yellow colour.

240. Prepare two glasses of very dilute nitrate of copper; into one drop a little liquid ammonia, and into the other some diluted arsenite of potash. The mixture of these two colourless solutions will pro-

duce very different effects; for the one glass will have an abundant precipitate of a beautiful grass green and the other a precipitate of a brilliant sapphire blue.

241. Take potassium, make it very hot within a small glass vessel of oxygen gas. Here a rapid combustion, with a brilliant white flame, will be produced, and the metallic globules will be converted into a white and solid mass, which will be found to be pure potash.

242. Place a small piece of potassium within a dry wine-glass, and in order to acquire an idea of its specific gravity pour a little alcohol ether, or naphtha upon it; when, quitting the bottom of the glass, it will immediately rise to the surface of the liquid, it being, notwithstanding its metallic appearance, the lightest solid body known.

243. If a little potassium be dropped into a jar of chlorine gas, it burns spontaneously, and emits a bright red light. In this experiment a white salt is formed, the chloride of potassium.

244. If a globule of potassium be thrown upon water, it is decomposed with great violence: an instantaneous explosion is produced with brilliant flame, and a solution of pure potash is the result.

245. If a similar globule be placed upon ice, it will spontaneously burn with a bright flame, and perforate a deep hole in the ice, which will contain a solution of potash.

246. Take a piece of moistened turmeric paper, and drop a globule of potassium upon it. At the moment that it comes into contact with the water, it burns and moves rapidly upon the paper, as if in search of moisture, leaving behind it a deep reddish brown trace.

247. When a globule of sodium is thrown into hot water, the decomposition of the water is so violent that small particles of the metal are thrown out of the water, and actually burnt with scintillations and flame, in passing through the atmosphere.

To read or practise the foregoing experiments merely for the sake of amusement, may, occasionally, have its advantages; but a resolution to repeat them, and examine all the phænomena, for the sole purpose of receiving instruction, is what the author would principally inculcate.

TABLES.

THE following Tables exhibit a collective view of all the frigorific mixtures in the publication of Mr. Walker, who made a great many experiments upon the artificial production of cold.

TABLE,

Consisting of Frigorific Mixtures, having the power of generating or creating Cold, without the aid of Ice, sufficient for all useful and philosophical purposes, in any part of the World, at any Season.

FRIGORIFIC MIXTURES WITHOUT ICE.

Mixtures.	Parts.	Thermometer sinks.	Degree of cold produced.
Muriate of Ammonia Nitrate of Potash Water	5 . 16	From $+$ 50° to $+$ 10°	. 40°
Muriate of Ammonia Nitrate of Potash Sulphate of Soda Water	5 5 8 16	From $+$ 50° to $+$ 4°	. 46°
Nitrate of Ammonia Water	1 1	From $+$ 50° to $+$ 4°	. 46°
Nitrate of Ammonia Carbonate of Soda Water	1 1 1	From $+$ 50° to $-$ 7°	. 57°
Sulphate of Soda Diluted Nitric Acid	3 2	From $+$ 50° to $-$ 3°	. 50°
Sulphate of Soda Muriate of Ammonia Nitrate of Potash Diluted Nitric Acid	6 4 2 4	From $+$ 50° to $-$ 10°	. 60°
Sulphate of Soda Nitrate of Ammonia Diluted Nitric Acid	6 5 4	From $+$ 50° to $-$ 14°	. 64°
Phosphate of Soda Diluted Nitric Acid	9 4	From $+$ 50° to $-$ 12°	. 62°

Mixtures.	Parts.	Thermometer sinks.	Degree of cold produced.
Phosphate of Soda	9		
Nitrate of Ammonia	6 } From + 50° to — 21°	.	71°
Diluted Nitric Acid	4		
Sulphate of Soda	8 } From + 50° to — 0°	.	50°
Muriatic Acid ..	5		
Sulphate of Soda	5 } From + 50° to + 3°	.	47°
Diluted Sulphuric Acid	4		

N.B.—If the materials are mixed at a warmer temperature than that expressed in the Table, the effect will be proportionably greater; thus, if the most powerful of these mixtures be made when the air is + 85°, it will sink the thermometer to + 2°.

TABLE,

Consisting of Frigorific Mixtures, composed of Ice, with Chemical Salts and Acids.

FRIGORIFIC MIXTURES WITH ICE.

Mixtures.	Parts.	Thermometer sinks.	Degree of cold.
Snow, or pounded Ice	2	to — 5°	. •
Muriate of Soda	1		
Snow, or pounded Ice	5	to — 12°	. •
Muriate of Soda	2		
Muriate of Ammonia	1		
Snow, or pounded Ice	24	to — 18°	. •
Muriate of Soda	10		
Muriate of Ammonia	5		
Nitrate of Potash	5		
Snow, or pounded Ice	12	to — 25°	. •
Muriate of Soda	5		
Nitrate of Ammonia	5		
Snow	3 } From + 32° to — 23°	.	55°
Diluted Sulphuric Acid	2		
Snow	8 } From + 32° to — 27°	.	59°
Muriatic Acid	5		
Snow	7 } From + 32° to — 30°	.	62°
Diluted Nitric Acid	4		

(From any temperature.)

Mixtures.	Parts.	Thermometer sinks.	Degree of cold.
Snow . . .	4 }	From + 32° to — 50° .	72°
Muriate of Lime . .	5 }		
Snow . . .	2 }	From + 32° to — 50° .	82°
Crystallized Muriate of Lime	3 }		
Snow . . .	3 }	From + 32° to — 51° .	83°
Potash . . .	4 }		

TABLE,

Shewing the Dimensions which a Bar takes at 212°, whose length at 32° is 1·000000.

Bars.	Authorities.	Expansions.	Dilatation in Vulgar Fractions.
Glass Tube	Smeaton	1·00083333	
Do.	Roy	1·00077615	
Do.	De Luc's mean	1·00082800	$\frac{1}{1116}$
Do.	Dulong and Petit	1·00086130	$\frac{1}{1148}$
Do.	Lavoisier and Laplace	1·00081166	$\frac{1}{1122}$
Plate Glass	Do. Do.	1·000890890	$\frac{1}{1143}$
Do. Crown Glass	Do. Do.	1·00087572	$\frac{1}{1114}$
Do. Do.	Do. Do.	1·00089760	$\frac{1}{1090}$
Do. Do.	Do. Do.	1·00001751	
Do. Rod	Roy	1·00080787	
Deal	Do. as Glass	. .	
Platina	Borda	1·00085655	
Do.	Dulong and Petit	1·00088420	$\frac{1}{1131}$
Do.	Troughton	1·00096180	
Do. and Glass	Berthoud	1·00110000	
Palladium	Wollaston	1·00100000	
Antimony	Smeaton	1·00108300	
Cast Iron Prism	Roy	1·00110940	
Cast Iron	Lavoisier by Dr. Young	1·00111111	
Steel	Troughton	1·00118990	
Steel Rod	Roy	1·00114470	
Blistered Steel	Phil.Trans.1725,p.428	1·00112500	
Do.	Smeaton	1·00115000	
Steel, not tempered	Lavoisier and Laplace	1·00107875	$\frac{1}{917}$
Do. Do.	Do. Do.	1·00107956	$\frac{1}{916}$
Do. tempered yellow	Do. Do.	1·00136900	

Bars.	Authorities.	Expansions.	Dilatation in Vulgar Fractions.
Steel, tempd. yellow	Lavoisier and Laplace	1·00138600	
Do. at a higher heat	Do. Do.	1·00123956	$\frac{1}{807}$
Steel	Troughton	1·00118989	
Hard Steel	Smeaton	1·00122500	
Annealed do.	Muschenbrock	1·00122000	
Tempered do.	Do.	1·00137000	
Iron	Borda	1·00115600	
Do.	Smeaton	1·00125800	
Soft forged Iron	Lavoisier and Laplace	1·00122045	
Round iron wire drawn	Do. Do.	1·90123504	
Iron Wire	Troughton	1·00144010	

TABLE

Of some of the principal Effects of Heat.

	Wedg.	Fah.
Extremity of the scale of Wedgwood's thermometer	240°	32277°
Greatest heat of an air furnace, 8 inches in diameter, which neither melted nor softened Nankin Porcelain . . .	160	21877
Chinese Porcelain softened, best sort . .	156	21357
Cast Iron thoroughly melted . .	150	20577
Bristol Porcelain not melted . .	135	18627
Cast Iron begins to melt . .	130	17977
Greatest heat of a common smith's forge .	125	17327
Plate Glass furnace, strongest heat .	124	17197
Bow Porcelain vitrifies . .	121	16807
Chinese Porcelain softened, inferior sort .	120	16677
Flint Glass furnace, strongest heat .	114	15897
Derby Porcelain vitrifies . .	112	15637
Chelsea Porcelain vitrifies . .	105	14727
Stone Ware baked in . . .	102	14337
Welding heat of Iron greatest . .	95	13427
Worcester Porcelain vitrifies . .	94	13297

	Wedg.	Fah.
Welding heat of Iron least	90	12777°
Cream-coloured Ware baked in	86	12257
Flint Glass furnace, weak heat	70	10177
Working heat of Plate Glass	57	8487
Delft Ware baked in	41	6407
Fine Gold melts	32	5237
Settling heat of Flint Glass	29	4847
Fine Silver melts	28	4717
Swedish Copper melts	27	4587
Silver melts, Dr. Kennedy	22	3937
Brass melts	21	3807
Heat by which enamel colours are burnt on	6	1857
Red heat, fully visible daylight		1077
Iron, red hot in the twilight		884
Heat of a common fire		790
Iron, bright red in the dark		752
Zinc melts		700
Quicksilver boils ⎰ Irvine		672
⎱ Dalton		660
⎱ Crichton		655
Lowest ignition of Iron in the dark		
Linseed Oil boils		
Lead melts, Guyton, Irvine		612
Sulphuric Acid boils, Dalton		620

TABLE *

OF CHEMICAL EQUIVALENTS, ATOMIC WEIGHTS, OR PROPORTIONAL
NUMBERS, HYDROGEN BEING TAKEN AS UNITY.

(From Dr. TURNER's System of Chemistry.)

FROM the full account already given of the laws of combination
and of the atomic theory, it will be superfluous to describe the uses of
a table of equivalents. The only explanation required in connexion
with this subject relates to the ingenious contrivance called the *Scale
of Chemical Equivalents*, devised by the late Dr. Wollaston.
This useful instrument is a table of equivalents, comprehending all
those substances which are most frequently employed by chemists in
the laboratory; and it only differs from other tabular arrangements of
the same kind, in the numbers being attached to a sliding rule, which

Q

is divided according to the principle of that of Gunter. From the mathematical construction of the scale, it not only serves the same purpose as other tables of equivalents, but in many instances supersedes the necessity of calculation. Thus, by inspecting the common table of equivalents, we learn that 87·15 parts, or one equivalent of sulphate of potash, contain 40 parts of sulphuric acid and 47·15 of potash; but recourse must be had to calculation, when it is wished to determine the quantity of acid or alkali in any other quantity of the salt. This knowledge, on the contrary, is obtained directly by means of the scale of chemical equivalents. For example, on pushing up the slide until 100 marked upon it is in a line with the name sulphate of potash on the fixed part of the scale, the numbers opposite to the terms sulphuric acid and potash will give the precise quantity of each contained in 100 parts of the compound. In the original scale of Dr. Wollaston, for a particular account of which I may refer to the Philosophical Transactions for 1814, oxygen is taken as the standard of comparison; but hydrogen may be selected for that purpose with equal propriety, and scales of this kind have been prepared for sale by Dr. Boswell Reid of Edinburgh. A very complete scale of equivalents has been drawn up by Mr. Prideaux.—(Phil. Mag. and Annals, viii. 430.

EQUIVALENTS OF SIMPLE AND COMPOUND BODIES.

Acid			Acid, citric,		
acetic, $4C+3H+3O$	-	51	c. 2 aq.	-	76
c. 1 aq.	-	60	columbic, $Cb+3O$	-	209
antimonious, $Sb+2O$	-	80·6	cyanic, $(2C+N)+O$	-	34
antimonic, $Sb+2\frac{1}{2}O$	-	84·6	cyanuric, -	}	64·5
arsenic, $As+2\frac{1}{2}O$	-	57·7	$1\frac{1}{4}(2C+N)+3O+1\frac{1}{4}H$		
arsenious, $As+1\frac{1}{4}O$	-	49·7	fluoboric, $B+3F$	-	64·04
benzoic, $15C+6H+3O$	-	120	hydro-fluoric, $H+F$	-	19·68
boracic, $B+2O$	-	24	formic, $2C+O)+(H+O)$	-	37
c. 2 aq.	-	42	fluo-silicic, $Si+Fl$	-	26·18
carbonic, $C+2O$	-	22	hydriodic, $H+I$	-	127
chloric, $Cl+5O$	-	75·45	hydrobromic, $H+B$	-	79·26
chloro-carbonic,	}	49·45	hydrocyanic, $H+(2C+N)$	-	27
$(C+O)+Cl$			hydrosulphuric, $H+S$	-	17
chromic, $Cr+3O$	-	52	hydroselenic, $H+Se$	-	41
citric, $4C+2H+4O$	-	58	hyposulphurous, $2S+2O$	-	48

* c means crystallized, aq. water, and the numeral before aq. indicates the number of equivalents of water which the crystals contain.

Acid,		
hyposulphuric, 2S+5O	-	72
iodic, I+5O	-	166
malic, 4C+1H+4O	-	57
manganic, Mn+3O	-	51.7
molybdic, Mo+3O	-	71.7
muriatic, H+Cl	-	36.45
nitric, N+5O	-	54
liquid with 2 aq. (Sp. gr. 1.5).	-	72
nitrous, N+4O	-	46
oxalic, 2C+3O	-	36
c. 3 aq.	-	63
perchloric, Cl+7O	-	91.45
permanganic, 2Mn+7O	-	111.4
phosphorous, P+1½O	-	27.7
phosphoric, P+2½O	-	35.7
pyrogallic	-	63?
selenious, Se+16O	-	56
selenic, Se+24O	-	64
succinic, 4C+2H+3O	-	50
sulphuric, S+3O	-	40
liquid, 1 aq.(Sp.gr. 1.8485)		49
sulphurous, S+2O	-	32
tartaric, 4C+2H+5O	-	66
c. 1 aq.	-	75
titanic, Ti+2O	-	40.3
tungstic, Tu+3O	-	123.7
uric, 6C+2N+1O	-	72
c. 2 aq.	-	90
Alcohol, (2H+2C)+(H+O)	-	93
Alumina, Al+1½O	-	25.7
Antimony	-	64.6
sesquichloride, Sb+1½Cl	-	100.05
oxide, Sb+1½O	-	76.6
sesquisulphuret, Sb+1½S	-	88.6
bisulphuret, Sb+2S	-	96.6
persulphuret, Sb+2½S	-	104.6
Arsenic	-	37.7
sulphuret, (realgar) As+S	-	53.7
sesquisulphuret, As+1½S	-	61.7
persulphuret, As+2½S	-	77.7
Barium	-	68.7
chloride, Ba+Cl	-	104.15
oxide, (baryta) Ba+O	-	76.7
peroxide, Ba+2O	-	84.7
sulphuret, Ba+S	-	84.7
Bismuth	-	71
chloride, Bi+Cl	-	106.45
oxide, Bi+O	-	79
sulphuret, Bi+S	-	88
Cadmium	-	55.8
chloride, Cd+Cl	-	91.25
oxide, Cd+O	-	63.8
sulphuret, Cd+S	-	71.8
Calcium	-	20.5
Calcium,		
chloride, Ca+Cl	-	55.95
oxide, (lime) Ca+O	-	28.5
sulphuret, Ca+S	-	36.5
phosphuret, Ca+P	-	36.2
Carbon	-	6
chloride, C+Cl	-	41.45
perchloride, 2C+3Cl	-	106.35
oxide, C+O	-	14
bisulphuret, C+2S	-	38
Cerium	-	46
oxide, Ce+O	-	54
peroxide, Ce+1½O	-	58
Chloral, 9C+6Cl+4O	-	212.7
Chlorine	-	35.45
oxide? Cl+O	-	43.45
peroxide, Cl+4O	-	67.45
Chromium	-	28
chloride, Cr+1½Cl	-	45.72
terchloride, Cr+3Cl	-	134.35
terfluoride, Cr+3F	-	84.04
oxide, Cr+1½O	-	40
Cobalt	-	29.5
chloride, Co+Cl	-	64.95
oxide, Co+O	-	37.5
peroxide, Co+1½O	-	41.5
sulphuret, Co+S	-	45.5
Copper	-	31.6
dichloride, 2Cu+Cl	-	98.65
chloride, Cu+Cl	-	66.05
dioxide, 2Cu+O	-	71.2
oxide, (black) Cu+O	-	39.6
disulphuret, 2Cu+S	-	79.2
sulphuret, Cu+S	-	47.6
Cyanogen, 2C+N	-	26
Ether, 2(2C+2H)+(H+O)	-	37
Glucina, G+O	-	25.7
Gold	-	200
chloride, Au+Cl	-	235.44
terchloride, Au+3Cl	-	306.85
oxide, Au+O	-	208
teroxide, Au+3O	-	224
tersulphuret, Au+3S	-	248
Hydrogen	-	1
arseniuretted, As+H	-	38.7
carburetted, (light) C+2H		8
carburetted, (heavy) 2C+2H		14
Iron	-	28
chloride, Fe+Cl	-	63.45
perchloride, Fe+1½Cl	-	80.7
oxide, Fe+O	-	36
peroxide, Fe+1½O	-	40
sulphuret, Fe+S	-	44
bisulphuret, Fe+2S	-	60
Lead	-	103.5
chloride, Pb+Cl	-	138.95

Vanadium,			Carbonate of		
binoxide, V+2O	-	84·5	manganese	-	57·8
acid, V+3O	-	92·5	potash		69·15
bisulphuret, V+2S	-	100·5	Bicarbonate of potash	-	91·15
tersulphuret, V+3S	-	116·5	c, 1 aq.	-	100·15
Uranium -	-	217	Carbonate of soda	-	53·3
oxide, U+O	-	225	c. 10 aq.	-	143·3
peroxide, U+1½O	-	229	Bicarbonate of soda	-	75·3
Water, H+O -	-	9	c. 1 aq.	-	84·3
Yttria, Y+O -	-	40·2	Carbonate of strontia	-	73·8
Zinc -	-	32·5	zinc	-	62·5
chloride, Zn+Cl	-	67·95	Chlorate of baryta	-	152·15
oxide, Zn+O	-	40·5	lead	-	186·95
sulphuret, Zn+S	-	48·5	mercury	-	283·45
Zirconia, Z+O	-	38	potash	-	122·6
			Chromate of baryta	-	128·7
			lead	-	163·5
SALTS.			mercury	-	260
			potash	-	99·15
Acetate of ammonia	-	68	Bichromate of Potash	-	151·15
c. 7 aq.	-	131	Muriate of ammonia	-	53·45
baryta	-	127·7	baryta	-	113·15
c. 3 aq	-	154·7	c. 1 aq.	-	122·15
cadmium	-	114·8	lime	-	64·95
c. 3 aq.	-	132·8	c. 6 aq.	-	118·95
copper, (neutral)	-	90·6	magnesia	-	57·15
c. 1 aq.	-	99·6	strontia, +8 aq.	-	160·25
—— (diacetate) c. 6 aq.	-	184·2	Nitrate of ammonia	•	71
—— (triacetate) c. 1½ aq.	-	183·3	baryta	-	130·7
lead	-	162·6	bismuth	-	133
c. 3 aq.	-	185·9	c. 3 aq.	-	160
—— (diacetate)	-	274	lead	-	165·5
—— (triacetate)	-	385·5	lime	-	82·5
lime	-	79·5	magnesia	-	74·7
magnesia	-	69·7	mercury c. 2 aq.	•	280
mercury	-	259	potash	-	101·15
potash	-	98·15	silver	-	170
silver	-	168	soda	-	85·3
strontia	-	102·8	strontia	-	105·8
zinc	-	91·5	Oxalate of ammonia	-	53
c. 7 aq.	-	154·5	c. 2 aq.	-	71
Arseniate of lead	-	169·2	baryta	-	112·7
lime	-	86·2	Binoxalate of baryta	-	148·7
potash	-	104·86	Oxalate of cobalt	-	73·5
Binarseniate of Potash	-	162·56	lime	-	64·5
c. 2 aq.	-	180·56	nickel	-	73·5
Arseniate of soda	-	89	potash	-	83·15
Binarseniate of soda	-	146·7	c. 1 aq.	-	92·15
c. 12½ aq.	-	259·2	Binoxalate of potash	-	119·15
Arseniate of silver	-	463·4	c. 2 aq.	-	137·15
Carbonate of baryta	-	98·7	Quadroxalate of potash	-	191·15
copper	-	61·6	c. 7 aq.	-	254·15
iron	-	58	Oxalate of strontia	-	87·8
lead	-	133·5	Phosphate of ammonia	-	88·55
lime	-	50·5	c. 3 aq.	-	115·55
magnesia	-	42·7	baryta	-	148·1

Phosphate of lead	-	147·2	Sulphate of mercury	- 248
*lime	-	442·29	Bipersulphate of mercury	- 296
†magnesia	-	112·8	Sulphate of potash	- 87·15
c. 14 aq.	-	238·9	Bisulphate of potash	- 127·15
Diphosphate of soda	-	134·1	c. 2 aq.	- 145·15
c. 1 aq. basic	-	143·1	Sulphate of soda	- 71·3
do. c. 24 aq.	-	359	c. 10 aq.	- 161·3
Sulphate of alumina	-	65·7	strontia	- 91·8
ammonia	-	57·25	zinc	- 80·5
baryta	-	116·7	c. 7 aq.	- 143·5
copper	-	79·6	alumina and potash	- 258·60
c. 5 aq.	-	124·6	c. 24 aq. (alum)	- 474·60
iron	-	76	Tartrate of lead	- 177·5
c. 6 aq.	-	130	lime	- 94·5
lead	-	151·5	potash	- 113·15
lime	-	68·5	Bitartrate of potash	- 179·15
c. 2 aq.	-	86·5	c. 1 aq. (cream of tartar)	188·15
lithia	-	58	Tartrate of antimony and	
magnesia	-	60·7	potash	- 333·31
c. 7 aq.	-	123·7	c. 2 aq. (tartar emetic)	351·31

* 8 Lime+8 phosphoric acid   † 2 Magnesia+1 phosphoric acid.

A VOCABULARY

OF

CHEMICAL TERMS.

Acetates—Salts formed by the combination of any base with the acetic acid.

Acids.—For the nature of acids, see page 106.

Aeriform fluids.—Fluid substances combined with an additional portion of caloric sufficient to give them the gaseous form.—See *Gas.*

Affinity is the term used synonymously with attraction, to denote the property of bodies, in consequence of which they combine together.

Aggregates—Substances whose parts are united by cohesive, and not by chemical attraction. See *Affinity of Aggregation.*

Albumen.—That peculiar animal substance which exists in the serum of the blood, the white of eggs, and other compounds.

Alcohol.—Spirit of wine, highly rectified to 66°. When purest, its specific gravity is only 0·7947.

Alembic.—The term given to the still used by chemists for their sublimations. *b* is the body and *a* the capital. The substance to be sublimed is placed in the body, and heat applied, the vapours rise into the head, where they are condensed.

Alkalies.—Peculiar substances which have an urinous, burning, and caustic taste, and a strong tendency to combination. When united with acids they form mild alkaline salts.

Alloys.—A combination of any two metals, except mercury, is called an alloy. Thus gold is alloyed either with silver or copper, for the purposes of coinage.

Alluvial.—By alluvial depositions, is meant the soil which has been formed by the destruction of the mountains, and the washing down of their particles by torrents of water.

Amalgam.—A combination or mixture of mercury with any other metal, is called an Amalgam.

Ammoniacal salts.—Salts formed by the union of an acid with ammonia, or volatile alkali.

Analysis.—The resolution of a substance into its constituent parts.

Annealing.—The art of rendering substances tough which are naturally hard and brittle. Glass and iron are annealed by gradual cooling ; brass and copper by heating, and then suddenly plunging them in cold water.

Apparatus, chemical.—This term is descriptive of all the utensils made use of in a chemical laboratory. The principal are stills, furnaces, crucibles, retorts, receivers, matrasses, worm-tubs, pneumatics, troughs, thermometers, &c.

Areometer.—A graduated glass instrument with a bulb, by which the specific gravity of liquids is ascertained. Baumé's areömeter is that which is chiefly referred to when the French writers speak of this instrument.

Argillaceous.—A term descriptive of those earths which contain alumina or clay.

Aroma.—A term used for the odour which arises from certain vegetables, or their infusions.

Arsenites.—Compounds of the arsenious acid (white arsenic) and bases.

Arseniates.—Salts formed by the combination of any base with the arsenic acid.

Atmospheres.—We use this term to express the degree of additional pressure given to fluids. Thus, if, in order to impregnate water with any of the gases, I give it a pressure of 15lbs. upon every square inch of surface, I am said to give it *one* atmosphere ; if 30lbs. *two* atmospheres, &c. &c.

Attraction, chemical.—A term used to express that peculiar propensity which different species of matter have to unite with each other, or with portions of matter of their own species.

————*of aggregation.*—A force by which two bodies of the same kind tend to combine, and by which an aggregate is formed without the *chemical* properties of the substances being at all changed.

Attraction of composition.—A force by which substances of different kinds unite, and by which matter is formed whose properties are different from those of the bodies before their combination. This attraction is stronger in proportion as the nature of the bodies is different, between which it is exerted.

Azote.—A name given by the French chemists to *nitrogen*, to which the reader is referred.

Balloon.—A term given by the French to their spherical chemical receivers.

Balsams.—Certain aromatic resinous substances, which are obtained from some trees by incisions. Of this kind are the Canada balsam, the balsam of Copaiva, the balsam of Tolu, &c.

Barometer.—An instrument which shows the variation of the pressure of the atmosphere, by the rise or fall of a column of mercury in a glass tube attached to a graduated plate.

Base.—A chemical term, usually applied to denote the earth, the alkali, or the metal which is combined with an acid to form a salt.

Baths.—Vessels for distillation or digestion, contrived to transmit heat gradually and regularly.

Bath sand.—Vessels filled in part with dry sand, in which those retorts are placed which require a greater heat than can be given by boiling water. In large works iron plates are used instead of vessels of capacity. They are often called sand-heats.

Bath water.—Vessels of boiling water, in which vessels containing the other matters to be distilled or digested are placed, in order that the same heat may be kept up throughout the whole of any particular process.

Benzoates.—Salts formed by the combination of any base with the benzoic acid.

Bittern.—The mother-liquor which remains after the crystallization of muriate of soda (sea salt). It generally contains sulphate of magnesia, and a small portion of sulphate of soda.

Bitumen.—A generic term, applied to a variety of fossil inflammable substances.

Blow-pipe.—An instrument to increase and direct the flame of a lamp for the analysis of minerals, and for other chemical purposes.

Bolt-head.—A round chemical vessel with a long neck, usually employed for digestions. It is also called a matrass.

Borates.—Salts formed by the combination of any base with the acid of borax.

Button.—A name given to the small round piece of metal which is found at the bottom of a crucible after a metallic ore or an oxide of metal has been reduced.

Calcareous.—A chemical term formerly applied to describe chalk, marble, and all other combinations of lime with carbonic acid.

Calcination.—The application of heat to saline, metallic, or other substances; so regulated as to deprive them of moisture, &c., and yet preserve them in a pulverulent form.

Caloric.—The chemical term for the matter of heat.

Caloric, free.—Caloric in a separate state, or, if attached to other substances, not *chemically* united with them.

Caloric, latent.—Is the term made use of to express that portion of caloric which is chemically united to any substance, so as to become a *part* of the said substance.

Calorimeter.—An instrument for ascertaining the quantity of caloric disengaged from any substance that may be the object of experiment.

Calx.—An old term made use of to describe a metallic oxide.

Camphorates.—Salts formed by the combination of any base with the camphoric acid.

Capillary.—A term usually applied to the rise of the sap in vegetables, or the rise of any fluid in very small tubes; owing to a peculiar kind of attraction, called capillary attraction.

Capsules.—Are small saucers of clay for roasting samples of ores and for smelting them to ascertain their value.

Caput Mortuum.—A term signifying *dead-head*, being that which remains in a retort after distillation to dryness. See *Residuum*, which is the modern term.

Carbon.—The basis of charcoal.

Carbonates.—Salts formed by the combination of any base with carbonic acid.

Carburets.—Compound substances, of which carbon forms one of the constituent parts. Thus plumbago, which is composed of carbon and iron, is called carburet of iron.

Causticity.—That quality in certain substances by which they burn or corrode animal bodies to which they are applied. It is best explained by the doctrine of chemical affinity.

Cementation.—A process by which metals are purified or changed in their qualities by heat, without fusion, by means of a composition, called a cement, with which they are covered. Thus iron, by being kept a long time in a certain degree of heat, surrounded by charcoal powder, is converted into steel.

Chalybeate.—A term descriptive of those mineral waters which are impregnated with iron. See *Martial.*

Charcoal.—Wood burnt in close vessels: it is an impure carbon, and generally contains a small portion of salts and earth. Its carbonaceous matter may be converted by combustion into carbonic acid gas.

Chatoyant.—A term much used by the French chemists to describe a property in some metallic and other substances of varying their colours according to the way in which they are held; as is the case with the feathers of some birds, which appear very different when seen in different positions.

Chert.—A term made use of in describing a species of siliceous stones, which are coarser and softer than the common silex. It is often found in large masses in quarries of limestone.

Chromates.—Salts formed by the combination of any base with the chromic acid.

Citrates.—Salts formed by the combination of any base with citric acid.

Coal.—A term applied to the residuum of any dry distillation of animal or vegetable matters.

Cohesion.—A force inherent in all the particles of all substances, excepting light and caloric, which prevents bodies from falling in pieces. See *Affinity.*

Cohobation.—When a distilled fluid is poured again upon the matter from which it was distilled, in order to make it stronger, it is called cohobation. The term is not much used by modern chemists.

Combination.—A term expressive of a true *chemical* union of two or more substances; in opposition to mere mechanical mixture.

Combustibles.—Certain substances which are capable of combining more or less rapidly with oxygen, or other supporters of combustion.

Combustion.—The act of absorption of oxygen by combustible bodies from atmospheric or vital air. The word decombustion is sometimes used by the French writers to signify the opposite operation.

Comminution.—The reduction of hard bodies into small particles.

Concentration.—The act of increasing the specific gravity of bodies. The term is usually applied to fluids which are rendered stronger by evaporating a portion of the water which they contain.

Condensation.—The act of bringing the component parts of vapour or gas, nearer together by pressure, or by cold. Thus atmospheric air may be condensed by pressure, and aqueous vapour by the subtraction of caloric, till it is converted into water.

Crucibles.—Vessels of indispensable use in chemistry in the various operations of fusion by heat. They are made of baked earth, or metal, in the form of an inverted cone.

Crystallization.—An operation of nature, in which various earths, salts, and metallic substances, pass from a fluid to a solid state, assuming certain determinate geometrical figures.

Crystallization, water of.—That portion, which is combined with salts in the act of crystallizing, and becomes a *component* part of the said saline substances.

Cupel.—A vessel made of calcined bones, mixed with a small proportion of clay and water. It is used whenever gold and silver are refined by melting them with lead. The process is called cupellation.

Decomposition.—The separation of the constituent principles of compound bodies by chemical means.

Decrepitation.—The sudden decomposition of salts attended with a a crackling noise when thrown into a red-hot crucible, or on an open fire.

Deflagration.—The vivid combustion that is produced whenever nitre, mixed with an inflammable substance, is exposed to a red heat. It may be attributed to the extrication of oxygen from the nitre, and its being transferred to the inflammable body; as any of the nitrates or oxygenized muriates will produce the same effect.

Deliquescence of solid saline bodies, signifies their becoming moist, or liquid, by means of water which they absorb from the atmosphere in consequence of their great attraction for that fluid.

Deliquium—Is the state of potash, or any deliquescent salt, when it has so far deliquesced by exposure to the air as to have become a liquid.

Delite.—A term used by some of the French writers, signifying to break, by the action of the air, like a soft stone into layers.

Deoxidize (formerly Deoxidate).—To deprive a body of oxygen.

Deoxidisement.—A term made use of by some writers to express that operation by which one substance deprives another substance of its oxygen. It is called unburning a body by the French chemists.

Depuration.—The purging or separating any liquid in a state of purity from its faeces or lees.

Detonation.—An explosion with noise. It is most commonly applied to the explosion of nitre when thrown upon heated charcoal.

Digestion.—The effect produced by the continued soaking of a solid substance in a liquid, with the application of heat.

Digester, Papin's.—An apparatus for reducing animal or vegetable substances to a pulp or gelly expeditiously.

Distillation.—A process for sepa-  rating the volatile parts of a substance from the more fixed, and preserving them both in a state of separation; *b* the retort, *a* the receiver.

Docimastic Art.—The art of assaying metals.

Ductility.—A quality of certain bodies, in consequence of which they may be drawn out to a certain length without fracture.

Dulcification.—The combination of mineral acids with alcohol. Thus we have dulcified spirit of nitre, dulcified spirit of vitriol, &c.

Edulcoration.—Expressive of the purification of a substance by washing with water.

Effervescence.—An intestine motion which takes place in certain bodies, occasioned by the sudden escape of a gaseous substance.

Efflorescence.—A term commonly applied to those saline crystals which become pulverulent on exposure to the air, in consequence of the loss of a part of the water of crystallization.

Elasticity.—A force in bodies, by which they endeavour to restore themselves to the position from whence they were displaced by any external force.

Elastic Fluids.—A name sometimes given to vapours and gases. Vapour is called an *elastic* fluid; gas, a *permanently* elastic fluid.

Elective Attractions.—A term used by Bergman and others to designate what we now express by the words chemical *affinity;* which see. When chemists first observed the power which one compound substance has to decompose another, it was imagined that the minute particles of some bodies had a *preference* for some other particular bodies; hence this property of matter acquired the term *elective* attraction.

Elements.—The simple, constituent parts of bodies, which are incapable of decomposition; they are frequently called principles. See *Simple Substances.*

Eliquation.—An operation whereby one substance is separated from another by fusion. It consists in giving the mass a degree of heat that will make the more fusible matter flow, and not the other.

Elutriation.—The operation of pulverizing metallic ores or other substances, and then mixing them with water, so that the lighter parts which are capable of suspension may be poured off, and thus separated from the grosser particles. The metallic substances which are reduced to an impalpable powder are prepared by this process.

Empyreuma.—A peculiar fluid of a disagreeable smell, arising from the burning of animal and vegetable matter in close vessels.

Eolipile.—A copper vessel with a small orifice, and partly filled with water. It is made hot, in order that the vapour of the water may rush out with violence, and carry a stream of air with it to increase the intensity of fires. It is an instrument of great antiquity.

Essences.—What are called essences, in chemistry and pharmacy, are the essential oils obtained by distillation from odoriferous vegetable substances.

Essential Salts.—The saline substances found in plants, and which are held in solution by the water wherein they are infused. They are obtained by evaporation and cooling.

Ethers.—Volatile liquids formed by the distillation of some of the acids with alcohol.

Evaporation.—The conversion of fluids into vapour by heat. This appears to be nothing more than a gradual solution of the aqueous particles in atmospheric air, owing to the chemical attraction of the latter for water.

Eudiometer.—An instrument invented by Dr. Priestley for determining the purity of any given portion of atmospheric air. The science of investigating the different kinds of gases is called *eudiometry*.

Expression.—A term used in pharmacy, denoting the act of forcing out the juices and oils of plants by means of a press. By a similar term the *expressed* are distinguished from the *essential* oils.

Exsiccation.—The act of drying moist bodies. It is effected in two ways; by exhaling the aqueous particles by the application of heat or atmospheric air, and by absorbing the moisture with soft and spongy substances. Thus, small matters are dried by chemists with bibulous paper; and larger masses, by spreading them on tablets of chalk.

Extracts.—The soluble parts of vegetable substances, first dissolved in spirit and water, and then reduced to the consistence of a thick syrup, or paste, by evaporation.

Fermentation.—A peculiar spontaneous motion, which takes place in all vegetable matter when exposed for a certain time to a proper degree of temperature. The changes which are effected by saccharine fermentation.

Fibrine.—That white fibrous substance which is left after freely washing the coagulum of the blood, and which chiefly composes the muscular fibre.

Filtration.—A chemical process for the depuration of liquid substances. Bibulous paper supported by a funnel is commonly made use of; but for dear and expensive liquors chemists generally use a little carded cotton lightly pressed into the tube of a glass funnel. The valuable concentrated acids should be filtered through pounded glass.

Fixity.—A term applicable to that property of some bodies of bearing a great heat without being volatilized.

Flowers.—In chemical language are solid dry substances reduced to a powder by sublimation. Thus we have flowers of arsenic, of sal ammoniac, of sulphur, &c. which are arsenic, sal ammoniac, and sulphur unaltered except in appearance.

Fluates.—Salts formed by the combination of any base with fluoric acid.

Fluidity.—A term applied to all liquid substances. Solids are converted to fluids by combining with a certain portion of caloric.

Flux.—A substance which is mixed with metallic ores, or other bodies, to promote their fusion: as an alkali is mixed with silex in order to form glass.

Fossil.—Substance extracted from the earth. Term generally applied to organic remains.

Fuliginous.—A term sometimes made use of in describing certain vapours which arise in chemical operations, having the thick appearance of smoke.

Fulmination.—Thundering or explosion with noise. We have fulminating silver, fulminating gold, and other fulminating powders, which explode with a loud report by friction, or when slightly heated.

Funnel.—A glass vessel of the shape here given, for receiving a filter.

Furnaces.—Chemical vessels of various forms for the fusion of ores, or other operations which require heat.

Furnaces, blast.—Are built for making iron, smelting ores, &c. They are so contrived that their heat is much increased by means of powerful bellows. A blacksmith's forge is a kind of blast furnace.

Furnaces, wind.—Chemical furnaces for intense heat, so constructed that they draw with great force, without the use of bellows.

Fusion.—The state of a body which was solid in the temperature of the atmosphere, and is now rendered fluid by the artificial application of heat.

Gallates.—Salts formed by the combination of any base with gallic acid.

Galvanism.—A new science which offers a variety of phenomena, resulting from different conductors of electricity placed in different circumstances of contact.

Gangue.—A term made use of to denote the stony matter which fills the cavities, and accompanies the ores in the veins of metals.

Gas.—All solid substances when converted into permanently elastic fluid by caloric are called gases.

Gaseous.—Having the nature and properties of gas.

Gasometer.—A name given to a variety of utensils and apparatus contrived to measure, collect, preserve, or mix the different gases. An apparatus of this kind is also used for the purposes of administering pneumatic medicines.

Gasometry.—The science of measuring the gases. It likewise teaches the nature and properties of these elastic fluids.

Gelatine.—A chemical term for animal jelly. It exists particularly in the tendons and the skin of animals.

Glass.—Some metallic oxides when fused are called *glass.* They have somewhat of resemblance to common glass.

Glass, phosphoric.—A vitreous, insipid, insoluble substance, procured by boiling down phosphoric acid to a syrup, and then fusing it by an increased heat.

Glass, gall.—See *Sandiver.*

Gluten.—A vegetable substance somewhat similar to animal gelatine. It is the gluten in wheat flour which gives it the property of making good bread, and adhesive paste. Other grain contains a much less quantity of this nutritious substance.

Graduation.—A process by evaporation, of bringing fluids to a certain degree of consistence, in order to separate more easily the substances they hold in solution.

Graduation.—The division of a scale or measure into decimal, or other regular parts.

Grain.—Weight made use of by chemical writers. Twenty grains make a scruple; 3 scruples a drachm; 8 drachms, or 480 grains, make an ounce; 12 ounces, or 5760 grains, a pound troy. The *avoirdupois* pound contains 7000 grains.

Granulation.—The operation of pouring a *melted* metal into water, in order to divide it into small particles for chemical purposes. Tin is thus granulated by the dyers before it is dissolved in the proper acid.

Gravity.—That property by which bodies move towards each other, in proportion to their respective *quantities* of matter. This is the property by which bodies fall to the earth.

Gravity, specific.—This differs from absolute gravity, inasmuch as it is the weight of a given *measure* of any solid or fluid body, compared with the *same measure* of distilled water. It is generally expressed by decimals.

Gums.—Mucilaginous exudations from certain trees. Gum consists of lime, carbon, oxygen, hydrogen, and nitrogen, with a little phosphoric acid.

Heat, matter of.—See *Caloric.*

Hepar.—The name formerly given to the combination of sulphur with alkali. It is now called sulphuret of potass, &c., as the case may be.

Hepatic Gas.—The old name for sulphuretted hydrogen.

Hermetically.—A term applied to the closing of the orifice of a glass tube, so as to render it air-tight. Hermes, or Mercury, was formerly supposed to have been the inventor of chemistry; hence a tube which was closed for chemical purposes, was said to be hermetically or chemically sealed. It is usually done by melting the end of the tube by means of a blow-pipe.

Hydrogen.—A simple substance; one of the constituent parts of water.

Hydrogen Gas.—Solid hydrogen united with a large portion of caloric. It is the lightest of all the known gases. Hence it is used to inflate balloons. It was formerly called inflammable air.

Hydro-carbonates.—Combinations of carbon with hydrogen were formerly described by this term. Hydro-carbonate gas is procured from moistened charcoal by distillation.

Hydrometers.—Instruments for ascertaining the specific gravity of spirituous or other liquors.

Hygrometers.—Instruments for ascertaining the degree of moisture in atmospheric air.

Incineration.—The burning of vegetables for the sake of their ashes. It is usually applied to the burning of kelp on the coasts for making mineral alkali.

Inflammation.—A phenomenon which takes place on mixing certain substances. The mixture of oil of turpentine with strong nitrous acid is an instance of this peculiar chemical effect.

Infusion.—A simple operation to procure the salts, juices, and other virtues of vegetables by means of water.

Insolation.—A term sometimes made use of to denote that exposure to the sun which is made in order to promote the chemical action of one substance upon another.

Intermediates.—A term made use of when speaking of chemical affinity. Oil, for example, has no affinity to water unless it be previously combined with an alkali; it then becomes soap, and the alkali is said to be the *intermedium* which occasions the union.

Kali.—A genus of marine plants which is burnt to procure mineral alkali by afterwards lixiviating the ashes.

Laboratory.—A room fitted up with apparatus for the performance of chemical operations.

Lactates.—Salts formed by the combination of any base with lactic acid.

Lakes.—Certain colours made by combining the colouring matter of cochineal, or of certain vegetables, with pure alumina, or with oxide of tin, zinc, &c.

Lamp Argand's.—A kind of lamp much used for chemical experiments. It is made on the principle of a wind furnace, and thus produces a great degree of light and heat without smoke.

Lens.—A glass, convex on both sides, for concentrating the rays of the sun. It is employed by chemists in fusing refractory substances which cannot be operated upon by an ordinary degree of heat.

Levigation.—The grinding down of hard substances to an impalpable powder on a stone with a muller, or in a mill adapted to the purpose.

Liquefaction.—The change of a solid to the state of a fluid, occasioned by the combination of caloric.

Litharge.—An oxide of lead which appears in a state of vitrification. It is formed in the process of separating silver from lead.

Lixiviation.—The solution of an alkali or a salt in water, or in some other fluid, in order to form a lixivium.

Lixivium.—A fluid impregnated with an alkali or with a salt.

Lute.—A composition for closing the junctures of chemical vessels to prevent the escape of gas or vapour in distillation.

Maceration.—The steeping of a solid body in a fluid in order to soften it, without impregnating the fluid.

Malates.—Salts formed by the combination of any base with malic acid.

Malleability.—That property of metals which gives them the capacity of being extended and flattened by hammering. It is probably occasioned by latent caloric.

Martial.—An old term for chemical preparations of iron. See *chalybeate.*

Massicot.—A name given to the yellow oxide of lead, as minium is applied to the red oxide.

Matrass.—Another name for a bolt-head; which see.

Matrix.—The bed in which a metallic ore is found.

Matt.—That mass of metal which separates from the scoriæ in smelting ores without previous roasting.

Menstruum.—The fluid in which a solid body is dissolved. Thus water is a menstrum for salts, gums, &c., and spirits of wine for resins.

Metallic Oxides.—Metals combined with oxygen. By this process they are generally reduced to a pulverulent form; are changed from combustible to incombustible substances; and receive the property of being soluble in acids.

Metallurgy.—The art of extracting and purifying metals.

Mineral.—Any natural substance of a metallic, earthy, or saline nature, whether simple or compound, is deemed a mineral.

Mineralogy.—The science of minerals.

Mineral Waters.—Waters which hold some metal, earth, or salt, in solution. They are frequently termed medicinal waters.

Minium.—The red oxide of lead, commonly called red-lead.

Molecule.—The molecules of bodies are those ultimate particles of matter which cannot be decomposed by any chemical means.

Molybdates.—Salts formed by the combination of any base with the molybdic acid.

Mordants.—Substances which have a chemical affinity for particular colours; they are employed by dyers as a bond to unite the colour with the cloth intended to be dyed. Alum is of this class.

Mother-Waters or *Mothers.*—The liquors which are left after the crystallization of any salts.

Mucilage.—A glutinous matter obtained from vegetables, transparent and tasteless, soluble in water, but not in spirit of wine. It chiefly consists of carbon and hydrogen, with a little oxygen.

Mucites.—Salts formed by the combination of any base with the mucous acid.

Muffle.—A semi-cylindrical utensil, resembling the tilt of a boat, made of baked clay ; its use is that of a cover to cupels in the assay furnace, to prevent the charcoal from falling upon the metal, or whatever is the subject of experiment.

Muriates.—Salts formed by the combination of any base with muriatic acid.

Natron.—One of the names for mineral alkali, or soda.

Neutralize.—When two or more substances mutually disguise each other's properties, they are said to neutralize one another.

Neutral Salt.—A substance formed by the union of an acid with an alkali, an earth, or a metallic oxide, in such proportions as to saturate both the base and the acid.

Nitrates.—Salts formed by the combination of any base with nitric acid.

Nitrogen.—A simple substance, by the French chemists called azote. It enters into a variety of compounds, and forms more than three parts in four of atmospheric air.

Ochres.—Various combinations of the earths with oxide, or carbonate, of iron.

Oil.—A fluid substance well known. It is composed of hydrogen, oxygen, and carbon.

Ores.—Metallic earths, which frequently contain several extraneous matters ; such as sulphur, arsenic, &c.

Oxalates.—Salts formed by the combination of any base with oxalic acid.

Oxide.—Any substance combined with oxygen, in a proportion not sufficient to produce acidity.

Oxidize.—To combine oxygen with a body without producing acidity.

Oxidizement.—The operation by which any substance is combined with oxygen, in a degree not sufficient to produce acidity.

Oxygen.—A simple substance composing the greatest part of water, and part of atmospheric air.

Oxygen Gas.—Oxygen converted to a gaseous state by caloric. It is also called vital air. It forms nearly one-fifth of atmospheric air.

Oxygenize.—To acidify a substance by oxygen. Synonymous with Oxygenate; but the former is the better term.

Oxygenizable.—A term applicable to all bodies that combine with oxygen, and do not emit flame during the combination.

Parting.—The operation of separating gold from silver by means of nitrous acid, and other mediums.

Pelican.—A glass alembic, with a tubulated capital, from which two opposite and crooked arms pass out, and enter again at the swell of vessel. The instrument is designed for operations of cohobation, and is calculated to save the trouble of frequently luting and unluting the apparatus. It is now seldom used.

Pellicle.—A thin skin which forms on the surface of saline solutions and other liquors, when boiled down to a certain strength.

Phlogiston.—An old chemical name for an imaginary substance, supposed to be a combination of fire with some other matter, and a constiteunt part of all inflammable bodies, and of many other substances.

Phosphates.—Salts formed by the combination of any base with phosphoric acid.

Phosphites.—Salts formed by the combination of any base with phosphorous acid.

Phosphurets.—Substances formed by an union with phosphorus Thus we have phosphuret of lime, phosphuretted hydrogen, &c.

Plumbago.—Carburet of iron, or the black lead of commerce.

Pneumatic.—Any thing relating to the air and gases.

Pneumatic Trough.—A vessel filled in part with water or mercury, for the purpose of collecting gases, so that they be rapidly removed from one vessel to another.

Precipitate.—Any matter which, having been dissolved in a fluid, falls to the bottom of the vessel on the addition of some other substance capable of producing a decomposition of the compound, in consequence of its attraction either for the menstruum, or for the matter which was before held in solution.

Precipitation.—That chemical process by which bodies dissolved, mixed, or suspended in a fluid, are separated from that fluid, and made to gravitate to the bottom of the vessel.

Principles of Bodies.—Synonymous with *Elements;* which see.

Prussiates.—Salts formed by combination of any base with prussic acid.

Putrefaction.—The last fermentative process of nature, by which organized bodies are decomposed so as to separate their principles, for the purpose of reuniting them by future attractions, in the production of new compositions.

Pyrites.—An abundant mineral found on the English coasts, and elsewhere. Some are sulphurets of iron, and others sulphurets of copper, with a portion of alumina and silex. The former are worked for the sake of the sulphur, and the latter for sulphur and copper. They are also called Marcasites and Fire-stone.

Pyrites, Martial.—That species of pyrites which contains iron for its basis. See a full account of these minerals in Henckel's Pyritologia

Pyrometer.—An instrument invented by Mr. Wedgwood for ascertaining the degrees of heat in furnaces and intense fires.

Pyrophori.—Compound substances which heat of themselves, and take fire on the admission of atmospheric air.

Quartation.—A term used by refiners in a certain operation of parting.

Quartz.—A name given to a variety of siliceous earths, mixed with a small portion of lime or alumina. Mr. Kirwan confines the term to the *purer* kind of silex. Rock crystal and the amethyst are species of quartz.

Radicals.—A chemical term for the *elements* of bodies; which see.

Reagents.—Substances which are added to the mineral waters or other liquids as tests to discover their nature and composition.

Realgar.—Red sulphuret of arsenic.

Receivers.—Globular glass vessels adapted to retorts for the purpose of preserving and condensing the volatile matter raised in distillation.

Rectification is nothing more than the re-distilling a liquid and abstracting a part of it only.

Reduction.—The restoration of metallic oxides to their original state of metals; which is usually effected by means of charcoal and fluxes.

Refining.—The process of separating the perfect metals from other metallic substances, by what is called cupellation.

Refractory.—A term applied to earths or metals that are either infusible, or that require an extraordinary degree of heat to change or melt them.

Refrigeratory.—A contrivance of any kind, which, by containing cold water, answers the purpose of condensing the vapour or gas that arises in distillation. A worm-tub is a refrigeratory.

Registers.—Openings in chimneys, or other parts of chemical furnaces, with sliding doors, to regulate the quantity of atmospheric air admitted to the fire-place, or to open or shut the communication with the chimney at pleasure.

Regulus.—In its chemical acceptation, signifies a pure metallic substance, freed from all extraneous matters.

Repulsion.—A principle whereby the particles of bodies are prevented from coming into actual contact. It is thought to be owing to *caloric*, which has been called the repulsive power.

Residuum.—What is left in a pot or retort after the more valuable part has been drawn off. Thus the sulphate of potash which remains in the pot after the distillation of nitrous acid is called the residuum. It is sometimes called the *caput mortuum*.

Resins.—Vegetable juices concreted by evaporation either spontaneously, or by fire. Their characteristic is solubility in alcohol, and not in water. It seems that they owe their solidity chiefly to their union with oxygen.

Retort.—A vessel in the shape of a pear, with its neck bent downwards, used in distillation; the extremity of which neck fits into that of another bottle called a receiver.

Reverberatory.—An oven or furnace in which the flame is confined by a dome which occasions it to be beat down upon the floor of the furnace before it passes into the chimney, so that it returns or reverberates upon the matter under operation.

Revivification.—See *Reduction*, which is a synonymous term: though "revivification" is generally used when speaking of quicksilver.

Roasting.—A preparative operation in metallurgy to dissipate the sulphur, arsenic, &c. with which a metal may be combined.

Rock-crystal.—Crystallized silex.

Salifiable bases.—All the metals, alkalies, and earths, which are capable of combining with acids, and forming salts, are called salifiable bases.

Saline.—Partaking of the properties of a salt.

Salts neutral.—A class of substances formed by combining to saturation an acid with an alkali, an earth, or other salifiable base.

———— *triple.*—Salts formed by the combination of an acid with two bases or radicals. The tartrate of soda and potash (Rochelle salt) is an instance of this kind of combination.

Sand bath. } See *Bath.*
—— *heat.* }

Sandiver.—A matter, composed of different salts, which rises as a pellicle on the surface of the pots in which glass is melted. It is used as a flux in the fusion of ores, and for other purposes. The term is probably a corruption of " Sel de verre."

Sap-colours.—A name given to various expressed vegetable juices of a viscid nature, which are inspissated by slow evaporation for the use of painters, &c.; sap-green, gamboge, &c. are of this class.

Saponaceous.—A term applied to any substance which is of the nature or appearance os soap.

Saturation.—The act of impregnating a fluid with another substance, till no more can be received or imbibed. A fluid which holds as much of any substance as it can dissolve, is said to be saturated with that substance. A solid may in the same way be saturated with a fluid.

Sebates.—Salts formed by the combination of any base with sebacic acid

Selenite.—A salt existing in spring water, formed by sulphuric acid and lime. Its proper chemical name is sulphate of lime.

Semi-metal.—A name formerly given to those metals which, if exposed to the fire, are neither malleable, ductile, nor fixed. It is a term not used by modern chemists.

Siliceous earths.—A term used to describe a variety of natural substances which are composed chiefly of silex; as quartz, flint, sand, &c.

Simple substances.—Synonymous with *Elements;* which see.

Smelting.—The operation of fusing ores, for the purpose of separating the metals they contain from the sulphur and arsenic by which they are mineralized, and also from other heterogeneous matter.

Solubility.—A characteristic of most salts.

Solution.—The perfect union of a solid substance with a fluid. Salts dissolved in water are proper examples of solution.

Spars.—A name formerly given to various crystallized stones; such as the fluor spar, the adamantine spar, &c. These natural substances are now distinguished by names which denote the nature of each.

Specific gravity.—See the word *Gravity.*

Spelter.—The commercial name of *zinc.*

Spirit.—A term used by the early chemists to denote all volatile fluids collected by distillation.

—— *proof.*—A term made use of to describe such ardent spirits as are of the same strength as the brandy of commerce, or of the specific gravity of 0·930, water being 1·000.

Stalactites.—Certain concretions of calcareous earth found suspended like icicles in caverns. They are formed by the oozing of water through the crevices, charged with this kind of earth.

Steatites.—A kind of stone composed of silex, iron, and magnesia. Also called French chalk, Spanish chalk, and soap-rock.

Stratification.—A chemical operation by which bodies are placed in a condition to act mutually upon each other by being arranged layer by layer, stratum super stratum, as is practised by metallurgists.

Sub-salts.—Salts with less acid than is sufficient to neutralize their radicals.

Suberates.—Salts formed by the combination of any base with the suberic acid.

Sublimate.—A name given to several mercurial preparations.

Sublimation.—A process whereby certain volatile substances are raised by heat, and again condensed by cold into a solid form. Flowers of sulphur are made in this way. The soot of our common fires is a familiar instance of this process.

Succinates.—Salts formed by the combination of any base with the succinic acid.

Sugar.—A well-known substance, found in a variety of vegetables, composed of oxygen, hydrogen, and carbon.

Sulphates.—Salts formed by the combination of any base with the sulphuric acid.

Sulphites.—Salts formed by the combination of any base with the sulphureous acid.

Sulphures or *Sulphurets.*—Combinations of alkalies, or metals, with sulphur.

Sulphuretted.—A substance is said to be sulphuretted when it is combined with sulphur. Thus we say sulphuretted hydrogen, &c.

Super-salts.—Salts with an excess of acid, as the supertartrate of potash.

Synthesis.—When a body is examined by dividing it into its component parts, the process is called analysis; but when we attempt to prove the nature of a substance by the union of its principles, it is called synthesis.

Syphon.—A bent tube used by chemists for drawing liquids from one vessel into another. It is sometimes called a *crane*.

Tartrates.—Salts formed by the combination of any base with the acid of tartar.

Temperature.—The free caloric which is attached to any body occasions the degree of temperature of that body.

Tenacity, is a term used when speaking of glutinous bodies. It is also expressive of the adhesion of one substance to another.

Test.—That part of a cupel which is impregnated with litharge in the

R

operation of refining lead. It is also the name of whatever is employed in chemical experiments to detect the several ingredients of any composition.

Test-papers.—Papers impregnated with certain chemical re-agents; such as litmus, turmeric, radish, &c. They are used to dip into fluids to ascertain by change of their colour the presence of acids and alkalies.

Thermometer.—An instrument to show the relative heats of bodies. Fahrenheit's thermometer is that chiefly used in England. Other thermometers are used in different parts of Europe.

Tincal.—The commercial name of crude borax.

Tinctures.—Solutions of substances in spirituous menstrua.

Torrefaction.—An operation similar to roasting; which see.

Triturium.—A vessel used for the separation of two fluids which are of different densities. The same operation may be performed by a common funnel.

Trituration.—An operation whereby substances are comminuted by friction.

Tubulated.—Retorts which have a hole at the top for inserting the materials to be operated upon, without taking them out of the sand heat, are called *tubulated* retorts.

Tungstates.—Salts formed by the combination of any base with tungstic acid.

Tutenag.—An Indian name for zinc. Chinese copper is also called by this name, which is a compound of copper, tin, and arsenic, much resembling silver in colour.

Vacuum.—A space unoccupied by matter. The term is generally applied to the exhaustion of atmospheric air by chemical or philosophical means.

Vapour.—This term is used by chemists to denote such exhalations only as can be condensed and rendered liquid again at the ordinary atmospheric temperature, in opposition to those which are *permanently* elastic.

Vats.—Large chemical vessels, generally of wood, for making infusions, &c.

Vital Air.—Oxygen gas. The empyreal or fire air of Scheele, and the dephlogisticated air of Priestly.

Vitrification.—When solid substances have undergone very intense heat, so as to be fused thereby, they frequently have an appearance resembling glass, they are then said to be vitrified, or to have undergone vitrification.

Vitriols.—A class of substances, either earthy or metallic, which are combined with the vitriolic acid. Thus there is vitriol of lime, vitriol of iron, vitriol of copper, &c. These salts are now called Sulphates, because the acid which forms them is called sulphuric acid.

Vitriolated Tartar.—The old name for sulphate of potash.

Volatile Alkali.—Another name for ammonia.

Volatile Salts.—The commercial name for carbonate of ammonia.

Volatility.—A property of some bodies which disposes them to assume the gaseous state. This property seems to be owing to their affinity for caloric.

Volume.—A term made use of by modern chemists to express the space occupied by gaseous or other bodies.

Union, Chemical.—When a mere mixture of two or more substances is made, they are said to be mechanically united; but when each or either substance forms a competent part of the product, the substances have formed a *chemical* union.

Ustulation.—The roasting of ores, to separate the arsenic and sulphur which mineralize the metal. When the matter is preserved which flies off, the process is called sublimation; but when this matter is neglected, the operation was formerly called ustulation.

Water.—The most common of all fluids, composed of 8 parts of oxygen and 1 of hydrogen.

Water, mineral.—Waters which are impregnated with minerals and other substances are known by this appellation. These minerals are generally held in solution by carbonic, sulphuric, or muriatic acid.

Way, dry.—A term used by chemical writers when treating of analysis or decomposition. By decomposing in the dry-way, is meant, by the agency of fire.

Way, humid.—A term used in the same manner as the foregoing, but expressive of decomposition in a fluid state, or by means of water, and chemical re-agents, or tests.

Welding Heat.—That degree of heat in which two pieces of iron or of platina may be united by hammering.

Wolfram.—An ore of tungsten containing also manganese and iron.

Worm-tub.—A chemical vessel with a pewter worm fixed in the inside, and the intermediate space filled with water. Its use is to cool liquors during distillation.

Woulfe's apparatus.—A contrivance for distilling the mineral acids and other gaseous substances with little loss; being a train of receivers with safety pipes, and connected together by tubes.

Zaffre.—An oxide of cobalt, mixed with a portion of silicious matter. It is imported in this state from Saxony.

Zero.—The point from which the scale of a thermometer is graduated. Thus Celsius's and Reaumur's thermometers have their Zero at the *freezing* point, while the thermometer of Fahrenheit has its zero at that point at which it stands when immersed in a mixture of snow and common salt.

INDEX.

ERRATA.

Page 58, line 7, for " soda" read " sodium."

  – 70, – 17, for " sufficating" read " suffocating."

  – 72, – 17, for " pouring sulphuric acid" read " diluted sulphuric acid."

  – 77, – 17, for " 2,524 grains" read " 252.458 grains at temp. 62°.

  – 93, – 11 from below, for " charges it with" read " charges with it."

  – 107, – 5 from below, for " paper" read " papers."

  – 110, – 16 from below, for " specific of" read " specific gravity of."

  – 120, – 3 from below, for " pain" read " pane."

  – 122, – 2 after " fluochromic" read " acid."

  – 129, – 4 from below, after " it ;" dele semicolon.

  – 135, – 11 from below, for " basis" read " beta ; and line 10 from below, for " zostrea" read " zostera."

  – 149, – 3, for " acids" read " acid."

  – 151, – 16 from below, for " Therphrastus" read " Theophrastus."

  – 186, – 11, for " Ethiop's minerals" read " Ethiops mineral."

  – 188, – 9 from below, for " alumina" read " calamine."

  – 188, – 17 from below, for " is the white" read " is sugar or the white."

  – 315 – 5 – top – " died " – " dried "

Dublin : Printed by John S. Folds, 5, Bachelor's Walk.

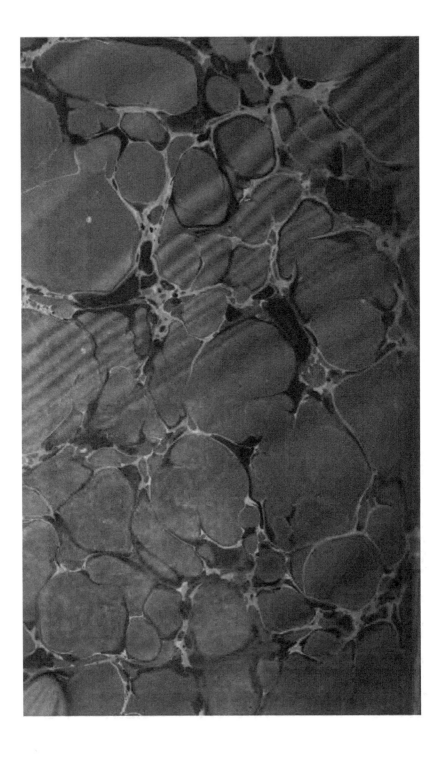